THE 1968 EXCAVATIONS
AT MOUND 8
LAS COLINAS RUINS GROUP
PHOENIX, ARIZONA

Prepared for Arizona Department of Transportation

Edited and Assembled by
Laurens C. Hammack and Alan P. Sullivan

Contributions by

Kim E. Beckwith
Patricia L. Crown
David A. Gregory
Laurens C. Hammack
Nancy S. Hammack
Richard J. Harrington
Bruce B. Huckell
Paul C. Johnson
Sandra Olsen

Amadeo M. Rea
William J. Robinson
Marilyn B. Saul
Benjamin W. Smith
Edward Staski
George A. Teague
Lynn S. Teague
Sharon F. Urban
Jamie L. Webb

Submitted by

Cultural Resource Management Section
Arizona State Museum
University of Arizona

September 1981

Archaeological Series No. 154

Frontispiece. Extent of 1968 excavations at Las Colinas (top of photo is South)

iii

ABSTRACT

This report describes the nature, extent, and results of archaeological excavations conducted at Mound 8 of the Las Colinas Ruins Group, Phoenix, Arizona. The excavations, undertaken in 1968, and subsequent analyses carried out during the following decade, were supervised by Laurens C. Hammack, then of the Arizona State Museum, University of Arizona. The Arizona State Museum excavations were authorized by the Arizona Department of Transportation as part of an annual Statewide Archaeological Contract between the two agencies.

Las Colinas is a Classic period (A.D. 1100-1450) Hohokam site located between Interstate 17 and 27th Avenue, south of McDowell Road, in Phoenix. The site consists of a specially constructed platform mound, habitation structures, and assorted features. These prehistoric remains were damaged by the construction of a historic adobe house in the 1880s and by vandalism through the following years. Mound 8, and the remains in the immediate vicinity, are threatened by the proposed construction of a segment of Interstate 10 known as the Papago Freeway.

Excavations focused on Mound 8, although the flat area east of the mound was tested; a single cremation area was discovered there. Habitation structures on and around the mound were excavated also.

It was determined that the mound was composed of post-reinforced, adobe-walled cells and encircling walls that formed the core of the structure. Various additions were made to this core, the most notable of which was a massive, solid-adobe wall. The top of the mound was capped with a layer of adobe on four different occasions.

At least 22 habitation structures, both pit houses and houses with solid-adobe walls, were discovered during the excavations. The range of structure morphology for any given period of occupation is much greater than that previously reported for other Classic period Hohokam sites. These and numerous other architectural features are discussed in this report.

Substantial collections of ceramic, chipped stone, and ground stone artifacts were recovered. These assemblages were thoroughly analyzed. The methods and results of these analyses are reported in this volume.

In addition, specialized analyses were performed on a wide range of materials recovered from the excavations. These analyses, described in appendices, pertain to human osteological remains, disposal of the dead, mammalian remains, bone artifacts, avian remains, shell artifacts, pollen identification, charcoal identification, and historic artifacts. A final appendix lists Arizona State Museum catalogue numbers for many of the artifacts and illustrations found in the volume.

PREFACE AND ACKNOWLEDGMENTS

Many people were involved in the production of the Las Colinas report and it is my pleasure to acknowledge their contributions to it.

David A. Gregory shared his extensive knowledge of the architecture of Las Colinas, and of related data, whenever called upon. His advice concerning the depiction of the complex architectural forms, especially the mound construction sequence, was absolutely invaluable. While I know that he might have done some things differently, I feel confident that he can use this volume as the basis for his forthcoming reanalysis and synthesis of the evolution of Hohokam platform mounds.

Bruce B. Huckell was interrogated intensively about events of the early 1970's when much of the laboratory analysis of the Las Colinas material was initiated. His ability to recall the locations of unaccessioned artifacts in deep stash and to decipher arcane and ritualistic provenience designations enabled us to provide a much expanded photographic record of the Las Colinas artifacts.

Benjamin Smith, editor, and Joseph Stevens, editorial assistant, diligently edited the volume, after overcoming severe pulmonary arrest upon viewing the manuscripts. Exasperation and frustration were controlled as they struggled to ensure that modern English usage prevailed in the final copy. Ben Smith was particularly adept at identifying and excising embedded and often recalcitrant non-sequiturs.

A platoon of illustrators was assembled. Charles Sternberg drafted the site map and rendered the construction sequence of Mound 8. Charles' talent for turning scribbled and murky field drawings into meaningful and informative illustrations is legendary and need not be expanded upon here. Phil Chase drafted the intricate pollen diagrams in his typically meticulous fashion. He also oversaw the paste-up phase of the manuscript's production. I frankly admit to exploiting his notorious attention to detail, which is reflected in the highly accurate layout of the illustrations. Ron Beckwith drew the Tonto Polychrome jar from a photograph provided by the pot hunters who removed it from Mound 8. Ron exposed, developed, and printed all of the artifact negatives with the exception of those that had been provided some time ago by Helga Teiwes and L. C. Hammack. He also printed all the architecture photographs from negatives supplied by Teiwes and Hammack. With the exception of those figures noted above, Brian Byrd drafted all of the illustrations which appear in the volume. He was most efficient in promptly producing high quality illustrations of artifacts, plan drawings, profiles, and various diagrams. Brian also was responsible for dealing with the technical reproduction companies in town, thereby ensuring rapid production of camera-ready figures. Joan Kusek provided the frontispiece, which was re-photographed from a Jerry Jacka print.

The onerous task of typing and correcting the final manuscript was cheerfully and efficiently handled by María Abdín. As many people are aware,

María is far more than a typist; problems of content and editing often came to our attention through María's diligence. The monograph benefitted immensely from her attention.

Kim Beckwith played a major role in the production of the volume. She was responsible for compiling the List of Figures and the List of Tables, and for checking for consistency and correspondence between these lists, the text content, and caption designations. This was truly a Herculean task considering the large number of tables and figures that are included in the volume. She was also responsible, in large part, for performing the "archival" work upon which the revisions and additions to the site map were based. In short, she was essential to the successful completion of the project.

Ray Pers, CRMS administrative assistant, bore the responsibility of dealing with the paperwork involving personnel procedures and of accounting for all receipts and accounts payable during the term of the project. His knowledge of the University of Arizona's labyrinthian accounting and payroll methods was both remarkable and indispensable.

Dave Gregory and Lynn Teague discuss (Chapter 1) the general editorial philosophy that guided the production of the Las Colinas monograph. I would like to add several comments to their general discussion. First, I am solely responsible for all editorial decisions pertaining to the content of the chapters and appendices. I actively, and frequently, solicited advice and information from all of the above-mentioned people (and others) in the process of forming an editorial decision. By and large, all suggestions were followed. Second, the volume is lavishly illustrated. This was done to facilitate comparison of various aspects of Las Colinas with other Classic period Hohokam sites. Third, Gregory and Teague mention that manuscript preparation dates accompany each contribution to the volume. This is true with the exception of their chapter and the appendices by Harrington, Saul, and Beckwith and Smith, which were submitted during July 1981. Finally, the reader should be aware that we had under five weeks to prepare a camera-ready manuscript for duplication. During this time, one chapter and two appendices had to be written; all chapters and appendices had to be edited for content, consistency, and style; and all illustrations drafted and photos processed. These factors should certainly be considered in evaluating the final product.

We thank the Arizona Department of Transportation for releasing the funds for publication of this volume. The interest and participation of Mr. Thomas Willett of the Federal Highway Administration is gratefully acknowledged.

Alan P. Sullivan
Arizona State Museum
University of Arizona
August, 1981

TABLE OF CONTENTS

LIST OF FIGURES

LIST OF TABLES

CHAPTER 1

INTRODUCTION

by David A. Gregory and Lynn S. Teague
Arizona State Museum
University of Arizona

Las Colinas and the Papago Freeway

Between April 1 and October 1, 1968, Laurens C. Hammack of the Arizona
State Museum directed excavations at Las Colinas (AZ T:12:10 ASM), a large
Hohokam site located within the Phoenix urban area (Figure 1). The excavations were conducted because the site lay within the proposed right-of-way of
that segment of Interstate 10 known as Papago Freeway, the planned construction
of which threatened the site. A substantial increase in vandalism of the site,
some of which involved the use of heavy equipment, dictated that the excavations be started at once. Following the terms of an existing salvage
archaeology agreement between the Arizona State Museum and the Arizona Department of Transportation, a contract was negotiated and work commenced.

The excavations focused on the feature designated Mound 8--a platform
mound. This feature was one of the 12 large mounds that had been recorded at
the site prior to the destruction wrought by the last century of agricultural
and urban development in the area. Numerous trenches were also dug in the
area to the east of Mound 8. Other portions of the site within the proposed
right-of-way were not investigated, both because land had not been acquired by
the State and because vandalism was a less pressing problem where conspicuous
features were not present.

The balance of the site has remained unexcavated in the ensuing years,
and the construction of the proposed freeway has not progressed as originally
planned. During this time, state and federal legislation designed to protect
cultural resources and provide for their prudent management has become
increasingly complex, and the Papago Freeway has become embroiled in controversy. This is due in part to divergent opinions about the proper treatment
of the prehistoric archaeological resources that still remain within the
highway corridor. The final disposition of these resources has not yet been
decided.

As a part of the decision-making process regarding the future treatment
of the remaining archaeological resources in the freeway corridor, a testing
program was designed and implemented. The purpose of this testing was to
provide information concerning the distribution and character of the remaining
subsurface resources that lie outside the immediate area of Mound 8. The
research design constructed to guide the testing (Gregory and McGuire 1980)

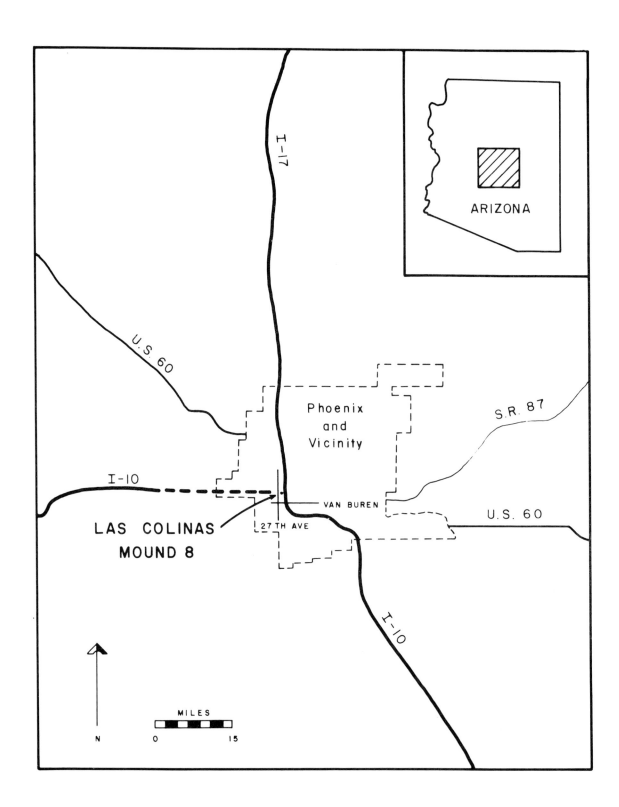

Figure 1. Location of Las Colinas

and the full report on the results of the testing (Schreiber and McCarthy 1981) provide supplementary information about the site of Las Colinas, Mound 8, and adjacent areas.

For those whose primary interest is the information that Las Colinas provides about Hohokam prehistory, these more recent documents may be profitably read as adjuncts to the present report. For those involved in the decision-making process now underway regarding the ultimate disposition of the remains of this site, this report of the 1968 excavations is a secondary but important source of information that supports the syntheses and recommendations presented by Gregory and McGuire (1980) and by Schreiber and McCarthy (1981).

It was decided by the Federal Highways official in charge of the project that, while copies of existing manuscripts and reports would suffice, a published report would be the most desirable form in which to present this portion of the necessary documentation. Consequently, funds were made available for the long-delayed publication of the complete report on the 1968 excavations at Las Colinas.

A History of This Report

Upon the completion of the 1968 excavations, a brief preliminary report was published (Hammack 1969), and a projected outline for a full scale site report was prepared. Between 1968 and 1973 various analyses were undertaken and manuscripts or reports were prepared and submitted. These dealt with such topics as an overview of the site of Las Colinas, ceramics, ground stone artifacts, shell, mammalian faunal remains, pollen, identification of wood charcoal, and vegetal remains. Between 1973 and 1977 additional manuscripts covering architecture and chipped stone artifacts were submitted; a second ceramic study was completed, as was a report on the dating of archaeomagnetic samples. The reports on the historic materials, bone artifacts, burials, and avian faunal remains were completed between 1977 and 1980. It was intended that these manuscripts and reports would be reviewed and returned to their authors for revision prior to publication. This process was never completed, and most of the chapters and appendices that appear in the present report are edited versions of these first drafts.

There are several exceptions that should be noted. Three separate ceramic analyses were originally done and three manuscripts were submitted; these have been incorporated in part into the ceramic chapter that appears here, which itself is the result of yet another analysis of the ceramic materials. It was completed in 1979 (see Crown, this volume). The chapter on vegetal remains was submitted and returned to the author for revisions in 1974. The revisions were never completed, and the results of this study are not available. The original outline projected a chapter on the dating of the site, and a chapter containing a summary and conclusions based upon the corpus of the report. These too were never completed. The appendices that present data on species identification of charcoal and that list archaeomagnetic dates have been compiled from the information contained in brief letter reports submitted prior to 1973. The original dates of submission and revision, if any, are given at the beginning of each of the chapters and appendices.

Because of the somewhat unusual circumstances under which the present manuscript was compiled and prepared for publication, the reader should be aware of the philosophy which guided editorial decisions. No changes have been made that affect the various authors' interpretations of their data. Except for changes made in format to improve readability of the various chapters and appendices, no liberties have been taken with the authors' original intentions. In many cases, figures, tables, and photographs have been added; and some original figures have been clarified for ease of reference and more complete documentation.

The material contained in Chapter 3, Architecture, was originally two separate chapters--one dealing with the mound itself and the other concerned with the rest of the architectural features recorded at the site. Because of the close relationship between the mound and the other architectural features and because of redundancies in the two chapters, they have been combined under joint authorship. When possible, the author was consulted when a question concerning a particular manuscript arose. If consultation was impossible, the original field notes or other pertinent documents were consulted.

Conclusion

A glaring lacuna in the present report is the absence of the customary chapter containing summary and conclusions. This chapter normally provides the investigator with an opportunity to give an overview of the investigation, to relate a site or group of sites to current thought on various research problems, and to point out new problems raised or implied by a particular set of data. It is also customary for the investigator to assess the relation of new data to current interpretations of prehistoric events and processes.

The explosive growth of contract work in the Hohokam area, and the resurgence of interest in Hohokam archaeology have given rise to new research concerns, and have promoted the reevaluation of old problems and interpretations regarding the development and achievements of Hohokam culture. The absence from this report of a summary of work done and conclusions to be drawn merely serves to make more obvious a fundamental characteristic of both archaeological interpretation in general, and of Hohokam interpretations in particular--that they are intrinsically incomplete.

It is reasonable to expect that the information in this report will generate no small amount of interest and will be a source of data for a variety of research problems in years to come. It is uncertain what disposition will be made of the materials remaining in the Papago Freeway corridor, but it is possible that an effort will be undertaken to recover additional data from Las Colinas. With this possibility in mind, it is appropriate that the present volume should be published without the traditional concluding chapter, for the story of Las Colinas as a focus of archaeological research is still unfolding.

CHAPTER 2

LAS COLINAS--THE SITE, ITS SETTING, AND
EXCAVATION PROCEDURES

by Laurens C. Hammack*
Complete Archaeological Services Associates
Cortez, Colorado

The Ruin Group

Casas de las Colinas was the name given to a group of Classic period
Hohokam mounds situated west of downtown Phoenix. Probably named by O. A.
Turney, the group consisted of ten artificial mounds and surrounding villages
and composed the largest cluster of such mounds in the Salt River Valley.

The naming of major village sites in the valley was initiated by
Cushing during the excavations of Los Muertos in 1887 and 1888. Later investigators, including H. R. Patrick, O. A. Turney, and Frank Midvale, continued
the tradition of using Spanish names for new sites found while mapping the
extensive canal system.

Although it is not as large in extent or in number of mounds as other
Valley sites, the Las Colinas ruins group was unique in its number of large,
artificial mounds in a relatively big area. Turney's map of the Prehistoric
Irrigation Canals published in 1929 (Figure 2) located ten mounds in a two-
square-mile area. Midvale, in a sketch done in 1968, added two more. In terms
of the contemporary Phoenix street system, the Las Colinas group is bounded
by 19th Avenue on the east, 27th Avenue on the west, Thomas Road on the north,
and Van Buren Street on the south. Only Mound 12, as defined by Midvale, lies
outside these boundaries (Figure 3).

As early as the 1920s, extensive deterioration of a number of these
mounds had already occurred. In a lengthy discussion of prehistoric irrigation,
Turney briefly described each mound as it appeared in 1929 (Turney 1929, Part
3:16-18):

Mound 1.   Graded down and used as a haystack yard (no dimensions
            given).

Mound 2.   Removed except for a slight terrace on which a house was
            was built (no dimensions given).

Mound 3.   Originally 105 feet by 105 feet, and 14 feet high, but
            it had been partially destroyed.

Mound 4.   Remains 180 feet by 150 feet, and 30 feet high.

*Draft completed: May 1973

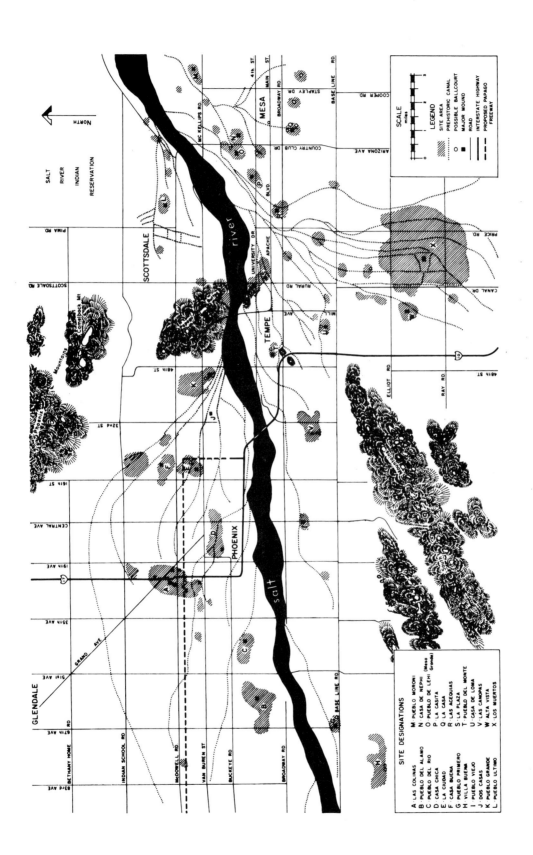

Figure 2. Turney's map of the prehistoric irrigation canals (updated)

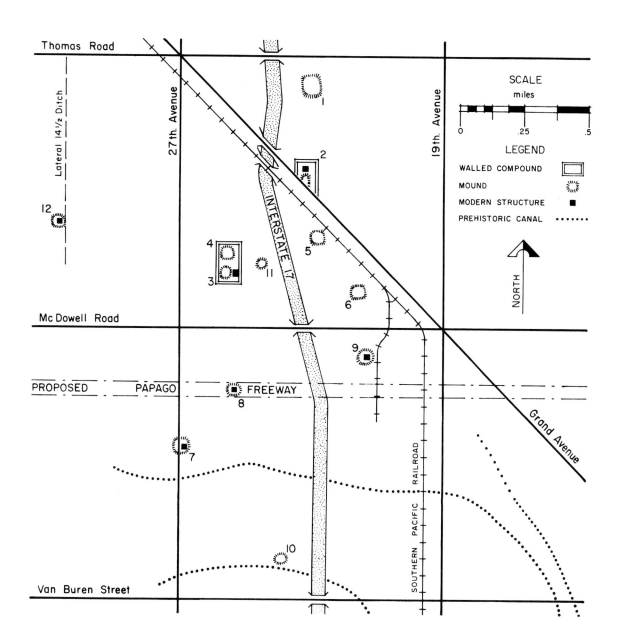

Figure 3. Locations of mounds

Mound 5. Slight elevation with a house within a date orchard (no dimensions given).

Mound 6. Entirely disappeared (no dimensions given).

Mound 7. Can be dimly seen; the county paved a road through its middle (27th Avenue) with a house built on its eastern slope; 250 feet by 180 feet, and 25 feet high previously.

Mound 8. Still remains, because a house was built on it; 90 feet by 115 feet, and 10 feet high.

Mound 9. Graded down by Col. William Christy in building his ranch home in 1884; 300 feet by 200 feet, and 5 feet high (in 1929).

Mound 10. Had disappeared before 1888. (Turney gives the location as just north of Van Buren Street and 15th Avenue, which does not agree with his map published with this description. An earlier edition of this map [1924] does show this location; however, it had been changed by the 1929 map.

Up to 1968, almost forty years later, destruction had continued until only Mound 8 remained in more or less its original, though disturbed, condition. Sherd, stone, and shell fragments can still be found at these locations in areas that have not been paved over.

From the various maps and meager descriptions it is possible to gain some additional information on the Las Colinas group. Three of the 12 mounds were apparently enclosed by compound walls (Figure 3). Mounds 3 and 4 were enclosed by a single wall, which is 520 feet north-south by 260 feet east-west (Midvale n.d.). Mound 2 was apparently also enclosed by a compound wall; however, no other information is available. That these were the only compounds within the group cannot be stated with certainty. Numerous house and trash mounds, most of which have long since been removed by agricultural activities, are also shown on Turney's map (Figure 2).

One final item represented on the prehistoric irrigation maps is what Turney (1924:5) refers to as "sun temples." He describes these as each having a "depressed, hardened, bowl-shaped floor, with a fire hole in the center covered with a slab, and gems beneath, all surrounded by a breast high, elliptical wall..." These "sun temples" are now generally acknowledged to be ball courts. The only excavated and preserved example in the Salt River Valley is at Pueblo Grande. Turney's map locates a ball court to the east of Mound 8, but extensive trenching of this area failed to confirm its existence. This area has been heavily plowed in the past, however, so it may indeed have existed at one time.

In 1906, Warren K. Moorehead published a brief account of some archaeological excavations in the Salt River Valley, in the vicinity of Phoenix. Working under the auspices of Robert Peabody of the Phillips Academy of Andover, Massachusetts, the excavations were conducted on the Kalfus Ruins (Las Colinas) "three miles due west from Phoenix" (Moorehead 1906:98-103). Moorehead's work on Mounds 3 and 4 was the only excavation of the Las Colinas group recorded prior to the work reported here. The main purpose of Moorehead's excavation was to obtain specimens for comparative purposes; but some architectural information was also collected. In addition to confirming the presence of two large mounds enclosed by a compound wall, Moorehead gave some indication of the nature of one of them. Concerning a trench placed in the larger of the two mounds (Mound 4), he commented:

> When the main trench was down about three meters we observed numerous pottery fragments, ashes, charcoal, and broken bones. These were in little packets or ash pits ranging from half a bushel to as much as three or four bushels. One large ash pit was three feet in depth. No floors could be traced and no walls found in the central cut save at the ends. We cleaned out the central cut to the original base, exposing six meters by 19 meters, and found little or nothing. It was even difficult to find the original base. No general floor seemed to have existed and we abandoned the central cut completely mystified as to the purpose of the ruin at this point (Moorehead 1906:102).

Although Moorehead was unaware of it at the time, he had made the first reference to the artificially constructed platform mounds that have become one of the hallmarks of the Classic period Hohokam.

Las Colinas Mound 8

Originally one of the least impressive of the mounds of the Las Colinas group, Mound 8 remained relatively intact despite the onslaught of agriculture and industrialization. A residence that was built on top of the mound as early as the 1880s remained until 1956 when it burned down. By that time the agricultural potential of the area was marginal, and housing developments began to encroach. The immediate vicinity of Mound 8 remained relatively undisturbed, even though a trailer court and fraternal lodge were constructed just west of the site. At the time of this writing (1973), open fields extend from Mound 8 to the Black Canyon Freeway (Interstate 17) on the east and almost to McDowell Road on the north. A number of housing developments have been built west of 27th Avenue.

The mound and its immediate environs had received some damage as a result of recent activities. Although not plowed because of the house there, the central portion of the mound had been damaged considerably when the structure was built. The residence has a four-foot-deep basement or cellar--an architectural feature rare in Arizona. Digging this cellar completely removed the center of the mound, thereby eliminating any hope of obtaining prehistoric structural features from the major use surface (Figure 4). In addition, a privy had been placed outside the northeast corner of the residence. The excavation made in conjunction with this structure removed most of a prehistoric burial. On the eastern periphery, an oval cinder block trough was built into the massive adobe retaining wall, and a well with a concrete pad was constructed nearby.

A number of concrete foundation slabs that served as bases for a series of outbuildings were present off the mound to the south. The slabs

Figure 4.   Destruction in Mound 8 by excavation of historic cellar

were probably the floors of chicken coops that were built during the 1940s when the place was a chicken ranch. A large oval pit approximately 70 feet by 30 feet by 2 feet had been excavated east of these slabs. At the time the fieldwork was done, the pit had already been filled with modern garbage.

After the house burned in 1956, the mound and surrounding area were used for trash dumping. The remains of the burned structure collapsed into the basement, and additional trash was deposited on top. Children playing in and around the mound occasionally dug small holes. Treasure hunters also probed the mound, but they did relatively little damage.

In March 1968, pothunters using a tractor dug a large hole in the northeast side of the mound. This excavation disclosed a complex series of walls and considerable cultural debris. The Arizona State Museum was subsequently notified that the site was situated in the path of Interstate 10, and fieldwork began on April 1, 1968.

The Setting

Las Colinas, Mound 8, AZ T:12:10 in the Arizona State Museum system (Wasley 1957), is located in the NW 1/4, NW 1/4 of Section 1, Township 1 North, Range 2 East, Maricopa County, Arizona. The elevation of this area (1079 feet) places the site within the Lower Sonoran Life Zone. As all native vegetation has long since disappeared, a description of the plant community for the general vicinity must suffice. Before extensive modern irrigation in the Salt River Valley had reclaimed much of the valley floor, the native vegetation consisted almost entirely of creosote bush (Sellers 1960). Mesquite thickets were to be found along the Gila River bottoms and in some of the dry washes to the south. The succulent Lower Sonoran vegetation types of the sahuaro/paloverde community are common on the nearby desert hills (Sellers 1960).

Climatological data for the city of Phoenix, based on a 63-year period, indicates a dry desert climate with precipitation averaging somewhat less than seven inches annually. Mean temperature is a warm 84.5 degrees F, with a high of 118 degrees F and a low of 16 degrees F recorded. An average of 152 days per year show temperature above the 90 degree F mark. The rainfall pattern is generally summer-dominant, with most of the precipitation falling in July and August (Sellers 1960).

Little is known of the paleoclimatic situation in the Salt River Valley during prehistoric times. The use of dendroclimatology is not applicable to the vegetation in a low desert (Weaver 1972:44), and palynology is in its infancy in this area. According to Schoenwetter and Doerschlag (1971), the Salt River Valley is already arid so that drought does not significantly affect the natural vegetation, although an increase in effective moisture will be observable in the pollen record (Weaver 1972:44). It is believed that during the period of occupation of Las Colinas the effective moisture in the valley was similar to the present, except during the period of increased rainfall from A.D. 1025 to 1075 and A.D. 1325 to 1475 (Weaver 1972:46).

Field Research Procedures

The standardized excavation techniques used at Las Colinas were no different from those of previous archaeological projects undertaken by the Arizona State Museum. Both power machinery and hand tools were used. All excavation of architectural or other prehistoric cultural features was done by hand. A backhoe was used for trenching the plowed field to the east of the mound, and for removing the modern fill within the cellar of the farm house. The backhoe was also used extensively as a photographic platform.

The locally recruited labor force had no previous archaeological experience. The daily work force averaged seven men during the six-month field season. Work began at dawn during the hot summer months when the temperature by 10:00 A.M. was well over 100 degrees F. The year of excavation, 1968, broke most of the temperature records for Phoenix. It was not uncommon to record temperatures of over 150 degrees on top of the mound during this period in the direct sunlight. The supervisory staff included the archaeologist, two assistant archaeologists, and two student archaeological assistants. A part-time recorder and a watchman were also employed.

All excavations were recorded in units called "features," a term that refers to either architectural features or to arbitrarily designated areas of excavations. Each feature was numbered consecutively starting with Feature 0, a designation for all surface materials. At AZ T:12:10, 125 features were designated. The initial feature numbers (1 to 5) were given to large stripping or broadside areas around and on top of the mound. These areas had been thoroughly disturbed and provided little definitive data. However, the large amounts of sherd and lithic material recovered in these areas served as the basis for the ceramic and lithic typologies for the site. This material could easily be handled and reworked without endangering the quality of the samples from specific architectural units.

Feature numbers were assigned in order of discovery by the supervisory archaeologist, with each designation identified physically by a marked tag or stake. Bulk material recovered from each feature was placed in double-strength paper bags labeled with exact provenience. All artifacts were bagged individually; large stone items were marked with a field specimen number on an unworked surface. A detailed field catalog was kept on each feature, each artifact was given a specimen number, and its date, provenience, and locus were recorded. In this way everything obtained from a specific unit was recorded in one place and was readily available. During the course of the project, 3679 field specimen numbers were assigned.

A daily excavation record was kept by the supervisory and assistant archaeologists detailing all aspects of the day's work. In addition, standard Arizona State Museum excavation forms were prepared on each feature when specific units were completed. Semipermanent datum points were established on top of the mound and on the flats. All measurements, both horizontal and vertical, were made from these points. Mapping was kept current with the use of an alidade and a plane table, and all measurements were taken in the metric scale. Individual architectural units were also drawn to scale to accompany the feature forms. A photographic record of the excavation was kept, resulting in over 1000 black and white and 600 color photographs. A 4 by 5 Speed Graphic,

2 1/4 by 2 1/4 Hasselblad, and a 2 1/4 by 2 1/4 Rollicord were used in the black and white coverage. Color work was done with the 4 by 5 and a 35 mm Zeiss-Icon. Aerial photography was provided at various intervals by the Arizona Highway Department (now the Arizona Department of Transportation).

All excavated fill material was removed from the site by wheelbarrows and placed in backdirt piles south of the mound. Stratigraphic separation was a highly complex matter, except in the interior of the platform mound. Excavation was accomplished in natural or cultural stratigraphic layers when possible; otherwise arbitrary level designations were used. All recovered materials were boxed and taken to the Arizona State Museum for cleaning and processing. Analysis was not begun until all fieldwork had been completed. The following chapters and appendices describe these analyses in detail.

CHAPTER 3

ARCHITECTURE

by Laurens C. Hammack and Nancy S. Hammack*
Complete Archaeological Services Associates
Cortez, Colorado

Introduction

The only visible architectural feature at Las Colinas prior to excavation was the platform mound. Rising slightly more than 2 m above the valley floor, the mound could not be considered inspiring (Figures 5 and 6). Because of extensive modern activity, little prehistoric cultural material remained on the surface. Excavations revealed that the mound consisted of a series of semi-circular and rectangular post-reinforced adobe-walled "cells" which were purposely filled with trash and capped with caliche-adobe. A series of such caps or surfaces was visible in cross-section. A massive, caliche-adobe wall enclosed the "cellular" portion of the mound, forming a rectangular structure approximately 25 m by 30 m in size. To the north and west as well as on top of the mound there were habitation structures, work areas, and burials. A brief architectural sequence for the site begins with simple pit houses excavated into sterile soil, followed by rectangular, post-reinforced adobe-walled rooms (similar to the cells of the mound itself), solid caliche-walled rooms, and finally a return to simple pit house structures with thin adobe walls (see Map 1).

The complexity of the architectural forms at Las Colinas necessitates a rather lengthy discussion supplemented by numerous plans and photographs. Initial discussion will center on the construction of the platform mound. Habitation structures will then be described in sequence from earliest to latest. It will become clear through the discussion that radical innovations were introduced into Hohokam architecture during a period of 300 years. House forms changed and a new type of architectural feature, an internally structured platform mound, was added. These changes in architecture and also in the artifact assemblages mark the end of the Sedentary period and the beginning of the Classic period (A.D. 1100 - 1450).

In the following discussion, all architectural features will be described in terms of the feature number designated during the excavation. As feature numbers were assigned in order of discovery, the numbers will not necessarily be in sequence. Construction details of the habitation structures are provided in Part II of this chapter.

---

*Draft completed: June 1976

Figure 5. Mound 8, before excavation (looking east)

Figure 6. Mound 8, before excavation (looking south)

Part I

The Platform Mound

Indications of architectural features within the mound were apparent
on arrival at the site since, in the northeast portion, vandals had gouged a
large hole almost to the foundations of the historic house. This hole
revealed a somewhat confusing mass of adobe walls and, when viewed in cross-
section, a number of sloping surfaces. A cut the width of a small tractor
had been made through the massive adobe outer wall, and the fill of the mound
had been hauled out with a scoop on the front of the tractor. This dirt was
piled just east of the mound. A single Tonto Polychrome jar associated with
a burial was reported to have been uncovered during this operation. Another
was found by local children poking around in the backdirt after the vandals
left.

This gaping hole, made just prior to the Museum's excavations, provided us with some initial information regarding the type of mound about to
be investigated. It was obvious that a unique situation confronted us--the
excavation of an internally structured mound of an architectural style
previously unreported.

The initial excavations into the mound were made in the hole created
by the collectors and their tractor, which was affectionately labeled Pot
Hunters' Gap (PHG). The remaining fill was hopelessly mixed. Fortunately,
the pot hunters had not quite reached the base level of the mound, and a
number of wall stubs and posthole patterns revealed the original plan. Concurrently, initial stripping on the east and north sides of the mound and
removal of modern garbage from within the foundations of the historic house
were begun. Datum points were established on the concrete south wall and
the cobble north wall of the historic house. These areas were left in place
during excavation and provided ideal reference points for both horizontal and
vertical measurement. On the flats west of the mound the Arizona Highway
Department had established a benchmark which provided the permanent datum.
An elevation of 1078.7 feet above sea level was recorded on this benchmark.
Aerial photogrammetric mapping by the Highway Department of the site during
excavation indicated that the datum point established on the south concrete
wall of the historic house had an elevation of 1086.5 feet leaving a vertical
height of 7.8 feet (2.37 m) from the top of the mound to the flats.

A number of problems complicated the excavations on top of the mound.
The modern structure had effectively removed most of the surface where prehistoric architectural features would be expected. To what extent the fill
from the digging of the cellar had been scattered across the mound, thus compli-
cating the sequence, was not known. Also, the amount of disturbance caused
by earlier relic hunters and the inhabitants of the historic dwelling during
its 70-year life span was not known.

The initial stripping on top of the mound and on the flats immediately
surrounding the mound indicated a rather complete mixing in the upper 30 cm to
40 cm and in some cases even more. Glass, tin cans, buttons, marbles, and
occasional coins were located in association with Gila Polychrome and other

prehi
ceram
recov
ceram

of the
Twelv
of the
recen
of the

of the
the f

the p
the u
at th
a max

on wh
1078.
is th
Highw

adobe
archi

retai
These
well
35 cm
for s
under
an un
morta
thous
The h
mound
above
towar

the p
vary
35 cm

6. Caps. Prepared, adobe-caliche surfaces placed over the retaining cells (walls and fill) and connected to an exterior wall. Two major, well-defined caps and two lesser caps are present in most areas of the mound.

Mound Construction

The overall plan of Mound 8 (Figure 8) details the layout of the subsurface architecture as excavated. The dashed lines represent probable wall locations not substantiated by actual excavation. Solid lines delineate actual walls uncovered. Postholes within solid lines indicate walls which were removed during excavation. Portions of the mound which were only excavated to the sloping caps have no interior architectural featues on the plan.

The prehistoric construction activities, which resulted in the final mound as excavated in 1968, can be divided into two main phases. Phase A, construction of the basic mound and its first capping, took place during the early Soho phase. This phase is subdivided into three stages. Construction of, and additions to, the massive outer wall, and the application of three adobe caps, are Phase B building events. This activity, which essentially stabilized the exterior of the mound and enlarged the upper portions, was carried out during the late Soho phase. Phase B is subdivided into one minor and four major stages.

Mound 8 may have been preceded by an earlier structure which was almost totally dismantled and removed when the present mound was erected. Two areas on the south side of the mound (Features 72a and 72b) show posthole alignments that do not conform to the general pattern exemplified elsewhere within the structure.

Phase A

Stage 1. Construction of the mound centered on an unusual wall which formed the nucleus around which the retaining cells were constructed. This east-west wall (labeled A on Map 1) divides Features 49 and 62 and provides the logical departure point for describing the building sequence of the mound. Although of post-reinforced adobe construction like all other retaining cell walls, Wall A exhibited structural strength and cohesiveness matched only by the massive outer wall. Wall A is 4.70 m in length, stands 1.57 m above basal level, measures 1.40 m wide at the base, and tapers to .20 m wide at the top. In cross-section it resembled an inverted ice cream cone (Figure 9). The top was rounded and smoothed, and the exterior surfaces were well plastered without the usual finger and hand impressions. A thick plastering of caliche applied in horizontal levels had run slightly, forming a banding effect on the surface of the wall. Wall A was cut on its east end by Wall C, and on its west end by Wall D. There was no attempt made to bond Wall A to either Wall C or Wall D at their points of intersection. It appears that Wall A was deliberately cut and at one time may have extended further. The cross walls are the typical, post-reinforced walls that comprise the retaining cells in the rest of the mound.

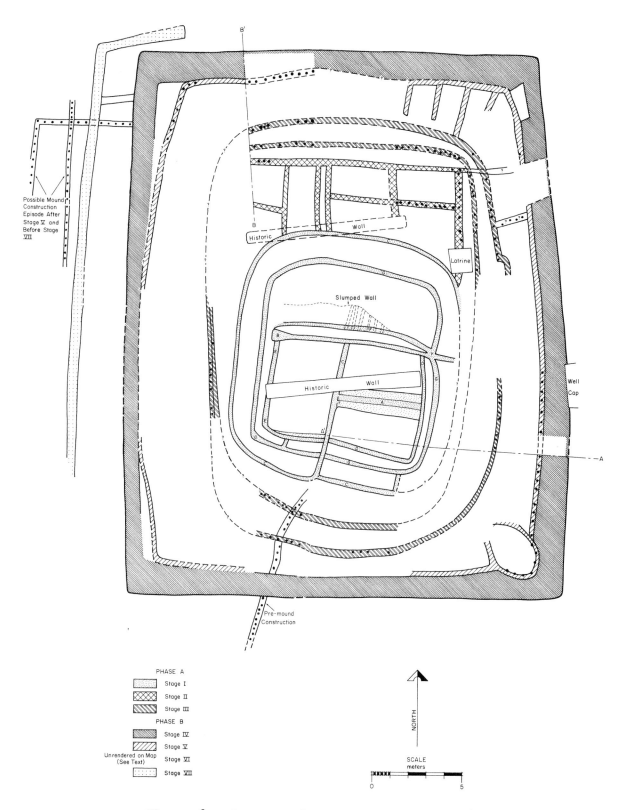

Figure 8. Construction sequence of Mound 8

Figure 9. Wall A, cross-section

Figure 10. Feature 16, postholes

The construc
previously (

Fea
stubs remair
outside the
impossible

The
the full he
from Featur
north walls
Feature 60

The
to those of
.50 m towar
level, whil
south doubl

Aga
disparate n
deposits wi
sterile des
Basal level
and contain

Sta
structed ar
on the nort
and west si
the east si
revealed se
poorly buil
only picked

Ins
described,
wash, and a
the basal 1
This wall v
the origina
Thus it app
struction a
the mound.
first porti
from Cap 1
of construc

A thick, prepared surface extended from 10 cm below the top of Wall A over the entire area of Feature 62. This surface consisted of two layers of sterile adobe 30 cm thick containing a series of postholes (Figure 10). These postholes are not indicative of a post-reinforced wall, but may show the location of a loom support. No other features or cultural materials were associated with this surface. On the other side of Wall A, a similar but thinner surface slopes off toward the north in Feature 49. These are the only instances of prepared surfaces within the retaining cells below the caps. They were probably used only temporarily, as they were covered by Cap 1.

The initial construction stage of the mound resulted in a central area of circular- and rectangular-walled cells consisting of Wall A and Features 37 and 46, 45, 47, 48 and 73, 49, 62, 63, and 75 (Map 1). This is the core area of the mound, and it represents the highest portion of the structure during the initial construction stage. All walls must have been constructed concurrently in a short period of time considering the lack of weathering visible on them. After excavation, these same walls began to crack and slough off, and rainfall caused immediate and recognizable damage.

The sequence of construction is based on wall abutments, which at first glance are confusing. It will be necessary to refer to Map 1 during the following descriptions. The abutment patterns indicate that various walls were under construction simultaneously. The postulated sequence of construction around Wall A begins with Wall B, an east-west wall delineating the north sides of Features 45 and 49. Wall C, next in the sequence, is the longest continuous wall. It begins in the center as a north-south wall, dividing Features 63 and 45 on the west from Features 62 and 49 on the east. Wall C continues southward, forming the east wall of Feature 73, and then turns west to form the major encircling post-reinforced wall of the core area of the mound. Walls D and E were built concurrently and form the central, rectangular retaining cells. Wall D forms the east wall of Feature 49 and the east and south walls of Feature 62. Wall E forms the south and west walls of Feature 63. Feature 45 is actually a continuation of Feature 63 and was separated by the historic house wall. Wall F, probably added to provide additional support to the main interior cells, had serious problems. The whole north portion collapsed just after construction (Figure 11). This collapse evidently took place during filling of Features 46 and 37, since intentional fill up to 30 cm deep lay below the fallen portion of Wall F.

No effort was made to rebuild the wall. Wall F was rather a failure as a supporting wall; however, this seemed to make little difference to the builders. Wall G abuts Wall C at the east end of Feature 73 and parallels Wall C, ending as the second major encircling wall dividing Features 48 and 46.

Upon completion of a particular section, the retaining cells were immediately filled with either trash or sterile desert soil. The three central cells (Features 45/63, 62, and 49) were filled with cultural material. Prodigious amounts of debris, including over 26,000 sherds and numerous shell and lithic artifacts, were recovered from the black, ashy fill. This material, probably obtained from trash mounds in the immediate vicinity, was stratigraphically homogeneous with no apparent differentiation from the top of the deposit to basal level. Features 62 and 63, which were not disturbed by the modern house foundation, contained 1.47 m and 1.66 m of fill respectively.

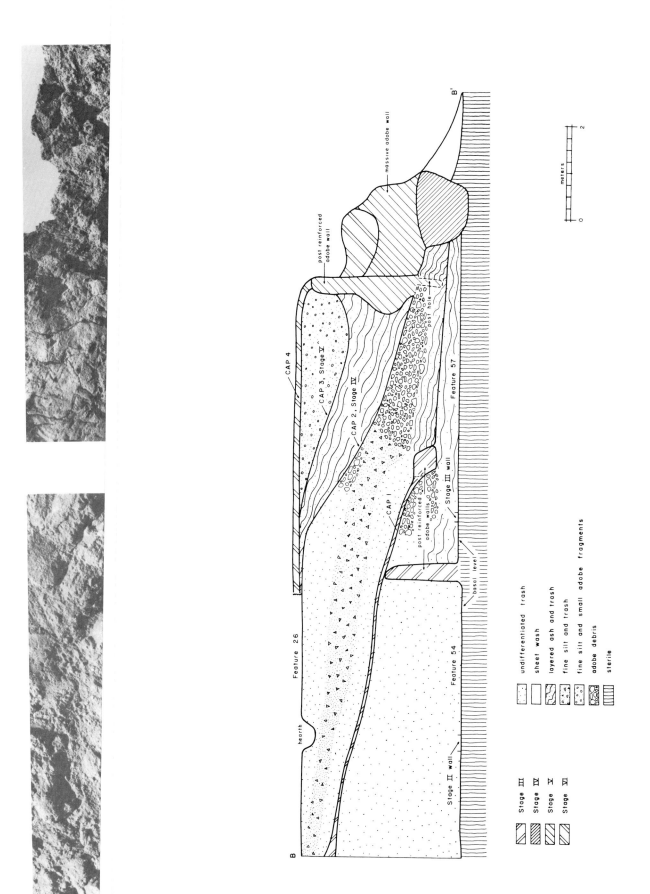

Figure 15. North cross-section of mound (B-B')

The construction of the post-reinforced walls in this area was similar to that previously described, although they exhibited fewer finger and hand prints.

Features 36 and 64 were located in Pot Hunters' Gap, and only the wall stubs remained. The east wall of Feature 36 was also cut by the privy built outside the northeast corner of the historic house (Map 1). Thus, it is impossible to discuss wall heights or abutments for this area.

The remaining features in this area sustained only minor damage, and the full height of most walls remained. Features 60 and 61 were separated from Feature 54 by a double wall running north-south. This wall abutted the north walls of Features 60, 61, and 54 (Map 1). The cross wall separating Feature 60 from 61 abutted the eastern wall of the north-south double wall.

The southern portions of the walls in this area were equal in height to those of the central core, but gradually decreased in height by about .50 m toward the north. The south wall of Feature 54 is 1.70 m above base level, while the north wall of the same feature is 1.20 m high. The north-south double wall described above slopes gradually downward to the north.

Again, the material used to fill these retaining cells was of a disparate nature. Features 60 and 61 contained the typical, ashy trash deposits with large amounts of cultural debris. Feature 54, however, contained sterile desert soil. No stratigraphy was present in any of these features. Basal level here was slightly more irregular than in the central core area and contained fewer puddling pits.

Stage III. During this stage low, post-reinforced walls were constructed around the central core (Map 1). These were uncovered by excavation on the north and south sides, whereas they can only be inferred on the east and west sides. On the west side there was no excavation below the cap. On the east side, Pot Hunters' Gap and Feature 115 (test trench through the mound) revealed several encircling walls. These walls were relatively low and very poorly built. They were almost impossible to see in cross-section and were only picked up by horizontal excavation.

Instead of undifferentiated artificial fill as in the areas previously described, the fill here consisted of stratified ash layers, lenses of adobe wash, and adobe chunks (Figure 14). There was 15 cm to 30 cm of trash between the basal level and the outermost of these post-reinforced encircling walls. This wall was extremely low (30 cm on the north and 15 cm on the east) and was the original exterior mound wall, into which Cap 1 (Figure 14) tied directly. Thus it appears that there was a short period of time between the rapid construction and filling of the central retaining cells and the first capping of the mound. There was another hiatus between construction of Cap 1 and the first portion of the massive outer wall, evidenced by thin lenses of sheet wash from Cap 1 appearing in cross-section (Figure 14). Cap 1 was the last episode of construction during Phase A.

28

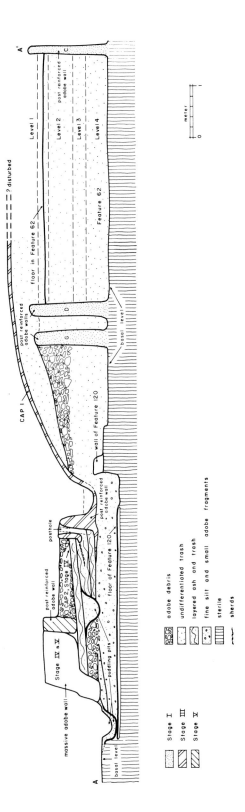

Figure 14. East cross-section of mound (A-A')

Phase B

Stage IV. The massive outer wall attained its present dimensions through several successive building stages. Its massiveness (1 m thick) was probably excessive for purposes of containing the fill of the mound; however, overcompensation was a typical practice of the builders of the mound. This wall also may have served to prevent erosion of the base of the mound and subsequent damage to its interior due to flooding. Later additions to the wall combined this function with that of raising the sides of the mound to extend the flat, usable surface on top.

The base of the massive wall was set into a shallow, rounded trench dug into the basal level. This trench, approximately 50 cm wide and 15 cm deep, was then filled with solid adobe and the wall built up an additional 35 cm above the basal level and widened out to a maximum thickness of 70 cm (Figure 15). At this stage of construction, the basic outline of the mound changed from the oval formed by the post-reinforced interior walls to a rectangle with sharply squared corners. Lumps of adobe, trash, and sandy fill, a meter thick in places, were piled in back of this wall and on top of Cap 1. Cap 2 covered this fill and was attached to the first portion of the massive adobe wall, enlarging the mound horizontally and vertically.

Stage V. The next building stage of the massive wall was the most ambitious, consisting of a vertical enlargement of the mound. A post-reinforced wall was set on top of Cap 2, approximately 50 cm inside the massive outer wall. As the base of the wall rests directly on the cap, separated by no more than 2 cm of fill, and its postholes are sunk through the cap, it can be assumed that little time elapsed between building stages. This post-reinforced wall was 1.80 m high where historic disturbance did not occur. It was slightly thicker (25 cm to 30 cm) than the interior retaining cell walls, since its function appears to have been to support the massive amounts of wet adobe which were piled against it. This wall ran parallel to the solid-adobe outer wall, except at the corners, where it angled inward, leaving a large gap between the two walls.

The additional quantities of solid adobe that were placed then on the exterior of this post-reinforced wall extended over Cap 2 and formed a massive wall more than twice as thick as the original (Figure 15). This solid-adobe mass was placed directly against the post-reinforced wall, except in the corners of the mound where the two walls separated from their parallel alignment (Map 1). This addition to the massive outer wall resulted in an extra meter of height and one-half meter of thickness.

There is no evidence of coursing in the wall construction, and it appears that it would have been necessary to use forms or some other device to contain the adobe in its proper place. No traces of such devices remain, undoubtedly due to the extensive erosion on the exterior of the massive wall.

As revealed in a profile trench through the north side, over a meter of layered ash and trash was placed on Cap 2 against the interior of the post-reinforced wall behind the massive wall (Figure 15). Due to the slope of

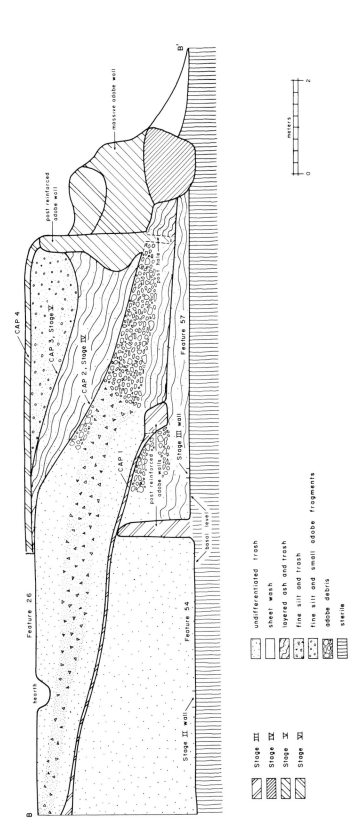

Figure 15. North cross-section of mound (B-B')

Cap 2, this layer thinned out to less than 25 cm near the top of the mound. This trash was then sealed by Cap 3, a slightly sloping, almost horizontal cap which abuts the post-reinforced wall 35 cm below its top.

In three of its four corners, the post-reinforced wall lining the massive outer wall departs from its parallel alignment, leaving a trapezoidal space between it and the massive outer wall. These areas were filled with loose trash, but do not appear to have been capped, except by the final surfacing (Cap 4). It is very difficult to determine whether this pattern was followed in the southeast corner of the mound due to the extreme leveling in this area in historic times. It appears that in this corner the entire space between the post-reinforced wall and the massive wall was filled with solid adobe. The post-reinforced wall, instead of being continuous, is interrupted by a bay-like structure into the corner of the massive wall and extending up the sides of Cap 2 (Figures 16, 17). The floor of the cap within this bay contains several postholes, which may have been supports for a corner structure on top of the mound.

In addition to the various cappings used to enlarge and raise the mound, an alternate method was utilized in the northeast corner during Stage V. Here, solid-adobe walls were built on top of Cap 2 (Figure 18). A series of four walls was placed at right angles to the north massive wall, forming rectangular cells which were filled with trash and surfaced with a layer of adobe. This surface correlates with Cap 4 on the northwest portion of the mound. The base of the walls described above followed the slope of Cap 2, which was anchored into the first construction of the massive wall. Thus, close to the massive wall, these walls are comparatively tall, tapering off as the cap slope rises. These walls, which can be considered as a type of retaining cell, are the only complete examples of solid adobe walls built on top of a cap. Their function was apparently to raise and flatten the surface of the mound in this area.

Stage VI. The final surfacing, Cap 4, is a horizontal layer of adobe 10 cm thick which ties directly into the top of the post-reinforced wall. Undifferentiated silt and small lumps of adobe compose the fill between Caps 3 and 4.

The massive wall shows one addition after the construction of Cap 3. This third addition is made up of 50 cm of adobe placed on top of the second addition. Since erosion and weathering have taken their toll on the upper portions of this wall, it can only be assumed that the massive outer wall originally attained the same height as Cap 4 and the top of the post-reinforced wall.

This sequence of cap construction cannot be confirmed for all sides of the mound because historic disturbance, especially on the south side, removed an unknown amount of the massive wall. Cap 4, the uppermost cap, was definitely present only on the north side of the mound (Figure 15). The successive capping or surfacing of the mound just described is found in part on the east and south sides; however, only Caps 1 and 2 are distinguishable in these areas (Figure 14).

Figure 17.   Same as Figure 16, (looking southeast)

Figure 16.   Bay-like structure in southeast corner of the massive wall (looking west)

Figure 18.   Adobe walls built on top
of Cap 2

Stage VII. A solid-adobe wall was built approximately 2.10 m to the west of the base of the massive outer wall, and directly on top of the layers of sheet wash and the remnant of a post-reinforced wall (pre-Stage VII construction; see below). This solid-adobe wall curved around the northwest corner of the mound and continued a short distance along the north face before abruptly ending.

The area between this solid-adobe wall and the massive wall (Features 19 and 122) was filled with unstratified, Civano phase trash. It appears that a cap was put on top of the trash, thus extending the mound slightly westward. In Feature 122, a definite sloping surface was uncovered, and in Feature 19, several areas of thick adobe were exposed.

Pre-Stage VII. After construction of the massive outer wall, a thin layer (10 cm) of trash was deposited on the west side of the mound. On top of this layer a series of post-reinforced walls (Features 113, 116, 118, and 117) were constructed, abutting the massive outer wall (Map 1). Although a thin layer of fine ash was noted in profile (Figure 19), it is not known whether the walled-off areas were used as rooms or were built as cells to support a capped extension to the mound. These walls were then either deliberately destroyed or extensively damaged by flooding, as only stubs remain, and these are overlain by a thick deposit of adobe sheet wash. This sheet wash is deposited in front of the vertical face of the massive adobe wall to a depth of 30 cm.

Unlike the four other Phase B stages, pre-Stage VII has no definite architectural linkage to the mound. The other stages are characterized by capping of the mound or by additions of adobe to the massive wall. The only architectural evidence relating pre-Stage VII to the massive wall is the abutment of the post-reinforced wall. For these reasons, pre-Stage VII is considered a minor stage in the overall construction sequence of Mound 8.

Dating of Mound Construction

Accurate dating of the various stages of mound construction at Las Colinas is difficult. The sequence of construction was developed through cross-sections and wall abutments, but these gave no indication of absolute temporal relationships. The only stratigraphic relationships between the mound and the habitation structures was the superimposition of the massive outer wall upon Features 119 and 121. But these two pit houses, although considered to be early Soho in date because of their architecture and the high proportion of Santan design elements in their pottery assemblages, have no archaeomagnetic dates or stratigraphic relationships to other habitation structures. The only hearth associated with the mound construction was Feature 18, an isolated firepit on Cap 2. It was originally given an archaeomagnetic date of A.D. 1220 ± 30, but this was later rejected (see Table 1).

The hearth associated with Feature 26, a pit house or jacal structure cut through Caps 3 and 4, has been given a good archaeomagnetic date of 1335 ± 38 (Table 1). This indicates that the final capping of the mound was accomplished before this date.

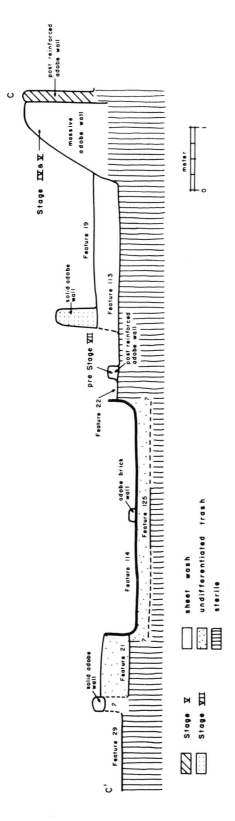

Figure 19. West cross-section of mound (C-C')

Table 1. Archaeomagnetic dates from Las Colinas

Feature Number	Feature Type	Location	Ceramic Phase	Date*	Comment
15	Hearth in pit house	Top of mound, NE corner	Early Civano	1390 ± ?	Date rejected (large dispersion)
18	Hearth (isolated)	On Cap 2 within mound	---	1220 ± 30	Date rejected (large dispersion)
26	Hearth in pit house	Top of mound, NW corner	Early Civano	1335 ± 38	Date acceptable
34	East hearth in pit house	Flats NW of mound	Early Civano	1415 ± 23	Date acceptable
34	West hearth in pit house	Flats NW of mound	Early Civano	1390 ± 36	Date acceptable
35	South hearth in pit house	Flats NW of mound	Late Civano	1395 ± 12	Date acceptable
35	East hearth in pit house	Flats NW of mound	Late Civano	1370 ± 27	Date acceptable
39	Hearth in solid-adobe wall room	West of mound	Early Civano	1365 ± 24	Date acceptable
40a	Hearth in pit house	West of mound	Late Soho-Early Civano	1410 ± 23	Date acceptable

*Samples processed and dates provided by Robert L. Dubois, Earth Sciences Laboratory, University of Oklahoma.

Table 1. (continued)

Feature Number	Feature Type	Location	Ceramic Phase	Date*	Comment
41	Hearth in pit house	Northeast of mound	Civano	1400 ± 17	Date acceptable
74	Hearth in pit house	North of mound	Late Civano	1450 ± 17	Date acceptable
76	Well-burned firepit in post-reinforced adobe-walled room	Northwest of mound	Soho	1180 ± ? 1370 ± ?	Ambiguous curve configuration
80	Hearth in post-reinforced adobe-walled room	West of mound	Soho	1230 ± 30	Date acceptable
100	Hearth in pit house	West of mound	Early Soho	1180 ± 25	Date acceptable
114	Firepit in pit house	West of mound	Civano	1385 ± 22	Date acceptable
125	Hearth in post-reinforced adobe-walled room	West of mound	Early Soho	1180 ± 25	Date acceptable

*Samples processed and dates provided by Robert L. Dubois, Earth Sciences Laboratory, University of Oklahoma.

Any attempt at more precise dating of the construction stages of the Las Colinas mound must rely upon pottery analysis. This approach is problematic due to the extremely disturbed nature and unknown origin of the fill of the retaining cells.

In Phase A of the mound construction, the fill appears to have been brought in from a variety of sources. There is no guarantee that it is contemporaneous with the mound itself, as it may have been obtained from trash deposits of an earlier occupation as yet undiscovered in the area of the mound. Phase B fill can be assumed to be contemporaneous with the various stages of construction of the massive outer wall.

To determine if there are any noticeable differences between Phase A and Phase B ceramics, the percentages of various decorated wares were calculated and compared (Tables 2 and 3). Decorated wares included only those sherds identifiable as to type and excluded undecorated body sherds, sherds which were too small, and unidentified buff wares and white ware sherds

Included in the tables is the frequency of pottery with Santan design elements recovered from each feature. These design elements, which indicate a transition between Sacaton Red-on-buff and Casa Grande Red-on-buff, are fully discussed in the pottery section (see Crown, this volume). The numbers in the Santan elements column do not correspond to individual sherds, but to individual design motifs. Two or more motifs may occur on a single sherd, thus the total number of Santan design elements for a feature may exceed the total number of individual Sacaton Red-on-buff or Casa Grande Red-on-buff sherds.

A major drawback to any comparison of Phase A and Phase B sherds is the discrepancy between sample sizes from these two major periods of mound construction. The average number of decorated sherds from Phase A features is 169.9, while the average for Phase B features is 9.7 sherds. The trash-filled cells from the center of the mound provide the bulk of significant pottery from Las Colinas. Areas of general stripping also yielded large numbers of sherds, but generally from a disturbed context. With the exception of Feature 100, the habitation structures had relatively low sherd counts, as did the Phase B areas of mound construction.

In comparing Phase A and Phase B decorated ceramics, several trends are evident. The most obvious trend is that intrusive black-on-white and black-on-red types are abundant in Phase A features, averaging 3.7 percent of the class total, but are completely absent in Phase B. The relative balance of Sacaton Red-on-buff and Casa Grande Red-on-buff is also indicative of a time difference. In Phase B the average percentage of Sacaton Red-on-buff is almost 20 percent less than in Phase A, while Casa Grande Red-on-buff increases 20 percent. Tanque Verde Red-on-brown is present in small amounts in Phase A, along with almost equal amounts of Santa Cruz Red-on-buff and Gila/Tonto Polychrome. In Phase B, Tanque Verde Red-on-brown and Santa Cruz Red-on-buff are completely absent, and Gila/Tonto Polychrome is well represented. Santan design traits are present in consistently higher numbers in Phase A than in Phase B, indicating a probable early Soho phase date for the former construction period. Phase B, although later, is still placed within the Soho phase due to the high incidence of Casa Grande Red-on-buff and the low percentage of Gila/Tonto Polychromes.

Table 2. Phase A retaining cell ceramic data

Feature	Total Sherds	Total Decorated Sherds	Sacaton Red-on-buff n	%	Casa Grande Red-on-buff n	%	Tanque Verde Red-on-brown n	%	Santa Cruz Red-on-buff n	%	Gila/Tonto Polychrome n	%	Santan Red-on-buff Elements	Intrusive Black-on-white (B/W) and Black-on-red (B/R) Types — Type	n	%
45	986*	350	100	28.6	232	66.3	1	0.3	6	1.7	1	0.3	162	Black Mesa B/W (4), Holbrook B/W (1), Tusayan B/W (1), Tusayan B/R (4)	10	2.9
46	1132	44	12	27.3	27	61.4	0	0	2	4.6	0	0	16	Black Mesa B/W (2), Tusayan B/R (1)	3	6.8
48	4087	134	75	56.0	42	31.3	0	0	7	5.2	0	0	78	Black Mesa B/W (2), Sosi B/W (1), Holbrook B/W (1), Tusayan B/W (3), Tusayan B/R (1), Medicine B/R (1), Prescott B/Gray (1)	10	7.5
49	3598	568	112	19.7	435	76.6	0	0	4	0.7	3	0.5	310	Kana'a B/W (1), Black Mesa B/W (3), Holbrook B/W (3), Flagstaff B/W (1), Tusayan B/W (7), Tusayan B/R (1)	16	2.8
51	1703	67	21	31.3	39	58.2	0	0	0	0	0	0	41	Kana'a B/W (1), Black Mesa B/W (2), Holbrook B/W (1), Tusayan B/W (1), Tusayan B/R (2)	7	10.4
60	1518	67	22	32.8	43	64.2	0	0	0	0	0	0	54	Black Mesa B/W (1), Tusayan B/R (1)	2	3.0
61	1992	133	17	12.8	110	82.7	0	0	5	3.8	0	0	82	Tusayan B/R (1)	1	.8
62	12591*	494	225	45.5	235	47.6	1	0.2	1	0.2	5	1.0	561	Black Mesa B/W (4), Holbrook B/W (10), Tusayan B/W (5)	19	3.8
63	4114	141	58	41.1	68	48.2	0	0	4	2.8	0	0	77	Tusayan B/W (5), Tusayan B/R (6)	11	7.8
72a	6772* A & B	94	24	25.5	65	69.1	0	0	3	3.2	1	1.1	124	Medicine B/R (1)	1	1.1
73	256	11	4	36.4	6	54.5	0	0	0	0	1	9.1	6		0	0
75	764	59	8	13.6	48	81.4	0	0	2	3.4	0	0	33	Black Mesa B/W (1)	1	1.7
77	936*	47	7	14.9	40	85.1	0	0	0	0	0	0	24		0	0
AVERAGE	3499.9	169.9	52.7	29.6	111.5	63.6	0.2	0.04	2.6	2.0	.8	.9	120.6		6.2	3.7

*Plain wares sampled

Note: frequency = n
percentage = %

Table 3. Phase B retaining cell ceramic data

Feature	Total Sherds	Total Decorated Sherds	Sacaton Red-on-buff		Casa Grande Red-on-buff		Tanque Verde Red-on-brown		Santa Cruz Red-on-buff		Gila/Tonto Polychrome		Santan Red-on-buff Elements	Intrusive Black-on-white and Black-on-Red	
			n	%	n	%	n	%	n	%	n	%		n	%
30	136	7	0	0	5	71.4	0	0	0	0	2	28.6	0	0	0
81	167	23	0	0	23	100.0	0	0	0	0	0	0	1	0	0
90	23	5	1	20.0	4	80.0	0	0	0	0	0	0	8	0	0
91	89	6	1	16.7	5	83.3	0	0	0	0	0	0	3	0	0
95	95	6	1	16.7	5	83.3	0	0	0	0	0	0	3	0	0
97	75	7	2	28.6	4	57.1	0	0	0	0	1	14.3	3	0	0
104	514	21	2	9.5	19	90.5	0	0	0	0	0	0	8	0	0
108	92	6	0	0	5	83.3	0	0	0	0	1	16.7	2	0	0
109	76	6	0	0	6	100.0	0	0	0	0	0	0	1	0	0
AVERAGE	140.8	9.7	.8	10.2	8.4	83.2	0	0	0	0	0.4	6.6	3.2	0	0

Habitation Structures

Introduction

Twenty-two habitation units were excavated around the base and on top of Mound 8 at Las Colinas. The primary criterion used to distinguish between units utilized for domestic purposes and units constructed primarily as integral components of the mound structure itself, was the presence of a hearth or firepit in conjunction with a recognizable floor. Other diagnostic features, although not always present, were postholes, storage pits, entryways, and floor-contact artifacts. An excellent example of this differentiation is seen in the series of contiguous, Civano phase, solid adobe-walled units attached to the west side of the massive outer wall (Map 1). Feature 27, containing firepits, postholes, and a metate associated with the floor, is included with the habitation structures, while adjacent Features 9, 19, and 122 which lack these components, are assumed to be extensions of the main mound structure.

The ordering of these structures within phases was based upon three factors. Of primary importance was pottery analysis, in which relative type percentages and the occurrence of trade wares were used to establish phase designations. This classification was further confirmed by stratigraphic placement and archaeomagnetic dates, when feasible (see Table 1). Architectural type and construction methods were also considered valid dating indicators.

A variety of construction techniques was used in habitation structures during the almost 300-year occupation of the area of Mound 8. The earliest structure is a traditional Sacaton pit house (Feature 112). The early Soho phase is characterized by large, post-reinforced adobe-walled rooms, often built within pits, while the later Soho and Civano phase rooms are all above ground. In the Civano phase both pit houses and above-ground, solid adobe-walled rooms are utilized for dwellings, with the former type being most prevalent. Late Civano phase structures at Las Colinas were exclusively pit houses, located both on top of the mound and around its base. Thus, although both post-reinforced and solid-adobe construction was utilized at various times, the pit house in diverse forms appears throughout the occupation of Las Colinas. There appears to have been a continuous use of this traditional Hohokam dwelling, while experimentation went on with a variety of other construction techniques during the Classic period.

Sacaton Phase

The earliest structure excavated at Las Colinas, Feature 112 (Figure 20), was a small, oval pit house. Although no archaeomagnetic date was obtained for this unit, its entryway was destroyed by construction of Feature 100, which has one of the earliest (A.D. 1180 ± 25) archaeomagnetic dates collected at the site (see Table 1). Very little pottery was recovered from Feature 112 and the disturbance from intrusive pits and structures makes ceramic dating problematic.

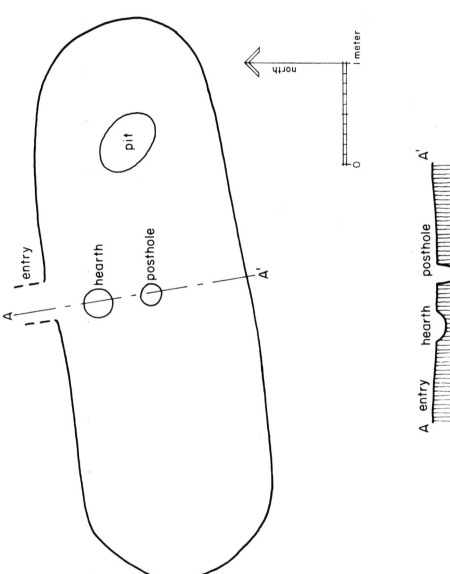

Figure 20. Feature 112

Although extremely small, this pit house resembles Sacaton phase structures at Snaketown. The floor is saucer-shaped with no groove, and the walls are unplastered. Roof support consisted of a single, central post, with no evidence of posts around the edge of the pit. The hearth was located immediately inside the entryway in the north wall. The size and shape of the entry could not be determined.

Early Soho Phase

Feature 100, one of six early Soho phase structures, overlies the entry-way of Feature 112. Ceramic data show a high concentration of Santan Red-on-buff sherds (a transitional type; see Crown, this volume) in Features 100, 119 and 121; Features 125, 76 and 84, however, did not yield sample sizes large enough to interpret.

Features 100, 125, and 76 are located on the west side of the mound, and are not attached to it structurally. Although the archaeomagnetic dates for all three cluster around A.D. 1180 ± 25, Feature 100 postdates Feature 125, since in constructing the north wall of Feature 100, the south wall of Feature 125 was removed. There are no archaeomagnetic dates for Feature 119 or Feature 121, but they are located beneath the massive outer wall, and the west wall of Feature 119 appears to intrude into an outer wall of an earlier mound construction. Feature 84, on the south side of the mound, cannot be dated by archaeomagnetic, stratigraphic, or ceramic data, but has been placed in the early Soho because of the conformity of its general construction to the other houses of this period.

That these structures were inhabited during the initial construction and expansion of Mound 8, is indicated by the fact that Santan Red-on-buff traits and intrusive trade wares are concentrated both in the structures themselves and in the central core cells of the mound. There is also a higher relative percentage of Sacaton Red-on-buff to Casa Grande Red-on-buff in these structures. Features 119 and 121 were both abandoned prior to the construction of the massive outer wall.

These early Soho houses are spaced fairly evenly around the perimeter of the mound, and, with the exception of Feature 100, their long axes are at right angles to it (Map 1). There is no indication of compound walls or compact grouping of the structures other than their association with the central mound itself. This arrangement of these houses reflects the somewhat casual plan of earlier Hohokam periods.

The only generalizations that can be made about the six early Soho structures are that they are large and rectangular, and that the hearth is in each case positioned near the center of a long wall. In other respects the dwellings are architecturally diverse (see Part II).

Features 119 and 121 are very much alike. Both are pit houses dug into sterile caliche and both have corner postholes. Their greatest similarity lies in the presence of a shallow pit located between the hearth and the nearest wall (Figures 21 and 22).

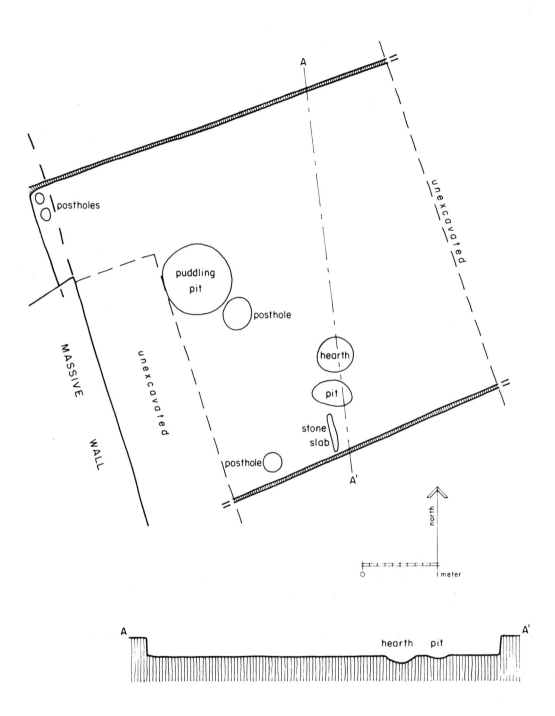

Figure 21.   Feature 119

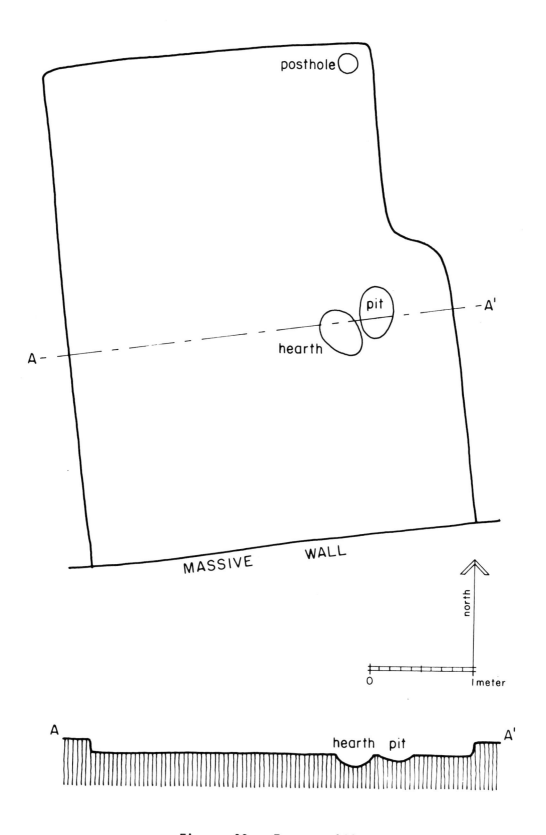

Figure 22. Feature 121

Features 84, 100, and 125 were constructed in approximately the same manner: a pit was dug into sterile soil, posts were erected around the interior edge of the pit, and the posts were finally plastered with caliche and adobe to form the post-reinforced adobe walls typical of the Soho phase (Figure 23, B). Each hearth was large and round, was lined with adobe, and had a raised rim. Feature 100 was the only house of this time period to have a definite entryway, consisting of a raised sill and a small exterior overhang (Figure 23, A-A'). It can be assumed that access to the other houses was through an opening immediately in front of the firepit. But erosion of the walls has left no indication of entryways.

The remaining structure, Feature 76, was an above-ground, post-reinforced adobe-walled house. Its wall posts were set in a trench dug into sterile soil and were left exposed inside the room (Figure 24).

Middle and Late Soho Phases

There is little evidence of occupation in the vicinity of Mound 8 between the late 1100s and early 1300s. Only one structure (Feature 80), a post-reinforced adobe-walled room, was uncovered that dated to the middle Soho phase. After its original construction (A.D. 1230 ± 30, see Table 1), it was extensively remodeled to form two contiguous rooms, Features 80 and 59 (Figure 25). All walls were constructed of post-reinforced adobe, and were similar to those in the core cells of the mound construction. There was no evidence of entryways, although wall stubs were so low that all traces may have been destroyed.

Civano Phase

The immediate area of the mound was apparently inhabited during the major part of the 13th Century. It is assumed that the major construction of the mound was completed by the early 1200s. It is not known whether there was any early ceremonial or other use of the surface of the mound. The earliest dated occupation of the mound is Feature 26, a pit house or jacal, the floor of which was excavated through Caps 3 and 4. It has an archaeo-magnetic date of A.D. 1335 ± 38 (see Table 1). Like all of the structures located on top of the mound, it was in poor condition, and few definite con-clusions could be drawn about its size, shape, or construction.

During the mid-14th Century, two radically different types of house construction were used at Las Colinas. Although the majority of structures excavated were pit houses, two rectangular, solid adobe-walled rooms were located on the west side of the mound. Feature 39, although not completely excavated, appears to be detached from all the other structures. Feature 24 abutted the west mound extension. In both structures the wall bases were placed in shallow trenches and were thicker than the upper portions. Doorways were well defined, with hearths located directly inside. Feature 24 had two hearths as well as an open-ended trough metate lying on the east end of the floor (Figure 41).

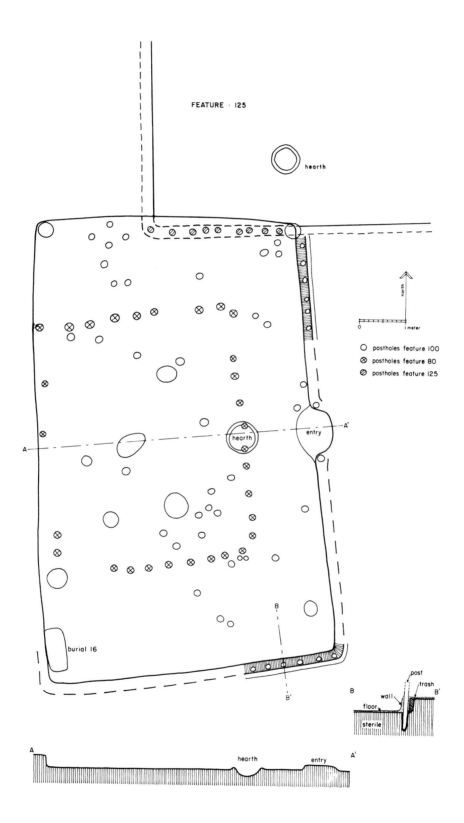

Figure 23. Feature 100: a. hearth and entry cross-section; b. post-reinforced wall cross-section

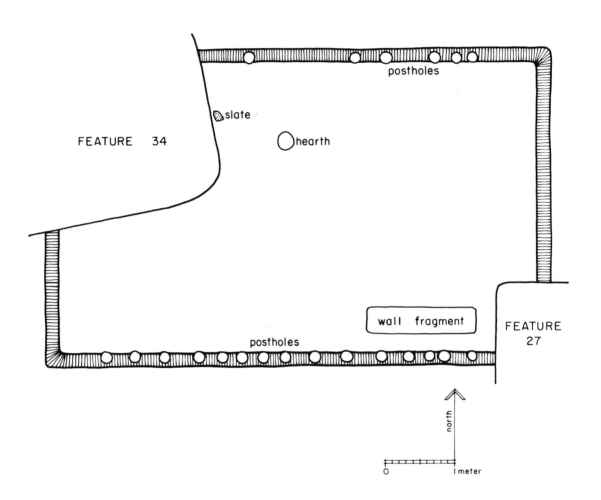

Figure 24. Feature 76

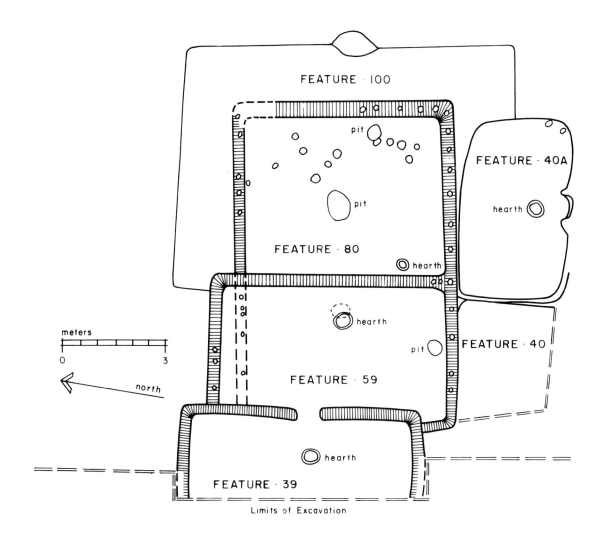

Figure 25. Features 80, 59, and 39, showing post-
reinforced adobe walls

Nine of the thirteen Civano structures are pit houses scattered on top and to the north and west of Mound 8. They are smaller than Soho phase structures, are shallow, and are lined with thin adobe that slopes from the walls onto the floor. While they are all roughly rectangular in shape, some have sharply delineated corners and others have broadly rounded corners. The method of upper wall construction cannot be determined, but the absence of postholes in the floor and around the exterior suggests that they were constructed of brush, reeds, or other flimsy material. There is no evidence of entryways, and the location of hearths is random. The hearths are small, round, and adobe-lined, and there are usually two in each house (Figures 26 and 27).

Feature 114 is an exception: this small, rectangular house was extremely well preserved with walls standing to a height of 50 cm. Sections of wall lying on the floor indicated an even greater original height. Features include an entryway with sloping floor, a firepit, corner postholes, and a plastered-over subfloor storage pit. Perhaps the most unusual feature is a low, adobe floor ridge bisecting the house just east of the entryway and firepit (Figure 51).

The three pit houses or jacal structures on the top of the mound (Features 15, 16, and 26) may have been used as cooking or work areas; they contain storage pits, mealing bins, and numerous superimposed hearths. Feature 40, attached to Feature 40a, is probably a similar work and storage area (Figure 28).

Two of the late (post A.D. 1400) Civano phase houses (Features 74 and 40a) have lateral stepped-entryways with hearths immediately inside. This design appears to be a return to a pit house form of earlier Hohokam periods.

In summary, the Civano phase at Las Colinas can be characterized by simple, brush-walled pit houses. These structures were randomly distributed, conforming to the casual arrangement of the earlier Hohokam villages.

Miscellaneous Architectural Features

Puddling Pits

The most common architectural features at Las Colinas were puddling pits. Between 75 and 100 of these pits were identified, although many were left unexcavated.

Puddling pits are basin-shaped excavations into trash middens or sterile soil. They were used to mix adobe for post-reinforced and solid-wall adobe construction during the Soho and early Civano phases. They are randomly scattered and are often intrusive into earlier features. The majority of puddling pits found at Las Colinas were intrusive into the basal level of the mound. Many of the outer walls of the mound were superimposed upon pits that had been utilized for the construction of interior mound walls (Figure 29).

Puddling pits within the mound were filled either with the caliche-adobe left from construction, or with the same fill used in the mound cells.

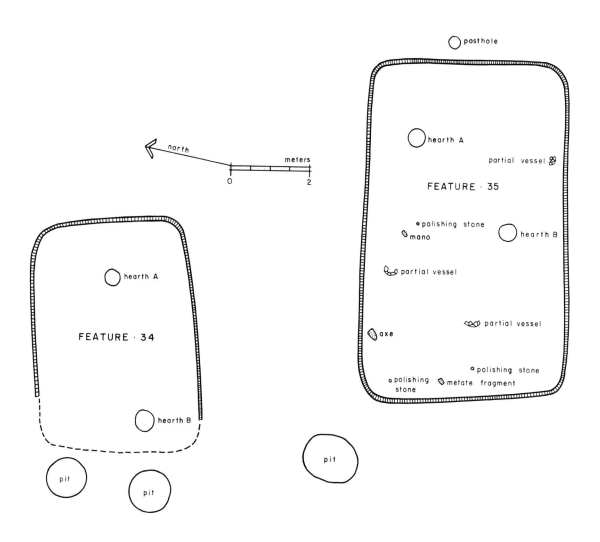

Figure 26.   Features 34 and 35

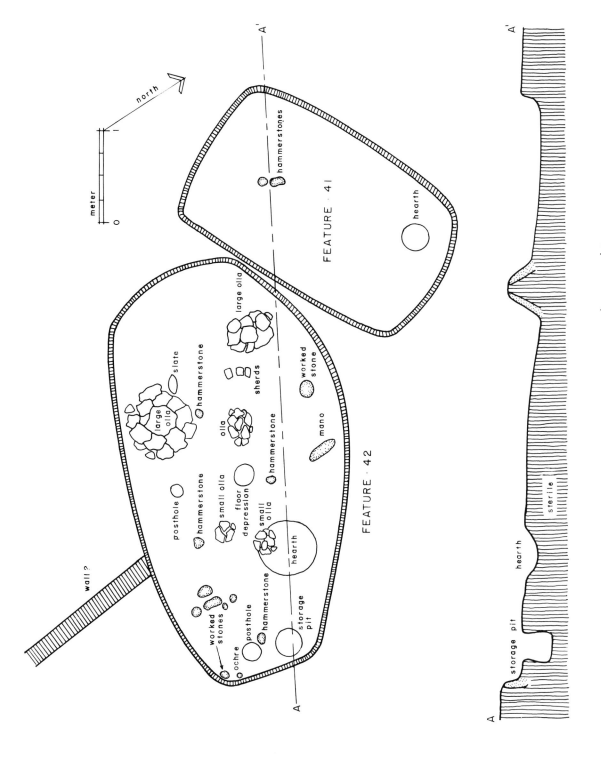

meter

north

FEATURE · 41

hammerstones

hearth

A'

large olla

slate

hammerstone

sherds

worked
stone

large
olla

olla

hammerstone

mano

posthole

hammerstone

small olla

floor
depression

small
olla

wall?

worked
stones

hammerstone

posthole

hearth

ochre

storage
pit

FEATURE · 42

A

A'

A

storage pit

hearth

sterile

Figure 27.   Features 41 and 42

53

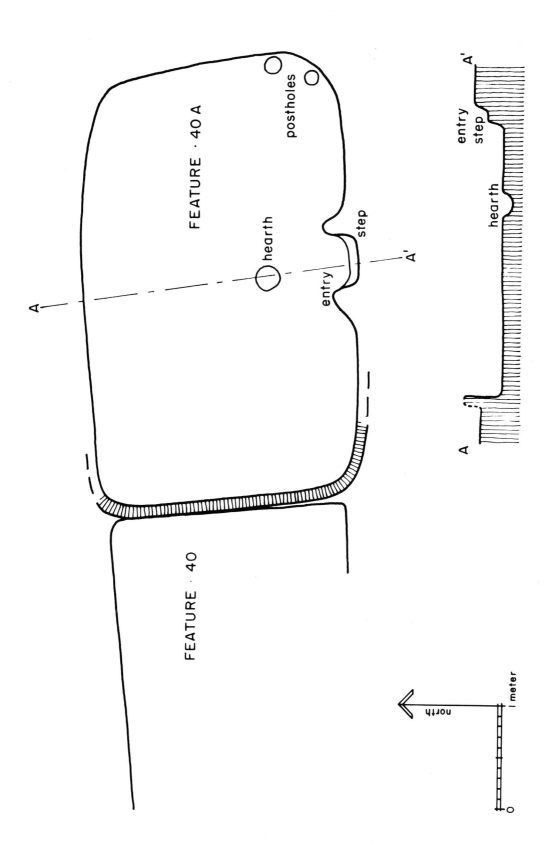

FEATURE · 40 A

postholes

hearth

entry

step

A

A'

FEATURE · 40

entry
step

hearth

A'

A

Figure 28.   Features 40 and 40a

north

0   1 meter

Figure 29. Walls superimposed upon puddling
pits

Pits on the exterior of the mound were often reused. In Feature 5, north of the mound, several puddling pits appeared to have been used to roast corn; they contained charred kernels and had slightly burned rims. Caches of worked stone were commonly found in pits on the west side of the mound.

Puddling pits usually had sloping sides and a flat bottom. Because the adobe lining terminated at the associated use-level, there were no adobe rims. The average diameter was 50 cm to 100 cm and the average depth equalled 20 cm to 50 cm.

Storage Pit

Feature 38 was a shallow, bell-shaped storage pit located just north-west of Feature 35. It was only 12 cm deep and contained a ground stone crusher and mano (Figure 30).

Walls

The south end of a post-reinforced adobe wall, 2.5 m long and 20 cm wide, was attached to the northeast corner of the massive outer wall. It probably was built during the Soho phase, although it does not appear to be directly related to any Soho phase structures. Its north end is cut by the wall of Feature 42, a Civano phase pit house.

The low, solid-adobe wall extending south as a continuation of the south wall of Feature 27 was of unique construction. It has horizontal grooves across its width as if it once supported a floor or other construction. The average width of the wall was 27 cm and its average height was 17.5 cm. The grooves were 4 cm to 8 cm wide, and were spaced approximately 60 cm apart (see Figures 31 and 32).

Several bases of post-reinforced adobe walls (Features 72a and 72b) were found which do not appear to be related to the mound construction (see Figure 33). They protrude through the basal level of the mound and extend beneath and outside the massive outer wall. They may be remnants of an earlier mound structure that was destroyed before construction of the existing mound. The limited area which was excavated gave no indication of the shape of such an earlier structure.

Possible Houses

Feature 88, on the top of the mound west of the house foundation, was partially destroyed by construction of the historic house foundation. It may have been one of the original Soho phase structures on the mound. The north wall was thick, solid adobe, and the west wall was post-reinforced light-brown adobe. There appeared to be a floor level extending toward the historic house foundation from these walls. East of the post-reinforced wall was a row of four rectangular pits dug along an east-west axis. The southernmost pit contained Burial 14. The remaining three were empty, and since they had been cut by the historic house foundation, it is felt that the burials were removed

Figure 30. Feature 38, bell-shaped pit

Figure 31. Feature 27 (looking southeast)

Figure 32. Same as Figure 31 (looking east)

Figure 33. Features 72a and 72b--early post-reinforced adobe walls
intersecting later Stage III walls

at the time of its construction. The pits were intrusive into the floor of Feature 88 and are probably much later in date.

Feature 120, located in a test trench (Feature 115) through the east side of the mound, appeared to be a portion of a burned house floor beneath the basal level of the mound. The section visible in the trench was of hard-burned adobe 4.60 m wide. The walls were probably made of reeds or jacal, although there is no clear evidence for the type of construction used. A post-hole containing a burned post was located in the center of the exposed floor. A large amount of burned roofing material lay directly upon the floor, includ-ing grass, reeds, and small poles. This floor is tentatively dated to the Santa Cruz phase as a Santa Cruz Red-on-buff sherd was found upon it.

Prehistoric Features on the Mound

In the Civano phase the top of the mound seems to have been used extensively for a variety of activities. Civano pit houses have already been discussed in the section on habitation structures, and a possibly earlier house (Feature 88) has been discussed above. It is striking that no extramural hearths or ramada work areas were located outside the boundaries of the mound. The higher elevation of the mound apparently was preferred for these activities.

The northwest corner of the mound was the highest and best-preserved section remaining. In this area, Feature 31 had several elements which suggest a work area with associated ramada or windbreak. There was no pre-pared floor in this area, but three postholes were intrusive into Caps 3 and 4, and a comal resting on flat river cobbles was associated with Cap 4. Two of the postholes had slab bases. It is obvious that Cap 4 was treated in this area as a general use surface late in the history of the mound.

Although the east and south sides of the mound had been extensively disturbed by historic use, there are indications of use in these areas in the late prehistoric period. A shallow pit through Cap 3 on the east side con-tained a quartzite axe, hammerstone, and mano blank.

A further indication of the importance of the mound during the Civano phase is the high percentage of burials that are intrusive into the mound surface. Twelve of the 15 burials uncovered at Las Colinas were scattered on the top of the mound. These are dated to the Civano phase through their stratigraphic relation to the mound caps.

Summary and Conclusions

The Mound

The 1968 excavations at Las Colinas revealed that Mound 8 was an arti-ficial platform mound dating to the Classic period. The internal structure consisted of a series of post-reinforced adobe walls erected upon a prepared surface. The retaining rooms or cells thus formed had been immediately filled with trash, sterile desert soil, or mixtures of the two. This edifice was capped with a layer of caliche-adobe. Subsequent construction of additional, post-reinforced adobe-walled cells, of a massive adobe outer retaining wall, and of additional caps, resulted in a rectangular, flat-topped mound 2 m high, 24 m wide and 29 m long.

It can be assumed that construction of Mound 8 began early in the Soho phase (A.D. 1100-1300) and was completed by the end of that phase. There is some evidence of an earlier, post-reinforced structure that was leveled before the present mound was erected, but architectural and ceramic data indicate that the nucleus of the structure was built rapidly during the 1100s. In the late Soho phase sporadic additions were made to the mound; these included several recappings.

During the Civano phase of the Classic period (A.D. 1300-1450), a solid adobe-walled extension was added parallel to the west side of the massive wall, changing the shape of the structure from rectangular to square. The level top of the mound was used for domestic purposes, and both habitation structures and burials penetrated the upper adobe caps.

The original function of the mound during the Soho phase is unknown. Foundations of a historic house destroyed whatever structures may have existed on the central portion of the mound. The undisturbed portions of the mound top, except for a fragment of undated, post-reinforced adobe wall, yielded no evidence of pre-Civano use. However, by the Civano phase of occupation, the mound was being used for the same secular purposes as the surrounding low-lying areas. Even though the original function of the mound may have been non-domestic, its purpose had apparently been forgotten, or had changed, in the intervening years. It is possible, too, that the original builders were dispossessed and that the mound passed into a different cultural tradition.

Artificial platform mounds have a long history in Hohokam culture. Mound 40 at Snaketown had been capped with a layer of adobe by A.D. 500 during the Snaketown phase (Haury 1976). The first attempts at achieving an elevated floor were confined to covering existing trash mounds, but by the Sacaton phase these mounds were being used as the nuclei for extensive additions that raised and extended the elevated surfaces. The platform mound became increasingly significant to the Hohokam, and consequently consumed a greater proportion of their energy, during the Sacaton phase. Mound 16 at Snaketown was a low, artificial mound constructed of clay and sand and capped with eight separate facings. Except for a large hearth, there are no indications of structures on the flat surface of the mound. A row of postholes encircling the base indicates that the mound may have been surrounded by a palisade (Haury 1976).

The Sacaton platform mound at the Gatlin Site near Gila Bend represents a far more ambitious undertaking. Wasley (1960) has identified six stages of construction, which culminated in a large, rectangular, flat-topped mound 3 m high. The first stage was a low, artifically constructed, faced mound of oval shape, which was subsequently enlarged and embellished with ancillary mounds connected to the main structure by radial walls. Vast quantities of material, contained by thick caliche facings, were consolidated in these structures. There are no indications of structures built upon the facings at any stage, and no evidence of ceremonial usage.

During the Classic period (A.D. 1100-1450) of the Hohokam, artificial platform mounds may have been the principal structures unifying surrounding communities in either a social or religious network, since ball courts were no longer used. Within the Salt and Gila drainages, four mounds are known to have been built during the Soho phase (A.D. 1100-1300). Mound 8 at Las Colinas has been discussed above. Hayden (1957) describes both the Pueblo Grande and La Ciudad mounds as being cellular in structure. The Pueblo Grande mound consists of a massive outer wall around solid adobe-walled retaining cells filled with trash and desert soil. On the top of the mound are large, non-contiguous houses which appear to resemble the early Soho structures at Las Colinas. Overlying these are contiguous, solid adobe-walled Civano phase rooms. La Ciudad is described as being similar to Pueblo Grande both in construction of the mound itself and in the sequence of structures on the mound top.

Fewkes' (1912) description of Compound B at Casa Grande suggests that this structure dates from the Soho period. Mound A is constructed of artificially filled cells with a series of non-contiguous, post-reinforced rooms on top. Mound B, although lacking the interior retaining walls, is also surmounted by post-reinforced rooms.

The Sacaton and Soho phase mounds differ greatly in their construction. The inspiration for the Sacaton mounds seems to have been in the faced trash mounds of earlier Hohokam periods. The original mounds were enlarged and embellished by repeated additions and alterations.

In the Soho phase the mounds were structured internally with rooms that were filled immediately upon completion. Although this method of construction represented a completely new departure in technique, there is no evidence that it was occasioned by instability of the unstructured mounds. The idea may have come north from Nayarit where, at the site of Ampa, Meighan (1959) found adobe cell construction of house and temple mounds. A grid arrangement of adobe walls formed small rooms which were filled with dirt and refuse to form a platform.

The function of the mounds appears to have changed between the Sacaton and Soho phases. There are no indications that Sacaton mounds were utilized for secular purposes; but the Soho mounds, with the exception of Mound 8 at Las Colinas, had large, rectangular, post-reinforced houses on their tops. At Pueblo Grande and La Ciudad, these Soho rooms were later overlaid by massive, walled, Civano structures. At Las Colinas, Mound 8 was also used for habitation during the Civano phase, but in this case the structures were thin-walled pit houses constructed of flimsy reeds or brush.

Platform mounds constructed during the Civano phase (A.D. 1300-1450) were generally similar to those of the Soho phase. However, the large platform mound at Escalante Ruin on the Gila River did not have a cellular structure and was supported solely by massive outer walls. On the top were contiguous, solid-adobe rooms (Doyel 1974). Moorehead's (1906) report of his excavations in the early 1900s indicates that Mound 4 of Las Colinas was similar in construction to the Escalante mound. University Indian Ruin in the Tucson Basin includes a mound whose core is a habitation structure that was deliberately filled with trash, and then flanked by massive walls designed to contain additional fill. Contiguous, solid adobe-walled rooms were constructed on top of the edifice (Hayden 1957).

Although the big house in Compound A at Casa Grande is not considered a mound, it must be noted that the bottom set of rooms have been filled purposefully, that the upper stories are therefore resting upon a mound. In this sense Casa Grande may be regarded as the ultimate expression of the Classic period artificial platform mound with superimposed dwellings.

Habitation Structures

Twenty-two habitation structures were excavated at Las Colinas in addition to the internally structured mound. During the Soho phase these structures were situated around the base of the mound; in the Civano phase, however, they were built both around the base of the mound and on top of it. In both phases the houses were randomly oriented, and were not contiguous.

Soho phase houses have been dated by their architectural form, archaeomagnetic dates, and stratigraphy. The majority of the archaeomagnetic dates indicated an occupation date of A.D. 1180. The Civano phase houses were dated by an extensive array of archaeomagnetic dates ranging from A.D. 1335 to A.D. 1450, and by supporting ceramic data.

The single Sacaton phase structure has been dated solely on the basis of stratigraphy and architectural form. It consists of a small, oval, saucer-shaped floor with a central post-support, hearth, and possible entryway.

Six houses which are assignable to the early Soho phase were wholly or partially excavated. They are believed to have been occupied during the construction of the mound in the 12th century. All the houses are large rectangular rooms with the firepit opposite the middle of a long wall, and presumably in front of the entryway. The construction is varied, ranging from thin-walled pit houses to post-reinforced adobe-walled pit rooms to above ground houses.

During the 13th century, the area immediately adjacent to Mound 8 was almost wholly unpopulated, although some alterations were made to the mound itself. Only one room, a post-reinforced adobe-walled structure, was occupied during this period. There is no indication why the population declined so remarkably during the 13th century, although many hypotheses such as harassment or climatic change have been advanced to account for the abandonment.

The reoccupation of the area during the Civano phase followed a new pattern. The mound itself as well as the surrounding area was used for habitation. Various features, such as burials, dwellings, and work areas were intrusive into the upper caps of the mound.

Eleven of the 13 Civano phase structures were small, thin-walled pit houses constructed of flimsy reeds or brush. Only two of these houses had discernible entryways, while the firepits were variable in location and the house forms varied from rectangular to oval. Two of the Civano phase houses were rectangular, solid adobe-walled rooms with hearths opposite the doorway in the long wall. During this period, apparently, insubstantial domestic structures were preferred to the large, heavy-walled houses that became common in the Soho phase.

In general, the habitation structures of the Classic period in the Gila and Salt river valleys are characterized by experimentation and diversity of design. It has been generally accepted that above-ground, post-reinforced adobe-walled structures were typical of the Soho phase, and that contiguous, solid-wall complexes were the rule during the Civano phase.

In fact, however, neither Las Colinas nor the majority of Hohokam sites conforms to the proposed pattern. A brief discussion of work at other Hohokam sites is presented below to confirm this point.

Three small Soho phase villages were excavated by Doyel (1974) within the Escalante Ruin group. Although they were surrounded by compound walls, at AZ U:15:22 (ASM) and AZ U:15:27 (ASM) these walls were added after construction of the rooms. The rooms were non-contiguous and of random orientation. Both post-reinforced and solid-adobe walls were found. Structures were built in pits as well as above ground, and forms ranged from oval to rectangular. The centered hearth and doorway that are characteristic of Hohokam habitation rooms were common.

Two structures excavated at a Soho phase site on the lower Gila River (AZ U:13:9 ASM) further illustrate this diversity. Both were rectangular; one had jacal walls and the other had solid adobe walls (Johnson 1964). Compound B at Casa Grande, which is believed to date from the Soho phase, contained both post-reinforced and solid-adobe houses (Fewkes 1912). Both types were non-contiguous, randomly arranged, large, rectangular structures, with centered hearth and doorway.

The habitation structures of the Soho phase do not fall into a consistent pattern. There seems to have been experimentation with new wall-construction techniques, although traditional patterns of village structure and individual house plans were continued. The Soho houses at Las Colinas illustrate this.

This diversity continues into the Civano phase. Although many of the large sites such as Los Muertos, Escalante, and Casa Grande at first glance appear to conform to the cited pattern of contiguous, solid-adobe pueblo structures within compound walls, there are anomalies in all cases. The first structure built on top of the Civano phase platform mound at Escalante was a Sacaton phase pit house (Doyel 1974). At Los Muertos, "thin-walled rounded huts were scattered outside the main walls" of the compounds (Haury 1945). Although Haury feels these may be pre-Classic in age, similar findings at other Classic sites argue for their being contemporaneous. Steen's (1965) excavations in Compound A at Casa Grande revealed various types of contemporaneous, non-contiguous houses with no pattern of placement of the different house types.

Smaller Civano phase villages in the Gila and Salt drainages also exhibit heterogeneity. Haury (1976) excavated several small, late-Classic sites near Snaketown. One (AZ U:13:21 ASM) consisted of scattered, non-contiguous, post-reinforced houses with no compound wall, while another (AZ U:13:22 ASM) had contiguous, post-reinforced walls within a compound. The Fitch Site (Pailes 1963) consisted of rectangular, non-contiguous, solid adobe-walled houses in random placement. It also should be noted that various kinds of footings were employed for these walls. In many instances the bases were placed in trenches; otherwise, they were laid directly upon the surface.

The prevalent house type at Las Colinas during the Civano phase differed from the ones discussed above. Although two solid-adobe wall rooms were found at Las Colinas, the majority of habitation structures were pit houses with thin adobe walls and insubstantial superstructures. These latter structures were not contiguous, and there was no evidence of a compound wall. This type of house was popular for over 100 years, through the middle of the 15th century. There are several other examples of very late, flimsy structures in the Salt and Gila valleys. Weaver (1972) reports a possible jacal structure on top of the house mound at Pueblo del Monte, and shallow pit houses were excavated into the top of collapsed Civano phase walls in Compound F at Casa Grande (Haury 1945).

The prevalence of structures with flimsy walls at Las Colinas through the mid-15th century is a strong argument for a Hohokam-Pima continuum in the Salt and Gila valleys; for at the time of European contact, the Pima occupied round huts made of reeds and branches. Although the Las Colinas house forms were different from those of the Pima, house forms in general were in continuous fluctuation throughout the history of the Hohokam. The most important point to be made however is that pit houses with thin walls were being used in the late Civano phase in preference to structures with contiguous, solid-wall rooms.

The most interesting question about the Classic period is whether the architectural changes which took place following the Sedentary period are attributable to the influence of people from the Tonto Basin, or whether they were an indigenous development. The continued presence of the pit house in association with other styles of architecture and a prevalent ranchería village pattern, suggests a continuity of conservative Hohokam traits mixed with more progressive and experimental elements. During the final phases of occupation of Las Colinas, earlier, and perhaps more traditional elements of Hohokam culture reappear, suggesting that there occurred a revitalization of ways of life which had never been completely lost. Moreover, there is no conclusive evidence of major influence from any non-Hohokam group.

Part II

Characteristics of Habitation Structures
at Las Colinas

This part of the chapter presents detailed descriptive information about the habitation structures excavated at Las Colinas. The structures are grouped by phase. The single Sacaton phase structure is presented first, followed by discussion of features from successively later phases. Within each phase, the structures are ordered by ascending feature number. The phase assignment of each structure is presented in Table 4.

Table 4.   Phase assignments of Las Colinas habitation structures

Feature	Phase	Feature	Phase
15	Civano	59	Soho
16	Civano	74	Civano
24	Civano	76	Soho
26	Civano	80	Soho
34	Civano	84	Soho
35	Civano	100	Soho
39	Civano	112	Sacaton
40	Civano	114	Civano
40a	Civano	119	Soho
41	Civano	121	Soho
42	Civano	125	Soho

Sacaton Phase

Feature 112 (Figure 34)

    Type: Oval pit house
    Location: West side of mound.
    Phase: Sacaton.
    Dating: Archaeomagnetic - none.
             Stratigraphic - underlying Features 100 and 40a.
    Dimensions: E-W = 5.60 m, N-S = 1.97 m.

    Construction:
            Walls: Pit excavated into trash, no prepared walls, no
                    evidence of walls.
            Roof: Posts on interior or exterior of pit, single central
                    post support, diameter = 30 cm, south of hearth.
            Floor: Saucer-shaped, rough, prepared adobe.
            Entryway: Center of north wall, width = 50 cm, shape
                       indeterminate as south wall of Feature 100 is
                       superimposed upon it.
            Hearth: Directly in front of entryway, small, circular,
                    adobe-lined with raised rim. Diameter = 25 cm,
                    depth = 11 cm.
            Floor Features: Subfloor pit - located in east end of floor,
                    oval, 90 cm by 60 cm. Puddling pits - three intrusive
                    pits cut east and south walls.

    Remarks: House appears to have burned after abandonment.

Figure 34. Feature 112 (looking south-southwest)

Figure 35. Feature 59 (middle), Feature 80 (foreground),
and Feature 39 (background; west wall in
Feature 39 is not a structural wall. It is
the limit of excavation)(looking west)

Soho Phase

Feature 59 (Figure 35)

    Type: Rectangular, post-reinforced adobe-walled room.
    Location: West side of mound.
    Phase: Late Soho.
    Dating: Archaeomagnetic - none.
           Stratigraphic - later remodeling of Feature 80, underlying
               Features 40, 40a, and 39.
    Dimensions: E-W = 3.5 m, N-S = 7 m, maximum height = 12 cm.

    Construction:
           Walls: Posts set into ground covered with adobe plaster.
                West and south walls are original walls of Feature
                80; east wall was partition constructed across center
                of Feature 80. The north wall of Feature 59 was then
                removed and a northern extension was added approxi-
                mately 1 m beyond original north wall. All construc-
                tion was done with post-reinforced adobe walls.
           Roof: No evidence.
           Floor: Two adobe floors, both original to Feature 80.
           Entryway: None.
           Hearths: A. Shallow ash lens, diameter = 30 cm, depth =
                      2.5 cm, intrusive into Hearth B.
                  B. Disturbed by Hearth A, deep, adobe-lined bowl,
                      diameter = 28 cm, depth = 8 cm.
           Floor Features: Postholes - line of 12 postholes just inside
                and parallel to west wall. May have been to strengthen
                wall and support roof. Storage Pit - bell-shaped
                subfloor pit at south end of room, oval mouth 25 cm
                by 32 cm, maximum interior width = 38 cm, depth =
                31 cm.
    Remarks: This feature is a result of later remodeling of Feature 80.

Feature 76 (Figure 36)

    Type: Post-reinforced adobe-walled room.
    Location: Northwest corner of mound.
    Phase: Early Soho.
    Dating: Archaeomagnetic - A.D. 1180 (questionable).
           Stratigraphic - underlying Features 34 and 27.
    Dimensions: E-W = 7 m, N-S = 4 m, maximum depth = 28 cm.

    Construction:
           Walls: Adobe-covered posts set 15 cm to 30 cm apart in trench
                dug into sterile soil. Posts exposed on interior of
                room.
           Roof: No evidence.
           Floor: Hard adobe.
           Entryway: None.

Figure 36. Feature 76 (looking west)

Figure 37. Feature 84 (looking north)

Hearth: Located 1 m south of center of north wall. It is round, adobe-lined with straight sides and flat bottom. Diameter = 25 cm, depth = 7 cm.
Floor Features: None.
Remarks: Construction of Feature 34, a Civano pit house, destroyed northwest quadrant.

Feature 80 (Figure 35)

Type: Post-reinforced adobe-walled room.
Location: West side of mound.
Phase: Soho.
Dating: Archaeomagnetic - A.D. 1230 ± 30.
          Stratigraphic - overlying Feature 100, underlying Features 40 and 40a.
Dimensions: E-W = 7 m, N-S = 5 m, maximum height = 20 cm.
Construction:
          Walls: Posts set into ground approximately 25 cm apart, then covered with adobe; average wall thickness = 25 cm.
          Roof: No evidence.
          Floor: Two separate floors. Lower floor was well-plastered, but broken in eastern half due to settling of fill of Feature 100. Upper floor was plastered directly upon the lower and consisted of adobe plaster 5 cm to 7 cm thick. Floor curves up into wall.
          Entryway: None evident, probably in center of south wall.
          Hearth: Center of and close to south wall, circular, adobe-lined, breast-shaped in cross-section, plastered over when Feature 80 was remodeled. Diameter = 30 cm, depth = 13 cm.
          Floor Features: Postholes - five postholes averaging 15 cm in diameter are scattered in a north-south line across center of room, perhaps to support a sagging roof. Plugged Holes - three parallel to east wall, average diameter = 15 cm. Pits - six subfloor pits in various locations, range in diameter from 62 cm to 20 cm.
Remarks: Wall constructed across center of house over both floors, became east wall of Feature 59. West half of room remodeled into Feature 59.

Feature 84 (Figure 37)

Type: Rectangular pit room.
Location: South side of mound.
Phase: Early Soho.
Dating: None (see remarks).
Dimensions: E-W = 6.40 m, N-S estimated at 9 m, but undetermined as southern half of feature unexcavated.

Construction:
        Walls: Pit dug into sterile soil, post-reinforced adobe walls erected inside pit.
        Roof: Fallen, burned adobe with reed impressions and burned mesquite beams lying directly upon floor.
        Floor: Hard, compact adobe.
        Entryway: None found.
        Hearth: Round, adobe-lined with raised rim. Diameter = 53 cm, depth = 15 cm.
        Floor Features: Two intrusive puddling pits located near firepit.

Remarks: Although no archaeomagnetic dates, stratigraphic superimpositions, or sufficient pottery for significant dating were available for this feature, its resemblance to Features 100 and 125 in construction and size indicates that it probably falls into the early Soho phase.

Feature 100 (Figure 38)

    Type: Rectangular pit room.
    Location: West side of mound.
    Phase: Early Soho.
    Dating: Archaeomagnetic - A.D. 1180 ± 25.
        Stratigraphic - overlying Feature 112, underlying Feature 59, 80, and 40a.
    Dimensions: E-W 9.5 m, N-S 6.0 m, maximum wall height = 37 cm.

Construction:
        Walls: Rectangular pit dug into sterile soil, vertical poles set 27 cm to 37 cm apart just inside pit wall, then covered with a 15 cm- to 35 cm-thick layer of adobe. This wall was completely independent of the pit wall, and the space between the two was filled with trash.
        Roof: Supported by two large (40 cm and 60 cm in diameter) central post supports, minor post supports in the northeast, southeast, and northwest corners, and scattered smaller posts. Numerous burned mesquite beams, masses of reeds and adobe, and the remains of a roof-top hearth were in the fill.
        Floor: Two floors had been laid; the lower was of rough adobe, never used, and immediately covered with an upper layer of smoothed adobe.
        Entryway: In center of east wall, a raised bulbous-shaped step, 1.8 m wide and 12 cm high. Postholes on the exterior suggest a covered entry.
        Hearth: In front of entryway, shallow circular, well plastered with a raised rim. Diameter = 50 cm, depth = 15 cm.
        Floor Features: Pits - seven shallow pits. Postholes - intrusive postholes from Feature 80, a post-reinforced room overlying Feature 100, are located in the central portion of the floor. Intrusive row of postholes inside eastern half of north wall associated with the

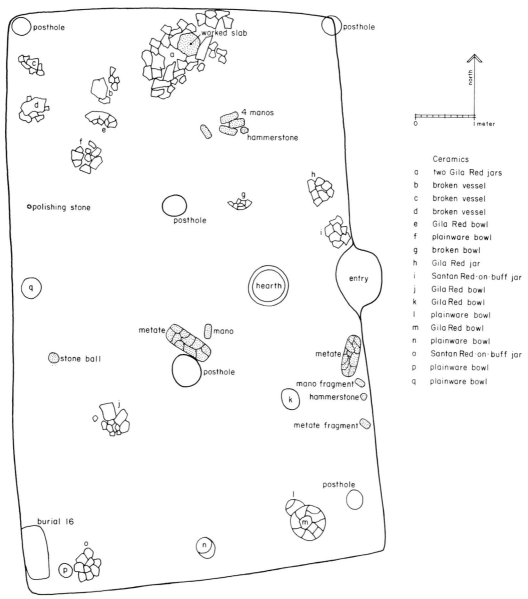

Ceramics
a   two Gila Red jars
b   broken vessel
c   broken vessel
d   broken vessel
e   Gila Red bowl
f   plainware bowl
g   broken bowl
h   Gila Red jar
i   Santan Red-on-buff jar
j   Gila Red bowl
k   Gila Red bowl
l   plainware bowl
m   Gila Red bowl
n   plainware bowl
o   Santan Red-on-buff jar
p   plainware bowl
q   plainware bowl

Figure 38. Feature 100 (looking east), and plan view

south wall of Feature 125 (partially excavated).
Burial 16 -intrusive along west wall in southwest
corner.

Remarks: Archaeomagnetic and archaeologic data suggest that this house
was rapidly consumed by fire. This is supported by the
abundance of cultural material in association with roof fill
and floor.

Feature 119 (Figure 21)

Type: Rectangular pit house.
Location: East side of mound.
Phase: Early Soho.
Dating: Archaeomagnetic - none.
           Stratigraphic - west wall underlies massive outer wall of
              mound and cuts into an earlier wall.
Dimensions: N-S = 4.60 m, E-W = cannot be determined as east end of
           house destroyed by historic activity. Maximum wall height =
           25 cm.

Construction:
           Walls: Pit dug into sterile caliche; west wall of pit
                   appears to have removed a portion of an earlier
                   exterior mound wall. Pit walls were plastered.
                   Average thickness of plaster = 5 cm. No evidence
                   of upper wall construction.
           Roof: No evidence.
           Floor: Well-plastered, slopes up into walls.
           Entryway: None.
           Hearth: Round, burned earth sides, diameter = 41 cm, depth =
                   10 cm.
           Floor Features: Postholes - two in northwest corner, one
                   along south wall, diameter = 12 cm to 22 cm, average
                   depth = 15 cm. Pits: shallow, oval pit just south
                   of hearth, diameter = 55 cm by 44 cm, depth 6 cm;
                   round pit at west end, diameter = 40 cm, filled with
                   burned adobe; intrusive puddling pit, diameter = 77 cm,
                   depth = 25 cm.

Remarks: High incidence of Santan Red-on-buff, and stratigraphic posi-
         tion of this structure indicate that it was constructed and
         occupied prior to final completion of mound.

Feature 121 (Figure 39)

Type: Semi-rectangular pit house.
Location: Northeast corner of mound.
Phase: Early Soho.
Dating: Archaeomagnetic - none.
           Stratigraphic - south wall underlies massive outer wall of
              mound.
Dimensions: N-S = 4.5 m, E-W = 3.75 m, maximum wall height = 13 cm.

Figure 39. Feature 121 (looking west)

Figure 40. Feature 15 (looking south)

Construction:

    Walls: Pit dug into sterile caliche, unplastered, no
          evidence of upper wall construction or support.

    Roof: Burned remains indicate construction with small
          logs, reeds, grass, and adobe.

    Floor: Packed caliche and adobe.

    Entryway: None.

    Hearth: Oval, burned earth sides, diameter = 45 cm by 37 cm,
          depth = 12 cm.

    Floor Features: Posthole - northeast corner, diameter = 18 cm,
          depth = 30 cm. Pit - directly east of hearth, shallow
          oval, diameter = 40 cm by 35 cm, depth = 7 cm.

Remarks: High incidence of Santan Red-on-buff and stratigraphic position indicate that this structure was inhabited prior to, or
during, early stages of mound construction.

Feature 125 (No Illustration)

    Type: Rectangular pit room.

    Location: West side of mound.

    Phase: Early Soho.

    Dating: Archaeomagnetic - A.D. 1180 ± 25.
          Stratigraphic - southwest corner and portion of south wall
          removed by construction of Feature 100, underlying Features
          21, 22, and 114.

    Dimensions: Unknown, maximum wall height = 10 cm.

Construction:

    Walls: Pit dug into sterile soil, post-reinforced adobe walls
          erected inside pit.

    Roof: Fallen burned adobe, reeds, sticks, and mesquite
          beams lying on floor.

    Floor: Hard, well-smoothed adobe.

    Entryway: None found.

    Hearth: Round, adobe-lined with raised rim. Diameter = 32 cm,
          depth = 13 cm.

    Floor Features: None.

Remarks: Although only the southwest quarter of this feature was
excavated, from the position of the firepit it can be estimated
that the long east-west axis measured approximately 7 m,
making it comparable in size to Feature 100.

Civano Phase

Feature 15 (Figure 40)

    Type: Pit house.

    Location: Top of mound, north of Feature 3.

    Phase: Civano.

    Dating: Archaeomagnetic - A.D. 1390 (discarded).
          Stratigraphic - intrusive into Caps 3 and 4.

Construction:
        Walls: Shallow pit dug into top of mound, plastered with thin
            adobe, maximum height = 24 cm. No evidence of upper
            wall construction.
        Roof: No evidence.
        Floor: Thinly plastered with adobe, continuous with walls.
        Entryway: None.
        Hearth: In southwest corner, along west wall, circular, clay-
            lined with raised rim, diameter = 27 cm, depth = 15 cm.
        Floor Features: Low (6 cm) clay ridge extending into house
            interior from south wall.

Feature 16 (Figure 10)

Type: Jacal.
Location: Top of mound, south of house foundation.
Phase: Civano.
Dating: Archaeomagnetic - none.
        Stratigraphic - intrusive into upper mound caps.

Construction:
        Walls: Indeterminate, no indication of adobe plaster. Two
            rows of postholes on northeast and southwest sides,
            which may indicate ramada-type structure.
        Roof: No evidence.
        Floor: Poorly prepared caliche-adobe.
        Entryway: None.
        Hearths: Eight hearths.
        Floor Features: Low (5 cm) clay ridge along southeast side.

Remarks: This feature appears to be a cooking area. Series of
        hearths may indicate seasonal or periodic use.

Feature 24 (Figure 41)

Type: Rectangular, solid adobe-walled room.
Location: Outside northwest corner of mound.
Phase: Civano.
Dating: Archaeomagnetic - none.
        Stratigraphic - overlying Feature 76.

Construction:
        Walls: Solid puddled adobe, base placed in trench 30 cm
            below floor level, wall base wider than upper portions.
        Roof: No evidence.
        Floor: Adobe-caliche plaster.
        Entryway: Door in middle of south wall, 49 cm wide.
        Hearths: A. Directly in front of doorway, breast-shaped,
               adobe-lined, diameter = 20 cm.
            B. Northwest of Hearth A, shallow unlined pit,
               diameter = 25 cm, depth = 8 cm.
        Floor Features: None.

Figure 41. Feature 24 (looking southeast)

Figure 42. Feature 26 (looking north)

Remarks: This room was added to the western extension of the mound.
The north and south walls are abutted to the west wall of
Feature 9. The west wall of this room extends south to
form the west wall of Feature 21.

Feature 26 (Figure 42)

Type: Pit house or jacal.
Location: Top of mound, northwest corner of house foundation.
Phase: Civano.
Dating: Archaeomagnetic - A.D. 1335 ± 38.
          Stratigraphic - cut through Caps 3 and 4.

Construction:
          Walls: Shallow pit excavated into top of mound. West and
                  south walls lined with adobe 15 cm thick and sloping
                  into floor, North and east walls unlined.
          Roof: No evidence.
          Floor: Caliche and some adobe plaster in southwest corner.
          Entryway: No evidence.
          Hearth: Cut by Feature 10, bowl-shaped, with burned earth
                  interior.
          Floor Features: Metate bin - U-shaped, thin-adobe ridge with
                  open end towards east. Subfloor pit - adjoining
                  south wall, semicircular with prepared-adobe walls.
                  Subfloor pit - along south wall, oval with prepared
                  walls and floor.

Remarks: Walls on south and west would have shaded work area from
         afternoon sun.

Feature 34 (Figure 43)

Type: Pit house, rectangular with rounded corners.
Location: Northwest of mound,
Phase: Late Civano,
Dating: Archaeomagnetic: Hearth A - A.D. 1390 ± 36, Hearth B - A.D.
          1415 ± 23. Stratigraphic: superimposed upon Feature 76.

Construction:
          Walls: Pit dug into sterile soil, approximately 45 cm deep,
                  lined with caliche-adobe 3 cm to 5 cm thick. West
                  wall indefinite.
          Roof: No evidence.
          Floor: Caliche-adobe, continuous with walls.
          Entryway: None.
          Hearths: A. Southwest corner of house, round, adobe-lined,
                       diameter = 28 cm, depth = 13 cm.
                    B. East end, round, clay-lined rim, sides and
                        bottom burned earth, diameter = 20 cm, depth
                        = 14 cm.
          Floor Features: None.

Figure 43. Feature 34 (looking west)

Feature 35 (Figure 44)

Type: Pit house, rectangular with rounded corners.
Location: Northwest of mound.
Phase: Civano.
Dating: Archaeomagnetic - Hearth A - A.D. 1370 ± 27, Hearth B - A.D.
           1395 ± 12.
           Stratigraphic - none.

Construction:
           Walls: Pit dug into sterile soil, lined with caliche-adobe
                   2 cm to 5 cm thick.
           Roof: No evidence.
           Floor: Caliche-adobe continuous with walls.
           Entryway: None.
           Hearths: A. Northwest corner, round, bowl-shaped, adobe-
                         lined, diameter = 25 cm, depth = 12 cm.
                     B. Center of south wall, round, bowl-shaped,
                         adobe-lined, diameter = 26 cm, depth = 15 cm.
           Floor Features: Subfloor pit, center of room, north of Hearth
                   B, rectangular, unlined, dimensions = 60 cm by 90 cm,
                   depth = 30 cm.

Feature 39 (Figure 45)

Type: Rectangular, solid adobe-walled room.
Location: West side of mound.
Phase: Civano.
Dating: Archaeomagnetic - 1365 ± 24.
           Stratigraphic - overlies Feature 59.

Construction:
           Walls: Solid puddled adobe, base placed in shallow trench
                   10 cm below floor level.
           Roof: No evidence.
           Floor: Adobe-caliche plaster.
           Entryway: Door in center of east wall, 70 cm wide.
           Hearth: Circular, adobe-lined with adobe collar. Located in
                   front of doorway, diameter = 24 cm, depth = 8 cm.
           Floor Features: None.

Remarks: Western half of room was not excavated because it was located
         on private property.

Feature 40 (Figure 46)

Type: Rectangular pit house.
Location: West side of mound.
Phase: Late Civano.
Dating: Archaeomagnetic - none.
           Stratigraphic - east wall contiguous to Feature 40a. North
               wall cuts into south wall of Feature 59.

Figure 44.   Feature 35 (looking west)

Figure 45.   Feature 39 (looking west)

Figure 46.   Feature 40 (looking west)

Figure 47.   Feature 40a (looking south)

Construction:

        Walls: Shallow (26 cm maximum depth) pit dug into trash,
                plastered with adobe approximately 5 cm thick. No
                evidence of upper wall construction.

        Roof: No evidence, one posthole on west side of house.

        Floor: Rough adobe, very poor.

        Entryway: No evidence.

        Hearth: None.

        Floor Features: Adobe-lined storage pit, oval, diameter =
                69 cm by 43 cm, depth = 21 cm. Storage pit - diameter
                = 30 cm by 25 cm. Pot impression - diameter = 25 cm,
                depth = 8 cm.

Remarks: This feature has no firepit, and the south and west walls
        were indefinite. It may not have been a habitation structure,
        but a storage and work area or jacal associated with Feature
        40a.

Feature 40a (Figure 47)

Type: Rectangular pit house.

Location: West side of mound.

Phase: Late Civano.

Dating: Archaeomagnetic - A.D. 1410 ± 22.
        Stratigraphic - overlies Features 80, 100, and 112.

Construction:

        Walls: Thin (5 cm) adobe-caliche plastered to sides of pit
                dug into trash. Maximum height = 40 cm. No evidence
                of upper walls.

        Roof: Adobe chunks resting on floor may have fallen from
                collapsed roof.

        Floor: Unprepared adobe, very rough.

        Entryway: Lateral step entryway in center of south wall.

        Hearth: In front of entryway, round, bowl-shaped, adobe-lined,
                diameter = 22 cm, depth = 11 cm.

        Floor Features: Two postholes in southeast corner.

Remarks: West wall contiguous to Feature 40.

Feature 41 (Figure 48)

Type: Pit house, rectangular with rounded corners.

Location: Northeast corner of mound.

Phase: Late Civano.

Dating: Archaeomagnetic - A.D. 1400 ± 17.
        Stratigraphic - may cut into Feature 42.

Construction:

        Walls: Unplastered pit dug into sterile caliche, approximately
                35 cm deep. No evidence of upper wall construction.

        Roof: No evidence.

        Floor: Unplastered except at east end around hearth.

Figure 48. Feature 41 (looking west)

Figure 49. Feature 42 (looking south)

Entryway: None.
Hearth: North corner, round, adobe-lined, diameter = 26 cm,
        depth = 17 cm.
Floor Features: None.

Feature 42 (Figure 49)

Type: Pit house, oval.
Location: Northeast corner of mound.
Phase: Civano.
Dating: Archaeomagnetic - none.
        Stratigraphic - may be cut by Feature 41.

Construction:
    Walls: Shallow pit dug into sterile caliche, plastered with
        adobe-caliche 2 cm to 5 cm thick. Walls 30 cm to 35
        cm high, but collapsed portions indicate height of
        approximately 70 cm.
    Roof: Adobe with reed impressions in fill. Two postholes,
        one in east end, one along south side.
    Floor: Adobe plaster continuous with walls.
    Entryway: None.
    Hearth: In northeast corner, shallow, unlined depression,
        diameter = 20 cm, depth = 8 cm, hearth had been
        plastered over.
    Floor Features: Storage pit, northeast corner, slightly bell-
        shaped, unplastered, diameter at mouth = 32 cm,
        depth - 35 cm.

Feature 74 (Figure 50)

Type: Pit house, rectangular with rounded corners.
Location: North of mound.
Phase: Late Civano.
Dating: Archaeomagnetic - 1450 ± 17.
        Stratigraphic - none.

Construction:
    Walls: Pit dug into sterile caliche, plastered with adobe-
        caliche 5 cm thick. Wall fall indicates height of at
        least 60 cm.
    Roof: No evidence, one posthole in northeast corner with
        adobe collar.
    Floor: Adobe, continuation of walls.
    Entryway: Center of east wall, lateral step entryway, width
        = 48 cm, length = 1.33 m.
    Hearth: In front of entryway, round, adobe-lined, raised rim,
        diameter - 26 cm, depth = 13 cm.
    Floor Features: None.

Figure 50. Feature 74 (looking south)

Figure 51. Feature 114 (looking east)

Feature 114   (Figure 51)

Type: Rectangular pit house.
Location: West side of mound.
Phase: Civano.
Dating: Archaeomagnetic - A.D. 1385 ± 22.
           Stratigraphic - overlies Features 21, 22, and 125.

Construction:
           Walls: Pit dug into trash, plastered with thin (3 cm to 4 cm
                   thick) adobe. Existing height - 50 cm, with further
                   portions lying on the floor indicating additional
                   height.
           Roof: No evidence except three post roof support, one central
                   and one each in northeast and southeast corners.
           Floor: Thick adobe-caliche plaster.
           Entryway: Center of north wall, just west of floor ridge.
                   Antechamber with sloping floor, plastered sides.
           Hearth: Directly in front of entryway, small, round, adobe-
                   lined. Diameter - 26 cm, depth - 13 cm.
           Floor Features: Floor ridge - low, 15 cm wide, running north-
                   south, constructed with rounded lumps of adobe,
                   constructed after walls and before floors were laid.
                   Plastered-over pit - just east of central ridge,
                   diameter = 55 cm.

Remarks: This late pit house is one of the most well constructed and
         preserved. It is believed to be contemporaneous with Feature
         24/27. This feature and Feature 114 are separated by a court-
         yard formed by the west wall of Feature 21 and the west mound
         extension.

CHAPTER 4

ANALYSIS OF THE LAS COLINAS CERAMICS

by Patricia L. Crown*
Arizona State Museum
University of Arizona

Introduction

The analysis of ceramics from the 1968 excavation of Las Colinas has been conducted almost continuously over the last 10 years by a number of researchers. At least eight different participants have examined some segment of the ceramic collection in detail during this decade. All have concluded that the Las Colinas material presents a rare view of Hohokam ceramics from the end of the Sacaton phase to the end of the Civano phase, and that this material exhibits tremendous variability while at the same time conforming largely to the reported material from other Classic period sites. This report will attempt to document the variability in a succinct manner. So much research has been done on this material and so many attributes have been recorded, that all of the data would not fit in one chapter. The complete collection is available, however, at the Arizona State Museum.

Before describing the Las Colinas ceramic material, it is important to describe the nature and extent of the previous research. The analysis of the material began soon after excavation ceased at Las Colinas. In the Spring of 1969, Laurens Hammack began sorting the ceramics from Feature 5. This feature was chosen for the initial sort because it contained a large number of sherds and its context--stripping around the mound--suggested that it might contain a mixed collection of types. Thus, it was possible that a detailed typology for analyzing the ceramics could be developed before the contents of other features were examined.

At this time, Hammack set up three typologies for sorting the material. For the decorated material he used the type designations given in the Los Muertos report (Haury 1945); for the red ware material he used the definitions given by Schroeder in his study of Salt River Valley trash mounds (1940:113, 183-186); but with the plain wares he found that little of the material could be adequately categorized on the basis of earlier reports. Hammack therefore set up a new typology based on attributes of temper, exterior surface treatment, and interior surface treatment. This typology will be described in detail in the section dealing with the plain ware ceramics.

In the summer of 1969, Frederick Gorman and Jonathan Haas began analyzing the remaining features (Hammack completed Features 5 and 10). Gorman sorted Feature 1 using Hammack's typology, and Haas sorted the remaining 121 features, 16 burials, and six cremations. During the course of this analysis,

*Draft completed: June 1979

Haas added several other plain ware and red ware categories to the typology. He completed this work and wrote a brief report on the plain ware and red ware ceramics in 1971 (n.d.).

In 1973, Carol Weed supervised a more detailed study of the decorated types, concentrating on the red-on-buff ceramics. In addition, she organized all of the information on the ceramics and wrote a detailed report on this work in 1974 (n.d.).

Also in 1973, Hayward H. Franklin wrote a paper entitled "The Use of Percentages in Ceramic Analysis: An Example from Las Colinas, Arizona." Using the data on Las Colinas plain ware and red ware, he compared the use of type/ware frequencies to type/total sherd frequencies in an attempt to determine the utility of each in ceramic analysis (Franklin n.d.).

In 1977, W. Bruce Masse did a detailed study of the red wares from Las Colinas for a seminar on Southwestern ceramics at the University of Arizona. His report was the first systematic attempt to examine the whole vessels from Las Colinas.

Work resumed on the Las Colinas material in 1979. Despite the plethora of data already available, further work was needed to collate and synthesize all of the previous work sheets and reports, to tally the sherd totals and frequencies, and to examine the whole vessels that had not been analyzed previously. Also, a fresh look was required because much work had been done on Classic period sites in the years since the initial reports of Haas and Weed, and other previously unavailable material had been published. It was necessary to review all of this recent literature and revise some of the conclusions reached in the initial reports.

Nevertheless, the bulk of the credit for the analysis of the Las Colinas material must go to Haas, Weed, and Masse. Haas's sherd analysis remains intact with modification only to his interpretations given the data. Weed's detailed examination of the red-on-buff ceramics, and her definition of Santan Red-on-buff is included with little modification. Much of her synthesis of the ceramic collection is retained in the following pages. Finally, Masse's excellent study of the red ware vessels is, with few exceptions, closely followed.

Plain Wares

Methodology

As described in the introduction, Hammack developed a typology to deal with material from the Las Colinas site. This typology included attributes of temper (sand, sand with mica, and schist), exterior surface treatment (striated versus non-striated), and interior surface treatment (smudged versus unsmudged). These seven attributes formed the 12 cell matrix (Table 5) used in classifying the majority of the sherds.

Table 5.   Plain ware typology following Hammack

Sand Striated Smudged	Sand with Mica Striated Smudged	Schist Striated Smudged
Sand Non-Striated Smudged	Sand with Mica Non-Striated Smudged	Schist Non-Striated Smudged
Sand Striated Non-Smudged	Sand with Mica Striated Non-Smudged	Schist Striated Non-Smudged
Sand Non-Striated Non-Smudged	Sand with Mica Non-Striated Non-Smudged	Schist Non-Striated Non-Smudged

Haas encountered a number of problems using this typology. As with all typologies, there were sherds that readily fit the categories and sherds that did not. It was difficult to distinguish sherds tempered with sand and mica from those tempered with sand alone, since almost all sand naturally has some mica in it. In the majority of cases, the difference was obvious, but when it was not, Haas placed in the mica category those sherds in which mica was immediately noticeable. If the mica was not immediately clear on inspection, the sherd was placed in the sand-tempered category. In addition, striations were often visible only when the sherd was held up to the light and examined for the shiny polish of individual lines. Sherds not obviously fitting either the striated or the non-striated category, were placed in the latter. The identification of smudging was often problematical. True forced smudging appears prehistorically when the potter packed the polished interior of a vessel with organic matter and inverted it, creating a reducing atmosphere inside the vessel and an oxidizing atmosphere outside the vessel. Besides producing a highly polished black interior, smudging deposits a carbon layer .5 mm to 1 mm thick on the vessel wall. A smudged appearance can also result from accidental fire-blackening during cooking. Conversely, blackening on smudged pottery can be burned out if it is refired in an oxidizing atmosphere. Haas placed in the smudged category only truly blackened pieces with a penetrated layer of blackened clay.

All of these sorting procedures were highly subjective, but exigencies of time dictated that the most efficient method be used. The procedures resulted, however, in correct placement in most instances. Haas sorted the vast majority of the material from Las Colinas by himself, so the sorting, if subjective, was at least consistently so throughout.

As well as the more traditional varieties of Gila Plain, Haas also devised four other categories to cover the variation found in the collection:

1. Micaceous-schist-tempered is a plain ware tempered with schist but with fine particles of mica included in the paste.

2. Muscovite-tempered differed from regular sand-with-mica-tempered in that the muscovite particles were large and flaky, while mica temper is usually characterized by fine particles.

3. Unknown plainware covered all sherds which could not be typed.

4. Too small to be identified included all sherds smaller than thumbnail size which could not be positively typed. Almost 20,000 sherds fit these criteria, attesting to the very complete recovery of ceramic materials at the site.

Only the first three categories that Haas established were used in the following analysis. It is not suggested that they are suitable for the analysis of material from other Hohokam Classic period sites. Because they are site specific, they should not be considered types in any formal sense. Should ceramics having these attributes be found to occur at other Classic period sites, Haas's categories might then be properly defined and codified as types.

After sorting the ceramics recovered from each feature, Haas recorded numbers of bowls and jar sherds. Separating rims into these categories was fairly simple, but separating body sherds was less reliable. He separated body sherds on the basis of interior surface treatment. Well-polished, smoothed, or striated sherds were considered to be bowls, and other sherds were placed in the jar category. This technique, unfortunately, was not reliable, since many types, especially unsmudged and/or schist-tempered types, had bowl interiors as rough as regular jar interiors.

All rim sherds and all large, representative sherds were saved. In addition, the material from eight habitation structures was kept and rebagged (Features 35, 40a, 71, 74, 112, 114, 119, 121) for future analysis. All of the material from all of the features was typed, with the exception of five of the trash-filled, uninhabited structures (Features 45, 49, 62, 72, 82). For these structures, all decorated sherds were typed, but only 10 percent of the red ware and plain ware collections were typed. All of the features had at least 2000 sherds, so a 10 percent sample was felt to be adequate. Haas removed a stratified random sample from each feature for analysis. Two other features were sampled and then completely analyzed to test the adequacy of the sampling procedure, which was found to be 95 percent accurate.

It is important here to discuss the relative merits of such an intensive analysis of the plain wares, since Haas's analysis is certainly one of the most intensive studies ever undertaken of Hohokam plain ware sherds. The final results of Haas's study showed that the model used to type plain ware sherds generated no additional information on the type. The only variable of the study found to have temporal or functional significance was temper. In addition, vessel and rim form were not included in the classification, but recorded independently by type; these traits were found to have probable temporal significance for the plain wares. Smudging and exterior polishing were found to vary independently of tempering material or passage of time. In conclusion, recording the attributes of temper and vessel form will generate as much significant information about variability in the plain ware assemblage as recording all of the attributes noted by Haas.

The problem arose of what to call the three major categories of plain ware. Haas called them sand-tempered, schist-tempered, and sand-with-mica-tempered brown ware, while Weed called them Gila Plain, sand-tempered plain ware, and schist-tempered plain ware. The technology used to manufacture these types was, apparently, identical, and, in many cases, the types inter-grade. It therefore seems most logical to adopt the strategy suggested by Opfenring (1965:4), and utilized by Weaver (1973:115) at the Midvale Site. Opfenring subdivided the type Gila Plain into three sub-types or varieties on the basis of temper. Gila Plain, Gila Variety is the designation given to the traditionally defined material with abundant mica particles and crushed rock or sand temper. Material with little mica in the temper, but abundant quartz sand temper is classified as Gila Plain, Salt Variety. Finally, phyllite- or crushed-micaceous-schist-tempered plain ware is classified under the rubric of Gila Plain, Wingfield Variety. Weaver (1973:115) feels that these varieties have regional significance: Salt Variety occurs primarily in the Salt River Valley, Gila Variety in the Gila River Valley and Queen Creek drainage, and Wingfield Variety in the lower Verde and Agua-Fria-New River drainages or in the Papagueria region around the Santa Rosa Mountains.

It may be argued at this juncture that the schist-tempered material should be designated as Wingfield Plain. As originally defined by Colton (1941:46), and later utilized by Di Peso (1956:34a), Wingfield Plain appears in the Sacaton phase distinguished from Gila Plain on the basis of very coarse mica schist temper. However, Colton notes Gila Plain as a synonym for Wingfield Plain (1941:46), and all researchers have noted the relationship between Gila Plain and Wingfield Plain in terms of manufacturing techniques. It seems more logical to expand the definition of Gila Plain to include a schist-tempered variety rather than utilize a different type designation. There is no evidence that the schist-tempered variety was manufactured outside of the site. Using Gifford's (1976:10) analysis of the varietal concept, the schist-tempered material has one minor attribute -- temper--distinguishing it from other plain wares. Apparently it also has a slightly different areal distribution, and, as will be demonstrated below, definite temporal significance in the Hohokam Classic period sequence. In summary, the schist-tempered plain ware from Las Colinas must be designated Gila Plain, Wingfield Variety until it can be demonstrated that it was not locally produced by methods identical to those used to produce Gila Plain, Salt Variety.

Analysis

A typical pattern for Hohokam Classic period sites is a gradual increase in the amount of plain ware being produced through time at the "expense of both decorated and red wares" (Hayden 1954:128). Schmidt correlated this rise in the quantity of plain wares with a rise in the occurrence of Gila Polychrome at the Classic period sites of La Ciudad and Pueblo Grande (1928:281). Schroeder also noted the rise of plain wares in the Salt River Valley survey (1940:120), but here it was accompanied by a drop in polychrome and decorated Hohokam types, and a rise in red wares. This general pattern is confirmed by investigations at other Classic period sites in the Gila-Salt Basin (Johnson 1964; Steen 1965; Weaver 1972, 1973; Doyel 1974, 1977).

In order to examine the material from Las Colinas for such patterning, the 124 features excavated were broken down into eight short time periods on the basis of stratigraphic relationships, archaeomagnetic dating, and architecture. The periods are as follows:

1. LSES = late Sacaton - early Soho

2. ES   = early Soho

3. S   = Soho

4. LS   = late Soho

5. LSEC = late Soho - early Civano

6. EC   = early Civano

7. C   = Civano

8. LC   = late Civano

Table 6. Feature frequency by ceramic period

Ceramic Period	Feature Frequency
LSES	6
ES	10
S	44
LS	6
LSEC	18
EC	15
C	19
LC	3

The number of features for each ceramic period is given in Table 6. All of the sherd totals were then compiled by type for each of these time periods. Only two of the features could not be included because of inconclusive evidence for dating. Table 7 presents the ceramic type frequencies by time period. The percentages of plain wares, red wares, and decorated wares for each time period are presented in Table 8. The figures reveal the characteristic rise in the percentage of plain wares from the end of the Sacaton phase to the interface between the late Soho and early Civano phases. At the beginning of the Civano phase, however, this percentage drops rapidly. It will be noted that it is the decorated wares which suffer primarily from the rise in abundance of plain wares, while the percentage of red wares remains constant throughout the Soho phase and rises abruptly during the Civano phase. Again, this pattern is the one described by Schroeder (1940).

The pattern is in itself interesting, but it becomes more so when the individual type frequencies are calculated through time. Table 9 presents the information on plain ware type frequencies by time period. The table reveals some very interesting patterns in the manufacturing and use of plain wares over time. Each will be discussed in detail below.

Gila Plain, Salt Variety

As stated above, the brown plain ware with sand tempering from Las Colinas will be designated Gila Plain, Salt Variety. This type constituted by far the largest amount of material in the entire site; 44,152 (32.9 percent) of the sherds were designated Gila Plain, Salt Variety. Of these sherds, 3770 (8.5 percent) were smudged and the remaining sherds were unsmudged. The sand-tempered sherds with smudging appeared to have use-smudging, and this blackening was present on both vessel interiors and exteriors. This blackened Gila Plain, Salt Variety was present through all excavated levels, but never exceeded more than 3 percent of the total amount of plain ware on any level at the site (Weed n.d.:43). Approximately 37 percent of the Salt Variety showed exterior striations due to intentional surface polishing. A study of rim forms revealed that four forms with recurved rims (E, G, H, and I) occurred only during the late Sacaton-early Soho levels and never in the later levels. During later time periods, straighter rim forms were dominant.

Table 7.   Ceramic type frequencies by period

	Ceramic Period				
	LSES	ES	S	LS	LSEC
Gila Plain, Salt Variety	1,742	3,471	4,610	1,256	7,929
Smudged	38	453	345	15	631
Gila Plain, Gila Variety	223	407	915	73	743
Smudged	4	31	167	2	194
Gila Plain, Wingfield Variety	3,252	6,725	8,186	1,456	6,322
Smudged	30	203	506	17	571
Micaceous Schist	16	18	21	2	19
Muscovite	46	16	3	2	6
Unknown Plain Ware	6	29	29	11	26
TOTAL PLAIN WARE	5,357	11,353	14,782	2,834	16,441
Gila Red/Mica	14	49	92	10	80
Smudged	85	147	267	41	241
Gila Red/Sand	36	117	249	60	655
Smudged	89	345	646	232	994
Salt Red	5	7	32	5	163
Smudged	5	12	64	14	250
Gila Plain/Slip	2	-	87	7	479
Schist w/Black Paint	370	699	721	105	338
Schist w/Slip	631	1,280	835	183	266
Red w/Surface Mica	173	114	275	22	138
Unknown Red Ware	219	230	178	38	243
Unnamed Red Ware	2	6	79	7	77
TOTAL RED WARE	1,631	3,006	3,525	724	3,924
Sweetwater Red-on-buff	-	-	-	-	-
Gila Butte Red-on-buff	-	-	-	-	1
Santa Cruz Red-on-buff	18	21	11	2	29
Sacaton Red-on-buff	540	190	137	25	91
Casa Grande Red-on-buff	1,674	682	953	156	717
Red-on-buff Body	504	853	658	140	717
Buff Paste w/Red	50	30	31	8	13
Gila Polychrome	10	12	55	5	192
Tonto Polychrome	-	2	7	5	66
Gila Polychrome/Hatched	-	-	1	-	2
Rincon Red-on-brown	-	-	-	-	-
Tanque Verde Red-on-brown	2	1	6	-	14
Jeddito Black-on-yellow	-	-	1	-	1
Hopi Orange	-	-	-	-	1
Kana'a Black-on-white	1	1	-	-	-
Sosi Black-on-white	-	1	1	-	-
Flagstaff Black-on-white	-	-	1	-	-
Holbrook Black-on-white	13	3	6	4	1
Black Mesa Black-on-white	12	7	5	-	3
Tusayan Black-on-white	7	3	2	-	2
Prescott Black-on-gray	-	1	8	-	-
La Plata Black-on-red	-	-	-	-	-
Medicine Black-on-red	1	1	-	-	-
Tusayan Black-on-red	24	7	11	2	6
Unidentified Black-on-white	6	2	2	-	4
Unidentified Black-on-red	-	-	1	-	1
TOTAL DECORATED	2,862	1,817	1,897	347	1,861
TOTAL SHERDS	9,850	16,176	20,204	3,905	22,226

Table 7. (continued)

	Ceramic Period			Total
	EC	C	LC	
Gila Plain, Salt Variety	2,734	21,364	1,046	44,152
Smudged	122	2,160	6	3,770
Gila Plain, Gila Variety	147	2,172	22	4,702
Smudged	15	566	-	979
Gila Plain, Wingfield Variety	1,329	8,223	124	35,617
Smudged	11	2,591	1	3,930
Micaceous Schist	4	15	-	95
Muscovite	6	17	1	97
Unknown Plain Ware	10	178	2	291
TOTAL PLAIN WARE	4,378	37,286	1,202	93,633
Gila Red/Mica	26	407	10	688
Smudged	123	1,282	18	2,204
Gila Red/Sand	341	2,006	94	3,558
Smudged	504	2,774	147	5,731
Salt Red	27	1,045	30	1,314
Smudged	86	1,552	61	2,044
Gila Plain/Slip	99	1,250	128	2,052
Schist w/Black Paint	109	443	24	2,809
Schist w/Slip	91	458	34	3,778
Red w/Surface Mica	12	72	4	810
Unknown Red Ware	125	542	27	1,602
Unnamed Red Ware	182	333	90	776
TOTAL RED WARE	1,725	12,164	667	27,366
Sweetwater Red-on-buff	-	2	-	2
Gila Butte Red-on-buff	-	3	-	4
Santa Cruz Red-on-buff	7	50	-	138
Sacaton Red-on-buff	25	136	3	1,147
Casa Grande Red-on-buff	202	1,295	11	5,690
Red-on-buff Body	168	1,247	21	4,308
Buff Paste w/Red	2	14	1	149
Gila Polychrome	131	722	22	1,149
Tonto Polychrome	27	210	7	324
Gila Polychrome/Hatched	4	12	-	19
Rincon Red-on-brown	-	3	-	3
Tanque Verde Red-on-brown	23	174	12	232
Jeddito Black-on-yellow	-	9	8	19
Hopi Orange	-	-	-	1
Kana'a Black-on-white	-	-	-	2
Sosi Black-on-white	-	-	-	2
Flagstaff Black-on-white	-	-	-	1
Holbrook Black-on-white	1	2	-	30
Black Mesa Black-on-white	1	6	-	34
Tusayan Black-on-white	-	6	-	20
Prescott Black-on-gray	1	9	-	19
La Plata Black-on-red	-	3	-	3
Medicine Black-on-red	-	1	-	3
Tusayan Black-on-red	1	7	-	58
Unidentified Black-on-white	3	-	-	17
Unidentified Black-on-red	-	2	-	4
TOTAL DECORATED	596	3,913	85	13,378
TOTAL SHERDS	6,699	53,363	1,959	134,382

Table 8. Ware percentages by time period

	LSES	ES	S	LS	LSEC	EC	C	LC
Plain Ware	54	70	73	73	74	65	70	61
Red Ware	17	19	17	19	18	26	23	34
Decorated Ware	29	11	9	9	8	9	7	4
TOTAL SHERDS/ TIME PERIOD	9,850	16,176	20,204	3,905	22,226	6,699	53,363	1,959

Table 9. Percentages of plain ware types by time period

	LSES	ES	S	LS	LSEC	EC	C	LC
Gila Plain, Salt Variety	33	31	31	44	48	62	57	87
Smudged	.7	4	2	.5	4	3	6	5
Gila Plain, Gila Variety	4	4	6	3	5	3	6	2
Smudged	.07	.3	1	.07	1	.3	2	-
Gila Plain, Wingfield Variety	61	59	55	51	39	30	22	10
Smudged	.6	2	3	.6	4	.3	7	.08
Micaceous Schist	.3	.2	.1	.07	.1	.09	.04	-
Muscovite	.9	.2	.02	.07	.04	.09	.04	.08
Unknown Plain Ware	.1	.3	.2	.4	.2	.3	.5	.2

Gila Plain, Gila Variety

The Gila Variety of Gila Plain is most commonly associated with Hohokam sites, particularly in the Gila Basin. Defined originally as having "abundant opaque angular fragments, smaller quantities water-worn sand; large proportions mica" (Colton and Hargrave 1937:174-175), it is the predominant plain ware type at Hohokam Classic period sites in the Gila River Valley (Gladwin and others 1937; Doyel 1974; Haury 1976). At Las Colinas, Gila Variety constitutes a relatively minor type, consisting of between 2 to 6 percent of the assemblage throughout all of the time periods (Table 9).

Jars are the predominant form within the Gila Variety at Las Colinas, with bowls forming a minor category of vessels. However, deliberate interior smudging of bowls occurs with some frequency, much like the Gila Plain from the Classic period sites near Snaketown (Haury 1976:204).

A floated surface which appears to be an accidental by-product of the technology is in evidence on the exterior of many of the Gila Variety sherds. It is probably the result of smoothing vessels that were not completely dry, since large sherds from the assemblage exhibit both smoothed and unsmoothed portions.

Gila Plain, Wingfield Variety

The schist-tempered variety of Gila Plain is designated Wingfield Variety. Fifteen of the 27 jar rim forms (Figure 52) are never found above the post-reinforced wall room level at the site (late Soho phase), while the remaining 12 rim forms occur almost entirely above this level. There are almost as many bowls as jars in the Wingfield Variety material, but the number of jars present declines in the later levels.

An examination of Table 8 reveals an inverse relation in the frequencies of Gila Plain, Salt Variety and Gila Plain, Wingfield Variety. At the late Sacaton phase-early Soho phase interface, Gila Plain, Wingfield Variety dominates the assemblage, constituting 61 percent of the total plain wares. Gila Plain, Salt Variety constitutes only 33 percent during the same time period. Throughout the following seven time segments, Gila Plain, Wingfield Variety gradually drops in frequency, while Gila Plain, Salt Variety increases in frequency to 87.5 percent of the assemblage by the late Civano phase.

The actual causes of this pattern are not known, but a number of speculations can be made, dealing with availability of temper, and functional distinctions. There is a possibility that schist temper became increasingly less available through time, due either to distance to the sources or control of these resources by other groups. Considering the high proportion of schist-tempered pottery produced throughout the Hohokam area, this possibility seems somewhat unlikely. Alternatively, there is some evidence that schist-tempered vessels had a different function from the sand-tempered vessels. Haas found that the sand-tempered jars were more widely diversified with respect to neck size and shape. The rim diameter of the sand-tempered jars ranged from 4 cm to 36 cm, and rim heights and shapes exhibited greater variety (Figure 53). In contrast, 90 percent of the schist-tempered jars had

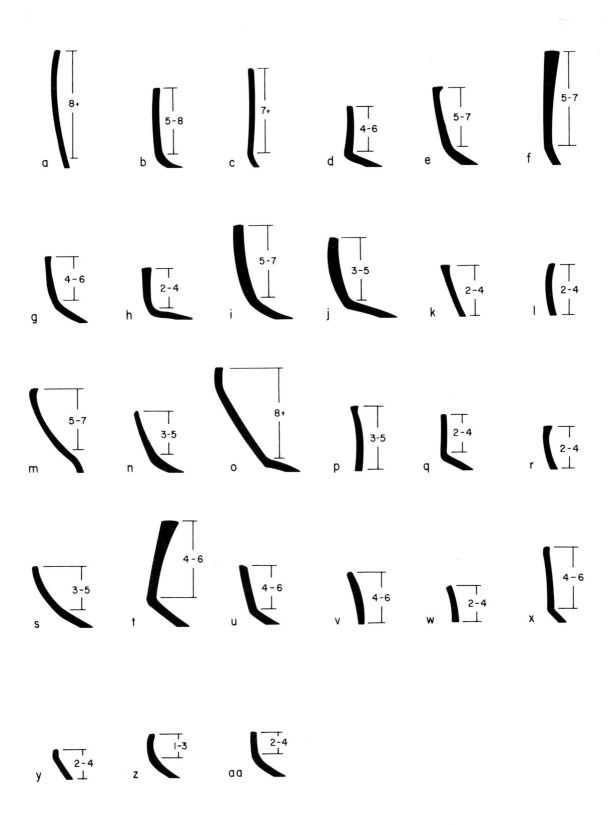

Figure 52. Gila Plain, Wingfield Variety jar rim forms

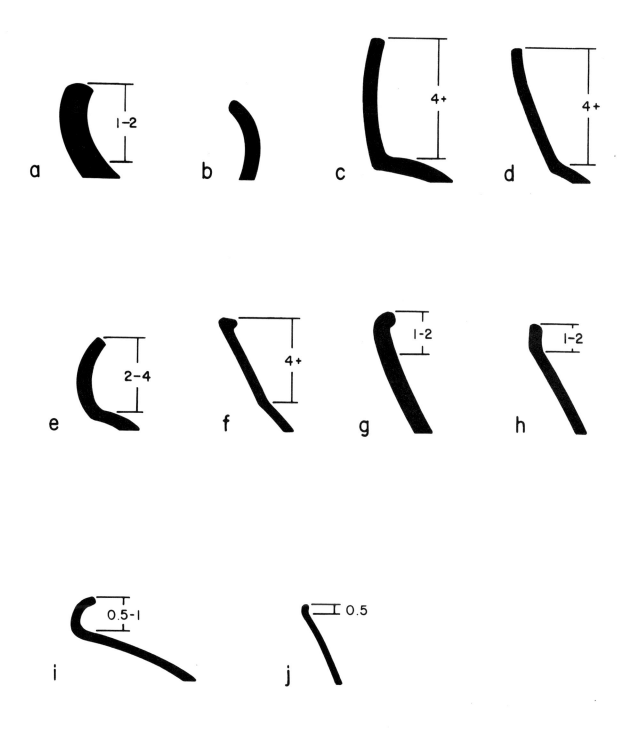

Figure 53. Gila Plain, Salt Variety jar rim forms

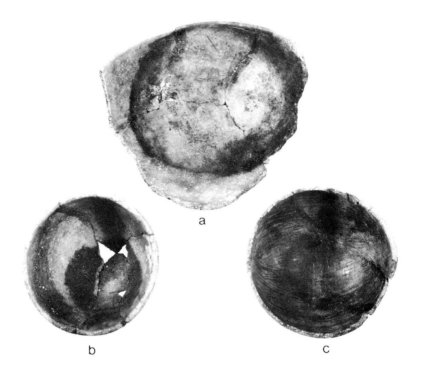

Figure 54.   Gila Plain, Salt Variety bowls (interior
view; diameter of c is 12.5 cm)

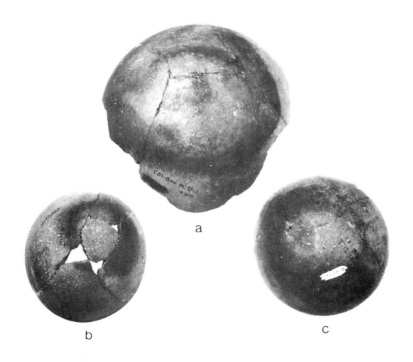

Figure 55.   Gila Plain, Salt Variety bowls
(same as Figure 54, exterior view)

diameters between 16 cm and 30 cm, with only one rim in the entire assemblage diverging considerably from this range; 80 percent of the jar rims were tall and almost straight, with a flattened lip. It is possible to postulate from these data that sand temper was used to manufacture medium-sized vessels with a variety of functions, while schist temper was used primarily to manufacture large stationary storage vessels. It may be that schist temper, because of its planar-like quality, was easier to paddle out into large thin vessels (Haas 1970:14). This conclusion is supported to some degree by the fact that Wingfield Plain occurs primarily as large storage vessels or wide-mouthed jars (Breternitz 1960; Weed and Ward 1970; Weed 1973). In addition, tests run by Weed (n.d.) and Raab (1973) suggest that schist conducts heat and allows for the even sweating of the vessel during contact with a fire.

Micaceous-Schist-Tempered Plain Ware

This category should probably be considered an adjunct to Gila Plain, Wingfield Variety. Since the schist is micaceous, the inclusion of mica in the paste of these sherds is not unusual. However, Haas did single these sherds out as a separate type, and they have been left as such here. The frequency of the micaceous-schist-tempered plain ware follows generally the pattern of the Gila Plain, Wingfield Variety material. Through time, the amount of this type present in the assemblage decreases.

Muscovite-Tempered Plain Ware

The final designated plain ware type, muscovite-tempered plain ware, also declines in popularity through time. Weed (n.d.:39) suggests that the sherds represent no more than two vessels. However, the type does appear consistently in all time periods of the site occupation, suggesting that a different temper source was utilized to produce a minor amount of this pottery in all time periods, or that a small percentage of trade vessels of this type entered the site consistently throughout the sequence.

Whole and Partial Vessels

Four out of the 24 plain ware vessels from Las Colinas come from Feature 100, an early Soho phase pit house. This pit house apparently was destroyed by fire, and the vessels were abandoned in the structure. Their remains should thus present a good picture of the household inventory of vessels during this time period.

Three of the four plain ware vessels from Feature 100 are Gila Plain, Salt Variety bowls. All three exhibit secondary burning or large fire clouds, and all three exhibit eroded bases indicative of use-wear. The sand temper is coarse and the finish dull on two of the bowls (Figure 54). Another vessel (Figure 55) also has coarse sand temper, but the interior is smudged, and the interior and exterior exhibit polishing striations identical to the pattern present on the vessel illustrated in Figure 51b of the Los Muertos report (Haury 1945:85).

The fourth vessel (Figure 56) is a large Gila Plain, Wingfield Variety jar, typical in size and shape of the sort of vessel that would be expected in the schist-tempered variety. The interior aperture diameter is 27 cm, while the greatest width of the vessel is just over 61 cm. Such a large vessel must have functioned as a storage container. Unfortunately, because of the burned nature of the assemblage from Feature 100, secondary firing occurs on all of the vessels from this structure, so it is impossible to distinguish those used over a fire from those with functions not involving contact with fire.

There are five vessels from Soho phase structures; two reconstructed bowls, and three partial vessels. The bowls tempered with extremely fine sand in a buff paste, are both miniatures, and are of relatively poor manufacture. Although the paste is quite fine, the overall shape and manufacturing quality of the vessels suggests that they are children's efforts (Figure 57). A third miniature bowl of unknown provenience has identical paste, temper, and overall quality, and probably belongs to the same genre. These vessels are not true Gila Plain, and will be left in an unnamed plain ware category due to the nature and small size of the sample.

The remaining three vessels are, unfortunately, only partial vessels, so little information can be gleaned from the overall sample of Soho vessels. The only Gila Plain bowl is of Wingfield Variety, smudged on the interior, but heavily burned both inside and out. The rim shape of this large, outcurving bowl resembles rim D (Figure 60) most closely.

The two Gila Plain jars (76-04, 42-27) from Soho phase features are both tempered with sand having flecks of gold mica. Gold mica occurs with less frequency in vessels from the Gila-Salt basin than does silver mica, and it might be indicative of trade in vessels or temper into the area. Both jars have blackened exteriors, and one (57-27) has three small stripes of red paint across three sherds near the vessel neck. Because of the partial nature of these vessels, it is impossible to determine their function; however, the large interior apertures of both suggest they may have been used for storage.

Only two vessels come from late Soho-early Civano phase features, and both are jars. The most complete of the two vessels (17-47) is a Gila Plain, Salt Variety pitcher. The bottom is worn and there is evidence of secondary firing on its exterior walls. The pitcher shape (Figure 59) is more typical of Classic period red wares than plain wares, but its occurrence is further evidence of the close relationship between the two wares (Haury 1976:225). The other late Soho-early Civano phase jar is a Gila Plain, Wingfield Variety vessel. Use-wear occurs on the vessel's interior and exterior base, and the exterior shows evidence of secondary burning. The jar is quite large, suggesting that the refiring may have occurred accidentally rather than over a hearth.

One Gila Plain, Salt Variety jar comes from an early Civano phase feature. The small jar has a straight neck, a globular, fire-blackened body, and a heavily eroded base. The sample is too small to make any generalizations about either late Soho or early Civano phase ceramic manufacture.

Civano phase features produced one whole plain ware bowl and six partial plain ware jars. The Gila Plain, Salt Variety bowl shows extensive wear on the exterior base and evidence of burning both inside and out (Figure 58, a). The interior was polished but not smudged.

Figure 56. Gila Plain, Wingfield Variety jar
(diameter is 61.3 cm)

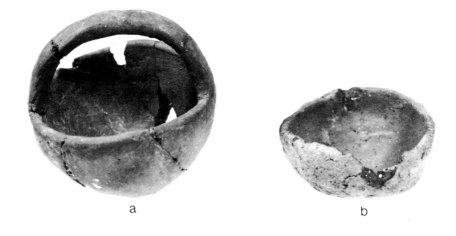

a   b

Figure 57.   Plain ware miniature bowls
              (diameter of b is 5.6 cm)

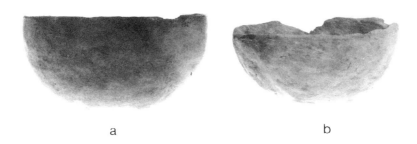

a   b

Figure 58.   Plain ware bowls (diameter
              of a is 13.5 cm)

Figure 59. Plain ware pitcher, with handle
attachment visible at top left
(diameter is 23.7 cm)

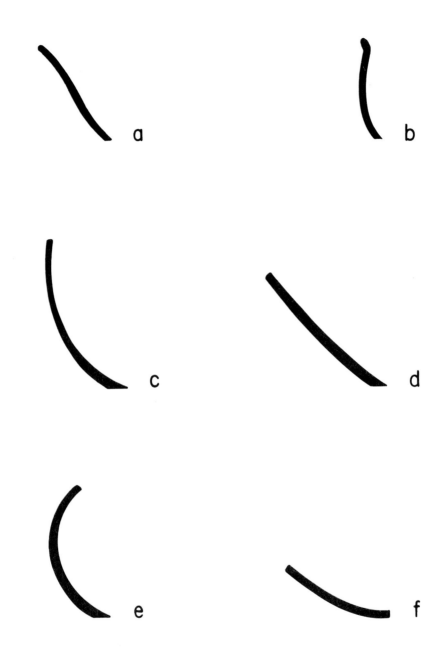

Figure 60. Plain ware bowl rims

Three of the partial jars are Gila Plain, Salt Variety, two of which have obvious polishing striations on the exterior. All three jars are fairly large, over 44 cm in diameter, with mouths 26 cm to 28 cm.

One Gila Plain, Gila Variety jar came from the Civano phase features. This vessel has a clearly floated surface, large fire clouds, and a well-polished exterior. Due to its very partial nature, no distinct shape could be discerned.

The two remaining jars are Gila Plain, Wingfield Variety. One vessel is a small jar (14 cm in diameter) with a globular body, but no neck. The second is a very large jar over 54 cm in diameter. The smaller vessel shows clear evidence of secondary burning, and from the evidence gleaned from the sherd materials, this shape is rather unusual for the Wingfield Variety of Gila Plain forms.

Perhaps the most interesting group of vessels comes from Feature 74, a late Civano phase pit house. An archaeomagnetic date of 1450 ± 17 came from this structure, making it the latest habitation structure known in a pre-historic context in southern Arizona. In his study of the red ware vessels from Las Colinas, Masse became interested in comparing these late prehistoric Hohokam vessels with the earliest known Pima ceramic vessels. He therefore examined the earliest historic material available at the Arizona State Museum from the Gila River Indian Reservation survey and the early Papago village of Batki. Although none of the material dates earlier than A.D. 1750, Masse believed that such a comparison might be of value. He found some strong similarities between the Papago material and the late red wares from Las Colinas, similarities which hold also for the plain wares from this structure (Masse n.d.:21-22).

Five plain ware jars come from Feature 74: one reconstructed jar and four partial vessels. All of these vessels are characterized by sand temper, thick walls, ellipsoidal bodies, and short to almost non-existent necks. They are poorly polished, have marks left by smoothing with the hand or some instrument, and show good evidence of secondary firing, probably over a cooking fire. The jars range in diameter from 30 cm to 40 cm, with mouths ranging from 12 cm to almost 19 cm in diameter. Masse noted the possible occurrence on one of the jars of a lip thickened by the addition of an extra coil of clay (Figure 61, a), a practice common on Papago jars, but heretofore unreported on Hohokam vessels (Masse n.d.:22). Following Masse's lead, we will designate this type "degenerate plain ware," although a larger sample will be required from other late prehistoric sites before the vessels can be considered more than a microtradition of Las Colinas. Nevertheless, the similarities between the form and technology of these jars and Pima ceramics are striking (Figure 61 a, b) and may be of significance in considering the question of a Hohokam-Piman continuum.

Conclusion

The plain ware assemblage from Las Colinas follows in general form the assemblages found at other Hohokam Classic period sites. Among the three varieties of Gila Plain, there is a clear shift through time from the use of schist temper to sand temper, while mica-tempered sherds occur in low frequency

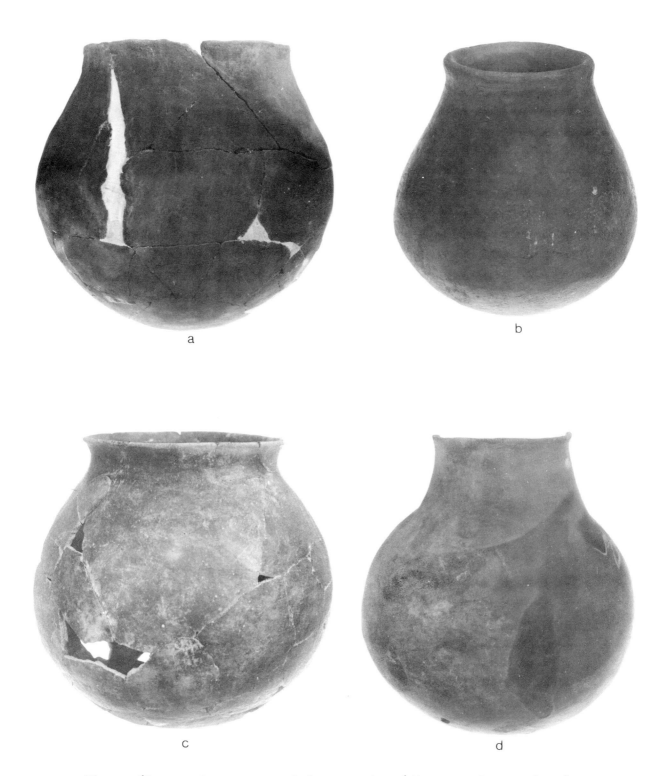

Figure 61.   a. Degenerate plain ware jar (diameter is 30.04 cm);
b. Papago jar (diameter is 18.5 cm);   c. Degenerate
red ware jar (diameter is 37 cm);   d. Papago jar
(diameter is 31.4 cm)

throughout the occupation of the site. The whole vessels reveal a wide variety of shapes and forms, most closely allied to the vessel forms of Gila and Salt Reds.

The whole and partial vessels also reveal the existence of a late degenerate plain ware which is close in form and technology to the plain ware vessels found on historic Piman sites in southern Arizona.

Red Wares

Methodology

In typing the red wares, Haas attempted to use the traditional distinctions developed for Classic period red wares. As with the plain wares however, he found difficulty in using the traditional typology. The distinctions between Gila Red and Salt Red were originally made by Schroeder (1940:113). Salt Red has a uniform polish and no visible polishing striations, while Gila Red has clear polishing striations. Haas, however, had difficulty determining striation frequency and polish uniformity. When the problem arose, he separated the sherds on the basis of quality of construction: Salt Red is better made than Gila Red (n.d.:4).

In addition to the traditional, micaceous-tempered Gila Red, Haas found that up to 49 percent of the red wares that could legitimately be classified as Gila Red actually had sand temper. Because of the absence of mica, Haas might have placed these sherds in the Salt Red category, but none of the other listed attributes of that type were observed. The type has readily apparent striations, yet fire-clouding was more restricted and less frequent than in the micaceous Gila Red. It was felt that the best solution was to place this material in the category of Gila Red, sand tempered. In addition to this type, Haas found five other categories of red-slipped material:

1. Gila Plain, Red Slipped is a thick, poorly fired type with a brown paste and abundance of sand temper. The slip (or wash) is deep red, but usually over half the vessel exterior is fire-clouded with just patches of red slip showing through. The exteriors of these vessels are poorly polished, producing a matte finish on the majority.

2. Schist-with-black-paint is a schist-tempered pottery type with black paint or slip applied on one or both surfaces. While the slip is usually smooth, it sometimes appears bubbly.

3. Schist-with-red-slip is a schist-tempered type with red slip instead of black. This slip is always smooth. In order to determine if the black paint was a metallic pigment which would fire red in an oxidizing atmosphere, Haas oxidized a number of the red-slipped and black-slipped sherds in a modern kiln. The results compounded the confusion concerning these two types. All but two of the schist-with-black-paint sherds burned out completely, reverting to the brown color of the paste. This would tend to suggest that the paint was a vegetal type which burns out in an oxidizing atmosphere. However, the remaining two sherds revealed red slip under the black paint. The schist-with-red-slip sherds also varied when refired. Two of these sherds retained

the red color when refired, but the third reverted to the brown color of the paste. This suggests that the red-painted category has both mineral- and carbon-painted sherds in it. The sherds with mineral paint rightfully belong with the schist-with-red-slip assemblage, but, unfortunately, all of the sherds would have to have been refired in order to find out which had mineral and which had carbon paint. The categories have therefore been left as originally set up, but should perhaps be considered as equivalent.

4. Thin-red-wash-with-surface-mica was represented by a very small number of sherds. The paste is fine, with sand and mica temper. The type has a red wash. but is unpolished. It may be related to Hayden's Huamanui Red (Hayden 1954:178), but the sherds are generally too small to be certain of such an affiliation. Huamanui Red is characterized by a red slip or wash which was applied by dipping the vessel into the wash. Such a technique resulted in drips of red wash at the base of the vessels. This attribute was not observed on the Las Colinas material, but this may be due to the size of the sherds. As will be discussed below, the vessel forms are more restricted than Hayden indicates for Huamanui Red.

5. Unnamed Red is the most baffling of the red ware categories created by Haas. It occurs almost exclusively in bowl form, but the vessels have recurved rims unlike typical Classic period Hohokam red ware forms. Instead, the form is identical to that found commonly in the Salado polychromes. In addition, the slip color is 7.5 R 5/6 (Munsell Soil Color Chart), the color which characterizes Salado Red. The exterior slip on the vessels is usually thin and polished over, and the gray-brown color of the paste often shows through. The interior slip is also thin, but usually not well polished. Although the material was originally called Las Colinas Red, and a type description was written by Masse (n.d.:Figure 10), it was felt that naming the material would be premature since it occurs in small numbers and restricted time periods at the site (see Table 10).

Before discussing the types in detail, it might be worthwhile to discuss the relationship between the red wares and the plain wares. As with the plain wares, the red wares have three distinct types of tempering material: sand, sand with mica, and schist, each with apparent temporal significance. The temper types should perhaps best be given the varietal status accorded the Gila Plain material described above which was also based on tempering material. In this case, however, the previously defined distinctions between Gila and Salt Red demand that they be kept as separate types. Furthermore, the schist-with-red-slip type might reasonably be argued to be Wingfield Red. Future work with red wares from other Classic period sites may find the same variability, and if these red wares can be shown to be locally produced, then it would perhaps be best to distinguish three varieties of Gila Red, based on temper categories, reflecting the plain ware distinctions. However, the Wingfield Red rubric will not be used here. First, it is a poorly defined type (Di Peso 1956:350). Second, it carries connotations of manufacture outside of the Gila-Salt basin. Until such time as the schist-tempered red ware can be demonstrated to be produced outside of the Gila-Salt basin, it is unnecessary to burden this material with a label which carries such connotations. Therefore, these types will be discussed with the appellations given them by Haas, which are merely descriptive.

Analysis

One of the continuing problems of Hohokam ceramics is the origin of the Classic period smudged red wares (Schroeder 1940, 1952; Haury 1945, 1976; Doyel 1977; Weaver 1978). The smudged red wares appear in the Hohokam sequence at the end of the Sacaton phase after a long period of ceramic production without red wares (Haury 1976:, ignoring the very early Vahki Red). Hypotheses developed to explain this phenomenon include: immigrations of new people into the area, either the Sinagua (Schroeder 1952), the Salado (Gladwin and Gladwin 1933), or the Mogollon (Haury 1945); in situ development of the type (Wasley and Johnson 1965; Wasley 1966), or introduction of the type by immigrants from outlying Hohokam settlements with earlier red ware traditions (Weaver 1972).

It was hoped that the red wares from Las Colinas might help to solve this mystery, since dated occupation of the site lasted from the end of the Sacaton phase to the end of the Civano phase. Unfortunately, the results of the red ware analysis from Las Colinas show the assemblage to be somewhat unique both in its stability and its variability.

As noted above, most Classic period sites have red ware which has been readily divided into Gila and Salt Reds. As originally defined by Schroeder, the distinction between Salt and Gila Red was temporal, Gila predominating during the Soho phase and Salt during the Civano phase (Schroeder 1940:113). Few researchers have found this distinction to hold absolutely, although Salt Red does tend to increase in frequency through time. There are sites, however, such as those in the Escalante Ruin group, which have Gila Red throughout the Classic period, and no true Salt Red. As illustrated in Table 10, Gila Red predominates throughout the sequence at Las Colinas, with a relatively low frequency of Salt Red. The red wares increase abruptly in frequency at the beginning of the Civano phase (Table 10), but this increase includes both Gila and Salt Red. This problem will be discussed further, after each of the types has been briefly discussed.

Gila Red, Mica-Tempered

The mica-tempered variety of Gila Red occurs in consistently low frequencies throughout the time periods represented at Las Colinas. Table 10 shows that the amount of mica-tempered Gila Red (unsmudged and smudged) in any one time period ranges from 5 percent to 14 percent of the sample. The percentage of the red ware which is smudged is consistently greater than the percentage which is unsmudged.

Gila Red, Sand-Tempered

The sand-tempered variety of Gila Red occurs in greater amounts than the Gila Red with micaceous temper, and the percentages of this type to other types of red wares increases steadily through time. Like Gila Red with mica temper, the sand-tempered variety is smudged more often than not. Both varieties of Gila Red show an extremely high incidence of bowls (over 95 percent) in the assemblages. When one considers that during the early Civano phase the two varieties represent 58 percent of the total red ware assemblages, this

Table 10. Redware type percentages by time period

Type	Time Period							
	LSES	ES	S	LS	LSEC	EC	C	LC
Gila Red/Mica	.9	2	3	1	2	2	3	2
Smudged	5	5	8	6	6	7	11	3
Gila Red/Sand	2	4	7	8	17	20	17	15
Smudged	5	11	18	32	25	29	23	22
Salt Red	.3	.2	.9	.7	4	2	9	5
Smudged	.3	.4	2	2	6	5	13	9
Gila Plain, Red Slipped	.1	-	2	1	12	6	10	19
Schist with Black Paint	23	23	21	15	9	6	4	4
Schist with Red Slip	39	43	24	25	7	5	4	5
Thin Red Wash with Surface Mica	11	4	8	3	4	.7	.6	.6
Unnamed Red Ware	.1	.2	2	1	2	11	3	13
Unknown Red Ware	13	8	5	5	6	7	5	4

indicates a very high number of bowls in the site. This also accounts for the high ratio of smudged to unsmudged sherds since bowls tend to be smudged more often than jars.

Salt Red

The Salt Red from Las Colinas is characterized by quartz sand temper, highly polished exterior surfaces, thick slip, and small fire clouds. As noted above, the amount of Salt Red relative to Gila Red increases somewhat through time. Like Gila Red, Salt Red is characterized by a preponderance of smudged materials, although the ratio of smudged to unsmudged sherds is rarely as high as it is for Gila Red. The fact that 31 percent of the sherds come from jars, as opposed to less than 5 percent jar sherds for Gila Red, may account for the difference in the ratios of smudged to unsmudged vessels. Because there is nothing in the Las Colinas material to indicate that Salt Red developed out of Gila Red or that Salt Red was at any time the dominant red ware at the site, it might be wise to consider reasons other than evolutionary ones for the differences between the two types.

The temporal distinctions between the two types, as developed by Schroeder, should be reexamined. His original placement of the types in evolutionary relation to one another was based on stratigraphic relations he found in trash mounds in the Salt River Valley. Dating was based on associated intrusive ceramics (1940:114). The dates for the intrusives were based on the dates then believed to hold for those types. A reevaluation of these dates, based on Breternitz (1966), shows that only 36 of the intrusive sherds found with the Gila Red sherds date solely to the Soho phase (A.D. 1150-1325), while the rest of the sherds (718) date to both the Soho and the Civano phases (Table 11). This fact is supported by the occurrence of Gila Red in all time periods at Las Colinas and at many other sites (see Doyel 1974; Pailes 1963:99).

If Gila Red and Salt Red occur simultaneously, and the distinction between them does not provide any information on temporal relations, what information might such a distinction offer? Doyel has argued that the distinction may have spatial significance, as there is some suggestion that Salt Red occurs primarily in the Salt River Valley and not in the Gila River Valley.

Table 11. Comparative dating of intrusive ceramic types recorded during Schroeder's survey (1940)

Intrusive Type	Frequency	Schroeder (1940)	Breternitz (1966)
Roosevelt Black-on-white	4	1200-1300	-
Pinedale Black-on-red	4	1200-1300	1275-1325
St. Johns Polychrome	1	1100-1200	1175-1300
San Carlos Red-on-brown	1	1300-1400	1275-1400
Pinedale Black-on-white	2	1250-1325	1275-1350
Deadman's Black-on-red	3	750- 900	775-1066
Salado Red	1	1150-1350	-
Pinedale Polychrome	1	1250-1325	1300-1350
Fourmile Polychrome	1	1350-1400	1300-1400
Tanque Verde Red-on-brown	1	1200-1400	1200-1400
Gila Polychrome	656	1300-1400	1300-1400
Pinto Polychrome	31	1200-1300	1200-1325
Tonto Polychrome	48	1300-1400	1300-1400

This proposition is supported by Masse (n.d.:14). Also, the information from Las Colinas suggests that the distinction might have functional significance. Gila Red was apparently manufactured almost solely in bowl form at Las Colinas while Salt Red was produced in both jar (31 percent) and bowl (69 percent) forms. It is of some importance to note that neither type shows extensive secondary firing or use-smudging, suggesting that they were used in household activities not involving fire. The jars are not, however, of the large storage type, but are rather small with wide mouths. The question of the relation between Gila Red and Salt Red will be explored further in the discussion of whole vessels from the site (below).

Gila Plain, Slipped

This is a distinct type which occurs frequently in later occupations at Las Colinas. The type occurs rarely in the early levels of the site, but increases to 12 percent of the red ware sample during the late Soho-early Civano interface and continues to occur throughout the late Classic period (when it is second in frequency only to sand-tempered Gila Red). Although Haas did not correlate this red ware with the degenerate plain ware of the late Civano levels discussed above, it is probable that this sherd material is part of the related degenerate red ware tradition described and defined by Masse (n.d.). Out of more than 2000 typed sherds, only 24 were rims; however, both the rim and body sherds indicate a preponderance of jar forms. All of the bowl forms occur in the late Civano features. As with the degenerate plain ware material, Masse (n.d.) suggests that this material is a probable ancestor of historic Piman ceramic material.

Schist-tempered with Black Paint

It is highly significant that, as with the plain wares, the schist-tempered varieties of red wares peak in frequency early in the occupation of Las Colinas and fall steadily to insignificant amounts by the late Civano phase.

Schist-tempered with Red Slip

This type is second only to Gila Red in overall frequency at Las Colinas. This type and the schist-tempered-with-black-paint sherds possess characteristics identical to the Gila Plain, Wingfield Variety; however, schist-tempered with red slip occurs predominantly in bowl form with the ratio of jars to bowls increasing slowly through time. As stated above, this material may in the future be reclassified under the term Gila Red, Wingfield Variety. The causes of the inversion in jar to bowl ratio from the red-slipped variety or schist-tempered ware to the plain-ware variety cannot be determined here, although it is possible that the increased number of Gila Red bowls served to replace the schist-tempered red ware bowls. Alternatively, the inversion in jar to bowl ratio may be a function of inadequate sample size in the later periods.

Thin-red-wash with Surface Mica

This type follows the general trend of the schist-tempered red wares through time; that is, a gradual drop was noted in frequency to insignificant amounts in the late Civano phase. As stated above, this type may be the elusive Huamanui Red defined by Hayden (1957:178), but the sample size and sherd size are too small to positively equate the two. Like Huamanui Red, thin-red-wash with surface mica appears to be a late Sacaton-early Soho type, but unlike the great range of shapes present in Huamanui (Hayden 1957:184), this type occurs primarily in bowl and plate form.

Unnamed Red Ware

One of the most interesting facets of the Las Colinas assemblage was the detection of a ceramic microtradition in the Civano phase features. This red ware type has a raspberry red slip like Salado Red. It first occurs in quantity in the early Civano phase and reaches its greatest frequency in the late Civano phase pit houses. As noted above, bowl forms are primarily ellipsoidal with recurved rims, a shape identical to Gila Polychrome bowls. A few rim sherds occur in an incurved bowl form also. Jar body forms are typically teardrop to globular with medium range vertical necks. Somewhat rounded Gila shoulders occur on the jars. There is no smudged variety of this unnamed red ware. The lack of smudging, combined with the distinct vessel forms and raspberry red color, distinguish this type from the other Classic period red wares. It has a restricted distribution both temporally and spatially within the site, which suggests that it is a local tradition produced by a few potters within the site for a short period of time. It is interesting that a small amount of red-on-brown decorated pottery with forms, color, and proveniences identical to the unnamed red ware also occurs at Las Colinas (see below). This type shows possible characteristics of coil-and-scrape production. Unless the red ware type is found at other Classic period sites it should be considered a microtradition of short duration at the Las Colinas site. It is especially intriguing that two of the whole vessels of unnamed red ware occur in a burial with no other ceramics. Perhaps this is the burial of one of the originators of this microtradition.

Unknown Red Ware

The unknown red ware category contains unidentifiable and somewhat questionable red ware sherds. All students of Classic period ceramics would agree that red wares are difficult, if not impossible, to separate from plain wares with complete accuracy. When slip was made by diluting the same clay used to construct the vessel, the distinction between red ware and plain ware is problematic. All counts and frequencies given, therefore, must be accepted with reservation. The relatively high frequency of unknown red ware sherds throughout the sequence at Las Colinas bears testimony to the difficulty of identifying red wares accurately. Most of the unknown red ware sherds have more variable color than is usual, making positive identification impossible.

The large number of types used to classify the Las Colinas red wares masks the more interesting trends in red ware production through time. Table 12 presents percentages for all of the red wares based on tempering material alone. The percentage of sand-tempered red ware was derived by adding Gila Red; sand tempered, Salt Red; and Gila Plain with red slip. The mica-tempered category is a conglomeration of micaceous Gila Red and thin-red-wash-with-surface mica variety. Finally, the schist-tempered totals were derived by adding the schist-with-black-paint and schist-with-red-slip types. Unnamed red and unknown red categories were eliminated from the totals due to the unknown origin and, in some cases, temper of these types. It is clear from Table 12 that much the same trends occur in the red wares of Las Colinas that occurred in the plain wares. Schist-tempered types have an early popularity which varies inversely with the rise in frequency of the sand-tempered type. The micaceous wares maintain a relatively stable proportion to all wares, declining somewhat at the end of the sequence.

Table 12.   Percentages of red ware temper types by time period

Temper	Time Period							
	LSES	ES	S	LS	LSEC	EC	C	LC
Sand-tempered	8	16	30	44	64	62	72	70
Mica-tempered	17	11	19	10	12	10	15	6
Schist-tempered	62	66	45	40	16	11	8	9

Whole and Partial Vessels

The red ware vessels from excavated structures provide information complementing that provided by the sherd material. As with the plain wares, however, the sample of whole and partial vessels is too small to provide a reliable picture of the range of vessels manufactured at the site. Rather, this material should be used to supplement information gleaned from the analysis of the sherds. There are 45 red ware vessels from Las Colinas, but because the site was occupied for 300 years, the source of most of the variability in the sample cannot be identified. It may be due to temporal, individual, functional, or spatial variability.

It is fortunate that the early Soho pit house which had burned (Feature 100) again provided a large proportion of the whole red ware vessels. Due to the manner of abandonment of this feature, we may consider this assemblage a complete red ware household inventory. Out of the nine red ware vessels present in this feature, six are bowls. There are two shouldered bowls in the assemblage which are almost identical in manufacture and shape (Figures 62, 63).

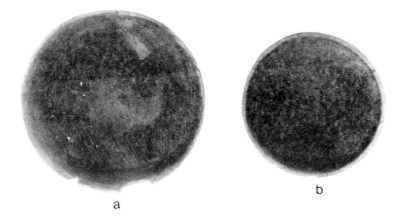

Figure 62. Two shouldered bowls from Feature 100 (diameter of a is 24.3 cm); interior view

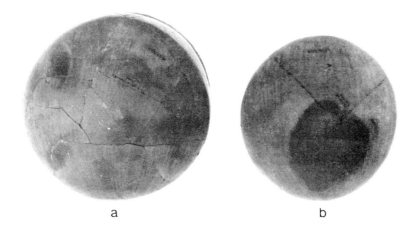

Figure 63. Two shouldered bowls from Feature 100 (exterior view)

Both are Gila Red with sand temper, with rounded bases outflaring to shoulders which incurve to small outcurving rims. Pattern polishing is present on both the interior and exterior of the vessels in a pattern identical to that illustrated in Figure 51b of the Los Muertos report (Haury 1945:85). On both vessels the interior aperture is approximately 2.5 cm smaller than the diameter at the shoulder. The bases are worn from use. The smaller bowl was smudged, and the larger was slipped on the interior.

Three of the bowls from the feature are shallow, outcurving bowls with rounded bottoms. These are all very large vessels with heavy use-wear on the bases. Two of the bowls are Gila Red with sand temper. These two bowls (Figure 64 a, b) are both smudged with interior pattern polish identical to Figure 51g (Haury 1945:85). The smaller of the vessels has this pattern of polishing on the exterior also, while the larger has the exterior pattern illustrated in Figure 51b (Haury 1945:85). Fire clouds occupy over 70 percent of the surface area of the bowls, but this may be due in part to the secondary firing of the vessels in the burning of the structure.

The third vessel with this shape is of the schist-tempered with red slip type. Unlike the other two bowls, this one is unsmudged, and the red slip on the interior and exterior of the bowl is not highly polished. No pattern to the finish could be discerned (Figures 65, a; 66, a). This bowl was so completely refired in the burning of the room that the true slip color shows through only in small patches near the rim.

The last bowl is also of the schist-tempered-with-red-slip type. This deep, incurved, hemispherical vessel has a slight suggestion of a shoulder. It is slipped on the interior and exterior, but the slip is thin and the polish all but gone. As with the other schist-tempered red ware vessel from this room, fire clouds cover most of the surface of the vessel, probably due to secondary firing (Figures 65, b; 66, b).

The three jars from Feature 100 are all large, sand-tempered Gila Red vessels. The smallest of the vessels has a low shoulder and rounded base. This shoulder separates two directions of polishing on the vessel (compare Haury 1945:Figure 52a). The other two jars also show extensive fire clouds (Figure 67). The interiors of these two vessels are heavily eroded, due probably to conditions of storage and use. Both vessels would have had large storage capacities and easy access through their relatively wide mouths. Polishing striations on these vessels were horizontal around the neck, and vertical over the body to the base (Figures 67, a; 68, b).

Based on the analysis of the sherd material, we might have expected more schist-tempered and fewer sand-tempered vessels in this early Soho phase structure. It is especially surprising that three of the seven Gila Red vessels are jars since only 5 percent of the Gila Red sherd sample consists of jars.

Only three vessels--two jars and a scoop--were recovered from other Soho phase features. The scoop is of the micaceous Gila Red type, and identical in form to the scoop from Los Muertos (Haury 1945:97, Figure 60b). The handle end of the scoop is slightly elevated. Both interior and exterior are slipped and well polished with a longitudinal polishing pattern. The exterior exhibits small, random fire clouds. There is no use-wear observable on the scoop.

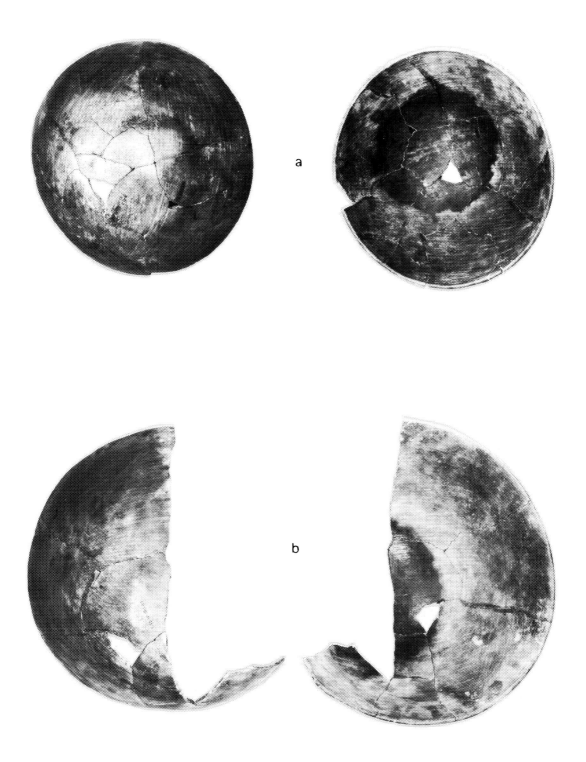

Figure 64.   Red ware bowls (exterior view on left; interior view on right; diameter of a is 36 cm)

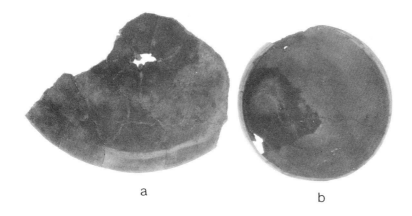

a

b

Figure 65. Red ware bowls (interior view;
            diameter of b is 27.5 cm)

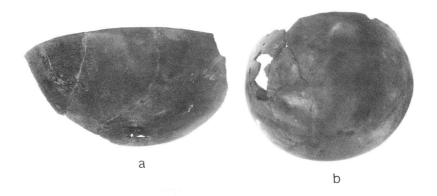

a

b

Figure 66. Red ware bowls (same as Figure 65;
            exterior view)

Figure 67. Sand-tempered Gila Red jars (maximum
diameter of a is 54 cm; b is 43.9 cm)

Both of the jars come from Feature 57, part of the mound fill, and both represent schist-tempered-with-red-slip red wares. As with the early Soho phase schist-tempered red ware jars, these are badly burned with only patches of slip showing through the blackened surface. The slip is thin and the finish matte, although vertical polishing striations are clearly present. The interiors of both vessels are blackened and show interior erosion due to use. One of the vessels has a high, vertical neck. The other vessel has a broken and reground neck. These vessel types are predictable given the norm suggested by the red ware sherd material. It is somewhat unusual, however, to find two jars of the schist-tempered red ware variety but no bowls, since bowls predominate in the early feature sherd material. The sample restricts adequate assessment, however.

The late Soho-early Civano features produced only two vessels, both sand-tempered Gila Red jars. The smaller of the two vessels is a tall-necked, small-mouthed, spheroidal jar with horizontal polishing around the neck and vertical polishing around the body. The second jar is badly eroded and has a dull slip. It is somewhat odd to find two jars of Gila Red in these features when this form is relatively rare in the sherd material.

An early Civano phase feature produced the first occurrence of a vessel which might be considered intermediate between Gila and Salt Reds (Figure 68,a). The sand-tempered smudged bowl has thin, spotty slip, a few large fire clouds on the exterior, but no visible polishing striations (compare Haury 1945:88, Figure 54m). Typing of this vessel and many others was difficult due to the intermediate nature of its appearance in relation to the attributes listed by Schroeder (1940:113) for separation of Gila and Salt Red.

Seven vessels, many of which also had traits intermediate to Gila and Salt Reds, came from Civano phase features. One of the vessels easily typed is a schist-tempered red ware bowl with pattern polishing on the exterior (compare Haury 1945:85, Figure 41k), and smudging on the interior. The occurrence of clear polishing striations is somewhat rare on the schist-tempered red wares since the slip is usually somewhat dull and poorly polished.

One of the remaining two bowls (5-144) has a well-polished exterior fitting the Salt Red type description (Figure 69,a), but a pattern-polished, smudged interior fitting the Gila Red type description (Figure 70, a). This sand-tempered vessel has large but irregular fire clouds. The final bowl from Civano phase features is a clear Salt Red smudged vessel, well slipped and polished (Figures 69, b; 70, b).

Four Salt Red jars came from Civano phase features. Two of these jars from Feature 42, a pit house, are of identical form and almost identical size. These high-necked, ellipsoidal jars both exhibit extreme variation in exterior slip color, with the color matching that on the unnamed red material in patches (Figure 71 a, b). It is interesting that such extreme ranges of color can occur on one vessel, and it suggests that some of the sherd material included in the unnamed red ware category may actually be segments from such Salt Red vessels.

This situation is repeated in Feature 29 which also produced two Salt Red jars. One of the jars (Figure 72) exhibited the same color variation

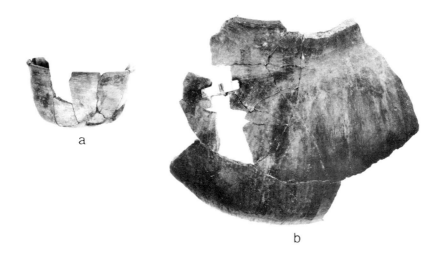

Figure 68. a. Gila Red/Salt Red bowl (diameter
12.5 cm); b. Gila Red jar

Figure 69. a. Bowl with Salt Red exterior and Gila
Red interior; b. Salt Red smudged bowl
(diameter is 16.2 cm); interior view

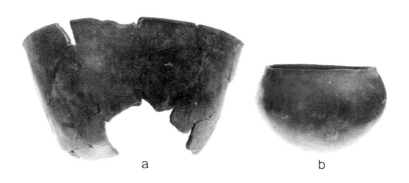

Figure 70. Same as Figure 69; exterior view

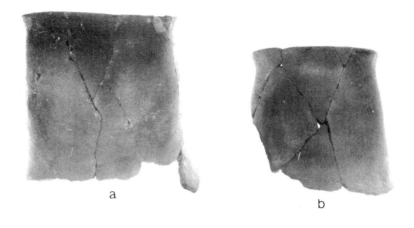

Figure 71. Salt Red high-neck jar forms
(height of a is 14.75 cm)

Figure 72. Salt Red low-neck ellipsoidal jar
(36.4 cm diameter)

which occurred on the vessels from Feature 42. This low-necked ellipsoidal jar has a dull finish and few, but relatively large, fire clouds. The second jar from this feature has a high vertical neck and low shoulder and exhibits some slip color variation (Figure 73, a) although not to the extent found on the other Salt Red jars described above.

The only vessel found in a late Civano feature is an unnamed red ware bowl (Figure 73, b). This vessel exhibits the characteristics of the type: recurved rim, raspberry red color, unsmudged dull-slipped interior, and no evidence of anvil marks on the interior.

The whole and partial red ware vessels from Las Colinas are in no way representative of the vast number of forms present in the sherd material. The whole vessels do, however, help to demonstrate the difficulty in utilizing the Gila Red/Salt Red distinction for this site. There is a considerable amount of intermediate material from Las Colinas, material which quite probably was typed as Gila Red using Haas's distinctions. This intermediate material appears primarily in contexts that occur just before and after the Soho-Civano interface.

Further evidence for an intermediate "type" comes from the large number of red ware vessels found in the burials and cremations at Las Colinas. Since the dating of the burials is based primarily on ceramic information, they will not be discussed in any temporal order. Sherd totals for the burials and cremations are presented in Tables 13 and 14.

Burial 4 has the largest number of ceramic grave goods, and this burial epitomizes the production of transitional Gila-Salt red ware (Masse n.d.:14). Four of the six vessels included in the burial are small bowls. The bowl in Figure 74, a is the only schist-tempered red ware vessel in the burial. Its smudged interior has polishing striations (compare Haury 1945:85, Figure 51b), while its exterior has a thin slip which is poorly polished. One of the sand-tempered Gila Red bowls (Figure 74, b has all the characteristics of good Gila Red: large amorphous fire clouds and polishing striations on the exterior and interior. The last small bowl (Figure 76), however, has characteristics of both Gila and Salt Reds. Polishing marks are clear on the interior, but the fire clouds are small, the break shattering, and the polishing marks indistinct on the exterior. A large, shallow, outcurved bowl (Figure 79) with sand tempering again has characteristics of both Gila and Salt Reds. Here the polishing marks on the smudged interior (compare Haury 1945:85, Figure 51g) and the exterior (Figure 51b) are distinct, but the fire clouds are small and patterned. One of the jars in the burial (Figure 76, b) is also of the transitional Gila-Salt type. Polishing patterns are clear on the jar exterior, but fire clouds are small and restricted to the vessel base. Also, the slip is thick, more often a characteristic of Salt Red than of Gila Red.

Vessels recovered from Burial 5 were of the transitional type. Both the small bowl (Figure 77, b) and the mug (Figure 77, a) were smudged and had well-polished exteriors and sand temper. The bowl has a pattern-polished interior and the mug has large, amorphous fire clouds, typical traits of Gila Red.

The two vessels associated with Burial 6 were significant because they were the only whole vessels of the unnamed red ware present in the assemblage.

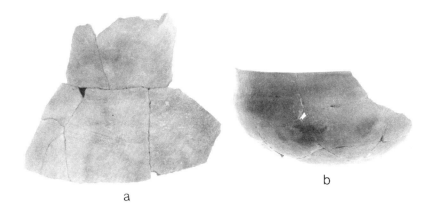

Figure 73. a. Salt Red jar neck; b. Unnamed
red ware bowl (diameter is 26 cm)

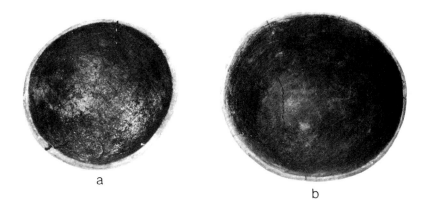

Figure 74. a. Schist-tempered red ware bowl;
b. Sand-tempered Gila Red bowl
(diameter is 14.9 cm); interior view

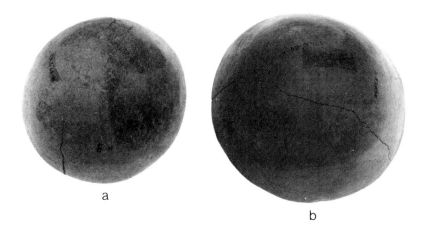

Figure 75. Same as Figure 74; exterior view

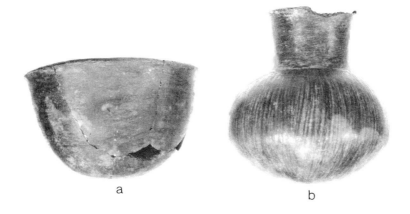

Figure 76.   a. Gila/Salt Red bowl; and b. jar
(height of b is 16.5 cm)

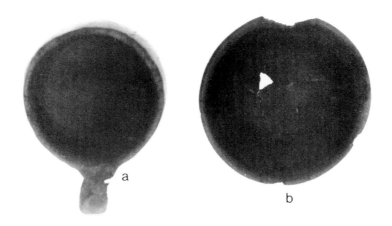

Figure 77.   a. Gila/Salt Red mug (diameter is 11.3 cm)
b. bowl.   Interior view.

Figure 78.   Same as Figure 77; exterior view

Figure 79. Gila/Salt Red bowl (diameter is 51.8 cm)

Table 13. Sherd counts for burials

Sherd Types	Burial							
	1	2	3	4	5	6	7	8
Gila Plain, Salt Variety	-	-	-	31	-	11	-	-
⎧ Smudged	-	-	-	-	-	-	-	-
Gila Plain, Gila Variety	-	-	-	3	-	-	-	-
Gila Plain, Wingfield Variety	-	-	-	54	-	13	-	-
⎧ Smudged	-	-	-	-	-	-	-	-
TOTAL PLAIN WARE	0	0	0	88	0	24	0	0
Gila Red/Mica	-	-	-	-	-	-	-	-
⎧ Smudged	-	-	-	5	-	-	-	-
Gila Red/Sand	-	-	-	-	-	-	-	-
⎧ Smudged	-	-	-	11	1	-	-	-
Salt Red/Smudged	-	-	-	-	1	-	-	-
Schist with Black Paint	-	-	-	3	-	2	-	-
Schist with Slip	-	-	-	6	-	-	-	-
Red with Surface Mica	-	-	-	-	-	-	-	-
Unknown Red	-	-	-	-	-	-	-	-
Unnamed Red	-	-	-	-	-	1	-	-
TOTAL RED WARE	0	0	0	25	2	3	0	0
Sacaton Red-on-buff	-	-	-	1	-	-	-	-
Casa Grande Red-on-buff	-	-	-	11	-	6	-	-
Red-on-buff Body	-	-	-	2	-	1	-	-
Gila Polychrome	-	-	-	-	-	-	-	-
Tusayan Black-on-red	-	-	-	1	-	1	-	-
TOTAL DECORATED	0	0	0	15	0	8	0	0

Table 13. (continued)

Sherd Types	Burial							
	9	10	11	12	13	14	15	16
Gila Plain, Salt Variety	1	-	16	5	9	23	-	-
Smudged	-	-	1	-	-	2	-	-
Gila Plain, Gila Variety	-	-	-	-	-	-	-	-
Gila Plain, Wingfield Variety	2	-	19	2	16	6	-	-
Smudged	-	-	-	-	1	-	-	-
TOTAL PLAIN WARE	3	0	36	7	26	31	0	0
Gila Red/Mica	-	-	-	-	-	-	1	-
Smudged	-	-	-	-	-	1	-	-
Gila Red/Sand	-	-	1	2	-	3	-	1
Smudged	3	2	2	8	1	4	-	-
Salt Red/Smudged	2	-	-	1	-	-	-	-
Schist with Black Paint	-	-	4	-	3	1	-	-
Schist with Slip	-	-	4	-	4	3	-	-
Red with Surface Mica	-	-	-	-	2	-	-	-
Unknown Red	-	-	-	3	6	1	-	-
Unnamed Red	-	-	-	-	-	-	-	-
TOTAL RED WARE	5	2	11	14	16	13	1	1
Sacaton Red-on-buff	-	-	-	-	1	-	-	-
Casa Grande Red-on-buff	-	-	1	-	1	-	-	-
Red-on-buff Body	-	-	1	-	1	3	-	-
Gila Polychrome	-	-	-	-	-	1	-	-
Tusayan Black-on-red	-	-	-	-	-	-	-	-
TOTAL DECORATED	0	0	2	0	3	4	0	0

Table 14.   Sherd counts for cremations

Sherd Types	Cremation					
	1	2	3	4	5	6
Gila Plain, Salt Variety	-	1	35	2	8	1
Gila Plain, Wingfield Variety/ Smudged	-	-	-	1	-	-
TOTAL PLAIN WARE	0	1	35	3	8	1
Gila Red/Sand	1	17	-	34	13	4
Gila Red/Sand/Smudged	-	1	-	-	3	22
Salt Red/Unsmudged	17	-	29	-	-	-
Salt Red/Smudged	1	-	-	-	-	-
Schist with Slip	1	-	3	-	-	-
TOTAL RED WARE	20	18	32	34	16	26

The bowl (Figure 80) is typical of the ellipsoidal vessel shape with a recurved rim. The interior of the vessel has a dull, raspberry red slip, while the exterior is somewhat polished, with slip ranging in color from raspberry red to orange and tan. The second vessel is a miniature tripod vessel (Figure 81), a form which, although rare, occurs in other Hohokam sites (see Haury 1945:100 for other examples). While the shape may be ultimately assignable to Mexican sources, the raspberry slip color is typical of unnamed red ware. Since other vessels of this type occur primarily in late Civano pit houses, it is interesting to speculate on the possible affiliation of this burial with those structures.

Four Gila-Salt Red smudged vessels were recovered from Burial 9. All four of the vessels are sand-tempered, but all four also have large, amorphous fire clouds. The three smaller bowls have well-polished interiors and exteriors (Figures 82 and 84), but the fourth vessel (Figure 85,a) has clear polishing striations on the exterior. Two of the bowls (Figures 82, b; 84, a) have flattened bases and small humps on the interior base.

Burials 10, 11, and 12 all produced Salt Red vessels. The two vessels from Burial 10 have smudged interiors, but dull exteriors apparently from use-wear (Figures 86 and 87). The vessel from Burial 11 appears to be a vertical-sided bowl (L.M. 54n), but the rim has been broken and reground so that the true vessel shape is not discernible (Figure 88, b). The bowl from Burial 12 is smudged and well polished, but has large, amorphous fire clouds covering almost one-half of the vessel surface (Figure 88, a).

Figure 80.   Unnamed red ware bowl
(diameter is 29.1 cm)

Figure 81.   Unnamed red ware miniature tripod
vessel (diameter is 6.4 cm)

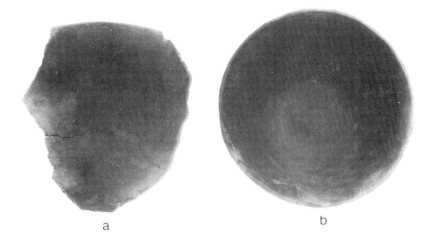

a   b

Figure 82. Gila/Salt Red smudged bowls (diameter of b is 24.3 cm); interior view

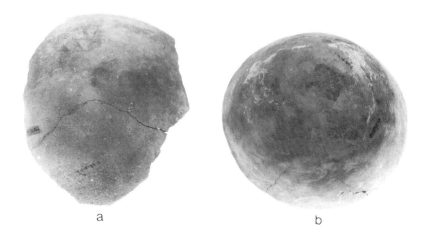

a   b

Figure 83. Same as Figure 82; exterior view

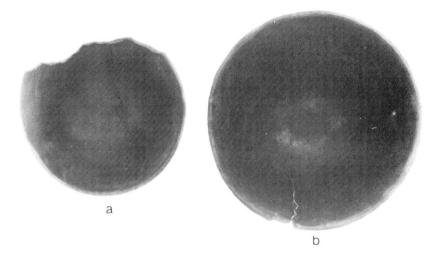

a

b

Figure 84. Gila/Salt Red smudged bowls (diameter
of b is 27.1 cm); interior view

a

b

Figure 85. Same as Figure 84; exterior view

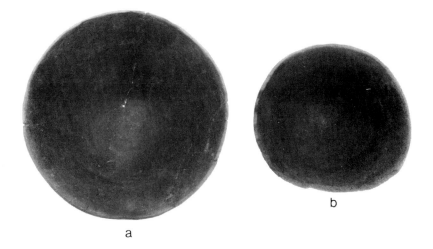

Figure 86. Salt Red bowls (diameter of b is
22.8 cm); interior view

Figure 87. Same as Figure 86; exterior view

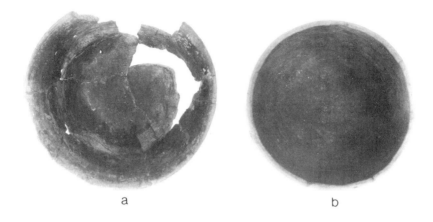

a   b

Figure 88. Salt Red bowls: a. Burial 12;
            b. Burial 11 (diameter of b is
            14.1 cm). Interior view

a   b

Figure 89. Same as Figure 88; exterior view

Only three jars were found in burials; two with Burial 4 and one with Burial 13. The Salt Red jar from Burial 13 is so fragmentary that the remaining base has almost a bowl form. There are extremely large fire clouds on this vessel, so that the slip color occurs only in patches on the polished surface (Figure 90, a).

Burials 14 (Figure 90,b) and 15 (Figure 91,a) again produced vessels typical of Salt Red smudged, but with large fire clouds covering over one-half of their exteriors.

Burial 16 intruded into Feature 100, an early Soho phase structure. A small hemispherical bowl from the burial has a slightly recurved rim and all of the characteristics of sand-tempered Gila Red, with patterned polishing, large fire clouds, and relatively thin slip (Figures 91, b; 92, b).

The only complete vessel recovered from a cremation is a low-shouldered Salt Red bowl, covered with thick, well-polished slip and many small fire clouds (Figure 93).

Conclusion

Before describing the decorated wares occurring at Las Colinas, it would be helpful to review the red ware material. Due to the different techniques and dates of analysis, the description of the red wares was somewhat disjointed. It is clear, however, that this assemblage exhibits much more variability than has been recorded for other Classic period sites. Whether this variability is due to the time depth of the site or the techniques of analysis is unknown.

Red wares at Las Colinas formed a significant percentage of the total assemblage for the entire occupation span of the site. Their gradually increasing frequency through time may be due to their absorption of the functions previously relegated to the decorated wares. It appears that by the late Civano phase, the functions of plain ware ceramics were also being absorbed by the red wares.

The red ware attribute with the most temporal significance appears to be tempering material. An early dominance by schist-tempered red wares gives way gradually to sand-tempered red wares. The micaceous variety remains a small but constant portion of the total assemblage throughout all time periods at the site.

Within the schist-tempered category, two types occur, one with black paint and one with red slip. These are probably the same type with the differences in color due to firing technique and/or paint types.

The most abundant red ware type at the site is Gila Red, both sand-tempered and micaceous varieties. Salt Red occurs in much lower quantities at the site in all time periods. The whole and partial vessels demonstrate the existence of many combinations of attributes which are transitional between Gila and Salt Reds, combinations which may have been placed in the Gila Red sherd category by Haas, accounting for the high frequency of this type. The

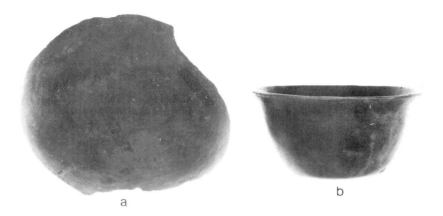

Figure 90. a. Salt Red jar; and b. bowl, from Burials
13 and 14, respectively; diameter of b is
18.3 cm.

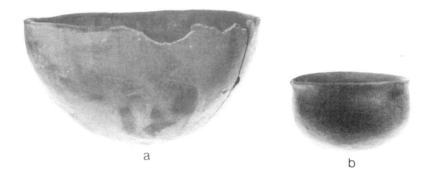

Figure 91. a. Salt Red bowl; b. Gila Red bowl, from
Burials 15 and 16, respectively; diameter
of b is 12.3 cm

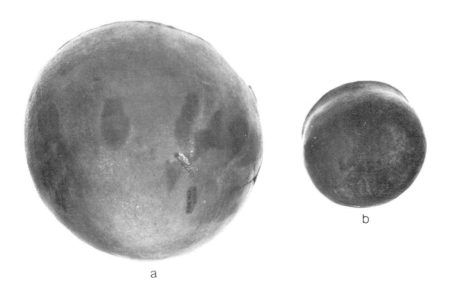

Figure 92. Same as Figure 91; basal view

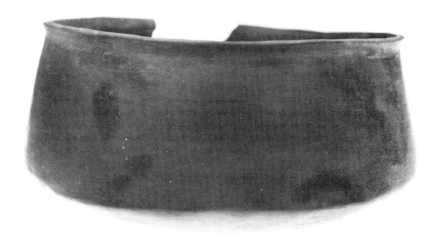

Figure 93.   Low-shouldered Salt Red bowl from
              Cremation 1 (diameter is 27.7 cm)

variability exhibited by these two types, however, and the fact that, at Las Colinas, Salt Red never supersedes Gila Red despite the known time depth, suggests that the accepted interpretation of these types does not hold for Las Colinas. It is generally argued that Gila Red and Salt Red form a sequence, the latter gradually replacing the former. At Las Colinas, this does not appear to be the case. Instead, Salt Red, as defined by Schroeder (1940: 113), appears to be only the best executed red ware on a continuum of red ware manufacturing techniques. All of the traits listed by Schroeder have been observed on the whole vessels, and no patterns of association emerge. Mica content, polishing striations, core color, pigment thickness, and fire cloud size, all vary independently of one another, resulting in good examples of both Salt and Gila Red, as well as a vast number of transitional forms. Perhaps, then, Gila and Salt Reds are not related in an evolutionary manner at all at Las Colinas. Instead, Salt Red occurs continuously as the apex of a manufacturing scale that has Gila Red at its base. Potters at Las Colinas seemed to be capable of producing red wares with any combination of the attributes listed above, and through time their preference for one end of the scale over the other changed only slightly. Salt Red is then only the most well-constructed variety of Gila Red, and Gila Red the less-accomplished version of Salt Red. It is significant to note here that true Gila Red occurs only once in a burial at Las Colinas; all other red wares fit the type description of Salt Red or some transitional type between the two. It seems unusual to have a preponderance of Salt Red in burials which date to the same time periods as features with a preponderance of Gila Red. One explanation would be that the dead were buried with the best of the red ware ceramics manufactured at the site. While the relationship between Gila and Salt Red may hold only for Las Colinas, it might help explain the anomalous frequencies of the two types found at other sites. In the Gila basin, for instance, Gila Red remains the only red ware type found at some Classic period sites throughout the sequence (Doyel 1974, 1977). Other sites in the Gila-Salt basin show stratigraphic relations between the two types which are unclear (Pailes 1963: 92-93).

It is interesting that schist-tempered red wares, the least technologically sophisticated of the red wares at the site, predominate early in the sequence, being replaced by the Gila-Salt Reds. Manufacturing quality tends to increase through time, but there is no trend towards greater production of Salt Red during any one time period.

Toward the end of the occupation, two new types appeared: Gila Plain with red slip, and unnamed red ware. Gila Plain with red slip is a degenerate red ware related to the degenerate plain ware produced at the site. Both are thick, poorly constructed types, with a thin slip and crude polish. Masse noted the relationship between the degenerate red ware and historic Pima and Papago pottery in vessel form, temper, presence of a carbon streak, and matte finish (n.d.:22). If the gap can be filled between the late prehistoric red ware and the historic Piman pottery, further support will be given to the notion of a Hohokam-Piman continuum (see Figure 61, c).

The unnamed red ware represents a distinct microtradition at Las Colinas. While this distinct red ware might be found at other sites in the future, it is likely that it represents the output of only a few potters living in the late Civano pit houses, possibly the individuals interred in Burial 6.

In conclusion, the red ware material from Las Colinas demonstrates the wide range of technological and formal traits the Classic period potters were capable of producing. Such variability in a Classic period site may be unique, but it is hoped that the typology presented here will be helpful in structuring future red ware classifications and will aid the interpretation of red ware manufacture in other Classic period sites.

Decorated Wares - Intrusive Types

Methodology

In contrast to the plain wares and red wares, where much of the material did not fit the established typologies, the decorated wares fit the established typologies with one exception. At Hohokam Classic period sites where independent dating techniques are not always available, ceramics often form a crucial means of dating the sites and their structures. It is important, therefore, to place the sherds, especially intrusive types, accurately within the accepted and usually well-dated typologies. The analysis of intrusive types thus serves the dual purpose of providing a means of dating structures as well as providing information on trade with cultures and regions outside of the Hohokam province. At Las Colinas, where archaeomagnetic dates are available and stratigraphic relationships between features are clear enough to provide a means of relative dating independent of the ceramic material, the intrusive sherds are more important in providing a picture of trade relations, than as a means of cross-checking dated structures.

The intrusive sherds were typed initially by Haas (n.d.) and Weed (n.d.) according to the traditional typologies. Most of the black-on-white sherds were sent for identification to three different archaeologists with experience in classifying Anasazi ceramics. The consensus of opinion was then accepted, even though there was some disagreement about the types (Figure 94).

Analysis

Table 15 presents a compilation of all the intrusive types recovered at Las Colinas, with dates given by Breternitz for these types and their known regional affiliation (Colton and Hargrave 1937; Breternitz 1966). It should be noted that the vast majority of these non-Hohokam intrusives are Anasazi in origin, but from a rather limited area of Anasazi occupation. All of the non-Anasazi intrusives (Verde Black-on-gray) originate apparently from the Verde Valley area. This is not an unexpected occurrence, as there is firm evidence of trade in other items from both the Verde and Agua Fria Rivers (Figure 99, a-c).

The Anasazi Black-on-whites are all either Tusayan or Little Colorado White Wares. A pattern of contact between these two areas and the Hohokam has been noted repeatedly in Hohokam sites (Schmidt 1928; Schroeder 1940; Haury 1976). It is somewhat surprising, however, that no Cibola White Ware material appeared in the assemblage, especially in view of the fact that Roosevelt Black-on-white has occurred in many Hohokam Classic period sites (Johnson 1964; Pailes 1963). The low number of Jeddito Black-on-yellow sherds is also

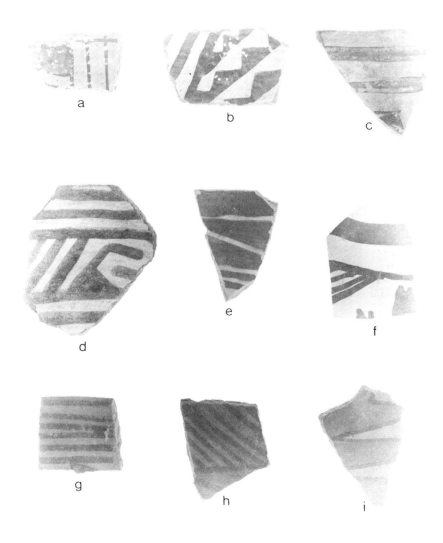

Figure 94. Anasazi intrusive sherds: black-on-white
(a-f); black-on-red (g-i); length of a is
4 cm

Table 15.   Non-Hohokam intrusive decorated ceramics at Las Colinas

Type	Number	Dates	Regional Affiliation
Jeddito B/Y	19	1300-1400	Hopi-Little Colorado
Hopi Orange	1	-	Hopi-Little Colorado
Kana'a B/W	2	725- 950	NE Arizona
Sosi B/W	2	1074-1200	NE Arizona
Flagstaff B/W	1	1066-1200	NE Arizona
Holbrook B/W	30	1075-1130	NE Arizona
Black Mesa B/W	34	875-1130	NE Arizona
Tusayan B/W	20	1150-1300	NE Arizona
Verde B/G	19	1050-1200	Verde Valley
Deadman's B/R	3	775-1066	Flagstaff
Medicine B/R	5	1075-1125	Flagstaff-Sunset Crater
Tusayan B/R	52	1050-1150	N Central Arizona
Tusayan Polychrome	4	1100-1300	N Central Arizona
Walnut B/W	1	1100-1300	NE Arizona
Unidentified B/W	14	-	-
Unidentified B/R	1	-	-
TOTAL	208		

Note: B/G = Black-on-gray; B/R = Black-on-red; B/W = Black-on-white;
B/Y = Black-on-yellow.

surprising; nine of the nineteen sherds are from one vessel, which appears to be a canteen.

The Anasazi Black-on-reds are all San Juan Red Wares (Figure 94, g-i).

The majority of the intrusives seem to be too early to occur in a Hohokam Classic period site, with the exception of Jeddito Black-on-yellow, Tusayan and Walnut Black-on-white, and Tusayan Polychrome. The other intrusives cluster in time between A.D. 725 and 1200, with the majority of them displaying design elements common for the period between A.D. 1150 and A.D. 1200 (Weed n.d.). An examination of the proveniences from which the black-on-whites were recovered indicates that almost one-half of the sherds were recovered from trash-filled retaining cells (Weed n.d.:21). This may point to an earlier component at Las Colinas. Since the retaining cells presumably were filled with trash material collected from the surrounding area, there may have been an earlier Sacaton phase component in the vicinity.

It is clear, however, that there was at least minimal trade with Anasazi groups prior to, and early in, the Classic period occupation of Las Colinas. After A.D. 1200, the amount of trade dropped rapidly, although Anasazi material was still entering the region. The Classic period withdrawal from colonized areas to the north may account in large part for this drop in trade wares. It is unusual, however, that no White Mountain Red Wares or Cibola White Wares were found at Las Colinas. Schroeder (1940:130) considers the occurrence of White Mountain Red Wares (along with Salado polychromes) as a hallmark of Soho phase occupation at Classic period sites.

Weed (n.d.:20) notes two sherds, both associated with late features, which, C. Meighan and C. A. Singer have informed me, apparently were manufactured in Mexico, either northern Nayarit or southern Sinaloa. These two sherds have not been relocated, and Weed does not provide any further information on provenience.

Decorated Wares - Hohokam and Hohokam-Related Types

Methodology

The Hohokam and Hohokam-related materials (including the Salado polychromes) were typed using the traditional classification scheme as much as possible. As with the plain wares and red wares, however, many sherds did not fit the established typology, and Haas created a number of types (described below) to classify this material.

A major exception to this strategy is the discussion of the elusive Santan Red-on-buff. Because of the controversy surrounding the establishment of this type, and the difficulty of separating it from the Sacaton Red-on-buff and from Casa Grande Red-on-buff, a detailed analysis is presented after all other Hohokam and Hohokam-related decorated types have been discussed.

1. Buff paste with painted-on-red has a fine, buff-colored paste with a thick, unpolished slip. This type is included with the decorated wares because the material is often decorated with parts of large design elements more generally associated with red-on-buff vessels. Only 150 sherds of this type were noted.

2. Red-on-buff body includes sherds which are known to be Hohokam red-on-buff types, but the precise type is not identifiable due to the fragmentary nature of the material.

3. Unnamed painted includes apparently locally produced red-on-brown sherds with forms, slip color, and manufacturing attributes identical to the unnamed red ware described above. Bands of red-on-brown decoration under the recurved rim on the exterior of the bowls characterize this type.

All other Hohokam decorated sherds were typed according to established descriptions: Santa Cruz Red-on-buff and Sacaton Red-on-buff (Gladwin and others 1937); Casa Grande Red-on-buff (Gladwin 1933; Haury 1945); Gila and Tonto Polychromes (Colton and Hargrave 1937; Haury 1945); Tanque Verde Red-on-buff (Danson in Hayden 1957); and Rincon Red-on-buff (Kelly 1975).

Analysis

Santa Cruz Red-on-buff

This early type (Gladwin and others 1937; Haury 1976) is present in
small amounts in almost all of the decorated assemblages at Las Colinas
(Table 16). Its occurrence suggests several possibilities: 1) the material
was recovered from temporally mixed features; 2) heirlooms or sherds were kept
by the inhabitants and found their way into these deposits; 3) rodent activity
caused a minor amount of mixing of the deposits.

Sacaton Red-on-buff

As would be expected, Sacaton Red-on-buff (Gladwin and others 1937;
Haury 1976) decreases in frequency through time (Table 16). This type is
well represented in the late Sacaton-early Soho features, but declines rapidly
in importance to a stable 4 percent of the assemblage in the Civano phase
features. Its occurrence during this late phase again suggests a minor amount
of mixing in the deposits. The general trend is, however, clear.

Casa Grande Red-on-buff

Except for two periods, Casa Grande Red-on-buff appears with the
highest frequency of any decorated type during the occupation of Las Colinas
(Table 16). It is clear that Casa Grande Red-on-buff was produced in quantity
up to the very end of the Classic period, although it steadily declined in
frequency during this time. In the late Sacaton-early Soho features, Casa
Grande Red-on-buff accounts for over half the decorated sherds. It drops in
percentage in the early Soho phase, but there is a concomitant increase in the
Red-on-buff body category, a considerable portion of which is probably
unidentifiable Casa Grande Red-on-buff. Up to the late Civano period, Casa
Grande Red-on-buff declines approximately 5 percent between each time period,
so that in the Civano features it forms only 33 percent of the decorated
assemblage. In the late Civano features this gradual trend ends with a major
drop in relative frequency to 13 percent of the decorated total, accompanied
by an increase in Salado polychromes and Tanque Verde Red-on-brown. It is of
interest that the Hohokam of the Gila-Salt basin appear to have discontinued
the production of their local Red-on-buff type in favor of imported Hohokam
types and the Salado polychromes of unknown origin.

The inhabitants of Las Colinas manufactured significant amounts of Casa
Grande Red-on-buff up to the end of the occupation of the site. It does appear,
however, as if the red-on-buff tradition was dying out in the Salt River basin
at the end of the Classic period.

Red-on-buff Body and Buff Paste with Red

These two unknown red-on-buff categories unfortunately contain consistently high amounts of decorated sherds throughout the sequence (Table 16).

Table 16. Percentages of Hohokam decorated types

Type	Time Period							
	LSES	ES	S	LS	LSEC	EC	C	LC
Santa Cruz R/Buff	.6	1	.6	.6	1	1	1	-
Sacaton R/Buff	19	11	7	7	5	4	4	4
Casa Grande R/Buff	59	38	50	45	39	34	33	13
Red-on-buff Body	18	47	35	40	39	28	32	25
Buff Paste w/Red	2	2	2	2	.7	.3	.4	1
Gila Poly-chrome	.3	.7	3	1	10	22	18	26
Tonto Poly-chrome	-	.1	.4	1	4	5	5	8
Gila Poly-chrome, hatched	-	-	.1	-	.1	.7	.3	-
Tanque Verde R/Brown	.1	.1	.3	-	.8	4	4	14

The percentage of total decorated wares found in the red-on-buff body category especially should be considered in any interpretations of ceramic production at Las Colinas. Even in the late Civano features, where it is clear that manufacture of red-on-buff ceramics is reduced, 25 percent of the assemblage is represented by unidentifiable sherds of Hohokam red-on-buff types.

Gila Polychrome and Tonto Polychrome

One of the most interesting facets of the Las Colinas decorated assemblage is the obvious change in the occurrence of the Salado polychromes through time. The Salado polychromes occur in negligible amounts in the features dating from the late Sacaton to late Soho phases (Table 16). From the end of the Soho to the end of the Civano, their frequency increases until together they account for 34 percent of the decorated assemblage. This fact tends to support the traditional dating and interpretation of the Salado polychromes in Classic period sites. Gila Polychrome is generally tree-ring dated as occurring after A.D. 1300. The transition from the Soho to the Civano phase is also believed to begin at A.D. 1300 (Schroeder 1940; Haury 1976:338). The Las Colinas material would strongly support placing the late Soho-early Civano phase boundary at A.D. 1300.

A variant of Gila Polychrome is also present at the site. It is represented by one partial vessel (Figures 95, 96,) and 19 sherds, which are portions of at least four other vessels. The design style is identical to Gila Polychrome, with the addition of fine red hatching on the vessel interior. Weed (n.d.:14) states that the paste and temper indicate a local origin for the type. Doyel has informed me that this variant of Gila Polychrome has been found at other sites in the Gila-Salt basin and there seems no reason to designate a new type from material which is obviously a minor variant of the traditional type.

This raises the question of the origin of the Salado polychromes at Las Colinas. Most technological analyses of the types show them to be locally made wherever they occur (Danson and Wallace 1956; Dickie 1965; Rogers n.d.). Weed states that spectrographic tests show the Las Colinas material to be locally made also (n.d.:15), although no further information on these tests was available. Most archaeologists now feel that the material was a trade ware from an area north of the Hohokam region (Doyel 1977:211; Wasley 1966:8; Johnson 1964:153; Schroeder 1952:329). The Las Colinas material unfortunately cannot provide additional information on this problem. Clearly, the occurrence of a coil-and-scrape manufactured type in a culture producing paddle-and-anvil pottery is anomalous, but not totally unprecedented. It is becoming increasingly clear that all groups in the Southwest were familiar with, and capable of, producing ceramics by both the paddle-and-anvil and the coil-and-scrape techniques, often producing each type for different functions. It is the uniqueness of the design style found on Gila and Tonto polychromes wherever they occur (and they have some of the widest distributions of any types in the Southwest) that argues against a local manufacture. The Gila and Tonto polychrome from Las Colinas do not depart from the established type and style descriptions (Haury 1945). However, to state unequivocally that the material was or was not produced at the site would be premature. Conclusions concerning the origin of these types must await detailed technological and stylistic analyses.

Tanque Verde Red-on-brown

There is a significant increase in the percentage of Tanque Verde Red-on-brown through time (Table 16). Small amounts were recovered from late Soho-early Civano phase features. However, the percentage of Tanque Verde Red-on-brown recovered from early Civano and Civano phase features increases to 4 percent and 14 percent, respectively, of the total decorated wares. Although only 233 Tanque Verde Red-on-brown sherds were found at Las Colinas, this increase in frequency still indicates a significant rise in the importance of this type.

Again, the question arises of the origin of this material. The Tanque Verde Red-on-brown sherds were defined using the typology set forth by Danson (1957) and Kelly (1975). Weed examined the paste, temper, and style present on

Figure 95.   Gila Polychrome variant bowl
(width is 21.5 cm); interior view

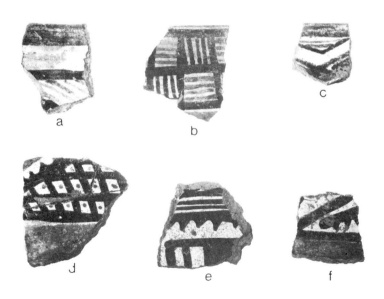

Figure 96.   Gila Polychrome variant sherds
(length of f is 4.5 cm)

the sherds and believed that approximately half of the sample was a locally-made variety. The design elements present on the local imitation were predominantly hatched triangles with adjacent pendant lines projecting at right angles from outlines of the main element. These sherds usually feature the "plaited" layout typical of Casa Grande Red-on-buff. The local imitation has a fine sand temper with large quartz and feldspar inclusions (Weed n.d.:17). (Figure 97).

Unnamed Decorated

One of the most interesting aspects of the decorated assemblage is the occurrence of a small amount of red-on-brown sherds definitely produced locally (Figure 98). Characterized by bowls with recurved rims, narrow bands of red-on-brown decoration on the exterior under the rim, and raspberry slip over the remainder of the vessel, the type appears to be closely related to the unnamed red described above. The vessel form, raspberry slip, and late Civano phase occurrence mirror the attributes of the unnamed red. There are no clear anvil marks on the interior of the vessels, but the profiles of the sherds show coil marks which are quite small and probably indicate a coil-and-scrape technique of manufacture. This type also may be a microtradition associated with late Civano phase pit houses, although the sample of six sherds is too small to provide a strong argument for temporal or functional associations.

In general then, the Hohokam and Hohokam-related types are found in increasingly lower frequencies through time at Las Colinas. As the decorated types decrease in overall quantity, the percentages of types known to be locally produced decirease also. The reason for this gradual cessation in the production of decorated wares is unknown and speculation would be, at this juncture, premature. The Hohokam-related types (Tanque Verde Red-on-brown and the Salado polychromes) increased in frequency at the site during the Civano phase. The origin of these two types remains unknown, but it is possible that the types were being produced by the inhabitants of Las Colinas. As noted, further technological and stylistic analyses of both types are needed to confirm the location of manufacture.

The general increase in the variability of the assemblage during the Civano phase may be due to a number of factors. It is clear from the amount of intrusive sherds that trade with northern areas decreased drastically before and during the Soho phase. The Civano phase was characterized by only minor trade with the Little Colorado region (Jeddito Black-on-yellow) and with the Kayenta region (Tusayan Polychrome). But trade with the Tonto Basin and with areas to the south, near Tucson, may be indicated by the relative increase in the frequency of the Salado polychromes and Tanque Verde Red-on-brown.

Unpainted Decorated

In addition to the decorated types described above, a number of pottery types have been included in this section which are decorated by the manipulation of the clay rather than with paint. Included in these types are corrugated, applique, and indented sherds (Figure 99).

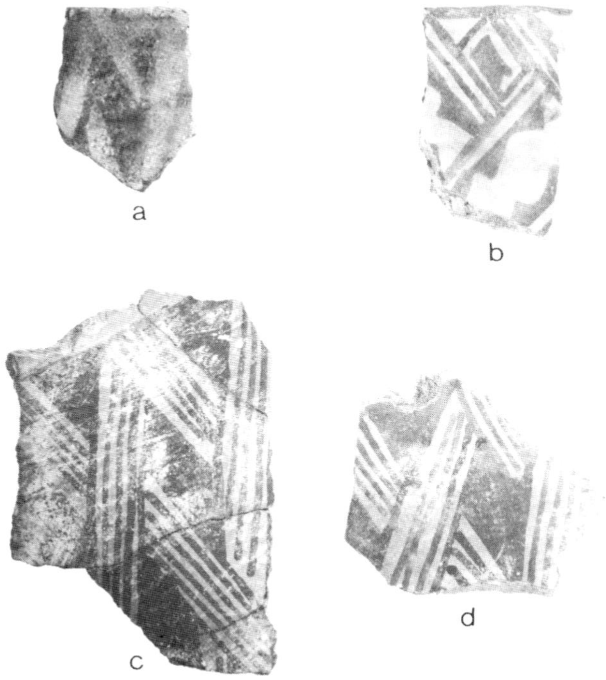

Figure 98. Unnamed decorated sherds (length of a is 15 cm)

Figure 97. Tanque Verde Red-on-brown sherds (length of a is 5.5 cm)

Corrugated. There are two types of corrugated sherds found at Las Colinas. The first is a brown plain ware with indented corrugations which have been partially obliterated by wiping. The interior of the three plain ware corrugated sherds is smudged, and these may represent sherds from one vessel. The five additional jar sherds were red slipped in a manner identical to Gila and Tonto polychrome. These indented, obliterated sherds probably are segments of Salado polychrome jars with corrugated necks. This vessel form occurs with some frequency in Salado polychrome assemblages and has been found in other Hohokam Classic period sites (such as Casa Grande, see Weed n.d.:19).

Applique. Thirteen applique sherds were found in features at Las Colinas (Figure 99, d-f). These plain, brown, sand-tempered sherds have applique bumps and are identical to material found at Snaketown (Gladwin and others 1937:Plate CXXXVI). The origin of this trait and the function of the vessels are unknown, although they may have been segments of small seed bowls (Weed n.d.:19). While the sherds show no evidence of paint, it is possible that they were painted with a fugitive paint like the material from Snaketown (Gladwin and others 1937:Plate CXXXVI).

Indented. One fingernail-indented sherd was found at the site. Such indented sherds occur at other Hohokam sites, but their origin remains unknown due to the extremely small sample available for analysis.

Santan Red-on-buff

The original classification of the red-on-buff assemblage was performed by Haas along the traditional lines set forth by Gladwin and Gladwin (1933); Gladwin and others (1937); and Haury (1976). Haas noted during the analysis that much of the material, particularly that from the earlier features, did not fit the Sacaton or Casa Grande Red-on-buff type descriptions, but seemed to have attributes of both types (Haas n.d.:12). In 1973, Weed began a detailed analysis of the red-on-buff sherds present at Las Colinas in an attempt to identify this transitional material. She was particularly concerned with the dating of the "transitional" sherds and the possibility that this material represented the elusive and ill-defined Santan Red-on-buff. She identified a quantity of material which not only could be isolated on the basis of unique features, but which occurred primarily in late Sacaton-early Soho features, dated by archaeomagnetic technique to between A.D. 1180 and 1225 (Weed n.d.:22-23). The temporal integrity, transitional nature, and identifiable features of the material reinforced the notion that the sherds were indeed a separate type. The analysis of this material was performed by Weed, and the description which follows is extrapolated from her description and recording forms (Weed n.d.:22-36).

Gladwin (1937:264) first postulated the presence of a transitional phase (Santan) between the Sacaton phase and the Soho phase. According to Gladwin, the Santan phase overlapped, but lasted longer than, the Sacaton phase. The clearest example of his notion lay in the eastern range of the Hohokam region near Casa Grande (Gladwin 1937:264). This "readjustment" phase was

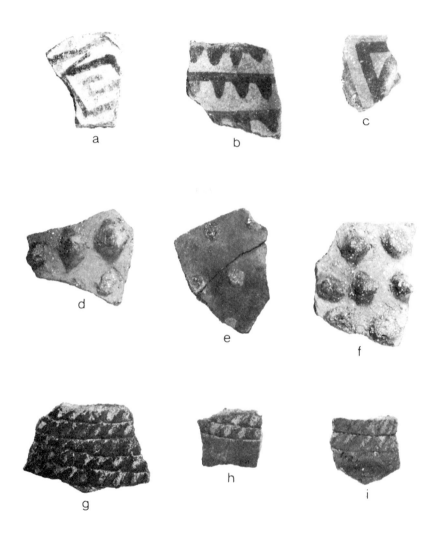

Figure 99.   Verde Black-on-gray (a-c), Applique
(d-f), and Red-slipped Corrugated
(g-i) sherds (length of g is 3.6 cm)

characterized by non-Hohokam architectural styles (contiguous rooms with post-reinforced walls in above-ground structures surrounded by compound walls); smudged red wares (Santan Red); and urn cremations (Gladwin 1937:264). Gladwin felt that the Santan phase heralded the arrival of the Salado incursion into the Hohokam heartland. Unfortunately, only a cursory definition was given the red-on-buff type which was to characterize the Santan phase (Gladwin and others 1937:170). Apparently little red-on-buff material was recovered in direct association with the red ware of the Santan phase.

Because the traits used to characterize the phase failed to co-occur with any consistency, later researchers abandoned the term "Santan," adopting instead terms such as late Sacaton or early Soho to identify this time period. Hayden has informed me, however, that work at a few late Sedentary-early Classic period sites has revealed a red-on-buff type with characteristics transitional between Sacaton Red-on-buff and Casa Grande Red-on-buff. This proposition is supported by Johnson (1964:158). Analysis of the red-on-buff material from Las Colinas also revealed a transitional type with characteristics of both Sedentary and Classic period red-on-buff types. This material closes the gap between Sacaton Red-on-buff and Casa Grande Red-on-buff, providing a final link in the ceramic continuum from Estrella Red-on-buff to Casa Grande Red-on-buff.

Weed recorded elements, motifs, and, wherever possible, layouts on the red-on-buff sherds from Las Colinas (Colton 1953). She was able, using this technique, to separate several repetitive "styles" which are loosely clustered in specific strata at Las Colinas. The clearest examples of Santan Red-on-buff occur in the early pit houses (Features 100, 119, 121), and in the trash-filled retaining cells. Unfortunately, Weed never recorded the numbers of sherds of Santan Red-on-buff for each feature that she analyzed, so that it is impossible to give precise frequencies for this type. Instead, the Santan material was included in the frequencies of Sacaton and Casa Grande Red-on-buffs. Along with her analysis of design elements and motifs, a rim form analysis was carried out. By contrasting this information with published descriptions and photographs of Sacaton and Casa Grande Red-on-buff (Gladwin and others 1937; Haury 1945), she was able to reach definite conclusions about the attributes of Santan Red-on-buff.

Weed recorded 10 specific design elements that occurred repeatedly on the red-on-buff sherds. These design elements are as follows:

1. Parallel lines

2. Thick lines

3. Parallel squiggles

4. Serrate border edge

5. Flags

6. Frets

7. Scrolls

8. Hatching

9. Isolated elements

10. Jog lines

The major hindrance to the study was the lack of a comparably large collection of whole vessels from Las Colinas. The importance of symmetry and layout in graphing the changes and continuities in Hohokam ceramic design has been stressed (Zaslow and Dittert 1977), but both attributes can rarely be recorded using sherd material alone. Weed also ran into problems in determining precisely which motifs were present from the portions available on sherd material.

Of the 10 elements, only two were type-specific: the thick line, which occurred only on Casa Grande Red-on-buff; and the curvilinear scroll, which occurred only on Sacaton Red-on-buff. Using this information and the results of the rim form and design study, Santan Red-on-buff material was separated from its neighbors.

Sacaton Red-on-buff jars are usually shouldered, with almost horizontal recurved rims on short to non-existent necks. Unshouldered vessels and straight-necked vessels represent minor variations. Design elements are rarely present on the vessel neck, but when neck designs are present, they are typically continuations of the body layout. Usually, the body design is bordered by an attached squiggle line or a line separated from the design by no more than 1.5 cm, with the line usually demarcating the shoulder.

According to Haury, bowls usually make up between 50 and 65 percent of any Sacaton assemblage. In flare-rimmed bowls, dominant designs are often restricted to either the exterior or interior of the vessel, although sometimes occurring on both. An interior design is usually carried all the way to the rim. Design elements frequently encountered on Sacaton vessels include hatching or parallel squiggle lines, combination lines, scrolls, life forms, and isolated repeated elements. Layouts are often panelled or plaited (Gladwin and others 1937; Haury 1945).

In contrast, Casa Grande Red-on-buff occurs almost exclusively in jar form. The recurved rim has been replaced by a tall, vertical rim (an average of 5.85 cm in height). Bands of design are present both around the neck and on the jar body. The shoulder has become more rounded in profile. Elements on Casa Grande vessels are predominantly rectilinear rather than curvilinear, utilizing lines, jog elements, and frets. Bands around the jar body can be above and/or below the vessel shoulder, while the shoulder itself is demarcated by a free-line squiggle (Gladwin 1933; Haury 1945).

The Santan Red-on-buff material represented at Las Colinas fills the obvious gap between these two types. It is transitional both in form and in decoration. Santan Red-on-buff does not differ from either of the above types from a technological standpoint. Colors appear identical to Sacaton Red-on-buff: the red varies from a weak red (10R4/3) to a red (10R 4/6) with the background termed very pale brown (10YR 8/4) in the Munsell color terminology (Munsell Soil Color Chart, 1949). The material is characterized by a quartzite sand temper coarser than the typically fine micaceous sand temper found in later Casa Grande Red-on-buff sherds. Toward the end of the Sacaton phase, more vessels occur with a free-line neck squiggle divorced from the body-design band. Santan Red-on-buff jars typically have medium vertical necks which do not exceed 5.5 cm in height, and a free-line neck squiggle which is present on over 90 percent of the necks. This line is separated from the body-design band by an average of 2.0 cm to 3.5 cm. A free-line squiggle (Figure 100) usually occurs also in very late Sacaton Red-on-buff vessels. On Casa Grande Red-on-buff jars these free-line squiggles are bracketed by bands of design at the neck, above and below the shoulder.

The medium vertical necks (which make up 67.1 percent of the jar rims from the Santan Red-on-buff sample) typically have a design composed of a continuous crenulated line or repetitive isolated elements. The banded design with framing lines is relatively rare (Figure 101).

Hatching, which is typically done with squiggle lines in Sacaton Red-on-buff and with straight parallel lines in Casa Grande Red-on-buff, is done with jog lines in Santan Red-on-buff. In addition, the serrate border edge, fret, and parallel line treatment occurs first in Santan Red-on-buff and continues to be utilized as design elements in Casa Grande Red-on-buff. Although the jog line treatment does occur in Sacaton Red-on-buff, it occurs usually on bowl interiors. On Santan Red-on-buff, the element occurs almost exclusively as a jar body design (Figure 102).

Relatively few bowls of Hohokam red-on-buff types were recovered at Las Colinas. However, the flare-rimmed form was definitely attributable to Sacaton Red-on-buff. Other forms appear to be Santan Red-on-buff or transitional types. These vessels show a high incidence of parallel line treatment, scrolls, and squiggle lines. Also, scrolls represent 15 percent of Santan Red-on-buff bowl designs, whereas they occur on only 5 percent of the jar designs.

Layout on Santan Red-on-buff vessels, as gleaned from sherd material, shows a shift to greater use of free space than in Sacaton Red-on-buff. Design panels and bands are more condensed so that the common plaited effect is more obvious. The Sacaton material exhibited primarily the use of reflexive structure in executing designs, while the Santan sherds exhibited primarily rotation of design elements.

In summary, Santan Red-on-buff is significant in bridging a rather wide gap between the vessel forms and design styles of Sacaton and Casa Grande Red-on-buff. Santan is transitional between the curvilinear, broad designs of Sacaton and the more stylized, rectilinear designs of Casa Grande Red-on-buff. The fact that such transitional forms have been recovered in other sites in a late Sacaton or early Soho phase context (Johnson 1964), suggests that the type is not just a site-specific ceramic type. Its occurrence at Las Colinas in features dated consistently earlier than the majority of the Classic period material, and in features and assemblages which produced high amounts of early black-on-white intrusives, supports a dating for this material consistent with Gladwin's original dating of the Santan phase, A.D. 1100-1200 (Weed n.d.).

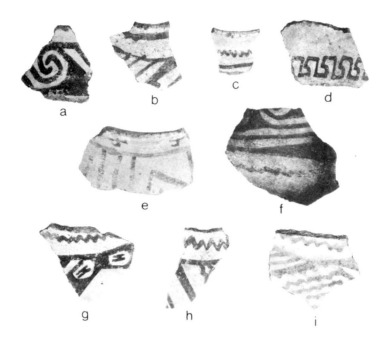

Figure 100.   Santan Red-on-buff jar neck sherds with
free-line neck squiggles (length of a is
7 cm)

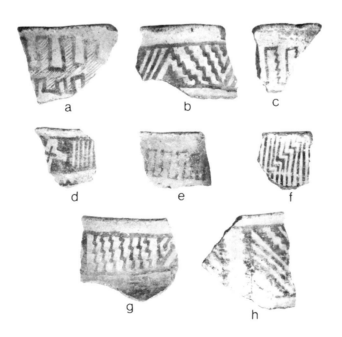

Figure 101.   Santan Red-on-buff jar neck sherds
with crenulated lines and repetitive
isolated elements (length of a is
8.5 cm)

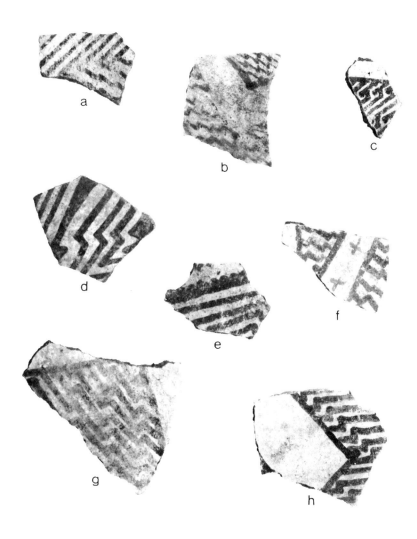

Figure 102. Santan Red-on-buff jar sherds with jog-line
hatching (length of a is 5 cm)

Whole and Partial Decorated Vessels

It is particularly fortunate that Feature 100, the burned pit house which contained a majority of the whole vessels from Las Colinas, also produced several vessels of Santan Red-on-buff. Four whole and partial red-on-buff jars were recovered from Feature 100, and all were good examples of Weed's Santan Red-on-buff type.

None of these vessels fit definitions of either Sacaton or Casa Grande Red-on-buff well, but have characteristics of each. The most complete vessel in the group is characterized by a short, recurved neck, which is almost vertical because the curve is so slight (Figures 103a, 104a). There is a definite design on the neck, although the design elements cannot be discerned because of the severe burning of the vessel and fugitive paint. It is certainly not a banded design, however, although it appears to be continuous around the rim. A free-line squiggle occurs at the point of greatest constriction on the vessel. There is a band of design on the vessel body and a free-line squiggle at the shallow, rounded shoulder. The basic layout is in a plaited pattern, with the plaiting bars filled with the negative thunderbolt motif and the scroll areas filled with jog-line hachure (see Zaslow and Dittert 1977).

Another vessel (Figure 105) has a short, vertical neck, with bands of design at the neck and body and squiggle lines between the bands and at the shoulder. Sacaton traits on this vessel include the use of scrolls in the band of design at the neck and the use of squiggle-line hatching, while Casa Grande Red-on-buff traits include the neck form and the use of banded designs.

The vessel in Figure 104,d) also has two bands of design on the medium vertical neck and from the neck to the shoulder. Again these are bordered by free-line squiggles. The plaited layout includes the negative thunderbolt motif in the bar areas and jog-line hachure in both the neck band and scroll area.

The last vessel from this feature is only 10 percent complete (Figures 103,c; 104,c). On this jar there is a definite band around the jar body, but the neck contains the crenulated line motif common on late Sacaton Red-on-buff jars. These areas of design are separated by a free-line squiggle. Jog-line hatching characterizes the motifs on the jar body.

These four vessels have formal and design characteristics which place them in a stage transitional to Sacaton and Casa Grande Red-on-buff. This transitional type has several characteristics of Sacaton Red-on-buff (recurved necks or lips, use of scrolls, unbanded shouldered vessels) as well as features of Casa Grande Red-on-buff (vertical necks, banded designs). Most significant are several features which appear to be unique to this type: free-line squiggles at the neck and shoulder, jog-line hachure, and short to medium height vertical necks.

It is of particular importance that two of these vessels were used to illustrate the true continuity of Hohokam design in terms of symmetry and layout. In their work on Hohokam pattern mathematics, Zaslow and Dittert (1977: 18-19) illustrate vessels 100 and 100-101 in demonstrating the relationship between Sacaton and Casa Grande Red-on-buff. These vessels and the two other

Figure 103.   Santan Red-on-buff (a, c) and Casa Grande Red-on-buff (b)
whole and partial vessels (diameter of a is 38.7 cm)

Figure 104. Santan Red-on-buff (a, c, d) and Casa Grande Red-on-buff vessels (b); diameter of d is 34.5 cm

Figure 105. Santan Red-on-buff vessel
(diameter is 38.1 cm)

vessels from Feature 100 truly do link Sacaton and Casa Grande Red-on-buff, so that the differences between the two types can now be seen as two points on an evolutionary continuum rather than qualitatively distinct forms. The storage rooms of the Arizona State Museum contain several vessels which fit Weed's criteria for Santan Red-on-buff, vessels whose significance was probably over-looked due to the transitional nature of their forms and designs. The sharing of features of both Sacaton and Casa Grande Red-on-buff might be overlooked in a large collection, but the material is available from other Classic period assemblages. In fact, the vessel used by Gladwin to illustrate his original type description of Casa Grande Red-on-buff fits well within the definition of Santan Red-on-buff (Gladwin and Gladwin 1933:Plate VIII).

Two Casa Grande Red-on-buff vessels were recovered at Las Colinas. Both had fugitive paint, and no evidence remains of design apart from ghost lines in some areas. The small jar from Feature 21 (Figures 103, b; 104, b) had two bands of design at the neck and body. The vertical neck of this vessel was broken and reground so that measurement is impossible. The design of the jar body was placed above the very low shoulder. The second jar was recovered from Burial 4, a burial which produced a number of Gila/Salt Red transitional vessels. This small jar displays two shoulders and large fire clouds. Unfortunately the paint is completely gone, although it is possible to discern that a band of design was painted between the neck and first shoulder. Both vessels have micaceous sand temper.

There was only one partial Gila Polychrome vessel recovered from the site, and this vessel displays the variety of design which includes red hatch-ing on the vessel interior. The bowl has a typical Salado paste and temper, and whole field focus in a finite design with four-fold rotation of the basic motifs. The exterior of the vessel exhibits a pattern polish and color reminiscent of Gila Red. It is impossible to tell whether this bowl was pro-duced by the paddle-and-anvil or coil-and-scrape technique.

At least one additional Salado polychrome vessel, a small Tonto Poly-chrome jar, was recovered at the site by pothunters. The jar was removed from one of the burials, located on the top of Mound 8 (Figure 106).

The final vessel in the assemblage from Las Colinas is of uncertain origin. While excavations were being conducted at Las Colinas, two Phoenix children told excavators that they had dug the vessel from the mound top; they donated it to the Arizona State Museum. The vessel is almost complete and is Bidahochi Polychrome type (Figures 107, 108). Although this type (Colton and Hargrave 1937:151) occurs in a time period consistent with the Las Colinas site dates, it is doubtful that the vessel could have been excavated from the area indicated by the pothunters since it would have required trenching through a concrete floor.

Miscellaneous Clay Objects

Griddles

Griddles, or comals, are commonly found in Classic period sites (Haury 1945:109-110; 1976:348), perhaps a result of West Mexican influence.

Figure 106.   Tonto Polychrome jar, from top of Mound 8
(height of jar is approximately 15 cm)

Figure 107. Bidahochi Polychrome bowl (diameter is
21.5 cm); interior view

Figure 108. Same as Figure 107; side view

Fragments of 40 griddles were found at Las Colinas in features dating to the Soho and Civano phases. The griddles are all composed of fine buff paste, six of which have schist temper. In contrast to the Los Muertos collection of griddles, most of which show evidence of use over a fire, none of the Las Colinas griddles are blackened or fire-clouded. The diameter of the specimens ranges from 20 cm to 42 cm. Eleven of the Las Colinas griddles have raised edges resembling other Classic period griddles (Haury 1945:110, Figure 67b and c) while the other 29 have only slightly curved edges (Haury 1945:110, Figure 67a) (see Figure 109).

Perforated Plates

Fragments of 69 perforated plates were recovered from Las Colinas. The fragments represent plates which would have varied from 22 cm to over 60 cm in diameter. The interior is smoothed on all of the plates, and the exterior is smoothed on the majority (Haury 1945:111, Figure 68d and 4). Of the 69 fragments, 25 have a raised ridge on the exterior edge, the result of thickening the last coil on the plates (Haury 1945:111, Figure 68c). The holes were punched through the plates from the inside while the clay was still wet. These holes were placed 1.4 cm to 3.8 cm apart, with smaller plates exhibiting closely set holes. No further clues to their function were recovered (Figure 109).

Spindle Whorls

Molded. Excavations at Las Colinas revealed 16 molded spindle whorls. These spindle whorls were identical in form and decoration to those from Los Muertos and are evidence of probable contact with west Mexico (Haury 1976:348). Eight of the spindle whorls are ellipsoidal in shape, four of these are medially grooved, three plain, and one medially grooved and vertically incised (Haury 1945:115, Figure 71b and c). Only one spindle whorl is discoidal in shape (Haury 1945:115, Figure 71d, e, and f), five are biconical (Haury 1945: 115, Figure 71g and h), and two are pulley shaped with vertical incising (Haury 1945:115, Figure 71i and j). Fourteen of the spindle whorls are plain ware, of which two have schist temper and the others a fine sand temper. The remaining two whorls are red slipped. Sizes range from .6 cm to 2.1 cm in width, and 2.2 cm to 4.2 cm in diameter. With one exception, all of the holes were centrally placed. The holes in three of the whorls were clearly punched while the clay was still wet but after molding was complete (Figure 109).

Perforated Sherd. A total of 30 perforated sherd spindle whorls was recovered from Las Colinas. These are all biconically perforated and range in size from 2.8 cm to 5.5 cm in diameter, and .2 cm to 1.0 cm in width. The majority (15) of the whorls are made of Gila Plain, Wingfield Variety sherds. Other pottery types present include: Gila Plain, Gila Variety (1); Gila Plain, Salt Variety (2); Gila Red (4); Salt Red (2); Schist-tempered Red Ware (1); Casa Grande Red-on-buff (3); and Gila Polychrome (1). In addition, one object which may be made of rubber was recovered. This was probably a part of an historic object that happens to resemble a spindle whorl.

Figure 110. Scoops, handles (length of b is 9 cm)

Figure 109. Griddle (a), perforated plates (b, c), and molded spindle whorls (d-g); (length of a is 18.7 cm)

Worked Potsherds

Discs. The excavations at Las Colinas led to the recovery of 105 discs. A dozen specimens have holes drilled partially through them, apparently to produce spindle whorls, although these were not completed. The discs range in size from 1.4 cm to 8.7 cm in diameter. Gila Plain, Salt Variety is the most common type (35), although Gila Plain, Wingfield Variety is also well represented (33). Other types present include Salt Red (20), Gila Red (8), Casa Grande Red-on-buff (4), and San Juan Red Ware (5).

Other Worked Sherds. A collection of 34 other worked sherds was recovered from the features excavated at Las Colinas. These are not discoidal, but appear in a number of other shapes from triangular and rectangular to ellipsoidal. The function of these sherds is unknown, but all have at least one, well-ground edge, and thus may have functioned as pottery scrapers used to smooth vessel walls (Haury 1945:121). Types present include: schist-tempered red ware (13); Gila Plain, Salt Variety (12); Salt Red (3); Gila Red (4); and Casa Grande Red-on-buff (2).

Handles. A large number of jar handles (90) were recovered from Las Colinas. Of these, 82 were simply flattened coils of clay. Where a small segment of the vessel was still attached to the handle, it is apparent that handles were often applied vertically to the vessel wall, with the upper end of the handle attached to the rim. The majority of the handles come from Gila Plain, Salt Variety jars (43), while the rest come from jars of Salt Red (24); Gila Plain, Wingfield Variety (6); and Casa Grande Red-on-buff (9).

Five handles from "bean pots" were present in the sample. The remaining three handles were erratic types: one exhibits a double handle, one a vertical knob with horizontal grooves, and one a small, horizontal, knob-like handle. All three are red wares.

Scoops. A total of 42 scoop fragments was recovered from Las Colinas features. A variety of red ware and plain ware fragments were found: 14 Salt Red; 6 Gila Red; 12 Gila Plain, Salt Variety; 7 Gila Plain, Wingfield Variety; and 1 Gila Plain, Gila Variety. One scoop appears to have been red-on-buff, but the sherd is so badly eroded that positive identification is impossible. One scoop fragment had an applique face (Figure 110). All of the scoop fragments appear to have come from scoops with horizontal rims (Haury 1945:97, Figure 60a), but most of the sherds are too small to identify positively. Two of the 42 fragments are handles, each of which has a vertical bar of clay across the interior portion, which would serve to protect the thumb of the individual holding it.

Conclusion

The Las Colinas assemblage has offered a rare, diachronic view of Hohokam ceramic variability and manufacture from the end of the Sacaton phase to the end of the Civano phase. This comprehensive collection, well dated and with excellent records of provenience, has permitted a thorough examination of changes in ceramic style, technology, and manufacturing frequency through time. The following discussion focuses on a number of interesting trends that may have significance for future analyses of Classic period ceramics;

1. <u>Changes in tempering material through time</u>. There is a definite shift in temper composition for both the plain wares and red wares. The shift is from an overwhelming majority of schist-tempered material at the end of the Sacaton phase to a preponderance of sand-tempered material at the end of the Civano phase. Since it is doubtful that these types were imported in mass, it is necessary to look for the causes of this shift elsewhere. Both functional differences and availability of temper materials might explain the shift, but further research is necessary before this change can be explained completely.

2. <u>Gila/Salt Red continuum</u>. The Las Colinas material demonstrates that Salt Red never constituted a majority of the vessels in any phase of the site's occupation. Instead, Gila Red is present in far greater amounts during the eight time periods differentiated at Las Colinas. It has been suggested on the basis of this information that Salt Red is not a temporally significant type, but rather a technologically superior variety of Gila Red. The whole vessels from Las Colinas exhibit a range of technical features combining elements of both Gila and Salt Reds. Again, it is interesting to note that burials are consistently found with the better-made varieties of Salt Red.

3. <u>Trade wares</u>. Trade in ceramics at Las Colinas was primarily with northern Anasazi groups of the Kayenta and Little Colorado branches, although some trade was carried out with groups from the Prescott region. Trade with these groups was more significant during the Sacaton phase than during the Soho and Civano phases. The reason for this decline in trade with the northern areas is unknown. Trade with Mexican groups was almost non-existent, although two sherds of probable Mexican origin were recovered at the site.

4. <u>Santan Red-on-buff</u>. A type transitional between Sacaton Red-on-buff and Casa Grande Red-on-buff, both in vessel form and design style, occurs at Las Colinas in late Sacaton-early Soho contexts. This material has been defined and described as Santan Red-on-buff and adds to our understanding of the late Hohokam ceramic sequence.

5. <u>Microtraditions</u>. At least two microtraditions occurred at Las Colinas during the late Civano phase. These microtraditions were probably associated. Both involved the use of raspberry red slip on recurved rim bowl forms, producing a matte red ware type and a stylistically unsophisticated red-on-brown type. Associated with only a few late Civano structures and one burial, this material probably represents a short-lived local ceramic fashion which originated and died with its makers.

6. <u>Household inventory</u>. Feature 100, a pit house which was destroyed by fire, contained a large number of whole vessels, which we may assume represent a household inventory for the early Soho phase. The room contained a total of 17 vessels including: 4 plain ware vessels (3 Gila Plain, Salt Variety bowls, and 1 Gila Plain, Wingfield Variety jar); 9 red ware vessels (4 Gila Red, sand-tempered bowls, 2 schist-tempered red ware bowls, and 3 Gila Red, sand-tempered jars); and 4 decorated vessels (Santan Red-on-buff jars).

CHAPTER 5

THE LAS COLINAS FLAKED STONE ASSEMBLAGE

by Bruce B. Huckell*
Arizona State Museum
University of Arizona

Introduction

The excavations at Las Colinas resulted in the recovery of a large collection of stone artifacts. Both flaked and ground stone proved to be well represented and, it was felt, offered an excellent chance for a detailed study of the Classic period Hohokam lithic industry. With the exceptions of Los Muertos (Haury 1945) and Casa Grande (Fewkes 1912), no single Classic site has produced a lithic assemblage as extensive as the one from Las Colinas. Weaver's work at Pueblo del Monte (1972) coupled with Pailes's analysis of the artifacts from the Fitch site (Pailes 1963) constitute much of the available data on Classic period lithic assemblages from the Salt River Basin area. Few good samples of Classic Hohokam lithic industries have been reported outside this area. Notable exceptions include sites in the Painted Rocks Reservoir area (Wasley and Johnson 1965), and University Indian Ruin (Hayden 1957) near Tucson.

The relatively rich assemblage from Las Colinas opened several important channels of inquiry into Classic period stone work. First, it permitted a rather complete overview of a typical Classic assemblage, which for purely comparative and descriptive purposes was quite important in and of itself. Second, the occurrence of Salado pottery types showed that there may have been contact with this group, and it was hypothesized that the lithic artifacts might reflect this Salado contact or influence as well. Third, examination of the collection of debitage, cores, hammers and finished tools provided an insight into the technological aspects of the assemblage. This study was qualitative rather than quantitative for the reasons which will be enumerated later.

Analysis began in the spring of 1970, and the majority of the work was carried out during the winter and spring of 1970-71 by Carol Weed. A specially designed Arizona State Museum form was used to conduct the analysis. This form enabled classification of each piece of stone by raw material type, and allowed for description of the specimen as unmodified, accidentally modified, a manufacture discard, or as an artifact or used flake. After the major part of the analysis was completed, the author undertook the final analysis of the tools and the drafting of a report on the flaked stone. George Teague did the same for the ground stone artifacts (see Teague, this volume).

Draft completed: July 1974

Despite the fact that they constitute an integral part of man's ability to survive in almost every environment, flaked stone tools have often been accorded only secondary value by archaeologists. This is understandable, for flaked stone has traditionally taken a back seat to pottery in the Southwest, due in part to the fact that potsherds are much more common at most sites than are pieces of flaked stone. As noted earlier, the flaked stone from Las Colinas offered an excellent opportunity to increase our knowledge and understanding of the Classic Hohokam lithic industry. The large size and completeness of the sample allowed the study of both functional and technological aspects of this industry. Because of the mixed nature of much of the site, this description of the flaked stone will treat the material as the product of a single industry. While this assemblage may encompass a period of 300 years, it is difficult to divide it into phases or distinct units of time. The majority of the flaked stone artifacts came from the trash-filled retaining cells of the mound, from strip areas, or from the general mound fill proveniences. The exact temporal association and origin of the material is therefore in doubt. In comparison with material from those features that could be assigned to a phase or portion of a phase, no apparent changes in the assemblage through time were noted, except for some possible variation in projectile point styles. Unfortunately, the sizes of the samples from dated features were relatively small.

Classification of Flaked Stone Artifacts

The following descriptions of the flaked stone artifacts organize the assemblage in a series of general categories of tools. When necessary, these categories are further subdivided into types based upon formal and metric attributes.

Projectile Points

Projectile points were relatively common artifacts at Las Colinas. Fifty-two whole, fragmentary and unfinished examples were recovered during the course of the excavations. Obsidian was the material favored for point manufacture. Sixty-seven percent of the points were made of this material. In contrast to the unifacially and bifacially retouched flake tools, most of these projectile points could be sorted into fairly consistent, patterned types. It was observed that more consistency in style was present in the obsidian points than in the points made of chert or other materials. A major part of this variation may be accounted for by the interpretation of some of the chert points as styles typical of earlier periods that found their way into the Classic context of the mound.

Most of the points were fairly simple technologically, and were produced by rather unpatterned pressure work on small flakes. Some points made on chert flakes showed more complexity or control in manufacture, but probably were not the products of Classic period stoneworkers. The following discussion of projectile points from Las Colinas deals with particular types or styles that are segregated on the basis of technological and stylistic attributes. Two broad groups have been established--points with notches and points without notches--and individual types are discussed under each group. Each type is described briefly and compared to projectile points from other Classic period (or earlier) sites when possible.

Points with Notches

Type 1. These points were short, wide triangles with fairly wide side notches: the type can be further separated by the treatment of the base.

The first subtype (1a) is characterized by a straight base (Figure 111, a-d). A total of 12 points, all complete, fit into this group, making it the largest category. The average length of these points is 18 mm, the average basal width is 10 mm, and the average thickness is 3 mm. Often they are slightly asymmetrical in outline, and on the whole do not display very careful workmanship. All were made of obsidian. At Las Colinas these points were found in both the earlier retaining cells of the mound and in the late pit houses, indicating that this style probably persisted through most of the Classic period. Haury (1945:125, Plate 35 f-i) reported the same style from Los Muertos, and noted "...the poorer quality of pressure flaking and...greater asymmetry in outline." He further stated that seven out of eight from that site were made of obsidian. Hayden (1957: Plate XL d) recovered one similar point from University Ruin, as did Weaver (1972: Plate VIII b) from Pueblo del Monte.

A single point of obsidian (subtype 1b) was found that closely resembled the subtype 1a style but that exhibits a basal notch rather than a simple straight base (Figure 111, e). This notch is equal in size to the side notches. Haury discussed four points from Los Muertos closely resembling the Las Colinas specimen (Haury 1945:125, Plate 35 j, k).

Type 2. Four points, two of obsidian and two of chert, are classified together in this group. They are united by being triangular in outline with a markedly concave base and small, shallow side notches, but may be divided into two subtypes based on relative length.

The first subtype (2a) is characterized by having shallow side notches located approximately midway up the point from the base. One complete specimen and one fragment were placed in this category (Figure 111, f). The complete specimen measures 23 mm long, 12 mm wide, and 3 mm thick.

This particular point style was very widespread in central and southern Arizona during the Classic period. For example, it is reported from such diverse areas as Los Muertos (Haury 1945: 125, Plate 35 b, c), from Tanque Verde phase sites in the Tucson area (Zahniser 1966: Figure 26c), and from sites in the upper Tonto Basin near Rye (Hammack 1969: Figure 15a, b).

The second subtype (2b) differs from the preceding one only in length: the two specimens included in this group are 14 mm long (Figure 111, g). However, they display the same base treatment and notching as the larger ones. Because they were made on smaller flakes they are noticeably shorter, but only slightly narrower at the base.

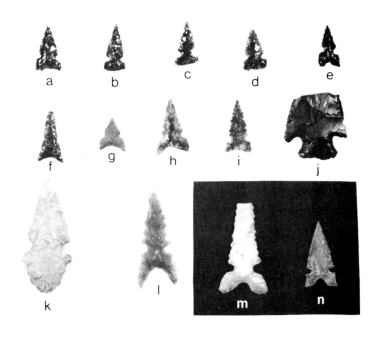

Figure 111. Points with notches (length
of k is 4.8 cm)

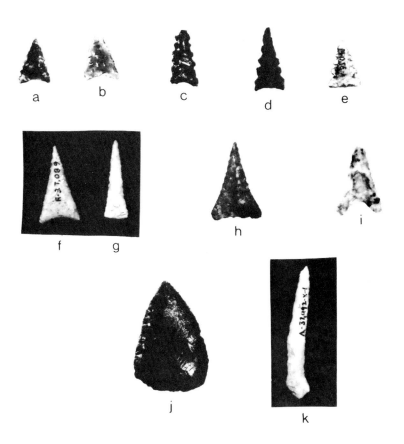

Figure 112. Points without notches, and drill
(length of c is 15.5 cm)

Type 3. Three points exhibit relatively long, serrated blades; wide, shallow side notches; and concave bases (Figure 111, h-i). They are all very close to 23 mm in length, and average 12 mm wide at the base. The notches are quite near the base, and mark the end of the serration.

Miscellaneous notched points. Six points cannot be classed with any of the previously discussed types. Each is unique and all represented earlier or non-local projectile point styles which found their way into the site. These points are described individually and, when possible, related to other sites or time periods.

The base of a large corner-notched dart point made of red petrified wood was recovered from a retaining cell of the mound (Figure 111, j). It was produced largely by direct percussion, but was shaped and notched by pressure flaking. In terms of style it resembles some Basketmaker dart points (cf. Morris and Burgh 1954: Figure 29 f), and it may have had its origins in the northern part of the state a few hundred years earlier than the occupation of the site.

A single leaf-shaped point with prominent side notches was also found in undifferentiated mound fill (Figure 111, k). Made of a banded gray quartzite, it too seems to be a dart point, although the style cannot be placed as to time or cultural affinity. It was worked largely by percussion and shaped by pressure. Possibly it is a preceramic Desert Culture point picked up by the Hohokam.

Three projectiles were found which seem to be Sacaton phase Hohokam in origin, as they are all much larger than the other notched points. One is made of brown chert and exhibits a deep basal concavity, a narrow, deeply serrated blade, and deep, wide side notches (Figure 111, l). It is rather thin, and suggests some of the more elaborate Sacaton phase points in shape. A second point, made of translucent white chalcedony, is definitely a typical Sacaton phase point (Figure 111, m). Its concave and widely notched base, deep, broad side notches, and lightly serrated blade duplicate a point illustrated in the Snaketown report (Sayles in Gladwin and others 1937: Plate LXXXVI k). The same may be said for a long triangular point of obsidian that has deep narrow side notches and a slightly concave base: its virtual twin may also be seen in the Snaketown collection (Sayles in Gladwin and others 1937: Plate LXXXVIII e, f). It was probably produced during the Sacaton phase.

Finally, a point superficially similar to subtype 1b was recovered from the thoracic region of a human burial, but was felt to differ sufficiently from that subtype to warrant its own description (Figure 111, n). It is made of a nearly transparent chalcedony and is exquisitely thin, measuring 28 mm long, 14 mm wide, and only 2 mm in thickness. It was produced by well-controlled pressure flaking of a quality superior to that seen on any other point in the Las Colinas assemblage. Beyond this little can be said; the point may or may not be Hohokam in origin.

Points without Notches

Type 4. This type was defined by the absence of notches for hafting, and by the presence of serration for the length of the blade. Three subtypes have been created to accommodate variations in base treatment, ratio of width to length, and type of serration.

Three points (subtype 4a), all of obsidian, were found at the site. These points were short (under 18 mm in length), wide (14 mm), triangular projectiles with concave bases. Typically the basal width is equal to two-thirds or more of the length, and the blade is finished with small, narrow serrations (Figure 112, a-b). Haury described nearly identical points from Los Muertos (1945:125-126, Plate 36 d), and from Los Pueblos Arriba (1945: Figure 124a).

Three points in the next group (subtype 4b) differ from those in the first subtype in two respects. First, they are much more slender, exhibiting narrower bases and longer blades, and second, they show larger and deeper serrations (Figure 112, c-d). One is of white chert, one of very fine-grained basalt, and one of obsidian. The single complete specimen is 23 mm long, 12 mm wide, and 5 mm thick. These seem less well made than the subtype 4a points.

While serrated points of a roughly similar nature are illustrated from Los Muertos, nearly identical points were present in Sacaton phase contexts at Snaketown (Sayles in Gladwin and others 1937: Plate LXXXV d, e). These points may be Sacaton phase projectiles deposited in Classic period contexts. It is more probable, however, that they are Classic period points produced in the enduring style of Hohokam serrated projectiles.

The subtype 4c point could be lost in a Sacaton phase group (Figure It bears serrations most similar to those seen on subtype 4b, but is short (17 mm) and has a rather wide (12 mm) straight base (Figure 112, e). It is made of obsidian.

A point from Los Muertos (Haury 1945: Plate 36 h) was quite similar but was larger. Points from Snaketown (Sayles in Gladwin and others 1937: Plate LXXXV e) also closely resembled the Las Colinas specimen.

Type 5. This type includes a group of projectiles which lack both notches and any sort of serration: they are simply long triangular points with straight or deeply concave bases. Two subtypes are constructed based on the ratio of width to length, and on basal attributes.

Three points, two of chert and one of obsidian, were included in subtype 5a. They have concave bases with sharp basal corners roughly one-third as wide as the point is long (Figure 112, f). The blade is fairly straight-sided and rather thin in comparison to the previously described points. On the average, the points are 24 mm long, 13 mm wide, and 3 mm thick.

This style of point was widespread in central and southern Arizona during the Classic period. Similar points were found at Los Muertos (Haury

1945: Plate 36 a), University Ruin (Hayden 1957: Plate XL e, g) and the Tucson Basin (Zahniser 1966: Figure 26 d) as well as at many other sites that have not been reported on in the literature. Undoubtedly, one reason for the wide distribution of this style was its simplicity of both shape and manufacture.

Two chert points (subtype 5b) are separated from the preceding group by their basal width-to-length ratios. Both exhibit very narrow, straight or slightly convex bases which are less than one-fourth as wide as the point is long (Figure 112, g). They are rather thick (5 mm), almost diamond-shaped in cross-section, and average 28 mm in length. One point from Los Muertos (Haury 1945: Plate 36 c) closely resembles these two specimens from Las Colinas.

Miscellaneous unnotched points. Two projectile points could not be easily placed in any of the preceding categories of points without notches. They most closely resembled the Type 5 specimens, but nevertheless display certain differences which set them apart from this type. One point made of jasper exhibits a slightly concave base with rounded corners, and a blade with concave sides. It is thin and well made (Figure 112,h). The other point (Figure 112, i) has a deeply concave base and a blade with fairly straight sides. This point is made of a mottled black and white chert, and bears a strong stylistic resemblance to early historic Papago projectile points (Haury 1950:274, Figure 56 q) although it is larger than most.

Heavy Projectile Point

A large obsidian flake was recovered which had been extensively bifacially retouched by pressure. It is essentially leaf shaped with a convex base and convex edges, and measures 39 mm long, 28 mm wide, and 6 mm thick. An effort was made to remove the bulb of percussion to thin the base, implying that the point was probably intended to be hafted. While it could have served as a knife, there is no wear pattern to confirm that use, and so it is interpreted as a heavy projectile point (Figure 112, j).

Miscellaneous Fragments

Six point fragments were too incomplete to allow their inclusion in any of the classes discussed above. One of these is a simple concave base fragment, which may originally have been a small subtype 5a point. Two very long, narrow, serrated tip fragments, and two short nonserrated tip fragments, otherwise unclassifiable, were recovered. A nearly complete specimen with a badly damaged base and a slightly broken tip was also grouped with these miscellaneous fragments. All these fragments are of obsidian.

Unfinished Points

Six additional obsidian flakes were found that show varying amounts of pressure work. One may be a completed point: it is a small triangular flake which has had its margins straightened and upon which a sharp tip has been formed. It received no basal thinning to remove the thick, cortical area. Three other flakes apparently broke during pressure flaking and were discarded. Two flakes showed incipient retouch, but were evidently abandoned due to thick areas on one lateral margin of the flake that could not be removed.

Drill

A single long, bifacially pressure flaked drill represents this common category of artifacts. Made of white chert, it is very narrow and exhibits a diamond shaped cross-section. No provision has been made for hafting it (Figure 112, k). It is 47 mm long and 7 mm wide, and it resembles a specimen from Los Muertos illustrated by Haury (1945: Plate 36 k). It is clearly smoothed from wear on portions of both faces and margins.

Large Primary Flake Tools

This category of tools encompassed 109 whole and fragmentary examples of implements made from large primary decortication flakes. They were common at Hohokam sites of all ages, and particularly so at those of the Classic period (Haury 1945, Hayden 1957, Pailes 1963, Weaver 1972). In the past, these implements have been classified using functional terms such as hoe, mescal knife, grass knife, saw, and so forth. Since these terms are restrictive, the decision was made to use a descriptive term that would admit the possibility of different uses for the same implement. All are united, nevertheless, by virtue of the fact that they were the products of the same technological manufacturing process. This process will be discussed in detail later, but it should be noted here that the process was used to produce only large primary flakes from river cobbles. The resulting flakes range in shape from circular to oval, and many are roughly twice as wide as they are long. They commonly exhibit a very flat bulb of percussion, no bulbar scar, and have a completely cortical exterior surface. Basalt and other igneous rocks, in addition to quartzite, were most commonly used in the production of these flakes. A sample of these implements is presented in Figure 113).

Many of the flakes were used just as they were removed from the core, without retouching. Others showed a conscious effort to shape the flake with a percussion retouch, or to thin or serrate the working edge using the same technique. Often the edge of the flake which served as the handle was blunted or backed by percussion. The working edge was commonly a long, thin margin of the flake that might be straight, concave, convex or sinuous in profile.

The function or functions that these primary flake tools served has been the subject of much debate in the past. Earlier workers (Fewkes 1912, Turney 1924) commonly referred to these implements as hoes, although more recently there has been a tendency to call some of them knives. Haury (1945) noted the wear patterns that some of these primary flakes exhibited, as did Hayden (1957). Both felt that at least some of the flakes served as knives rather than hoes, because of the direction of the striations from wear on the working edge. Hayden proposed that striations running parallel to the working edge implied use as a knife, and that striations aligned transversely to the

Figure 113.   Large primary flake tools (length of c is 15.5 cm)

Figure 114.   Tabular knives (length of a is 15.5 cm)

working edge indicated use as a hoe (Hayden 1957:142). The 109 complete and fragmentary examples of large primary flake tools from Las Colinas were examined to determine whether or not discernible patterns of wear were present. It was found that only about 10 percent showed distinguishable wear polish and striations when examined under a binocular microscope at 30x. Of these specimens, all but one exhibited striations running parallel to the working edge of the tool. In some cases wear polish extended nearly 30 mm up the faces of the tool. This suggests that at Las Colinas the majority of these large primary flake tools probably served as cutting implements. The single exception was a tool made on a large fragment of a flake that showed striations directed transversely across the working edge, indicating that the tool was used with a scraping or planing motion. These striations were evident only on the actual working edge -- had the flake been used as a hoe, the polish and striations would extend up both faces.

It is quite probable that the tools used for cutting had relatively long lives. A dulled or worn tool could be sharpened with relative ease by serrating the working edge with a percussion retouch. One tool showed this quite well: fresh percussion flake scars cut through the edges and surfaces of the tool that were dulled by wear. Serration was noted on eleven of the tools, although many more showed a simple, even percussion retouch on the working edge.

Thus, at Las Colinas, these large primary flake tools appear to have served for cutting, although there is some evidence that they were occasionally employed in tasks involving scraping or planing. There is nothing to suggest that these tools were used as hoes. The presence of wear polish and striations well up the faces of some of the tools suggests that relatively thick and somewhat abrasive materials were cut with them. The fibrous mescal or agave leaf might produce such wear, but experimental data on this point are lacking.

Rather than continue to call all of these tools hoes or mescal knives, it is suggested that the phrase "large primary flake tools" be used to designate these distinctive implements. While recognizing that the flakes were the result of a specific manufacturing process, the use of this phrase implies no particular function. Rather, it allows for a variety of possible functions for the same flake. Data gathered from wear pattern studies can be used in the future to determine the specific uses of these flakes.

Tabular Knives

These implements are quite similar in form to the large primary flake tools, but are distinguished by virtue of the fact that they are made on thin, natural slabs of material. They are typically oval or rectangular in outline, and have a working edge constructed by chipping or grinding along one of the long edges of the slab (Figure 114). These working edges were commonly produced by either a percussion or pressure retouch that created a series of fine serrations. Some specimens were shaped and backed by percussion in the same manner as the large primary flake tools. Still others exhibit grinding on both faces of the tool near the working edge. The materials used are apparently igneous in origin and are relatively fine-grained.

Twelve examples of tabular knives, four complete and eight fragmentary, were recovered at Las Colinas. These artifacts are common at Classic period Hohokam sites (Haury 1945, Hayden 1957, Pailes 1963, Weaver 1972) as well as sites of earlier periods, such as Snaketown (Gladwin and others 1937). Traditionally they have been referred to as knives, and no evidence uncovered at Las Colinas indicates otherwise. Three specimens which had obvious wear patterns were examined at 30x with the aid of a binocular microscope, and all proved to have prominent striations running parallel to the working edge. As with the large primary flake tools, there was no evidence that any of the tabular knives saw service as hoes. In fact, the virtual duplication of both form and wear patterns suggests strongly that the tabular knives and most of the large primary flakes served interchangeably for the same cutting functions.

Unifacially Retouched Flake Tools

This category consists of all those flakes or flake fragments that show an intentional modification of the original flake margin by unifacial retouching. Fifty-one specimens were recognized as having been retouched in various fashions. A further breakdown of this group of artifacts has been attempted in an effort ot illustrate the diversity of the tools included in this category.

One of the most striking aspects of the retouched flake tools was the obvious lack of standardization and patterning. Pailes (1963:156) brought up this point in discussing the lithic assemblage from the Fitch site. There is no apparent selectivity or preference for the type of flake used and there is no regularity in the retouching of the flake. It seems as though the nearest suitable flake or flake fragment was used to make a tool, and that little attention was given to its material or shape. The retouch was done in a haphazard fashion in most cases, creating an uneven sinuous edge with protrusions and concavities. For these reasons it is difficult to arrive at a satisfactory classification of the retouched flake tools. The following paragraphs represent an attempt to deal with the tools on a more specific level, by placing them in groups of similar implements.

Scrapers

Thirty-two retouched flake tools exhibited unifacial retouch which created a fairly steep edge angle. These have been classified as scrapers. There is very little regularity in these tools. Typically, they show a percussion retouch covering from one-half to three-quarters of the margin of the flake. Twenty-four of the scrapers were made from basalt, andesite, rhyolite, and other related igneous materials. Five were made from chert, two from quartzite, and one was made from petrified wood. For purposes of description, these implements have been segregated into four types distinguished by size and type of retouch.

Type 1. Fifteen of the thirty-two scrapers show a slightly irregular retouch with edge angles ranging from 50 degrees to 80 degrees, with an average of approximately 70 degrees. The flake or flake fragment selected is usually plano-convex or nearly lenticular in cross-section, and not over 35 mm in maximum dimension. Working edges tend to be straight or convex. The retouch does not appear consistently on any one portion on the flake margin. Figure 115, f, h-i) illustrates some typical examples of this group of scrapers.

Type 2. Five scrapers were segregated from the rest because they show a denticulate type of retouch (Figure 115, e). This retouch was apparently done deliberately by removing a series of widely spaced percussion flakes in order to create a sinuous or grossly serrated working edge. Usually the outline of the working edge is straight or convex. These denticulated scrapers show size, shape, and edge angle characteristics similar to the more evenly retouched scrapers discussed in the previous paragraph. Their specific function is not understood.

Type 3. Five larger specimens of scrapers were encountered which exhibit a relatively even retouch, as is found in the Type 1 scrapers. The major criterion for their separation was size. They are larger in maximum dimension, and they are thicker and heavier than the scrapers discussed previously. Hayden (1957:160, 163) illustrated what he referred to as scraper-planes that are of similar size and shape, but more extensively retouched than the Las Colinas examples (Figure 115, c, g). One of these large scrapers is prominently polished on the working edge. It is the only scraper in the assemblage with a wear pattern. Examination under a microscope reveals striations aligned transversely to the working edge, confirming that this tool was used as a scraper.

Type 4. Four circular or oval tools were found which may or may not have been used as scrapers. All four tools have steep edge angles, and all of them have heavily battered working edges. Whether this wear was acquired during the planing of resistant materials, or from pounding and chopping is open to question. They are grouped with the scrapers because they are smaller than choppers (under 80 mm in maximum dimension) and because their edge angles are steeper than is common on choppers. Two of the tools are made on flakes, while the other two are made on cobble fragments (Figure 115, a, b).

Knives

Two unifacially retouched tools were classified as knives because of the presence of a well-executed retouch along the thin flake margin.

A single basalt flake was found which bears a minute unifacial retouch along one lateral margin and a heavier "backing" along the opposite margin (Figure 116, g). The slightly convex cutting edge displayed an edge angle of between 30 degrees and 35 degrees. No wear was observed.

One long blade-like flake of petrified wood was apparently also used as a knife (Figure 116, a). It has a unifacial retouch on one lateral margin which creates an edge angle of approximately 20°. The cutting edge is straight to slightly convex.

Figure 115. Scrapers: Type 1 (f, h, i), Type 2 (d-e),
Type 3 (c, g), Type 4 (a, b); length of a
is 7.4 cm

Figure 116. Unifacial knives (a, g), notched flake (f), graver (d), small chopper-scrapers (h-i), bifacial knives (b-c), biface (e); length of a is 6.7 cm

Technologically these are very simple tools. It is possible that the retouch on the cutting edge was done only to resharpen the edge after it had become dulled through use. If that is true, these two tools are more closely related to what Weaver termed flake knives (Weaver 1972:70-75) at Pueblo del Monte. These he described as flakes that were used for cutting without retouching. Hayden discussed implements from University Ruin that he called retouched flake knives (Hayden 1957:164-166); these are apparently similar to the two Las Colinas specimens.

Notched Flakes

Two other flakes, one of quartzite and one of rhyolite, showed single large notches on one margin. This notching was achieved by striking a deep blow with a hammerstone to remove a great deal of the flake margin, thus creating a wide concavity or notch. It is probable that these implements were used to shape or smooth cylindrical objects made of wood, bone, or antler.

Three flakes of basalt showed an exaggerated type of retouch which amounted to multiple notching (Figure 116, f). All three are roughly circular in shape, and were retouched by percussion. Similar specimens from University Ruin are illustrated and described by Hayden (1957:162, 165).

Gravers

One graver made on a basalt flake fragment and one made on an andesite flake were found during the analysis. Unfortunately, the single spur on the basalt specimen, formed by retouching a projection between two shallow notches, had been partially broken off (Figure 116,d). The andesite graver was intact and less retouching had been used to form the single spur. Thirteen gravers were reported from Pueblo del Monte: none "...exhibited any retouch, but they did have indications of the typical wear pattern of gravers" (Weaver 1972:86). Hayden reported three gravers from University Ruin, although the spurs had been produced by intentional retouching as in the Las Colinas specimens.

Bifacially Retouched Flake Tools

Fourteen tools that had been bifacially worked were identified during the analysis. As with the unifacially retouched flake tools, very little patterning or standardization was observable. Nevertheless, enough clustering was observed in these implements to allow the construction of four categories. With three of these categories it is possible to assign tentative functions that the tools may have served; in some cases, however, one wonders if the tools were ever used. Still, they have clearly been modified from their original flake form, and are therefore included in this discussion of tools.

Small Chopper-Scrapers

Five bifacially retouched tools were grouped together because they exhibited an alternating bifacial retouch that created a sinuous working edge.

Four of these tools were made on fairly large, thick flakes (one of basalt, one of quartzite, two of andesite), while the fifth was made on a fragment of a three-quarter grooved axe of diorite. All have a convex working edge, and display edge angles averaging 40 degrees. Two of them have incipient wear patterns, suggesting that they might have served as light-duty scraping or chopping implements. These two are illustrated in Figure 116, h, i.

Knives

Three flakes, two of chert and one of obsidian, were classified as small bifacially retouched knives. Two of them were characterized by low edge angles and a random bifacial retouch composed of short flakes (less than 2 mm on the average) along one margin. The third knife showed a uniform bifacial pressure retouch on one lateral margin of the flake, and a somewhat thicker cutting edge. In addition, the opposite margin of the flake was backed by a random retouch. Two of these knives are illustrated in Figure 116, b, c.

Bifaces

Two other implements probably also functioned as knives. Both are fragmentary, and both are differentiated from the knives discussed in the previous paragraph by the presence of percussion flake scars that completely cover both faces of the implement, making them true bifaces. The larger specimen (Figure 116, e) is made of petrified wood, while the smaller fragment, representing only the tip of the knife, is of chalcedony. Large bifacial knives of this sort seem to be relatively uncommon on Classic period sites: Hayden reported only one from University Ruin (1957:173-174), and Weaver did not recover any from Pueblo del Monte.

Miscellaneous Bifacial Tools

Two implements defied classification because of their amorphous shape and retouch. One of these was a large andesite flake fragment, roughly a long rectangle in outline. It showed a partly bifacial retouch along its long edges, and gave the impression of being a tool that was never completed. Another tool was likewise constructed on a basalt flake fragment, and exhibits a gross bifacial retouch consisting of very large flakes with deep negative bulbs of percussion. A slight wear polish is present along one deep flake scar and suggests that the tool may have functioned as a scraper or spokeshave. Its amorphous shape and retouch, as well as its relatively small size (7 mm in maximum dimension), militate against its inclusion in any of the previously described categories of bifacially retouched tools.

A single tool showed a bifacial retouch consisting of random flakes under 2 mm in length. This retouch was constructed on a portion of a wedge-shaped basalt "chunk" that had an edge angle of approximately 65 degrees. Its function is unclear; it may have served for either scraping or cutting.

Choppers

Eighteen implements were identified as choppers. These tools are made on elliptical cobbles or cobble fragments (10 mm to 20 mm in size) and are characterized by edge angles of 50 degrees to 80 degrees. The rounded, convex working edges were sharpened by the removal of fairly large percussion flakes. Occasionally, if made on whole cobbles, a section of the cortical edge was left unflaked, presumably to serve as a handle or backing. Fifteen of the specimens show unifacial retouching, while three have bifacially constructed working edges. The retouched working edge usually encompasses from one-half to five-sixths of the cobble margin, and occasionally extends completely around it. Fifteen of the eighteen choppers were made of basalt, the material most frequently used for these tools. Of the remaining three, one was of quartzite, one was of porphyritic basalt, and one was of diorite. Wear patterns are almost non-existent on these tools. Figure 117 presents some typical examples of choppers from Las Colinas.

Weaver recovered 16 choppers from Pueblo del Monte, but does not specify whether they were unifacially or bifacially retouched (Weaver 1972: 67-70). Pailes reports only two choppers from the Fitch site (1963:163), but Hayden reports a total of 121 unifacial choppers and 112 bifacial choppers from University Indian Ruin (Hayden 1957:154-157).

The absence of wear patterns makes it difficult to establish specific functions for the choppers. Perhaps they were used like axes for tasks such as working wood and clearing land. They may even have been used for butchering larger animals.

Utilized Flakes

This group of artifacts includes all those flakes that were used in their unmodified state. They are tools, but differ from those previously described in that they have not been intentionally retouched on the working edge. Two types of utilized flakes can be distinguished, based on the wear exhibited by the working edge: use-smoothed or polished, and use-retouched.

Sixteen flakes which bore definite use polish were found. Fourteen of these were of relatively fine-grained basalt, while the remaining two were of quartzite. Twelve flakes had been used long enough and hard enough to develop a use polish with striations oriented parallel to the long axis of the working edge. This fact demonstrates that the majority of these flakes functioned as cutting instruments. The working edges vary from concave to convex, but are normally slightly convex. Edge angles range from 25 degrees to 60 degrees, and average 40 degrees. Wear polish is usually confined to the cutting edge itself and does not extend more than 2 mm up the faces of the tool. Figure 118 illustrates two flakes with prominent wear polish and striations. This category of artifacts from Las Colinas is probably equivalent to Weaver's "flake knives" from Pueblo del Monte (1972:70-75).

Twenty-nine flakes had margins that were apprently retouched during their time of use. This retouch commonly consists of a series of short (less than 2 mm) flakes removed either unifacially or bifacially at random intervals along the working edge. Eighteen of these flakes were of basalt, five of chert, four of rhyolite, one of porphyritic basalt, and one of quartzite. Their use remains uncertain--some may have served as knives, and some as scrapers. They are essentially identical to the utilized flakes that show use polish in the configuration of their working edges and their edge angles. The presence of the use retouch may indicate that they were used to work harder or more resistant materials such as wood or bone. This has not been experimentally

188

Figure 117. Choppers (length of a
is 11.8 cm)

189

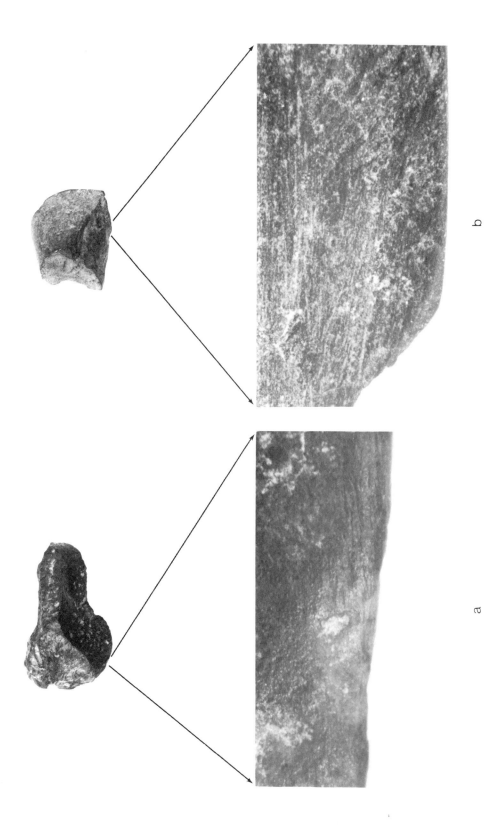

a

b

Figure 118. Utilized flakes with detail of wear (length of
flake a is 7.4 cm)

tested using coarser-grained materials akin to those found at Las Colinas, and so must remain a simple suggestion or untested hypothesis. It must also be kept in mind that such a wear pattern can be generated on the thin edge of any flake by other processes: accidental retouch of flakes can be produced by the tread of the occupants of the site, by blows from shovels or other tools during excavation, and by rough handling in the past.

Hammerstones

This rather varied category contains a large number of individual specimens, and is the most well-represented group of stone tools from the site. To describe the variation within this category of tools, four types of hammerstones were established: reused core, unmodified cobble, retoucher, and fragment. Each type is discussed separately below.

Reused Core

Hammerstones which exhibited several flake scars and battered edges or prominences were classified as reused cores. Some specimens had only three or four flake scars covering a small portion of the tool, while others exhibited numerous scars which completely covered the surface (Figure 119, a-c, f). These flake scars can be produced in three ways: intentional retouch to create a prominent edge, accidental fracturing during use, or reuse of cores as hammers. It is probable that this category contains specimens produced in each of these three ways, but it is often difficult to determine the relative importance of each process. Accidental fracturing during use was probably the least common of the three, judging from the hammerstone fragments recovered. The fragments commonly exhibited a plane type of fracture; only rarely did any of the fragments display the features of flakes. It is almost impossible to determine whether intentional retouching of cobbles or simple core reuse accounts for the majority of the specimens in this class of hammerstones. Both processes produce the same result: a spherical or oblong cobble with several sharp prominences or edges that could be used for pecking, chipping, or hammering. Weaver termed these same implements "flaked hammerstones," and felt that they were cobbles "...reduced in size by removing, intentionally or accidentally, by crude percussion techniques, large flakes from a portion of the boulder usually leaving a portion of the cortex intact" (Weaver 1972:63). He recovered 25 from Pueblo del Monte, and 178 were identified in the Las Colinas assemblage.

Since only a small proportion of the cores were of those materials commonly used for hammerstones, it was felt that many of the cores had been reused as hammerstones at Las Colinas. Of the total number recovered, 128 were of basalt, 22 of a porphyritic basalt, two of andesite, three of diorite, and 23 of quartzite. These reused core hammerstones averaged approximately 351 grams in weight and 7.8 cm in maximum dimension. The degree of wear varies greatly; some specimens show only incipient battering restricted to a small portion of the tool, while others have broad areas of wear covering nearly every ridge or prominence. In addition, there are differences in the nature of the wear. Some hammerstones have simple rounded areas of battering, whereas others display a flat or slightly convex bevel, implying that they were used to strike blows at an angle to the surface of the object being worked. It is quite possible that the hammerstones with rounded wear surfaces were used for pecking, and that those with beveled wear surfaces were used for chipping. This explanation should be tested experimentally. Three hammerstones included in

Figure 119. Cores reused as hammerstones (a-c, f);
retouchers (d-e); length of d is 6.7 cm

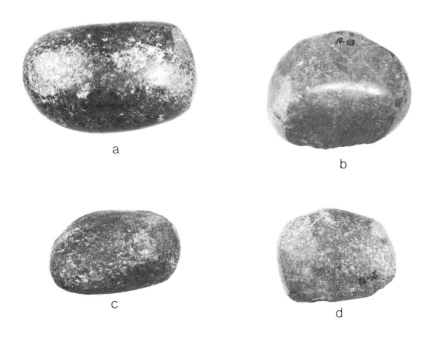

Figure 120. Unmodified cobble hammerstones (length
of a is 11.7 cm)

this type showed prominent red ocher stains, probably from use in preparing
this pigment.

Unmodified Cobble

The 34 specimens in this group were distinctive, for they bore no flake
scars but were noticeably battered on their ends or edges from service as
hammers (Figure 120). Most of these stream cobbles were apparently used just
as they were found, although some of the diorite examples show pecking and
grinding on naturally occurring facets (Figure 120). Whether this indicates
that the tool served more than one purpose or was a reject from the manufacture
of another type of tool is not clear. The Las Colinas specimens averaged 9.5
cm in maximum dimension, weighed an average of 581 grams, and were generally
elliptical in cross-section. Of these 34 specimens, six were of basalt, four
of porphyritic basalt, three of andesite, one of gabbro, one of epidote, eight
of diorite, and 11 of quartzite.

Hayden (1957:152) lists 20 hammerstones from University Indian Ruin
that seem to be comparable to these river cobble hammers. Weaver (1972:107)
recorded nine from Pueblo del Monte. Weaver noted that some of his hammerstones also displayed pecked and ground surfaces. Other than the pecking and
grinding on some specimens, there is nothing to indicate that these cobble
hammerstones served a different function than the reused core hammerstones.

Retouchers

This interesting group of hammerstones was easily separated from those
previously discussed on the basis of size and the nature of the material used.
All 12 of these specimens are small (less than 10 cm in maximum dimension) and
all are made on thin cobbles or flakes (Figure 119, d, e). Six are of basalt, one
is of porphyritic basalt, two are of diorite, and the remaining three are of
quartzite. All displayed wear on a thin edge or end of the piece of material,
and in some cases this wear took the form of a bevel. The term "retoucher" is
used here to describe them, for it is suggested that they functioned as chipping hammerstones, and more specifically as light percussion hammers for
retouching scrapers and knives, and for working small cores of obsidian and
chert. These have not been described previously, and appear to represent a
distinctive type of hammerstone.

Fragments

Sixty-eight hammerstone fragments were recovered during the excavations.
Most of these fragments exhibited simple breaks in the form of plane fractures
that probably occurred during use. Since no information was recorded other
than the material of which they were made, none of these fragments can be
accurately included in the previously described groups.

Cores

A total of 119 specimens were classified as cores. These artifacts
were typically globular in shape, and showed evidence of having had a number
of flakes removed from them. Most could be termed exhausted, meaning that
the removal of more flakes was either impossible or undesirable. In addition,

none of these cores showed any signs of having been subsequently used for other purposes, although it is quite likely that many exhausted cores did see further service. Table 17 classifies the 119 cores recovered on the basis of the type of rock from which they were made.

Table 17. Division of cores by material type

Material	Number of Cores
Basalt	49
Porphyritic basalt	20
Andesite	2
Rhyolite	2
Diorite	1
Quartzite	23
Chert	4
Obsidian	18
	119

The majority of these cores (62.2 percent) are of igneous materials, the most readily available local stone suitable for flaking. With the exception of obsidian, igneous rock is quite variable with regard to grain size, the presence of phenocrysts, and the occurrence of fault planes. Igneous rock is best suited for less sophisticated methods of flaking, such as decortication or simple percussion retouch. Quartzite, the next most common material, also varies noticeably in grain size but for the most part is similar to the coarser igneous rocks in quality.

The four chert cores and 18 obsidian cores were much smaller in size than the typical coarse igneous or quartzite cores, probably due in large part to the original size of the unworked material. While the Salt River yields fairly large cobbles of both the coarser igneous rocks and quartzites, chert and obsidian occur in much smaller cobbles or nodules, and should be considered nonlocal materials. The obsidian includes several distinct lithologic varieties, but at this time individual source areas cannot be determined. This is also true for much of the chert. It should be noted that the smaller flakes of chert and obsidian were desirable for projectile point manufacture, since they could be easily worked by pressure flaking. As mentioned above, the coarser-grained materials were generally suited only to percussion working, and for this reason larger flakes were detached for use as cutting and scraping tools.

The cores were usually worked in a very simple fashion. Natural cobble surfaces which were fairly flat commonly served as the initial striking platform. Often the cortical surface was the only platform used, and all flakes were removed in the same direction until the core was exhausted or unworkable. Occasionally when one striking platform became unusable the core was turned and another cortical surface was used as a platform. Large single flake scars, or points of intersection of two or more flake scars, were also used for the same purpose. A sample of the typical cores is illustrated in Figure 121.

The obsidian cores are very small (less than 30 mm maximum dimension) and with only one exception are totally exhausted (Figure 122). A number of them were so small that they were almost impossible to hold in the hand and work by freehand direct percussion. It is suggested that a more specialized technique was employed in the reduction of at least some of these obsidian nodules. Unworked nodules recovered from Las Colinas are normally under 3 cm in maximum dimension and are round or oval in shape. Their size and shape makes them very difficult to work by normal direct percussion techniques. There are indications that some of these nodules were flaked using a rest or anvil and a technique known as bipolar percussion (Crabtree 1972:40-42). This technique requires resting one end of the core or nodule on a stone anvil, supporting it with the fingers, and striking the other end of the piece with a hammerstone. The resulting flakes and shatter fragments tend to be thick and irregular in shape. A single blow will often produce several flakes and fragments. The cores, once exhausted, often show crushing, battering and incipient cones of percussion. The technique described here probably was not used on all the obsidian worked at Las Colinas, but may have been used to get the most out of any given piece of material, and to break into the rounded nodules at the start of the process of decortication.

Debitage

By far the majority of the flaked stone recovered from Las Colinas falls into this general category, which consists of all those specimens which show no obvious utilization, retouch, or other form of modification. Three categories were provided on the original lithic analysis form to further divide this mass of material: unmodified stone, accidentally modified stone, and manufacture discard. The first two categories proved highly unsatisfactory because of their vague, ambiguous nature. The category termed "unmodified" includes a universe of lithic materials which may or may not have any relation to the archaeology of the site. The category termed "accidentally modified" was not useful either, since it could refer to a simple gravel cobble retouched by a shovel, or to a flake struck by a pick. In either case, the value of such pieces of stone to the study of the Classic Hohokam lithic industry is rather dubious. Since these categories were used in the original analysis, they are included in this discussion. Taken together they account for less than five percent of the debitage from Las Colinas.

Manufacture discard is essentially synonymous with debitage, and is used to refer to the unused flakes, flake fragments, and chunks resulting from the flaking process. Because of the pressure of time, no flake-type classification or metric analysis was undertaken. Furthermore, since all the debitage had been discarded as the original analysis progressed, it was no longer available for examination. For these reasons, only the raw material composition of the debitage is presented in Table 18.

Figure 121. Cores (length of c is 4.5 cm)

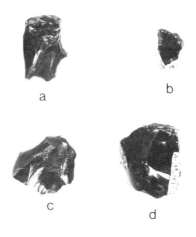

Figure 122. Obsidian cores (length of a
is 2.7 cm)

Table 18. Raw material breakdown of Las Colinas debitage

	Percentage	Count
Igneous Materials		
Dark fine-grained igneous (Basalt)	60.9	3,852
Rhyolite	.7	43
Andesite	.9	60
Diorite/Porphyritic basalt	15.3	970
Obsidian	6.1	384
Unidentified igneous	.9	56
Total Igneous Materials	85.0	5,364
Siliceous Materials		
Jasper	.1	5
Chert	1.4	91
Chalcedony	.4	27
Petrified wood	.1	6
Quartz	.1	8
Total Siliceous Materials	2.1	137
Quartzite	12.7	806
Sandstone	.2	13
Limestone	trace	1
TOTAL	99.8	6,322

Most of the flakes and flake fragments appeared to be the result of hard hammer decortication work. Typically they exhibited cortical or plain unprepared platforms, fairly prominent bulbs of percussion, and showed a wide range in shape. Often these flakes were roughly equal in length and width and tended to be fairly thick. No metric studies were carried out, so this account is necessarily qualitative in nature. Evidently there were very few bifacial thinning flakes recognized, and no tool retouch flakes were noted, although some were undoubtedly present.

No blades or microblades were identified, although some previous workers (Pailes 1963:167-168; Weaver 1972:90) have suggested the presence of these specialized flake types in Classic period sites. Pailes recovered four microblades of obsidian at the Fitch site, and Weaver reported two blades from Pueblo del Monte. Weaver stated (1972:90) that he separated these two blades from the other flakes because "...their presence implies the mastery of a complex manufacturing procedure involving careful selection of raw materials, preparation of a specific type of core, and the production of flakes of a predetermined size and configuration." It is suggested that since no blade cores were found on either site, and since only a small number of flakes that could be typed as blades were present, the proposal of any sort of blade industry is unsupportable. In all probability, the flakes described as blades or microblades are the fortuitous result of the same percussion decortication processes that produced the majority of the debitage.

Discussion

This section of the chapter is intended to serve as a general overview of the Classic period Hohokam flaked stone assemblage. It was felt that a consideration of the basic aspects of the assemblage would be of greater value than a summary or review of the preceding descriptions of tool types. Therefore, the following discussion will deal with material sources, manufacturing techniques, the utilization of flaked stone, and the question of Salado influences.

The Salt River channel probably provided the Hohokam stone workers with the majority of the material they used. Stream worn cobbles of basalt, quartzite, chert, and fine-grained metavolcanic rocks are quite common in various sizes all along the channel of the river where it passes through Phoenix. There can be little doubt that this was the major source area for the people at Las Colinas, since the material types found at the site can almost all be duplicated in the river gravels. However, there is no known local source for obsidian, petrified wood, or certain of the cherts, so these probably represent materials which were imported from outside the Salt-Gila basin. The obsidian may have come in small nodules from the Superior area or perhaps from as far away as Flagstaff. Its origin might be determined by trace element analysis. In all likelihood the petrified wood originated in the northeastern portion of Arizona. The nonlocal cherts, however, are almost impossible to trace at this time. In any case, over 90 percent of the flaked stone recovered at Las Colinas was made of locally obtainable materials, and the remainder was undoubtedly imported.

The Classic period chipped stone assemblage was produced by stone-workers employing a few relatively simple manufacturing techniques. Probable techniques that were used are summarized in Figure 123. This figure presents suggested manufacturing sequences for various tool types described earlier, and traces their fabrication from raw material to finished implement. There is, of course, some overlap, since certain implements could be produced by more than one technique.

As shown in this diagram, direct percussion (possibly freehand) is presumed to have been the most common technique. It was probably used for most of the decortication work, and also to modify flakes either unifacially or bifacially to create knives, scrapers, and other tools with retouched working edges. The majority of this work seems to have been done with a hard hammer. In addition, two other forms of percussion flaking may have been used in some situations to produce desired flake types or to more efficiently exploit certain raw materials. In the case of the large primary flake tools, a specialized form of direct percussion was employed: a large river cobble

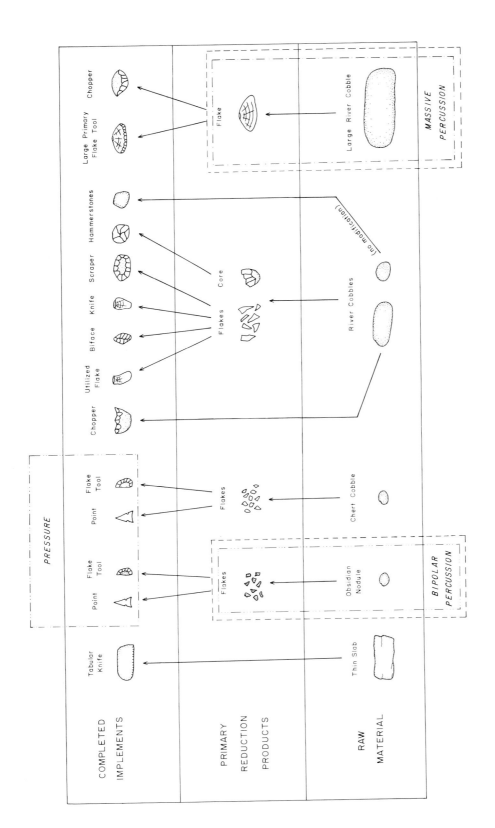

Figure 123. Schematic diagram of the Hohokam flaked stone industry, showing reduction sequences and manufacturing techniques (unless otherwise indicated, manufacture technique is direct percussion)

of suitable material was flaked with another slightly smaller river cobble. Replicative experiments conducted by the author indicate that a large river cobble of igneous or metamorphic rock, adequately supported by sand and other smaller cobbles, will yield the characteristic flakes when struck at a suitable angle with a large cobble hammer. The other specialized form of direct percussion is bipolar direct percussion, which seems to have been employed in an effort to efficiently utilize small nodules of obsidian. The use of an anvil or rest to support the core, and a small hammer to strike the platform area, allowed the stoneworker to efficiently reduce small pieces of material. In contrast to the technique used to produce large primary flakes, bipolar percussion was probably employed only when freehand direct percussion was ineffective or undesirable.

Pressure flaking is the only other major technique used by the Classic Hohokam stoneworkers. For the most part it was used in the manufacture of projectile points, but the serration of tabular knives and large primary flakes, as well as the fine even retouch on the cutting edges of knives, could also have been accomplished by pressure work.

What, then, can be said about the Classic Hohokam chipped stone assemblage in comparison to earlier Hohokam assemblages? Is there a discernible change in this assemblage that might reflect the influence of another industry? Carol Weed (1972) saw almost no evidence of Salado influence when she examined the flaked stone and ground stone artifacts from Las Colinas. The author believes that the Classic period assemblage is best viewed as the end point of a long tradition of stoneworking which began at least a thousand years earlier. While the origins of this tradition are not well understood at this time, it is apparent that it was adapted very early in the Hohokam occupation of the Salt-Gila basin to exploit the lithic resources of the area. During the Classic period these same resources were used by stoneworkers who practiced techniques established generations earlier, and who manufactured the same tool types in use since the Pioneer period. In fact, if most of the implements found at Las Colinas were mixed with tools from any of the earlier periods at Snaketown they would be indistinguishable in terms of both material and technique from their earlier counterparts. Only the projectile points made in the Classic period differ from those produced during the preceding periods. The typical Classic period point is a short, light side-notched form. Stylistically identical points are also found on Salado sites in the Tonto Basin and at most Classic period sites in southern Arizona. This may be taken as the only bit of tangible evidence of Salado influence on the Hohokam flaked stone assemblage if one assumes that this point style does have its origins in the Salado industry. However, it should also be noted that Hohokam projectile points changed through time and that there was a good deal of stylistic diversity at any given time. This was especially true during the Santa Cruz and Sacaton phases when this diversity reached its zenith. Numerous specimens found at Snaketown (Sayles in Gladwin and others 1937: Plates LXXXV, LXXXIX, and LX) support this observation. The Hohokam apparently enjoyed experimenting with different projectile point styles during this period of time.

Perhaps the most remarkable aspect of Classic period Hohokam flaked stone assemblages is the technological continuity that completely overshadows any variation that could be attributed to cultural change.

CHAPTER 6

THE NONFLAKED STONE ARTIFACTS FROM LAS COLINAS

by George A. Teague*
Western Archeological Center
National Park Service
Tucson, Arizona

Introduction

All of the nonflaked stone artifacts recovered at Las Colinas were analyzed. Among these artifacts were manos, metates, specialized grinding tools, ground stone axes, ornaments, and ground stone objects of uncertain function. End battered cobbles, edge trimmed tabular schist tools, and unmodified nonindigenous stone and mineral specimens were also among the subjects of this study.

During the formative stages of Southwestern archaeology, it was recognized that "[A]n ordered, consistent and generally understandable nomenclature is essential" (Kidder 1932:8). In order to achieve consistency I have chosen to employ already existing systems of classification. Definitions and terminology will closely follow Woodbury (1954) unless otherwise noted.

This chapter is divided into three parts. Part I is concerned with the terminology, classification, and analysis of the Las Colinas nonflaked stone artifacts. Also included in Part I are qualitative and quantitative data on the artifacts of each class.

Part II examines the spatial and temporal aspects of artifact classes within the Las Colinas site. The data in this section are presented in tabular form.

In Part III an hypothesis regarding the interpretation of mano variability is tested, and the Las Colinas assemblage is compared with similar material from other sites in the area of the Phoenix basin. Finally, the apparent absence of technological change at the site is discussed (compare Huckell, this volume).

*Draft completed: December 1973

Part I: Terminology, Classification, and Analysis
of the Las Colinas Nonflaked Stone Artifacts

Manos

Conventional Manos

A mano is a tabular piece of stone that is rubbed back and forth on another stone surface (metate) to grind food, such as corn, that has been placed between the two stones (Woodbury 1954:66).

Inspired by Haury's illustration of the essential mano types at Los Muertos (Haury 1945:28), I have devised a preliminary descriptive set of mano subclasses. These subclasses are as follows:

1. Relatively thick manos, used on one face (Figure 124:1)

2. Relatively thin manos, used on one face (Figure 124:2)

3. Relatively thin manos, often wedge-shaped in cross-section, and used on both faces (Figure 124:3)

4. Relatively thin manos, faceted in cross-section, and used on both faces

Each mano, with the exception of the multiuse and specialized forms, was assigned to one of the above subclasses.

Manos at Las Colinas were made from stones that approximated the required dimensions, and were used either without modification or with only rough trimming to shape. No pecked "finger grips" were noted, and no further modification was made beyond occasional surface pecking on fine-grained specimens. Because of the porous nature of vesicular basalt, manos made from this material were seldom pecked. The stones were used on one side continuously, then flipped over and used on the other side. That they were occasionally used as ad hoc battering or pecking tools is shown by the presence of the multiuse forms. As wear reduced the dimensions of the manos to unmanageable proportions, they were discarded. There are no examples of broken or worn out forms that had been reused, with the exception of one mano fragment that had subsequently served as a grooved abrader (Figure 125).

Data pertaining to various mano characteristics are provided in Table 19 through Table 25.

Multiuse Manos

Multiuse manos are identical to those described above, except that they show evidence of heavy wear from battering or pecking, in addition to the grinding that produced their working surfaces in the normal course of use. One specimen was heavily pecked in the center of its grinding surface. Tables 21 and 22 display data regarding this class.

Figure 124. Mano subclasses (length of 1 is 18.7 cm)

Figure 125. Mano fragment used as abrader (length is 7.5 cm)

Figure 126. Steatite abrading-straightening tool (length is 6.3 cm)

Table 19. Mano attribute frequencies (n = 174)

Attribute	Frequency
Condition	
Whole	30
Broken	144
	174
Material type	
Basalt	81
Vesicular basalt	52
Quartzite	33
Gneiss	4
Andesite	4
	174
Inferred metate form	
Trough	89
Flat	10
Indeterminate	75
	174
Size	
One-hand	18
Two-hand	104
Indeterminate	52
	174
Body shape in plan view	
Rectangle	3
Rounded rectangle	124
Oval	10
Indeterminate	37
	174
End shape	
Convex from working surface	85
Biconvex	26
Rounded rectangle	36
Indeterminate	27
	174
Longitudinal cross-section	
Biplano	169
Plano-convex	5
	174
Lateral cross-section	
Plano-convex	104
Biplano	51
Converging biplano	17
Multi-plano	2
	174

Table 20.   Mano measurements by subclass

Length of whole manos
(in centimeters,   n = 30)

Subclass	Range	Mean	Number
1	13.0-19.0	18.0	6
2	13.5-21.0	17.0	16
3	12.0-19.0	14.0	8
4	---	-	-

Width (n = 174)

Subclass	Range	Mean	Number
1	5.0-11.0	8.5	39
2	6.5-11.0	8.5	70
3	4.0-11.0	8.4	63
4	8.5- 9.0	8.7	2

Thickness (n = 174)

Subclass	Range	Mean	Number
1	3.0- 6.5	4.9	39
2	2.5- 5.5	3.8	70
3	2.5- 4.0	3.4	63
4	2.5- 3.5	3.0	2

Table 21.   Multiuse mano attribute frequencies (n = 9)

Condition

    Whole   3
    Fragmentary   6
                      9

Material

    Vesicular basalt 1
    Basalt   5
    Quartzite   3
                      9

Inferred metate form

    Trough   1
    Flat   5
    Indeterminate   3
                      9

Body shape in plan view

    Rounded rectangle 5
    Oval   4
                      9

Table 22.   Multiuse mano measurements (in centimeters)

Length

    Range   10.0-10.0
    Mean   10.0
    Number   3

Width

    Range   5.0-10.0
    Mean   7.9
    Number   9

Thickness

    Range   2.5-6.0
    Mean   4.3
    Number   9

Number of use faces

    Unifacial   4
    Bifacial   5

Specialized Manos

This class was created to embrace the ambiguous and overlapping tool types formerly designated as handstones, rubbing stones, polishing stones, etc. I believe that there are insufficient grounds for functional specification within this class. Specialized manos are formally differentiated from manos by their smaller size and by the material of which they are most often made--water worn cobbles. Specialized manos are generally made of a finergrained stone than conventional manos and in consequence are more apt to show striations, and evidence of light wear and polish.

Specialized manos from Las Colinas were segregated on the basis of use; no alteration of natural cobble form was observed with the exception of occasional light pecking on the surface (Figure 127). The wear indicates a great variety of possible uses that include food processing, tool polishing, pigment grinding, battering and pecking functions, and use as percussion flaking implements. This broad spectrum of function, combined with the fact that the vast majority of specialized manos are unbroken and exhibit light wear, leads me to believe the specialized manos are expedient tools that were used for an immediate purpose, then abandoned. A large fraction (25 percent) was discarded at their location of use.

Additional data are available in Tables 23 and 24.

Table 23.   Specialized mano attribute frequencies (n = 40)

Condition	
Whole	34
Broken	6
	40
Material	
Vesicular basalt	1
Quartzite	28
Diorite	11
	40
Number of use faces	
Uniface	17
Biface	20
Indeterminate	3
	40
Body shape in plan view	
Round	4
Oval	32
Rectangular	4
	40

Figure 127. Specialized manos (length
of a is 7.6 cm)

Figure 128. Palette fragments (length of b is
9.3 cm) (see also Figure 138)

Table 24. Specialized mano measurements (in centimeters)

Length (n = 34)

Range	5.0-11.0
Mean	7.6

Width (n = 40)

Range	2.0-10.0
Mean	5.8

Thickness (n = 40)

Range	1.5-5.0
Mean	3.8

Table 25. Frequency of use-wear types (grinding excluded)

Type	Frequency
Use-polish, any surface	14
Parallel striations	11
Unifacial pecking	9
Bifacial pecking	3
Edge grinding	9
End battering	11

Metates

Metates have been defined as implements that were modified by a mano in the process of grinding (Woodbury 1954:50; Weaver 1972:91). Metate subclasses include trough forms and flat forms. As with manos, the functional implication drawn from ethnographic analogy is that these implements were used primarily for the preparation of corn and other food.

The trough metates measured at Las Colinas were almost invariably pecked to shape from large slabs or small boulders of abrasive stone. In some cases, the interior grinding surface was first pecked to a shallow depth, but was subsequently ground down further through use. In other examples, it appears that the interior was initially dressed to produce the high sides found on some specimens. Trough metates stayed where they were used until the bottoms were worn through.

Flat metates were formed by grinding the surface of a relatively thin, flat piece of stone. In only one example was the stone edge-trimmed or dressed in any fashion. Use and discard patterns corresponded to those of the trough metates.

Information about the properties of the metates is available in Tables 26 through 31.

Table 26.   Attribute frequencies of whole and fragmentary trough metates (n = 8)

End character	
Open both ends	6
Open one end	2
	8
Condition	
Whole	4
Broken	4
	8
Material	
Basalt	2
Vesicular basalt	2
Gneiss	3
Granite	1
	8
Inferred wear stage	
Initial	2
Intermediate	4
Terminal	2
	8
Exterior treatment	
Pecked to shape	7
Unshaped	1
	8

Table 27.   Trough metate measurements (in centimeters)

Maximum length
    Range   35.0-55.0
    Mean   42.0

Maximum width
    Range   21.0-29.0
    Mean   52.3

Maximum thickness
    Range   11.0-18.0
    Mean   11.8

Grinding surface, maximum length
    Mean   36.1

Grinding surface, maximum width
    Mean   21.8

Grinding surface, maximum thickness
    Mean   8.5

Grinding surface area (in square
    centimeters)
    Range   400.0-1300.0
    Mean   726.0

Wall depth
    Range   1.5-7.0
    Mean   4.8

Table 28.   Metate fragment attribute frequencies (n = 94)

Material	
Basalt	54
Vesicular basalt	40
	94
Inferred metate form	
Flat	4
Trough	69
Indeterminate	21
	94
Exterior treatment	
Pecked/ground	67
Unmodified	6
Indeterminate	21
	94

Table 29.   Metate grinding surface measurements (n = 74)(in centimeters)

Mean thickness of grinding surfaces	3.6
Total area of grinding surface (in square centimeters)	4550.0

Table 30.   Flat metate attribute frequencies (whole and fragmentary) (n = 4)

Condition	
Whole	4
Broken	0
	4
Material	
Granite/Gneiss	4
Inferred wear stage	
Initial	2
Intermediate	2
Terminal	0
	4
Exterior treatment	
Edge-trimmed	1
Unshaped	3
	4

Table 31.   Flat metate measurements (whole and fragmentary)
            (in centimeters)

Maximum length

    Range   31.0-50.0
    Mean   35.3

Maximum width

    Range   20.0-27.0
    Mean   24.5

Maximum thickness

    Range   3.0-11.0
    Mean   7.0

Grinding surface, maximum length

    Mean   27.8

Grinding surface, maximum width

    Mean   18.8

Grinding surface, maximum thickness

    Mean   6.0

Grinding surface area (in square
    centimeters)

    Range   400.0-1000.0
    Mean   532.0

Palettes

Palettes are shaped, flat, rectangular pieces of stone with one worn surface and a raised border (Haury 1937:121-126).

Two slate palette fragments were recovered from Las Colinas. Both specimens had been finely ground, dressed and incised. The fragment depicted in Figure 128, a) has an incised border design of diamonds separated by triangular zones of hatching. The other fragment (Figure 128, b) was incised with zoned hatching and spirals (see also Figure 138).

Since no material was found adhering to the grinding surfaces, it is not possible to infer what substances were being ground or prepared on these palettes.

Also, only broken specimens were found, all in mixed trash proveniences. No use-discard cycle was reconstructible for these artifacts.

Palette fragment measurements are printed in Table 32.

Table 32. Palette fragment measurements (in centimeters)

Specimen	Length	Width	Thickness	Grinding Area (in square centimeters)
a	7.0	12.0	2.0	135
b	8.5	5.0	.5	Unavailable

Another artifact is included with palettes because of the square, shallow depression pecked into one surface. The depression measures 12.0 cm by 11.0 cm in plan, providing 132 square centimeters of grinding surface. The implement has been fashioned on a thin quartzite cobble which has maximum dimensions of 23.0 cm by 20.0 cm by 5.0 cm. The cobble was used as a chopper at some time, as indicated by bifacial percussion trimming and subsequent bruising along one edge.

Grinding Slabs

A grinding slab, as distinguished from a flat metate, is a stone slab, "generally irregular in shape, with one or both faces worn smooth and slightly concave as a result of grinding or rubbing" (Woodbury 1954:113).

Four grinding slabs were analyzed. Two of these are basalt slabs, one is of schist (Figure 129) and the other is a large, thin, granite cobble. All grinding slabs were unshaped and were formed of stone slabs or cobbles possessing at least one flat surface. The area of the grinding surfaces ranges from 25.0 to 150.0 square centimeters. Additional measurements are provided in Table 33.

It is interesting to note that the objects (in Figure 129) had been used to grind red pigment.

Bowl-shaped Mortars

A definition of bowl-shaped mortars offered by Woodbury (1954:116) requires a rounded exterior surface and relatively thin walls. These items may have been used as containers as well as mortars (Sayles 1937:101-120).

The one mortar recovered at Las Colinas was manufactured by extensive exterior and interior pecking and grinding that produced a symmetrical cylinder with one closed end. The implement is 14.0 cm in diameter, with a maximum thickness of 6.5 cm. Wall depth is 3.0 cm and estimated grinding surface is 16.0 square centimeters. The object was recovered from a mixed trash context; its use remains uncertain.

Figure 129.   Grinding implements with red pigment
(length of grinding slab is 20 cm)

a

b

c

Figure 130.   Ground stone axes: double-bit (a),
single-bit (b), blank (c); length
of a is 11.5 cm

Table 33. Grinding slab measurements (in centimeters, n = 4)

Length	
Range	8.0-19.0
Mean	13.0
Width	
Range	6.0-12.0
Mean	8.7
Thickness	
Range	2.5-8.0
Mean	4.4

Abrading-Straightening Tools

These objects are small, shaped blocks of stone with one or more grooves worn into them. Based on ethnographic analogy, these tools were probably used for abrading, smoothing, and straightening wooden shafts (Woodbury 1954:101-111).

Only two specimens representing this category were recovered. Their measurements are given in Table 34. One specimen was manufactured on a basalt mano fragment (Figure 125), and exhibits a groove measuring 2.0 cm by 1.0 cm by .5 cm.

Another specimen (Figure 126) made of dense black steatite had two grooves worn into it (groove dimensions are 4.5 cm by 1.0 cm by .5 cm; and 3.0 cm by 1.0 cm by .5 cm). Parallel hatching connects the two grooves. Striations within the grooves parallel their long axes. Polishing and multiple striations cover this specimen.

Both artifacts had been discarded in mixed trash proveniences.

Table 34. Abrading-straightening tool measurements (in centimeters)

Specimen	Length	Width	Thickness
Basalt	6.5	5.0	5.0
Shale	6.5	4.5	1.5

Ground Stone Axes

Single-Bit

Woodbury (1954:25) defined an axe as "a tool which was designed and used for chopping, and which was hafted by means of a wooden handle fitted against or into grooves or notches." Conventions of terminology follow Woodbury's adaptation of Kidder's (1932:45) classification.

The ground stone axes from Las Colinas were manufactured from hard stone cobbles with original dimensions slightly larger than required for the finished product. The cobble's surface was pecked to shape. While some specimens were left unground, or were ground only along the tip of the bit, about half of the objects were heavily ground and highly polished over the entire surface. All ground stone axes recovered from Las Colinas, both single and double bit varieties, were characterized by a hafting groove extending 3/4 of the way around the circumference of the poll (Figure 130, b).

Qualitative and quantitative data on the single-bit axes are presented in Tables 35 and 36.

Table 35.   Ground stone axe (single-bit) attribute frequencies (n = 13)

Attribute	Frequency
Condition	
Whole	4
Broken, reused	6
Broken, not reused	3
	13
Material	
Diorite	13
Surface treatment	
Pecked overall, unground	3
Pecked overall, superficially ground	3
Pecked overall, highly ground and polished	7
	13
Use wear, whole specimens	
Tip blunted	1
Bifacial microspalling	3
Striations perpendicular to width of bit	2
Tip resharpening, broken specimens	
Unifacial flake removal	4
Bifacial flake removal	2

Table 36.   Ground stone axe (single-bit) measurements
            (in centimeters)

Maximum length (whole specimens only)

    Range   15.0-16.0
    Mean   15.4

Maximum width

    Range   4.0-7.5
    Mean   5.6

Maximum thickness

    Range   3.0-5.5
    Mean   4.0

Mean poll length   3.1

Mean bit length (whole specimens only,
    n = 4)   8.9

Mean bit width   5.4

Examination of use-wear indicates that the tools were used for chopping. I suggest that the heavy spalls taken from the bit end of about one-half the specimens are the result of resharpening rather than breakage through use. The sample size is too small for reconstructing the use-discard cycle, but the tools are generally found in mixed trash regardless of their condition.

Double-Bit

One double-bit axe was found (Figure 130, a). The axe was pecked, ground, and polished to shape and is made of quartzite. Both bits exhibit bifacial microspalling, and one of them has been resharpened by the unifacial removal of three large flakes. Both bits are 5.0 cm long and 6.0 cm wide. Maximum dimensions of the axe are 12.0 cm by 6.5 cm by 3.0 cm. The groove is 2.0 cm wide.

Axe Blanks

Eight pieces of stone, five of which were broken, were found that are consistent in size and material with the ground stone axes. All of these objects were pecked and ground to some extent, and are thought to reflect the initial stages of axe manufacture (Figure 130, c). The amount of surface area ground or pecked ranges from 20 percent to 90 percent and averages 45 percent per specimen. Two of the specimens were employed as tools in their own right, as evidenced by battering and crushing on the ends.

Ornaments

Perforated Ornaments

With the exception of perforated schist objects, items in this class will be called beads if the perforations are centrally located, or pendants if the perforations are near the edge of the object (Woodbury 1954:143). Perforated schist discs will be included with ornaments for convenience, even though there has been debate about their function (compare Fewkes 1912:129-130; Haury 1945:142).

Classification of perforated schist objects was based both on form and stage of manufacture. The forms, and key abbreviations, are as follows:

A - Circular, center perforation

B - Rectangular and trapezoidal, and perforated

C - Subrectangular, center drilled

D - Irregularly shaped object

The manufacture stages are inferred from the occurrence of superposed technological elements. These stages are as follows:

1 - Rough chipping to shape

2 - Grinding initiated

3 - Grinding completed around perimeter and on faces

4 - Drilling started

5 - Object completed

6 - Object broken after manufacture

As an example of the above code, an object designated A4 is a circular center-perforated schist disc which is finished except for the completion of drilling. Examples of form classes are illustrated in Figure 131,a-c). Examples of manufacture stages are illustrated in Figure 131, 1-6. Data pertaining to each stage are presented in Table 37.

The perforated schist objects found at Las Colinas were manufactured by chipping pieces of tabular schist to rough shape and then grinding the edge and surfaces to the desired form. Perforation was accomplished by biconical drilling. The finished objects were found in proveniences similar to those of broken objects and objects in various stages of manufacture.

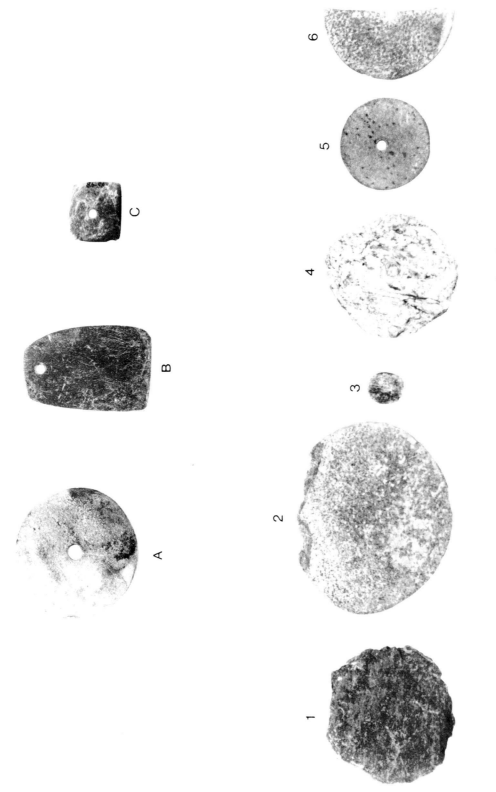

Figure 131. Perforated ornaments: classes of forms (a-c), stages of manufacture
(1-6); length of c is 2.1 cm

Table 37.   Perforated schist object measurements (in centimeters)

A Series (n = 55)

Stage	Frequency	Diameter (Mean)	Thickness (Mean)
A1	8	5.5	0.3
A2	8	4.3	0.2
A3	7	3.0	0.2
A4	2	4.3	0.2
A5	7	3.6	0.1
A6	23	4.1	0.1

B Series (n = 13)

Stage	Frequency	Diameter (Mean)	Width (Mean)	Thickness (Mean)
B1	3	6.0	4.3	0.4
B2	3	3.7	2.8	0.2
B3	3	2.5	2.5	0.1
B4	-	-	-	-
B5	2	2.8	2.2	0.1
B6	2	3.3	2.0	0.1

C Series (n = 6)

Stage	Frequency	Length (Mean)	Width (Mean)	Thickness (Mean)
C4	1	2.5	1.5	0.2
C5	5	2.0	1.7	0.1

D Series (n = 3)

Stage	Frequency	Length (Mean)	Width (Mean)	Thickness (Mean)
D6	3	2.3	1.5	0.2

Objects in production, as well as those already discarded, were found in a large number of proveniences. This fact leads me to suggest that extensive lateral recycling occurred among perforated schist objects. The occurrence of subrectangular center-drilled objects and irregular perforated objects that may be reworked schist discs gives support to my contention. Further clarification of the use for perforated schist discs is provided by the observation that the distribution of both center perforated discs and end perforated rectangular forms is nearly identical. I argue that if the discs were used as spindle whorls, as has been suggested by others, then functional context would differ from that of objects classed as ornaments. Since the distribution of discs and pendants of schist is remarkably similar, I conclude that these objects had similar uses.

Seven polished turquoise beads were found that had been drilled through the axis of width, rather than the axis of thickness (Figure 132, s-y). Mean dimensions are 1.0 cm by 0.7 cm by 0.2 cm.

Two elongated pendants with round cross sections, made from unidentified stone, were recovered (Figure 132, a-b). One is complete and one is fragmentary. The whole specimen is 3.0 cm in length.

Ten flat pendants of turquoise were found, four of which were broken (Figure 132, c-l) All were trapezoidal or oval in plan view and had been ground or polished to shape. Mean maximum dimensions are 1.9 cm by 1.2 cm by 0.3 cm.

Nine center-perforated beads were analyzed, seven of argillite, and two of turquoise (Figure 132, m-r). The diameter of the holes ranged from 0.1 cm to 0.2 cm.

Of the non-schist pendants, little can be said of the manufacturing process (since only finished forms were recovered) except that all had been ground to shape and polished. Nor can much be said about the turquoise and argillite beads, except that one double-thickness bead was incised around the perimeter of its outer face, indicating that a length of material may have been first ground into cylindrical form and then divided into beads. Beads and pendants were found in unusually high proportions in room floor and burial proveniences.

Unperforated Ornaments

Included in this category are polished stone rings, curved cylindrical objects, and irregularly shaped objects that may have served as decorations. These items will be individually described.

One unfinished cylindrical curved object recovered at Las Colinas had manufacture marks indicating that a small block of stone had been bifacially drilled to a common center, and then broken in half, with one-half of the drilled section serving as the interior of the elbow (Figure 133, a). The object was then ground and polished to a symmetrical shape. Use of these objects is unknown, but Di Peso (1951:183) has provisionally assigned similar objects to a category that includes ornaments.

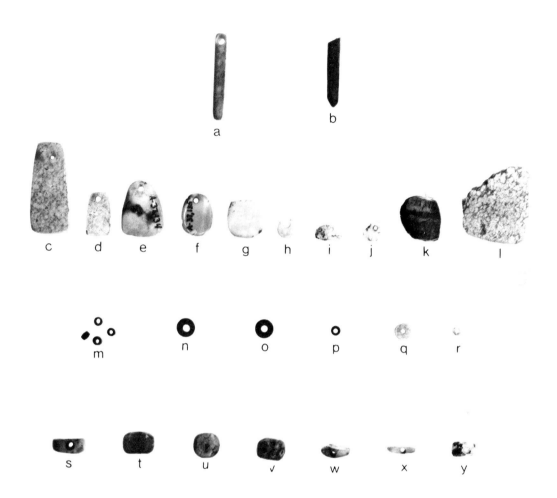

Figure 132. Perforated ornaments: pendants and beads
(length of a is 3.1 cm)

Three argillite specimens were recovered, each of which is in the form of an elbow. The objects are round in cross-section and all of their ends have been drilled to form conical depressions. Average largest dimension is 1.7 cm and mean diameter is 0.9 cm.

Two polished fragments of argillite were examined. Each has a lenticular cross-section measuring 0.2 cm in thickness, and each is 1.5 cm in longest dimension. The form of each is an arc that, if extended, would form a circle approximately 2.0 cm in diameter (Figure 133, b-c).

One T-shaped item was found with maximum dimensions of 2.5 cm by 1.5 cm by 0.5 cm. The item has been ground on all surfaces and is made of shale (Figure 133, d).

Ground Stone Objects of Uncertain Function

Included in this category are ground stone rings, stone balls, and miscellaneous objects also made of stone.

At Las Colinas the ground stone balls and miscellaneous objects (oblong forms) were pecked and ground to shape with no further modification. Ground stone rings were apparently made by grinding and pecking a hole through the center of an irregular slab of stone, and then grinding the object into a toroid.

Eighteen ground stone balls were found at Las Colinas, only one of which was broken. Eleven of the balls were of basalt, and the remaining objects were made of quartzite, granite, or a conglomerate. Two of the balls are relatively massive, having diameters of 17.0 cm and 19.0 cm. The remaining sixteen balls have diameters ranging from 2.0 cm to 6.0 cm, with a mean diameter of 3.9 cm. No use-wear was noted.

Six oblong forms of ground basalt were recovered that were identical to the ground stone balls, except for being oblate instead of spherical. Mean maximum dimensions are 6.2 cm by 4.2 cm by 4.0 cm.

Four stone rings made of vesicular basalt were examined, all of which were broken. Each had been biconically ground, but only in one example had the grinding perforated the stone to form a complete ring. All specimens were pecked and ground to shape. Two specimens had been grooved around the outer perimeter face. Diameters ranged from 4.5 cm to 6.0 cm, with a mean diameter of 5.6 cm. The mean thickness was 3.6 cm.

Four miscellaneous objects were analyzed. The first of these is a subrectangular piece of vesicular basalt measuring 8.0 cm by 4.0 cm by 3.0 cm. This object was biconically ground and was apparently broken during manufacture.

The second artifact is a plummet-shaped piece of ground basalt measuring 4.5 cm in length and 2.0 cm in diameter at the center of the long axis. Around the circumference are two shallow grooves (Figure 134, c).

Also recovered was a fragment of a ground stone cylinder which is rounded on the unbroken end and has a shallow groove around its circumference. It is 3.5 cm long and 1.5 cm in diameter (Figure 134, b).

The final artifact in this class is a naturally cylindrical pebble of diorite, rounded and battered on both ends and pecked along the long axis of one side. At 2.0 cm from one end a line has been incised around the object (Figure 134, a). Dimensions are 11.0 cm in length and 1.7 cm in diameter.

At Las Colinas no stone balls, oblongs, or rings were found in primary contexts such as room floors or burials. Therefore, the function of these objects remains unknown.

End-Battered Cobbles

Artifacts in this class are cobbles of stone unmodified except for battering on their ends.

Ten unworked cobbles of diorite and quartzite showed evidence of heavy battering on one or both ends. Two size ranges were noted: small cobbles have mean dimensions of 9.3 cm by 3.8 cm by 3.3 cm, while massive cobbles have mean dimensions of 28.0 cm by 10.3 cm by 8.1 cm.

Tabular Schist Tools

This class includes large, thin schist tools with one or more cutting edges formed by flaking or grinding. Objects in this class are identical with those elsewhere termed hoes, or mescal knives (Hayden 1957:142-146; Steen 1962:25).

The tabular schist tools from Las Colinas were fashioned by flaking and grinding one or more sharp edges, each about 10 cm long, on a piece of tabular schist (Figure 135). In only two specimens, possibly hoes (Figure 136), did shaping appear to go beyond the requirements of mechanical function. The primary use of these tools is thought to have been cutting, due to the four instances of striations parallel to the long axis of the use-edge, and to the character of microspalling and dulling along the edges. There is little evidence of resharpening. I suggest that these tools were used for cutting soft vegetal material. When they became dull, they were discarded rather than resharpened. This suggestion is supported by the fact that these tools are made from soft stone with casually produced working edges, and by the fact that the overwhelming majority of these tools are not broken or resharpened.

Thirty-two tools of tabular schist were analyzed, five of which were broken. All exhibited one or more use-edges that had been percussion flaked or ground to shape. The edge shaping is bifacial in twenty of the specimens. Mean maximum dimensions are 12.9 cm by 6.6 cm by 0.9 cm.

There are forty-eight discrete sections of edge which show use-wear. The average used edge section is 10.0 cm in length. Evidence of use is the presence of microspalling, crushing, or a combination of the two.

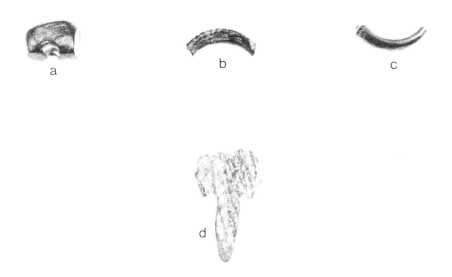

Figure 133.   Unperforated ornaments (length
of b is 1.5 cm)

Figure 134.   Ground stone objects of uncertain
function (length of c is 4.3 cm)

Figure 135. Mescal knife (length is 15.2 cm)

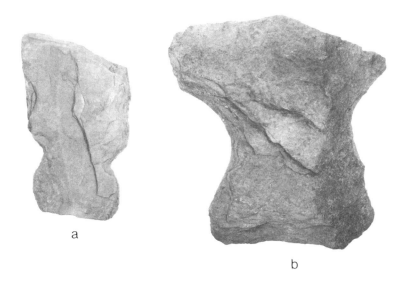

a

b

Figure 136. Tabular schist tools, possibly hoes
(length of a is 7.7 cm)

There were four edge sections which exhibited striations, and in all cases the striae were parallel to the length of the edge. Use-wear was evident on both faces in all but three cases.

Pigment Source Stones

These artifacts presumably were ground to produce pigment.

Two pieces of stone were found that had been faceted by grinding. One is a fragment of white volcanic tuff measuring 9.5 cm by 9.5 cm by 5.5 cm in maximum dimensions and possessing seven grinding facets. The other is a natural crystal of galena 2.5 cm in diameter and 2.0 cm in thickness that has been ground and striated on one surface (Figure 137, a).

In addition, traces of a ground oxidized red stone were found adhering to the surfaces of one trough metate, six trough metate fragments, one grinding slab and three specialized manos. Two hematite fragments were also recovered (Figure 137, b-c).

Stone and Mineral Specimens

Included in this category are unmodified stone and mineral specimens that presumably were gathered for later use as raw material for tools.

Three small, irregular pieces of turquoise were found. The largest dimension of any piece was 0.3 cm. In addition, five quartz crystals were recovered. One large specimen had dimensions of 9.0 cm by 2.5 cm by 2.5 cm, while mean dimensions of the four smaller specimens were 2.9 cm by 1.2 cm by 1.0 cm.

Ten water worn sandstone concretions were also found. All were unbroken and unmodified. Interbedded with the sandstone were bands of quartzite or basalt. Mean dimensions are 9.4 cm by 6.5 cm by 4.5 cm.

A total of 126 pieces of unworked and unused tabular schist were found. These objects conformed in size and material type to the class of perforated schist ornaments and are presumed to be raw material for ornaments. Mean maximum dimensions for these items are 7.4 cm by 6.4 cm by 1.0 cm.

Part II: Intrasite Distribution of Artifact Classes

Distributional information pertaining to the various artifact classes is presented in terms of temporal and spatial provenience. Relative temporal distribution is inferred by means of association with dated pottery types. Temporal phases are referred to by the following abbreviations:

229

Figure 137. Pigment source stones (diameter of a is 2.55 cm)

Sa = Sacaton

S   = Soho

C   = Civano

E   = Early

L   = Late

(M) = Mixed

In addition, a broader distinction between an Early and a Late time period is sometimes made in the discussion. The Early period refers to portions of late Sacaton and early Soho phases, while elements of late Soho and early and late Civano phases refer to the Late period.

Spatial proveniences will be indicated by the following abbreviations:

TI   = Trash-filled retaining cells

TII = Mixed trash locations

TIII = Mound fill

B   = Burial

F   = Feature

HI   = Habitation floors and floor fill

HII = Post-occupation habitation fill

When sufficient sample sizes exist, two frequency tables are provided for each artifact category. The spatial distribution of artifacts within each category is indicated by cross-referencing them against the provenience system described above. This method is also used to show the temporal distribution of artifacts, using the phase system described above. When the sample size is insufficient for this method of data presentation, a short description of the appropriate information will be substituted.

Manos

Conventional Manos

Table 38.   Spatial distribution of manos

Provenience	Mano Subclass				
	1	2	3	4	Total
TI	1	4	8	0	13
TII	23	38	37	1	99
TIII	1	8	7	3	19
F	4	1	6	0	11
HI	9	12	3	0	24
HII	0	2	6	0	8
TOTAL	38	65	67	4	174

Table 39.   Temporal distribution of manos (n = 168*)

Time Period	Mano Subclass				
	1	2	3	4	Total
LSa	0	1	2	0	3
ES	4	8	5	1	18
LS	1	6	2	0	9
EC	4	7	4	0	15
LC	1	1	6	0	8
C(M)	12	24	19	1	56
E/L(M)	14	21	23	1	59
TOTAL	36	68	61	3	168

*6 manos could not be assigned to a time period

Multiuse Manos

Table 40.   Spatial distribution of multiuse manos (n = 9)

Provenience	Frequency
TII	7
HI	1
HII	1

Table 41.   Temporal distribution of multiuse manos (n = 9)

Time Period	Frequency
Early	1
Late	8

Specialized Manos

Table 42.   Spatial distribution of specialized manos (n = 40)

Provenience	Frequency
TI	5
TII	19
TIII	3
F	2
HI	11

Table 43.   Temporal distribution of specialized manos (n = 40)

Time Period	Frequency
Early	3
Early/Late	4
Late	33

Metates

Table 44.   Spatial distribution of metates (n = 12)

| Provenience | Metate Subclass | | Total |
	Trough	Flat	
TI	1	0	1
TII	2	1	3
HI	4	2	6
HII	1	1	2
TOTAL	8	4	12

Table 45.   Temporal distribution of metates (n = 12)

| Time Period | Metate Subclass | | Total |
	Trough	Flat	
ES	2	1	3
LS	2	0	2
EC	2	2	4
C(M)	2	1	3
TOTAL	8	4	12

Table 46.   Temporal distribution of metate grinding area

Time Period	Square Centimeters
Early	1825
Late	6215

Table 47. Spatial distribution of metate fragments (n = 94)

Provenience	Frequency
TI	8
TII	62
TIII	7
F	1
HI	6
HII	10

Table 48. Temporal distribution of metate fragments (n = 94)

Time Period	Frequency
Early	9
Early/Late	27
Late	58

Table 49. Temporal distribution of metate fragment grinding area

Time Period	Grinding Area
Early	280 sq cm
Early/Late	1065 sq cm
Late	3205 sq cm

Palettes

All palettes were recovered from mixed trash locations (TII). Both slate fragments can be assigned to the early Civano phase, while the quartzite cobble specimen was recovered from a Soho phase context.

Grinding Slabs

Table 50. Spatial distribution of grinding slabs (n = 4)

Provenience	Frequency
TII	1
HI	2
HII	1

All grinding slabs were found in Soho or Civano phase associations.

Mortars

The single mortar recovered during the excavations is from a TII provenience, and was associated with pottery of the early Civano phase.

Abrading-Straightening Tools

Both specimens are from TII provenience types and were associated with pottery of both early and late Soho phases.

Ground Stone Axes

Single-Bit

Table 51. Spatial distribution of single-bit ground stone axes (n = 13)

Provenience	Frequency
TII	11
HI	2

Figure 138. Palette fragment (enlargement of Figure 128, b) (length is 9.3 cm)

Table 52.   Temporal distribution of single-bit ground stone axes (n = 13)

Time Period	Frequency
E/L	1
EC	2
LC	1
C	9

Double-Bit

The only double-bit ground stone axe was found in a cache pit of an unknown temporal affiliation.

Axe Blanks

All axe blanks (n = 8) were found in trash proveniences of the later temporal phases.

Ornaments

Perforated Ornaments

Table 53.   Spatial distribution of Series A perforated schist objects

Provenience	Manufacture Stage						Total
	A1	A2	A3	A4	A5	A6	
TI	2	2	3	-	-	10	17
TII	3	3	2	-	6	5	19
TIII	3	3	-	2	-	4	12
HI	-	-	1	-	-	-	1
HII	-	-	1	-	1	2	4
TOTAL	8	8	7	2	7	21	53

Table 54. Temporal distribution of Series A perforated schist objects

| Time Period | Manufacture Stage | | | | | | Total |
	A1	A2	A3	A4	A5	A6	
Early	-	2	1	-	1	11	15
Early/Late	2	-	3	-	-	3	8
Late	6	5	3	2	6	8	30
TOTAL	8	7	7	2	7	22	53

Table 55. Spatial distribution of Series B perforated schist objects

| Provenience | Manufacture Stage | | | | | Total |
	B1	B2	B3	B5	B6	
TI	1	-	-	-	-	1
TII	1	2	1	1	-	5
TIII	1	1	1	-	-	3
HI	-	-	1	-	-	1
HII	-	-	-	1	2	3
TOTAL	3	3	3	2	2	13

Table 56. Spatial distribution of Series C perforated schist objects (n = 6)

| Provenience | Manufacture Stage | |
	C4	C5
TI	-	5
TIII	1	-

Table 57.   Spatial distribution of Series D perforated schist objects (n = 3)

	Manufacture Stage
Provenience	D6
TI	1
TII	1
TIII	1

Table 58.   Temporal distribution of Series B, C, and D perforated schist objects (n = 22)

Time Period	All Manufacture Stages
Early	8
Early/Late	2
Late	12

Table 59.   Spatial distribution of non-schist pendants and beads (n = 28)

Provenience	Frequency
TI	3
TII	5
HI	14
HII	1
B	5

Table 60.   Temporal distribution of non-schist pendants and beads (n = 23)

Time Period	Frequency
Early	14
Late	9

Unperforated Ornaments

Table 61.   Spatial distribution of unperforated ornaments (n = 6)

Provenience	Frequency
TI	3
TII	3

Table 62.   Temporal distribution of unperforated ornaments (n = 6)

Time Period	Frequency
Early	4
Early/Late	2

Ground Stone Objects of Uncertain Function

Table 63.   Spatial distribution of ground stone objects of uncertain function (n = 29)

Provenience	Frequency
TI	6
TII	14
TIII	5
HI	2
HII	2

Table 64.   Temporal distribution of ground stone objects of uncertain function (n = 29)

Time Period	Frequency
Early	5
Early/Late	2
Late	22

Miscellaneous Objects of Ground Stone

All four specimens were recovered from Late period trash proveniences.

End-Battered Cobbles

All specimens (n = 10) were found in trash proveniences. Temporal associations include both Early (two specimens) and Late (eight specimens) periods.

Tabular Schist Tools

Table 65.   Spatial distribution of tabular schist tools (n = 32)

Provenience	Frequency
TI	5
TII	18
TIII	2
HI	2
HII	5

Table 66.   Temporal distribution of tabular schist tools (n = 32)

Time Period	Frequency
Early	8
Early/Late	8
Late	16

Pigment Source Stones

The volcanic tuff specimen was from an HI provenience in association with Early period pottery, while the galena crystal is from trash with late Soho phase associations.

Red Oxidized Pigment Stone

Table 67.   Spatial distribution of red oxidized pigment stone (n = 11)

Provenience	Frequency
TI	3
TII	2
TIII	1
HI	4
HII	1

All red oxidized stone associations were with pottery of the later phases at the site.

Stone and Mineral Specimens

Of the eight specimens of turquoise and quartzite recovered from the excavations, one (a large quartz crystal) was associated with a burial, while the rest were found in trash. One specimen was recovered from the Early period, three were from the Late period, and the remainder are of uncertain temporal association.

Concretions

All of the water worn sandstone concretions (n = 10) were found in TII provenience types and all are from the Civano phase.

Unworked Tabular Schist

Table 68.   Spatial distribution of unworked tabular schist (n = 126)

Provenience	Frequency
TI	20
TII	82
TIII	6
F	1
HI	5
HII	12

Table 69.   Temporal distribution of unworked tabular schist (n = 126)

Time Period	Frequency
Early	16
Early/Late	37
Late	73

Part III: The Significance of Hohokam Mano Classification: A Reevaluation

The Problem

It has long been assumed in Hohokam studies that mano morphology can serve as a useful indicator of change through time within a culture, or of change in cultural integrity due to intrusions, invasions, influences, and the like. However, it has been known for as long a time that mano forms may reflect change within a cycle of use (Bartlett 1933). The problem then, is to determine if the classes of manos from Las Colinas serve as a useful basis for making statements about culture-historical relationships, or about the functional life cycle of grinding tools, or about both.

Preliminary Data Reduction

The provisional classification of manos into four subclasses proceeded along traditional lines of morphological observation and measurement (see Part I). To make the problem operational, a reclassification of the mano subclasses is necessary to avoid sample size problems. Two mano "types" are proposed. Type 1 manos combine attributes of mano subclasses 1 and 2 and include the larger, two-hand manos with one use-face. Type 2 manos are a combination of subclasses 3 and 4 and include the smaller, two-hand manos with two use-faces that are sometimes wedge-shaped or faceted in cross-section.

In addition, it was felt that the greatest use could be made of temporal distribution data if relative time periods such as Early, Early/Late and Late, rather than phases were used.

Two Hypotheses

Hypothesis One

There are manos associated with both Early (late Sacaton and early Soho phases) and Late (late Soho, early Civano, and late Civano phases) periods at Las Colinas. Therefore, if manos are suitable indicators of change, then the distribution of the mano types will show change through time. Data on their distribution is given in Table 70.

Table 70.   Distribution of mano types through time

Period	Mano Type	
	Type 1	Type 2
Early	13 (12.5%)	8 (12.5%)
Early/Late	35 (33.7%)	24 (37.5%)
Late	56 (53.8%)	32 (50.0%)
TOTAL	104 (100.0%)	64 (100.0%)

Distribution of mano types by time period was examined by the chi-square method. No significant difference through time was demonstrated: it is therefore concluded that mano types cannot be appealed to with confidence as indicators of change through time at Las Colinas.

Hypothesis Two

It was suspected that the mano types reflect different stages in the use-cycle of grinding tools, and that Type 1 manos reflect an initial stage of use, while Type 2 manos are from the final stages of use. Manos in the terminal stages of wear (Type 2) are more likely to be discarded than manos which are in an initial stage of use (Type 1) because of their reduced mechanical efficiency.

An examination of refuse types provides an indication of location of discard. The term primary refuse refers to objects abandoned at the site of use, while the term secondary refuse refers to items transported for discard (Schiffer 1972). For purposes of this test, primary refuse includes objects from room floors and floor-fill, while secondary refuse is composed of objects which were clearly transported for discard: that is, items found in retaining cell trash-fill and in post-occupation trash-fill in rooms. Whole manos only will be used in the test of Hypothesis Two, to avoid confusing the pattern of discard.

I contend that if the mano types are suitable for explicating past lifeways, as reflected in cycles of tool use, then the distribution of them should vary between refuse types.

The distribution of mano types within each refuse type is given in Table 71.

Table 71.   Distribution of mano type by refuse type

Refuse Type	Mano Type	
	Type 1	Type 2
Primary	8 (61.5%)	1 (14.3%)
Secondary	5 (38.5%)	6 (85.7%)
TOTAL	13 (100.0%)	7 (100.0%)

Examination of the data indicates a distinct disparity between the spatial distributions of mano Types 1 and 2 at Las Colinas. There is a marked tendency for Type 2 manos to be associated with secondary refuse, while Type 1 manos are generally found in primary refuse proveniences. On the strength of this pattern, I conclude that mano types at Las Colinas have been found to be useful in the explication of past lifeways through functional analysis. It should be remembered, however, that the small sample size makes this conclusion tentative.

Summary and Conclusion

Intra-Regional Comparisons

In this section, a comparison of nonflaked stone items from the Las Colinas Site with similar objects from other sites within the region will be made.

In general, the milling equipment is very similar to that of Los Muertos (Haury 1945), Pueblo del Monte (Weaver 1972), the Fitch Site (Pailes 1963), the University Indian Ruin (Hayden 1957), and Classic period Hohokam sites in the Painted Rock Reservoir (Wasley and Johnson 1965).

The ground stone axes and ornaments share the same affinities, and in addition show similarities to the axes of the Upper Ruin at Tonto National Monument (Steen 1962) and of the later phases at Snaketown (Sayles 1937).

The slate palettes are similar to those at Snaketown (Haury 1937) and the occurrence of utilized lead is noted at both Snaketown (Hawley 1937) and at Las Colinas.

Water worn concretions similar to those at Las Colinas were found, usually in the context of "caches," at Los Muertos (Cushing 1890:179; Haury 1945:144-145), Pueblo del Monte (Weaver 1972:136-145), University Indian Ruin (Hayden 1957:169-170), and Pueblo Grande (Hayden 1957:152).

The single formal abrading-straightening tool was most like those found in the Upper Ruin at Tonto National Monument (Steen 1962) and at Casa Grande (Fewkes 1912:126).

Extra-Regional Influences

A currently vexing problem in Hohokam studies is the degree of influence brought by outside elements, especially as might be evidenced by the occurrence of "Salado traits" in a Classic period Hohokam site.

In dealing with this problem, Weed (1972) used data derived from her preliminary study of the Las Colinas lithics. She postulated a trait list of "Salado" lithic indicators which included, among other items, double-bit axes, arrow shaft straighteners, adzes, polishing stones, and a different sort of trough metate than those found at Classic Hohokam sites. Only one double-bit axe and one formal arrow shaft straightener fragment (abrading-straightening tool) were found at Las Colinas. No adzes or unusual metate forms were discovered. Weed concluded that Salado type indicators are not readily identifiable in the assemblage, and that the assemblage remains typically Hohokam.

Intra-Site Change through Time

There is little demonstration of change through time within any of the classes of ground stone objects. The formal and stylistic characteristics of most classes, especially milling equipment, axes, and palettes, are unchanged from those of the Sedentary period, and they exhibit little variation throughout the Classic period at Las Colinas. However, there is a decided tendency for intricate and carefully made ornaments of exotic material (pendants, beads, polished rings, etc.) to be confined to the earliest phases at Las Colinas.

APPENDICES

APPENDIX A

ANALYSIS OF THE HUMAN SKELETAL REMAINS
FROM LAS COLINAS

by Richard J. Harrington
Human Identification Laboratory
Arizona State Museum
University of Arizona

Introduction

The site of Las Colinas yielded 16 burials, six cremations, and miscellaneous osseous material. Part of these remains were recovered in 1968 and subsequently analyzed in 1969 by Walter H. Birkby at the Human Identification Laboratory, University of Arizona. Three of the burials (B-2, B-5, and B-6) and two of the cremations (5 and 6) were not recovered. One burial (B-3) consisted of nonhuman osseous remains. The breakdown by age and sex for the remaining 12 burials and four cremations is as follows: two females, four probable females, two males, two probable males, two adults of undeterminable sex, two children, and two infants. The above individuals referred to by sex are adults. No acceptable method for determining the sex of subadults had been devised at the time of writing. With two possible exceptions, none of the burials or cremations appears to represent more than one individual, nor does any individual appear to be represented in more than one burial. The possible exceptions, B-1 and B-4, are discussed in detail below.

Because of the paucity of osseous material from most of the burials and cremations, many of the fragments were added to the miscellaneous collection at the Human Identification Laboratory subsequent to their analysis in 1969. Only Burials 8, 9, 12, and 16, and Cremations 1 and 4 were retained as discrete burial units.

Criteria used for determining age and sex of the individuals are discussed in Bass (1971) and Brothwell (1963:68-69). Diagnoses of pathologies are based on Brothwell and Sandison (1967) and Steinbock (1976). Those burials and cremations brought in for analysis receive detailed discussion below.

Burials

Burial 1

Adult, probable male. Age is based on bone size and thickness. Sex is based on the robust nature of the tibiae and fibulae. The only other remains of this individual are two tarsal bones.

However, two immature phalanges were recorded, suggesting that two individuals are represented. Due to the very fragmentary state of this burial and its present inaccessibility, a definitive conclusion cannot be made. No pathologies, no anomalies, no metric, and no nonmetric data were recorded.

Burial 2

Not recovered (excavator's report indicates the presence of an adult's lower limb bones in a poor state of preservation).

Burial 3

Post-cranial remains of _Canis_ _sp_.

Burial 4

Child, less than seven years old. Estimate of age is based on the presence of nonerupted mandibular central incisors. Three phalanges, one metatarsal, and some long bone fragments comprise the rest of the recovered remains. According to the excavator's report, one infant and one adult (the infant represented by skull fragments--the adult by long bones) were present. The report indicates that the bones were not salvageable because of poor preservation. It cannot be determined from the scant information whether some of the remains (the child's) were exhumed and some (the adult's) were left in place, or whether the long bones were simply identified incorrectly in the field. Since immature long bone fragments were recovered, and since the excavator's rather crude map of the burial depicts only the long bones attributed to the adult, it seems most likely that only the child is represented.

Burial 5

Not recovered due to poor preservation. Identified by the excavator as a young adult female.

Burial 6

Not recovered due to poor preservation. Identified by the excavator as an adult female.

Burial 7

Infant, less than six months old. Estimate of age is based on the lack of eruption of deciduous teeth. The remains are very fragmentary and poorly preserved. No pathologies, no anomalies, no metric, and no nonmetric data were recorded.

Burial 8

Adult, male, 30 to 40 years old. Estimate of age is based on the extensive wear of the masticating surfaces of the molars. Determination of sex is based on the curvature of the subpubic angle, the diameter of the femoral head, and the robustness of the long bones. This individual was afflicted with dental caries, alveolar abscesses, antemortem tooth loss, hypertrophic lipping of several vertebrae, and hypertrophic lesions on both patellae. These hypertrophic changes are indicative of osteoarthritis. Given the fragmentary state of the cranium, it could not be ascertained if there had been any cranial deformation. One femur was sufficiently intact to measure, and an estimate of stature of approxmately 167.5 cm was determined from this measurement (Genovés 1967). Only a few nonmetric traits were observable.

Burial 9

Adult, female, 25 to 30 years old. Estimate of age is based on the degree of wear of the molar cusps. Determination of sex is based on the small size and lack of prominence of the supraorbital tori, occipital nuchal crest, and the mastoid processes. The cranium is severely afflicted with "lesions" that appear to be attributable to postmortem chemical activity that led to mineralization, cracking, and discoloration. Osteoporosis is evident on the frontal, parietal, and occipital bones, but other true pathological lesions on these bones are not discernible because of the postmortem damage. The dentition is extensively affected by caries, alveolar abscessing, cementum hyperplasia, and antemortem tooth loss. Hypertrophic changes attributable to osteoarthritis occur in joints involving the following bones: the innominates, humeri, ulnae, the right scapula, bones of the hands and feet, cervical and lumbar vertebrae, the sacrum, the right mandibular condyle, and the right temporo-mandibular joint. Lesions on the right tibia are probably due to osteomyelytis. Scars of parturition are evident on the dorsal surface of the right pubis. Cranial measurements were taken and nonmetric traits were recorded. There is some cranial deformation in the occipital region.

Burial 10

Adult, female. Estimate of age is based on the degree of wear of the masticating surfaces of the molars. Determination of sex is based on the diameter of the left femoral head. The remains are very fragmentary and in poor condition. Dentition is characterized by alveolar abscesses, cementum hyperplasia,

and antemortem tooth loss. Some of the vertebral fragments
show sign of osteoarthritic hypertrophy. A sizeable lesion
of unknown etiology is present on the diaphysis of one tibia.
No metric data were recorded save for the femoral head diameter
and no nonmetric traits were observable.

Burial 11

Adult, probably female. Estimate of age is based on the extent
of molar cusp wear. Determination of sex is based on bone
robustness. The remains were quite fragmentary and highly
mineralized. Hypertrophic lesions are evident on the lumbar
vertebrae and the right humeral coronoid fossa, two thoracic
vertebrae suffered from a compression fracture, and a left
rib is fused to a thoracic vertebra. The teeth are afflicted
with caries and cementum hyperplasia. No metric or nonmetric
data were recorded.

Burial 12

Adult, male, 30 to 40 years old. Estimate of age is based on
the degree of wear of the masticating surfaces of the teeth.
Determination of sex is based on the prominence of the supraorbital tori, the rounded supraorbital borders, the robust
mastoid processes, and the size of the femoral head. Pathologies include dental caries and enamel hypoplasia. Three
teeth show evidence of antemortem chipping, and there is some
cranial deformation in the occipital region. Nonmetric data
were recorded and a few measurements were taken.

Burial 13

Adult, probably female. Estimate of age is based on endocranially closed sutures and the degree of tooth wear.
Determination of sex is based on the size of the mastoid
processes and the overall gracile nature of the bones. No
pathologies, anomalies, or metric data were recorded. A few
nonmetric traits were observed.

Burial 14

Adult, probably female. Estimate of age is based on fused
epiphyses, and bone size and thickness. Determination of
sex is based on the sizes of the mastoid processes and left
femoral head, and on the shape of the supraorbital borders.
Pathologies include osteoarthritic hypertrophy of the vertebrae,
both shoulders, and the left knee; kyphosis of the lower
thoracic region; sinusitis (inflammation of the frontal sinuses);
hypertrophy of the cranial diploë; and cementum hyperplasia.

There is no cranial deformation. The cranium was observed
for nonmetric traits. The only measurement taken was of the
left femoral head.

Burial 15

Infant, less than six months.. Estimate of age is based on the
noneruption of the deciduous teeth. The remains of this
individual were sparse and extremely fragmentary. No pathologies, no anomalies, no metric, and no nonmetric data were
recorded.

Burial 16

Child, five to six years old. Estimate of age is based on the
stage of dental eruption. No pathologies or anomalies were
observed. No cranial measurements were taken because of
warpage, but post-cranial measurements and cranial nonmetric
data were recorded.

Miscellaneous Remains

These remains include one cranial fragment, six teeth, and
one nonhuman tooth. The excavator's report does not indicate
whether these remains were screen-recovered, scattered on the
surface, or found in proximity to any of the other burials and
inadvertently disassociated from their proper provenience.

Cremations

According to the excavator's reports, each cremation was found in
association with a ceramic pot, but the pots were broken and the debris scattered by plowing. Weights were obtained for cremations 1 and 4 to provide
a rough estimate of the percentage of the individual remaining. A typical
adult male will yield approximately 1750 g of cremated bone (Binford 1972b:385).
Cremations 2 and 3 are represented by only a few fragments each and were not
weighed. Cremations 5 and 6 were not recovered, but the excavator's reports
indicate that they also consisted of only a few fragments.

The color of cremated bone indicates both the intensity of the cremating
fire and the length of time the bones were exposed to it (Binford 1972a:376).
Chalky white, blue, and gray discolorations result from the calcination of the
bone due to intense or prolonged burning. The black color of charred bone
indicates only superficial firing.

A fresh or "green" bone will exhibit deep transverse cracking and
varying degrees of warpage when intensely burned. Defleshed or dry bone will
crack superficially and split longitudinally, but will not warp when fired
(Binford 1972a:376).

Cremation 1

Adult, probably male. Estimate of age is based on bone size and thickness, and the presence of fused epiphyses. Determination of sex is based on the curvature of the fragmented left sciatic notch, the robustness of the left femoral head, and the prominence of the occipital nuchal crest. The weight of the remains is 507 g. Fragments are warped, extensively cracked, and moderately calcined, indicating a flesh cremation. No pathologies, no anomalies, no metric, and no nonmetric data were recorded.

Cremation 2

Adult, unknown sex. Estimate of age is based on bone size and thickness. This cremation consists of four fragments (one cranial and three long bone fragments) that are moderately calcined. No pathologies, no anomalies, no metric, and no nonmetric data were recorded.

Cremation 3

Adult, unknown sex. Estimate of age is based on the presence of a fused neural arch, and bone size and thickness. The cremation consists of four fragments showing a range of calcination. No pathologies, no anomalies, no metric, and no nonmetric data were recorded.

Cremation 4

Adult, probably female. Estimate of age is based on bone size and thickness, fused epiphyses, and endocranially obliterated sutures. Determination of sex is based on the sharp supraorbital borders. Weight is 486 g. Pathologies include hypertrophy of the lumbar vertebrae, and antemortem tooth loss. Fragments are warped and extensively cracked with moderate calcination. No measurements were taken and no nonmetric traits were recorded.

Cremation 5

Not available for analysis.

Cremation 6

Not available for analysis.

APPENDIX B

DISPOSAL OF THE DEAD AT LAS COLINAS

by Marilyn B. Saul
Department of Oriental Studies
University of Arizona

Introduction

Fifteen inhumations and six cremations were discovered during the 1968 excavations at Las Colinas. This appendix describes these remains with respect to their location, depth, orientation, accompanying grave goods, and degree of disturbance. Also discussed is their relative sequence of interment during the prehistoric occupation of Las Colinas.

Inhumations

Fifteen inhumations that included the remains of seven adult females, three adult males, five subadults and two probable adults of unknown gender, were recovered. One other burial (B-3) proved to contain the remains of a dog. There were two instances of possible multiple inhumation--both of a child with an adult. Sex and age do not appear to have been factors in placement of the burials. Figure 139 shows the locations of the interments at Las Colinas.

Only one adult male (B-12) was accompanied by grave goods. Of the two infant burials (B-7 and B-15), the first was accompanied by two bone awls and the second by a bowl. The majority of the grave goods were associated with adult female individuals, with the exception of Burial 4 which contained only the remains of an infant; however, an adult may originally have been buried there as well.

The 23 vessels accompanying the burials included 17 bowls, three jars, two mugs, and one tripod vessel. All were red wares with the exception of one Casa Grande Red-on-buff jar (Table 72). Of the remaining 22 vessels, four were Gila Red, eight were Gila/Salt red ware, eight were Salt Red and two were of an unnamed variety of red ware (Table 72). Other grave goods included quartz crystals, shell ornaments, beads, awls, and a stone ball. Ocher was found in association with Burial 12 and Burial 14, an adult male and an adult female respectively. Asbestos was found with Burial 14.

The burials were clustered in four areas: the eastern section of the mound, the northern section of the mound, a centrally located area on the

257

258

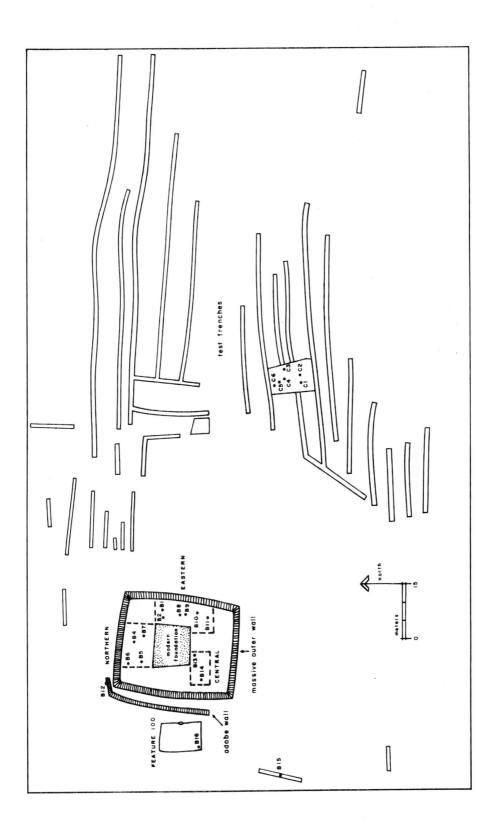

Figure 139. Locations of burials and cremations

Table 72. Whole vessel pottery types associated with burials at Las Colinas

Associated Pottery Types	Burials					
	4	5	6	9	10	11
Casa Grande Red-on-buff	B4-6					
Gila Red	B4-2					
Gila Red Smudged				B9-2 B9-3		
Gila/Salt Red	B4-1 B4-3 B4-5 B4-7					
Gila/Salt Red Smudged		B5-1 B5-2		B9-5 B9-6		
Salt Red						
Salt Red Smudged				B9-4	B10-1 B10-2	B11-2
Unnamed Red Ware			B6-1 B6-7			

Table 72. (continued)

Associated Pottery Types	Burials				
	12	13	14	15	16
Casa Grande Red-on-buff					
Gila Red					B16-2
Gila Red Smudged					
Gila/Salt Red					
Gila/Salt Red Smudged					
Salt Red		B13-4		B15-1	
Salt Red Smudged	B12-2		B14-7		
Unnamed Red Ware					

mound, and the western addition to the mound. One burial (B-15) was found in relative isolation (see Figure 139).

Description of Burials

Eastern Section of Mound

Six individuals were interred in this portion of the mound. Four of the inhumations (Burials 8, 9, 10, and 11) were extended burials, oriented east to west, with the head to the east, and the face upturned. The two other burials were grossly disturbed, and no data could be obtained concerning their orientation. Three of the interments were above the uppermost adobe cap, one was in the cap, and one was in a clay-lined pit. The excavation record of the sixth burial yielded no data concerning its position in relation to the latest cap (see Table 73).

Burial 1. Burial 1 was located in an adobe-lined pit. Burial pits were encountered at Los Muertos that penetrated several overlapping floor levels, giving the impression that they had been deliberately lined with adobe (Haury 1945:44). The situation was clearly different at Las Colinas because the pit of Burial 1 did not penetrate the thick adobe layer of Cap 4. Had the pit in fact penetrated Cap 4, it would at first have been uncertain, as at Los Muertos, whether the adobe lining was deliberate or simply a consequence of digging through the overlapping, hardpacked surfaces. This was the only burial encountered in association with a lined pit. Little data were available on the pit, and it does not appear to have been fully delineated. No data on the orientation of this burial were recovered.

Although the excavator identified only an infant burial, final analysis suggests a multiple burial of a possible adult male with an immature individual. No grave goods were encountered.

Burial 2. Burial 2 was disturbed by a historic well on the east side of the mound that eliminated all evidence of the inhumation except for the lower limbs. Field analysis determined that the burial was of an adult. The orientation of the remains suggest an extended burial. No grave goods were encountered.

Burial 8. Burial 8 was interred above Cap 4 (see Table 73). No artifacts accompanied this adult male (Figure 140).

Burial 9. Burial 9 was also interred above Cap 4 (see Table 73). No pit was found. The burial was of an adult female, 25-30 years of age. Two Gila Red smudged bowls (B9-2, B9-3), were located 25 cm east of the cranium. A Salt Red smudged bowl (B9-4) was directly to the left of the cranium, nestled in the shoulder area. Two Gila/Salt red ware smudged bowls (B9-5, B9-6) were on the left side of the individual by the knee and lower limb.

Table 73. Depth of burials at Las Colinas

Burial Number	Eastern Section	Northern Section	Central Section	Western Addition
1	68 cm below surface			
2	Disturbed by historic well			
4		68 cm below datum		
5		68 cm below datum (intruded into Cap)		
6		Data unavailable		
7		53 cm below surface (associated with Feature 18)		
8	87 cm below datum (above Cap 4)			
9	129 cm below surface (above Cap 4)			
10	116 cm below surface (above Cap 4)			
11	Intruded into Cap 4			
12				Pit intruded into solid adobe wall
13			Pit in Feature 63	
14			Intruded into Cap	
15				60 cm below surface

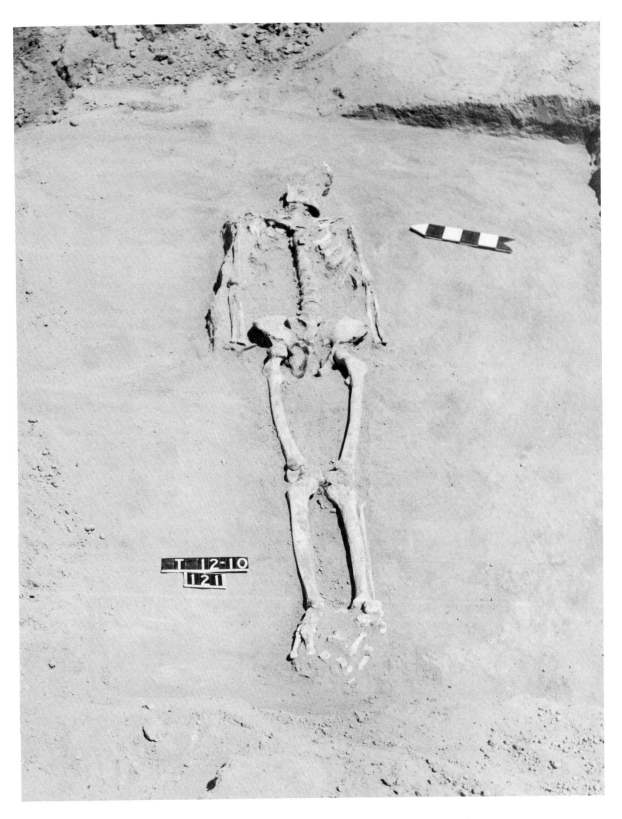

Figure 140. Burial 8 (looking east)

Burial 10. Burial 10 was located above Cap 4 (see Table 73).   One of two Salt Red smudged bowls (B10-1) associated with this burial was found directly east of the cranium. This interment of an adult female was the only burial in which the legs were splayed, presumably to accommodate a bowl (B10-2) placed between the ankles of the individual. The splayed position may have been natural, however, since analysis showed a lesion on the tibia that may have been a debilitating affliction during life (see Harrington, this volume). Five black stone beads were recovered during the bone analysis. There was no documentation of their provenience.

Burial 11. This burial was the only inhumation in this area which intruded into Cap 4. No depth was given. The burial pit was excavated at an angle into the cap, causing the cranium to protrude above the cap.

This burial of a probable adult female was greatly disturbed; the cranium, pelvis, right radius/ulna, and both hands were missing. Grave goods were negligible, and consisted of a Salt Red smudged worked rim (B11-2) (possibly from a mug) located at the left shoulder and a large red striated sherd (B11-5) found at the right foot of the individual. Although rodents were originally blamed for the absence of the skeletal remains listed above, the paucity of grave goods and disturbance of the cranial area where such things were likely to have been placed, may indicate that the grave was robbed.

Northern Section of Mound

Four burials were encountered in this section of the mound. Adequate data concerning orientation was available only for Burial 5 and Burial 6. These followed the orientation exhibited by the previous burials. Burial 5 was located in the latest cap, Burial 4 was below the cap, and Burial 7 was above the cap. No depth was recorded for Burial 6.

Burial 4. Burial 4 was a possible multiple interment located in a trash layer below the uppermost cap (see Table 73). No pit was delineated. The excavator's notes indicated an adult and an infant burial, although only infant remains were submitted for analysis.

A northeast by southwest orientation was determined on the basis of the reported adult limb stains, which the excavator had attributed to the presence of the original leg bones. The excavator indicated that the head was at the northeast end of the burial, although no cranium was recovered. This author believes that the data are insufficient to support any conclusion about the position of the head.

The infant was located at the western extent of the grave. Because of the paucity of remains and the confusing data, it was difficult to form a conclusion as to the orientation and arrangement of the burials.

Six vessels were found distributed throughout the grave. Their positions in terms of the human remains cannot be adequately specified. One Gila

Red bowl (B4-2), three Gila/Salt red ware bowls (B4-1, B4-3, B4-5), one Gila/ Salt jar (B4-7) and one Casa Grande Red-on-buff jar (B4-6) were recovered. In addition to the vessels, a quartz crystal, shell bracelet fragment, and shell ring were recovered.

Apparently the adult bones could not be recovered and therefore were not submitted for analysis. The quantity of grave goods associated with this interment suggests that an adult was indeed buried here along with the infant. It could not be determined whether these burials were simultaneous.

Burial 5. The remains in this burial were determined by the excavator to be those of an adult female. The burial was in a pit intruding into the uppermost cap (see Table 73). Preservation was poor, and the remains could not be recovered for analysis.

A Gila/Salt red ware smudged bowl (B5-1) was located on the right side of the individual just below the knees, and a Gila/Salt red ware smudged mug (B5-2) was found on the individual's right side by the shoulder.

Burial 6. Burial 6 was accompanied by two unnamed red ware vessels, a bowl (B6-1) found fragmented on either side of the cranium and a miniature tripod vessel (B6-7) located under the bowl fragments. A piece of ocher was discovered within the bowl. Other burial goods included a stone ball east and slightly north of the cranium, a turquoise bead by the left arm, and two shell rings on the second and third phalanges of the left hand. The bones were not submitted for analysis, but field estimates indicate the individual was an adult female (Figure 141).

Burial 7. Burial 7 was the only infant burial associated with a hearth, Feature 18 (see Table 73). Two bone awls were recovered, but their direct association with the burial was not established conclusively.

Central Section of the Mound.

Two inhumantions, Burial 13 and Burial 14, were discovered in a central location on the mound. Both burials appear to intrude into Cap 4, and their orientation is similar to that found in the eastern and northern sections of the mound.

Burial 13. An adult female was buried in a pit excavated through Cap 4, just below the tops of the walls in Feature 63. Accompanying the burial were five sherds 25 cm to the east and north of the cranium that proved, when reconstructed, to be the bottom of a Salt Red jar (B13-4). A small vessel was found by the left knee, but was subsequently mislaid and therefore not available for analysis. A pipestone disk bead was recovered from the area of the right ankle.

Figure 141. Burial 6 (looking east)

Burial 14. This burial of an adult female was accompanied by one vessel and a variety of artifacts which were recovered from a possible pouch found to the left of and slightly under the cranium. The pouch contained a large quartz crystal and a piece of asbestos. Other small artifacts were recovered from this area, but no details were given. A Salt Red smudged bowl (B14-7) was found, according to the top plan, slightly under the cranium.

The only anomaly in the orientation of this individual's remains was that the cranium faced slightly north with the chin tucked into the shoulder region. It is possible that the cranium originally rested face up on the bowl and achieved its final position upon decomposition. If that was the case, the pouch must originally have been placed under the individual's head. A piece of asbestos was found within the cranium, but was probably included originally in the pouch and was deposited in the cranium by subsidence or rodents. Hematite was found on the pelvis of the individual.

Western Addition to the Mound

Excavation in the area west of Mound 8 yielded two burials, Burial 12 and Burial 16. These burials differ from the standard pattern of orientation previously established.

Burial 12. Burial 12, an adult male, was found in a pit, and was oriented slightly northeast by southwest, with the head to the northeast and the face upturned. The pit intruded into the solid adobe wall associated with the Stage VII construction episode. The body was covered with hematite, a chunk of which was found under a Salt Red smudged bowl (B12-2) located to the right of the cranium. To the left of the cranium was an unnamed red ware sherd (B12-3). A projectile point was found in the individual's chest and a phalanx found in the mouth. The latter may be due to rodent activity which, according to the excavator, accounted for the loss of much of the skeleton. It was originally hypothesized, based on the presence of the projectile point, that the individual met a violent death. Of course, the projectile point may simply have been included with the burial goods.

Burial 16. This burial was of a child 5-6 years of age. The burial is intrusive in an early Soho phase pithouse, Feature 100, partially cutting into the floor and the west wall. The child was interred on its right side in a semi-flexed position, oriented in a north-to-south direction with head to the north and the face to the southeast. A Gila Red bowl (B16-2) lay directly west of the cranium. This individual was buried sometime between the occupation of the pit house and construction of Features 40 and 40A, the walls of which were constructed over the grave.

Extramural Area

Burial 15. An inverted Salt Red bowl (B15-1)was placed over the infant in Burial 15 which was found approximately 23 m south-southwest of Burial 16 (see Figure 139). No pit was discerned.

Cremations

Six cremations were discovered during trenching operations east of the mound. All cremations were located at or slightly below the plow zone and thus had been heavily disturbed by historic agriculture in this area. Each of the six cremations was associated with funerary vessels. Cremations 1 and 4 contained abundant osseous material. Cremains were scarce, however, in Cremations 2, 3, 5, and 6. Four of the cremations (Cremations 1, 2, 3, and 4) were submitted for analysis, and each proved to be an adult (see Harrington, this volume).

Cremation 1. Cremation 1 was in a Salt Red smudged bowl (C1-2) and was covered with Salt Red sherds. A shell bracelet fragment was found in the funerary vessel.

Cremation 2. Cremation 2 was found in a pit along with sherds from a Gila Red vessel (C2-1).

Cremation 3. Cremation 3 was heavily disturbed by historic cultivation. Sherds of a Salt Red vessel (C3-1) and a striated red ware (Gila Red?) vessel (C3-2) were associated with this individual.

Cremation 4. Cremation 4 was accompanied by the lower portion of a funerary vessel; apparently, the upper portion and cover bowl had been removed by historic farming. A shell bracelet fargment was recovered from the vessel.

Cremation 5. Cremation 5 yielded two fragmentary Gila Red vessels (C5-1). Both vessels had been badly damaged by agricultural activities.

Cremation 6. Cremation 6 was associated with Gila Red smudged sherds (C6-1) found inverted over the cremains.

Conclusions

Fifteen inhumations and six cremations were recovered from Las Colinas. The inhumations were all interred within the primary occupation area, while the cremations were disposed of in an area outside the mound. This followed the accepted pattern of Classic Hohokam burial practices. An anomaly within this pattern, however, was that more inhumations than cremations were encountered. Agricultural disturbance in the cremation area, as well as extensive trenching rather than excavation of the entire cremation area, may account for the relatively low proportion of cremations recovered from Las Colinas.

The pattern of interment was similar to that found at Los Muertos and other Classic Hohokam sites. The individuals are oriented in an east-to-west direction, head to the east and face up. Two exceptions to this rule were found in the western addition to the mound.

Apparently, sex and age did not influence the placement of burials, although these factors may have affected the inclusion of grave goods. Burials that contain a large amount of artifacts are invariably adult females. Grave goods were regularly placed around the head, in the shoulder region, and near the knees and feet. With the exception of a Casa Grande Red-on-buff jar, the vessels accompanying the inhumations were exclusively red wares.

Although the cremation area was heavily disturbed, there appears to have been a pattern of interment of the cremains in funerary vessels, that were in turn covered with an additional vessel or sherds. The vessels and sherds associated with the cremations were red wares.

It appears that while cremation was practiced at Las Colinas, there was a gradual shift to inhumation. Haury (1945:43) noted a shift to inhumations at Los Muertos and other Classic Hohokam sites and attributes this to Puebloan influence in the area.

There were at least two phases of burials represented on the mound itself. The earliest of these is Burial 4, which was located beneath the uppermost cap on the north side of the mound. All other burials in the east, north and central areas are above or intruded into the last cap and are, therefore, contemporary with the most recent prehistoric occupation. It was difficult to determine when the burials in the western addition to the mound occurred, although it can be said that Burial 16 took place after the early phase occupation of the pit house and before construction of Features 40 and 40A. Burial 12 was intruded into the solid adobe wall associated with the Stage VII construction episode. No data are available concerning the temporal placement of Burial 15, or the cremations, within the occupation span of Las Colinas.

APPENDIX C

MAMMALIAN REMAINS FROM LAS COLINAS

by Paul C. Johnson*
Department of Geosciences
University of Arizona

Introduction

If minimum faunal counts based upon bones recovered from archaeological sites reflect the quantity of meat actually consumed, the people who occupied Las Colinas did not depend heavily upon game as a food source. A total of 922 bones and bone fragments were identified at the species or genus level. At least 165 individuals of 17 species are represented (Table 74).   However, 81 percent of the individuals were rabbit-sized or smaller. Only 16 individuals of species antelope-sized and larger were represented. Las Colinas was occupied during a 270 year period (A.D. 1180-1450) resulting in a mean time between large animal kills of about 17 years. This unlikely conclusion may be biased by the following factors: the site was not occupied continuously; skeletal material was discarded at the kill site; certain elements were retained for making tools and weapons; trash was deposited in areas not excavated; bone was not preserved because of dog and rodent scavenging, weathering before deposition, and leaching after deposition; elements were missed or broken during excavation; not all bone fragments recovered could be identified.

The 16 artiodactyls were represented by a total of only 54 bones. However, an estimated 70 percent to 80 percent of the bone recovered consisted of long bone fragments that could not be identified. The fragments are probably from deer (Odocoileus sp.) and bighorn sheep (Ovis canadensis).

Only a few artiodactyl pelvis fragments and no mandibles or frontals were recovered, precluding the determination of sex ratios and a detailed age structure. Several juvenile artiodactyls are represented, but unfortunately can not be identified below Order.

All of the artiodactyl elements referrable to genus or species have fused epiphyses; they are therefore adult. None of the bones, large or small, showed recognizable signs of having been butchered or gnawed by dogs, although a few had been gnawed by rodents. In general, the larger bones were in worse condition than the smaller ones, and surface markings may have been obscured. Table 74 details the frequency of burned and unburned bone. It is interesting that 60 percent of the deer (Odocoileus) elements were burned, but only 10 percent of the jackrabbit (Lepus) elements. Perhaps this reflects different cooking techniques for animals of different sizes.

*Draft completed July 1973

Table 74. Descriptive and inferential aspects of the mammalian remains from Las Colinas

Species	Number of Elements	Percent of Elements Burned	Minumum Number of Individuals	Total Estimated Pounds of Meat for Species*	Percent of Total for All Individuals
Lepus californicus (Black-tailed jackrabbit)	375	10	69	207	7.2
Sylvilagus audubonii (Desert cottontail)	156	13	41	62	1.6
Citellus sp. (Ground squirrel)	117	0	11	-	-
Thomomys bottae (Valley pocket gopher)	170	0	9	-	-
Perognathus sp. (Pocket mouse)	4	0	3	-	-
Dipodomys sp. (Kangaroo rat)	1	0	1	-	-
Sigmodon sp. (Cotton rat)	7	0	5	-	-
Neotoma sp. (Woodrat)	3	0	2	-	-
Canis sp. (Dog and coyote)	24	20	8	200	5.3
Canis familiaris (Domestic dog)	1	0	1	25	0.7
Taxidea taxus (Badger)	1	0	1	12.5	0.3
Lynx rufus (Bobcat)	3	0	1	15	0.4
Felis cattus (Domestic cat)	3	-	2	-	-
Odocoileus sp. (Deer)	37	60	8	800	21.7
Antilocapra americana (Prong-horned antelope)	2	0	1	55	1.4
Ovis canadensis (Bighorn sheep)	13	18	5	500	13.5
Bison bison (Bison)	2	0	2	1800	48.0
Sus scrofa (Domestic pig)	3	-	3	-	-
TOTAL	922		173	3676.5	100.1

*Data for pounds of usable meat from White (1953).

cannot be stored except as fat. Therefore, unless the bison meat is cured and eaten over an extended period, the daily or weekly ingestion of rabbit may be more important, even though the actual poundage of rabbit meat is much less.

Sylvilagus audubonii

Two partial skulls, 33 lower jaws, isolated teeth, nearly 100 post-cranial elements and three auditory bullae of Sylvilagus audubonii (desert cottontail) were recovered.

The three species of cottontail (S. audubonii, S. floridanus, and S. nuttallii) found in Arizona at present are difficult or impossible to distinguish without complete skulls because they exhibit marked morphological convergence in this part of their range (Hoffmeister and Lee 1963a, 1963b). The two partial skulls recovered are referred to S. audubonii for the follow-ing reasons: the sides of the mesopterygoid fossa pinch inward and a distinct submarginal ridge extends posteriorly from the palatal bridge, the postorbital constriction is larger than 12 mm, and the posterior extension of the supra-orbital processes are free. The auditory bullae are referred to S. audubonii because of their large size. The remaining elements have been referred to S. audubonii on the basis of contemporary ecological differences between the species, and on the assumption that most of the rabbits were killed in the vicinity of the village. It is possible that the other species were present in the fauna.

McGregor (1941:257) in an analysis of the fauna recovered from Winona and Ridge Ruin noted that "jackrabbits predominated as a food early in the history of the trash mound, and were relatively less abundant later." He suggested that this could be explained by differences in behavior of jack-rabbits and cottontail rabbits when hunted: the former tend to run to escape, while the latter tend to hide. McGregor suggested that since the jackrabbits were easier to catch, their ranks would have been depleted first (during the early stages of occupation of Winona and Ridge Ruin) and that with the passage of time the cottontails would, therefore, have been propor-tionately more important as a food resource.

The Las Colinas rabbits do not follow this pattern (Figure 142). Although the number of rabbits represented fluctuates through time, the pro-portion of jackrabbits to cottontails remains nearly constant. In fact, the largest proportion of jackrabbits occurs during the Civano phase--the last period of occupation. Only two jackrabbits and no cottontails were recovered from the features of late Soho phase. This may be evidence for a low level of occupation during that time.

Rodentia

All of the rodents recovered from Las Colinas with the exception of Sigmodon (cotton rat) are burrowing forms. None of the specimens are assignable to species except Thomomys bottae. However, all of the genera of rodents are found in the Phoenix area today. Since none of the elements show

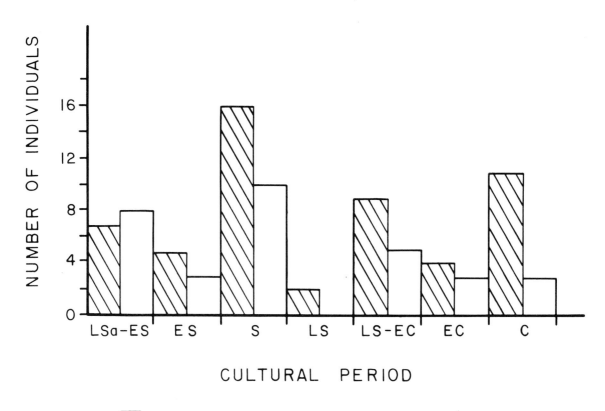

Figure 142.   Frequency of jackrabbits and cottontail rabbits
from the Las Colinas site by cultural period.
(L = Late, E = Early, Sa = Sacaton, S = Soho,
C = Civano)

evidence of burning or butchering, it cannot be established that the animals were utilized for food or that they were contemporaneous with human occupation of the site.

One nearly complete skeleton of Thomomys was recovered and almost certainly represents an animal which died in its burrow. In some sites in Arizona there is evidence that rodents may have been an important food source for the Hohokam people (Stein 1963:214; Olsen 1971:21).

Ammospermophilous harrisi or Spermophilous tereticaudus (Squirrels)

One partial skull, lower jaws, isolated teeth and one nearly complete skeleton that were referred to Ammospermophilous harrisi or Spermophilous tereticaudus (on the basis of size and morphology) were recovered at Las Colinas.

Perognathus (Pocket Mouse)

Three mandibles and one partial skull are referred to Perognathus. The very small size of the specimens suggests they may represent P. amplus.

Dipodomys (Kangaroo Rat)

Dipodomys is represented by a partial skull that may be D. merriami or D. ordi, both of which are found in the Phoenix vicinity today (Cockrum 1960). These two species are strongly convergent in Arizona and cannot be separated on the basis of size.

Sigmodon (Cotton Rat)

Sigmodon is represented by five lower jaws.

Neotoma (Wood Rat)

Neotoma is represented by two lower jaws.

Carnivora

Canis spp. (Dog, Coyote, Wolf)

Canis spp. are represented by isolated teeth and postcranial elements. All of the elements are within the size range of C. familiaris (domestic dog) and C. latrans (coyote). Four of the bones were burned, suggesting that some of the animals had been eaten. None showed butcher marks.

The only element definitely considered Canis familiaris is a complete lower jaw bone. The bone, in good condition, has not been burned and there are no apparent butcher marks. Olsen (1968:35) described specimens from Grasshopper Ruin that are similar in size (see Appendix J). The specimen is also similar in size to Allen's Plains Indian Dog (Allen 1920:453). Measurements are as follows: condylosymphysis length, 123.5 mm; alveolus, C-M$_3$, 82.2 mm; alveolus, P$_1$-M$_3$, 64.9 mm; length of carnassial (M$_1$), 20.0 mm; greatest thickness of jaw ventral to M$_1$, 10.0 mm; depth of jaw from alveolus of M$_1$ to ventral margin, 29.0 mm; alveolus P$_1$-P$_4$, 33.7 mm; alveolus M$_1$-M$_3$, 33.3 mm. The teeth do not appear crowded along the tooth row as they are in the short-nosed dog (Olsen 1968:36).

Taxidea taxus (Badger)

Taxidea taxus is represented by a partial squamosal including the glenoid fossa. The species is a burrowing form and may be intrusive. Badger probably was of little importance to the food economy and may have been sought for its skin as much as for its meat.

Lynx rufus (Bobcat)

Lynx rufus is represented by one fibula, one ulna, and one partial pelvis. The three elements were collected during stripping of the mound and may not be contemporaneous with Hohokam occupation of the site.

Artiodactyla

Odocoileus spp. (Mule Deer and White-tailed Deer)

Odocoileus spp. are represented by isolated teeth, and postcranial elements that include the following: partial femora, pelvis, metapodials, and phalanges.

None of the deer elements are complete enough to be assignable with certainty to either of the two species found in Arizona; Odocoileus hemionus (mule deer), and O. virginianus (white-tailed deer). In general, the mule deer is larger than the white-tailed deer in Arizona. However, without relatively complete pelvis or frontal bones, it usually is not possible to discriminate between a small female mule deer and a large male white-tailed deer. Since they represented 21.7 percent of the potential meat resource, deer undoubtedly were an important source of food. Although no butcher marks were observed, 60 percent of the deer bones showed evidence of having been burned. Only 10 percent of the jackrabbit bones were burned. A chi-squared test applied to the jackrabbit and deer samples indicated that the difference was not due to sampling error (significant at the .005 level). It is possible that the burning was caused by roasting meat without removing the bones. The condition may also have resulted from burning garbage, or from banking fires with midden material, as has been suggested by Parmalee (1972:48) for a site in Illinois.

Antilocapra americana (Prong-horned Antelope)

Antilocapra americana is represented by one complete phalanx and one complete calcaneum. Antelope are not found in the Phoenix area today, but probably would be were it not for human interference (Lowe 1964).

Ovis canadensis (Bighorn Sheep)

Ovis canadensis is represented by 11 phalanges, one partial horn core, and one metapodial.

Bighorn sheep were probably found primarily in mountainous areas. However, sheep move readily from one mountain range to another (Russo 1956:31) and may have been hunted in the intervening desert areas as well as in the mountains. The species is represented largely by foot bones, suggesting that the kill sites were not in the vicinity of the village. The metapodial probably was cut during a tool making procedure rather than during butchering. Approximately the same proportion of sheep and Canis sp. bones were burned-- 18 percent and 20 percent, respectively. These percentages are approximately one-third that of burned deer bone. Chi-squared tests indicated that the differences are not due to sampling error (significant at the .01 and .005 levels respectively).

Bison bison (Bison)

Bison is represented by the proximal one-third of a left tibia and by a pelvis fragment which includes the acetabulum. Based upon size, the tibia is from a female and the pelvis from a male. Both specimens are from the floor fill of rooms, and it is highly improbable that they are intrusive. The two rooms were not occupied contemporaneously: they have been tentatively dated at A.D. 1200 and A.D. 1380. Subfossil bison remains have been found in a number of sites in Arizona and Western New Mexico (Figure 143). The few historic documents that mention the presence of bison west of the Rio Grande Valley are based upon circumstantial evidence. Bancroft (1889) stated that Apache in Arizona were trading for buffalo hides from a people located seven days journey northward from the Gila River when they were visited by Vildosola's expedition in 1758. Roe (1970:275) believes that the source for the hides may have been an area called Mesa la Vaca north of Winslow, Arizona. However, the people living in the area may have been middlemen in the trading operation who received their hides from people to the east. There is no evidence that Mesa la Vaca was named for the presence of bison rather than cattle. The Cosgroves (1932:4) stated that they were told by a woman who had been a resident of Las Cruces, New Mexico from 1871 to 1874 that "One night a half grown buffalo calf came in with our herd of cows."

Coues (1867:540) stated, "There is abundant evidence that the Buffalo (Bos americanus) formerly ranged over Arizona, though none exist there now." However, Coues does not cite any evidence and in correspondence (1875) could not substantiate the statement (Roe 1970:275).

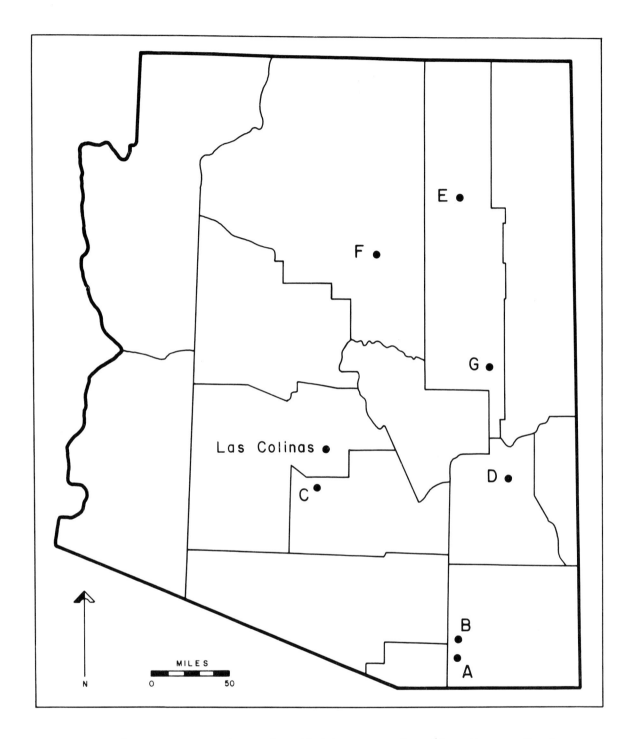

Figure 143. Sites with subfossil bison remains (A = Murray Springs,
B = Babocomari, C = Snaketown, D = Point of Pines,
E = Awatovi, F = Ridge Ruin, G = Bear Ruin)

It is possible that the early explorers in Arizona saw bison but did not record it in their journals. This seems unlikely, since bison sightings were commonly recorded by travelers in New Mexico (Bancroft 1889). Therefore, bison must either have been limited in numbers and restricted in distribution in Arizona, or some cultural mechanism (such as trade or hunting expeditions) must be postulated to explain the presence of their subfossil remains. Reed (1955) supported the latter view and implied that the "quantity and condition" of the bones were an index of the proximity of bison range. The author argues that the part of the skeleton remaining is at least as important as the quantity and condition of the bone. Not all skeletal elements of bison were equally useful; because bison bones are relatively heavy, it seems reasonable to assume that only those skeletal elements that were of greatest value would have been carried long distances. Generally, there is an inverse relationship between an animal's size and the number of bones by which it is represented in an archaeological site (called the Shlepp effect by Daly, 1969).

It is unlikely that the bison radius and pelvis found at Las Colinas were trade items. The historic Plains tribes processed radii to recover the marrow and occasionally used them for making tools (Wheat 1972:102, 103). The pelves, although customarily left at the kill site, were sometimes broken and used as "paint brushes" (Wheat 1972:102, 116). However, these elements probably were not traded as food items and any tools made from them could have been made from locally available materials. The radius showed no signs of having been cut before breakage, but instead looked as though it had been smashed.

Haury (1937:157) recorded elements of six bison recovered from Snaketown (Figure 143, c) including the following: four horn cores, one first lower molar, ear bones, and the end of a humerus. Concerning the head of bison, Haury (1937:157) made the following suggestion:

> it is possible that this part of the animal may have had some special significance to the Hohokam, not unlike the bison horns used today on certain masks of the Hopi. Whether they were actually used for food is an open question, but the presence of a humerus bone suggests the possibility. In this event, the bison must have ranged within one or two days journey of Snaketown.

Wheat (1972:102), in a detailed summary of bison hunting and butchering techniques of the historic Plains tribes, stated that almost invariably the skull was left at the scene of the kill:

> Horns, however were often removed to be used in a variety of ways: to make spoons, drinking vessels and even bows. Horns were also used as containers by the Blackfoot, in which to carry fire from one camp to another. Grinnell was told by his Cheyenne informants that they had a place where they piled up the horn sheaths after a kill.

The interest to the Plains tribes and apparently to the Hopi was in the horn sheaths and not the cores. If the Hohokam were primarily interested in the horn sheaths, it does not seem likely that traders would have bothered to carry the heavier horn cores as well.

Many historic tribes used bison brains as food and for curing hides (Wheat 1972; Oswalt 1966). It may be that the skull elements recovered at Snaketown were those of animals killed close enough to the village that it was convenient to carry in the skulls complete with the horn sheaths and brains. The recovery of ear bones suggests that at least an entire skull was present.

Sites in the Point of Pines area that have contained bison remains include AZ W:10:47, AZ W:10:50 (Stein 1962) and AZ W:9:69 (Gifford 1957). The sites have been given the dates that follow: A.D. 1400-1450; A.D. 1325-1400; and A.D. 900-1400, respectively. The first two sites contained bison vertebrae as well as other elements. The presence of vertebrae--which were not useful as tools, but were sometimes used to make bone grease--suggests that the kill site was not distant.

DiPeso (1951) reported the recovery of bison from the Babocomari Village site in southeastern Arizona (Figure 143, b). He stated:

> Hunting also played a most important role in their subsistence pattern as evidenced by the numerous outdoor cooking ovens filled with quantities of animal bones. It was most surprising to find that bison, commonly believed to inhabit the plains west of the Pecos River in New Mexico, were present in the upper reaches of the San Pedro River Valley during the occupation of the Babocomari Village. Their bones were very common in the trash fill of the cooking ovens, as well as in a single large ceremonial cache located in association with cremation area 5 (Di Peso 1951:240).

In the same report (DiPeso 1951:207) is a photograph of a pit containing the skull, leg bones, and ribs of a bison, with the comment that "some...show evidence of being burned, cracked, and painted." Assuming the species identification is correct (the analysis was done by Dr. W. H. Burt of the Museum of Zoology, University of Michigan), it seems highly probable that at least some of the bison present in the site were killed locally. The Babocomari site was occupied from A.D. 1200 to A.D. 1450 (DiPeso 1951).

A complete skeleton of a juvenile female Bison bison that was apparently pregnant at the time of death was discovered in the alluvium of the San Pedro River in southeastern Arizona near the Murray Springs Paleo-Indian site (Figure 143, a). Bruce Huckell has informed me that a Carbon-14 date and stratigraphic evidence indicate a date of approximately A.D. 1600. These data suggest there was a breeding population of bison in the region.

Bison remains represented at least 65 percent of the 1600 identifiable bones recovered from Bat Cave, located in the bluffs bordering the Plains of San Augustin in southwestern New Mexico (Dick 1965). Approximately 90 percent of the bison elements were found in midden levels I and II with dates indicating occupation during the first few centuries A.D. Dick suggested the bison were killed near the cave, and commented: "It is possible that the bison were driven into the cave area and trapped against the cliffs if not in the main chamber of the cave itself, especially during periods of heavy snow cover." Smith (1950:177-178), in an analysis of the plant remains from Bat Cave, stated: "Remains of plants requiring a permanent body of shallow water (Typha latifolia, Scirpus olneyi and Scirpus validus) indicates a higher amount of precipitation than at present for the time represented by level II and possibly for level III."

The lower jaw of a bison was recovered at Bear Ruin in east-central Arizona (Figure 143, g) with tree-ring dates of about A.D. 650 (Haury 1940). Haury stated: "It does not seem probable that this part of the animal would have been brought in to the village from far away and the evidence thus suggests that the bison ranged within striking distance of the Forestdale hunters."

The presence of bison in the Winona and Ridge Ruin (McGregor 1941) is problematical; although the identification was corroborated by a specialist, the genus listed for bison is Bos--the genus of cattle--which includes the animals most easily confused with bison. However in the text, the term bison was used. The skeletal elements identified were not given, but one individual was represented. Tree-ring dates from the Winona and Ridge Ruin indicate that the site was occupied about A.D. 1077-1173 (McGregor 1941).

Bison bones have been recovered from several other Southwestern sites: Mogollon Village, A.D. 700-900 (Haury 1936); Swartz Ruin, A.D. 950-1150 (Cosgrove and Cosgrove 1932); Hawikuh (Hodge 1920; Smith 1966:231); Chetro Ketl, A.D. 945-1116 (Hawley 1934:21; Brand and others 1937); Mesa Verde, Site 34 (O'Bryan 1950); and Awatovi (Lawrence 1951). Only at the Hawikuh site was bison represented by more than a few elements, including ribs and pelves. Unfortunately, the age of the bison material was not clearly stated in the reports and the site was occupied for many centuries.

If the presence of bison in the sites discussed above was not the result of trade or long distance hunting trips, then geographical range extensions of the species at certain times must be explained.

The range of an animal is a dynamic phenomenon that fluctuates constantly through time. The reason for this is that the interrelated physiographic, biological, and climatic factors which limit an animal to a certain area are not constant (Cockrum 1962:50-57). The exact reason why an animal is restricted to a certain range is difficult to determine and may never be determined for bison because the species is essentially extinct in the wild state. However, it is certain that climatic factors played an important role --either directly or indirectly--in establishing the limits of the species' range. It may be that the moisture and temperature conditions during most of the past 1000 years in Arizona have been too severe to support populations of bison. The dryness may have had two important consequences: dry conditions cause a lowering of the water table which reduces the number of streams with perennial flow, and the number of springs available for water supply; low rainfall results in sparse grass cover, which may be less than the minimum required to sustain bison from year to year. High summer temperatures combined with the above conditions probably created an environment that exceeded the physiological tolerances of bison. Thus, environmental factors which increased the effective moisture, and decreased the average summer temperature, would have been conducive to a range extension of bison. However, the change to cooler and wetter conditions had to continue for a long enough period that the vegetation and water table would be significantly altered. These changes might have required a decade or more, depending upon the magnitude of the change.

Recent advances in multivariate analysis and the availability of computers have resulted in new techniques for analyzing the relationship between tree growth and climate (Fritts and others 1971). These studies have made it possible to reconstruct variations in paleoclimate with relative precision based upon an analysis of tree rings. Since A.D. 1000, there have been eight periods during which the climate of the Southwest has been significantly cooler and/or moister: 1110-1129 (Robinson and Dean 1969); around 1200 and 1300-1400 (Dean and Robinson, in press); 1611-1625, 1641-1650, 1741-1755, 1826-1840, 1906-1920 (Fritts 1965). The moist periods most widespread and markedly above average were as follows: A.D. 1300-1400, A.D. 1611-1625, and A.D. 1906-1920.

Pollen analyses by Schoenwetter (1962) and Martin (1963) do not seem to corroborate the above hypothesized environmental changes, probably because most of the fluctuations are too short to be detected by present techniques. However, the pollen record does indicate that environmental shifts occurred. Schoenwetter (1962:196) suggests that during the period A.D. 1200-1350, "standing water must have been more common than it is today" in eastern Arizona and western New Mexico.

The author hypothesizes that bison were ranging into Arizona only during the periods of widespread above average moisture. After each moist period, the range of this species again contracted. There probably was a lag time of several years between the onset of wetter conditions and the appearance of bison in the state. Consequently, the periods of increased moisture and expansion of bison range do not coincide precisely. The dates of most of the sites containing bison after A.D. 1000 support this hypothesis, especially when allowance is made for small errors in dating. The author does not maintain that the time correlation has been generally established, but only that it is a possibility warranting further investigation.

The two bison recovered from Las Colinas represented 48 percent of the potential meat resource of the Hohokam inhabitants. This figure is probably misleading, since the two individuals were killed within a 270-year period of intermittent occupation. However, even if bison is under-represented in the archaeo-fauna, it may be that at certain times the species was an important animal food resource.

Modern Domestic Animals

Two skulls and one pelvis of domestic cat (Felis cattus) and one mandible, one ulna, and one humerus of domestic pig (Sus scrofa) were recovered from Las Colinas. All elements came from stripping and trenching operations around the mound, and from a retaining cell located in the center of the historic barn floor.

Summary and Discussion

The following observations may be made about the fauna as a whole.

1) Basing an estimate of the absolute size of a population occupying a site on an analysis of refuse is highly problematical (Guilday 1970).

However, if the relative abundance of animal remains may be taken as an indication of the relative size of the population at different periods, we can conclude that the population of Las Colinas fluctuated widely. Population was greatest during the middle Soho phase and least during late Soho (Figure 144). Table 76 presents a summary of the location by feature of the individual mammals recovered from the site.

2) The relatively small amount of meat represented by the animals recovered suggests that animals were supplemental to plants in the food economy.

3) Mammals predominated as the most important of the animal food resources. Deer and bighorn sheep were hunted primarily in the mountains that surround the area. Rabbits were probably plentiful within the vicinity of the village.

4) Rabbits, though they represented only 8.8 percent of the total meat resource, may have been the most enduring source of animal protein.

5) No muskrat, beaver, or otter remains were identified, suggesting that the mammalian fauna of the nearby Salt River was not exploited significantly.

6) There was no evidence for seasonal occupation of Las Colinas.

7) The inhabitants had a relatively large form of dog. Burned canid bones suggest some dogs or coyotes were eaten.

8) No butcher marks were observed on bones of any species.

9) A significantly larger proportion of deer bones were burned than those of other species. Perhaps this fact reflects different cooking techniques.

10) Except for bison, all species and genera in the fauna would be found in the Las Colinas (Phoenix) area today were it not for human interference. Therefore, no general climatic change is indicated.

11) Bison may have ranged within the immediate vicinity of Las Colinas around A.D. 1200, and between A.D. 1300-1400. Conditions of increased moisture at these times allowed bison to migrate into Arizona from New Mexico, and Sonora, Mexico. Combining the relative number of bison remains in Southwestern sites with details of the physiography and ecology of the region, it appears probable that bison were most abundant and remained longest in the southeastern part of Arizona.

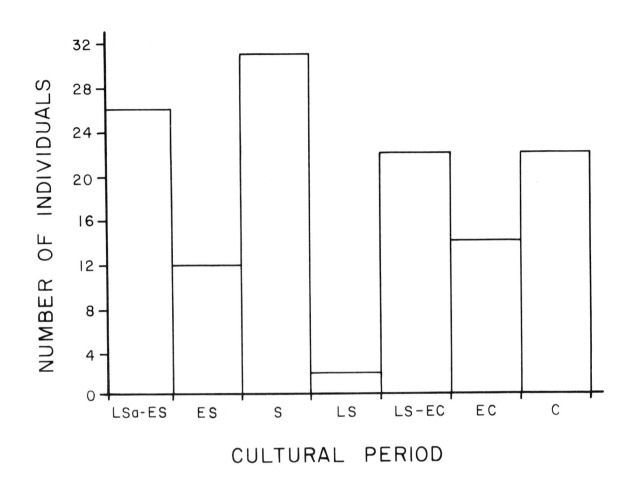

Figure 144. Population fluctuations at Las Colinas as indicated
by relative abundance of animal remains (L = Late,
E = Early, Sa = Sacaton, S = Soho, C = Civano)

285

Table 76. Distribution of individual mammals in the Las Colinas site by cultural feature

Species	Feature											
	0	1	2	3	4	5	8	9	10	11	12	13
Jackrabbit	1	1	1	1	1	2	1	1	5	1	-	2
Cottontail rabbit	-	-	2	1	1	1	-	-	-	1	1	-
Ground squirrel	-	-	-	-	-	-	-	-	-	-	-	-
Pocket gopher	-	-	-	-	-	1	-	-	1	-	-	-
Pocket mouse	-	-	-	-	-	-	-	-	-	-	-	-
Kangaroo rat	-	-	-	-	-	-	-	-	-	-	-	-
Cotton rat	-	-	-	-	-	-	-	-	-	-	-	-
Wood rat	-	-	-	-	-	-	-	-	-	-	-	-
Dog and coyote	-	-	-	1	-	1	-	-	-	-	-	-
Dog	-	-	-	-	-	-	-	-	-	-	-	-
Badger	-	-	-	-	-	-	-	-	-	-	-	-
Bobcat	-	-	1	-	-	-	-	-	-	-	-	-
Deer	-	-	-	-	-	-	-	-	-	-	-	-
Antelope	-	-	-	-	-	-	-	-	-	-	-	-
Bighorn	-	-	-	-	-	1	-	-	-	-	-	-
Bison	-	-	-	-	-	-	-	-	-	-	-	-
Total	1	1	4	3	2	6	1	1	6	2	1	2

Table 76. (continued)

Species	Features											
	14	17	19	20	21	23	24	26	33	40	45	47
Jackrabbit	-	1	1	1	2	1	1	-	1	1	3	-
Cottontail rabbit	1	-	2	-	2	-	-	1	-	1	1	-
Ground squirrel	-	-	-	-	1	-	-	-	-	1	-	-
Pocket gopher	-	-	1	-	1	-	-	-	-	1	-	-
Pocket mouse	-	-	-	-	1	-	-	-	-	-	-	-
Kangaroo rat	-	-	-	-	-	-	-	-	-	-	-	-
Cotton rat	-	-	-	-	-	-	-	-	-	-	2	-
Wood rat	-	-	-	-	1	-	-	-	-	-	-	-
Dog and coyote	-	-	-	-	-	-	-	-	1	-	-	-
Dog	-	-	-	-	-	-	-	-	-	-	-	-
Badger	-	-	-	-	-	-	-	-	-	-	-	-
Bobcat	-	-	-	-	-	-	-	-	-	-	-	-
Deer	-	-	-	-	1	-	-	-	-	-	-	1
Antelope	-	-	1	-	-	-	-	-	-	-	-	-
Bighorn	-	-	2	-	-	-	-	-	1	-	-	-
Bison	-	-	-	-	-	-	-	-	-	-	-	-
Total	1	1	7	1	9	1	1	1	3	4	6	1

Table 76. (continued)

Species	Features											
	48	49	51	54	55	56	57	58	59	61	62	63
Jackrabbit	2	5	1	1	1	1	1	-	1	2	6	1
Cottontail rabbit	1	3	1	-	-	-	1	-	-	-	6	1
Ground squirrel	-	1	-	-	-	-	-	1	-	-	3	-
Pocket gopher	-	1	-	-	-	-	-	-	-	-	1	-
Pocket mouse	-	2	-	-	-	-	-	-	-	-	-	-
Kangaroo rat	-	-	-	-	-	-	-	-	-	-	-	-
Cotton rat	-	1	-	-	-	-	-	-	-	-	2	-
Wood rat	-	-	-	-	-	-	-	-	-	-	-	-
Dog and coyote	-	1	-	-	-	-	-	-	-	-	-	1
Dog	-	-	-	-	-	-	-	-	-	-	-	-
Badger	-	1	-	-	-	-	-	-	-	-	-	-
Bobcat	-	-	-	-	-	-	-	-	-	-	-	-
Deer	-	-	-	-	-	-	-	-	-	-	1	-
Antelope	-	-	-	-	-	-	-	-	-	-	-	-
Bighorn	-	-	-	-	-	-	-	-	-	-	1	-
Bison	-	-	-	-	-	-	-	-	-	-	-	-
Total	3	15	2	1	1	1	2	1	1	2	20	3

Table 76 . (continued)

Species	Feature 65	71	72	75	77	80	82	83	90	94	100	103
Jackrabbit	4	1	1	1	1	1	-	1	-	1	2	1
Cottontail rabbit	2	1	1	-	-	-	1	1	1	1	2	-
Ground squirrel	-	-	-	-	-	-	1	-	-	1	-	-
Pocket gopher	-	-	1	-	-	-	1	-	-	-	-	-
Pocket mouse	-	-	-	-	-	-	-	-	-	-	-	-
Kangaroo rat	-	-	-	-	-	-	-	-	-	-	-	-
Cotton rat	-	-	-	-	-	-	-	-	-	-	-	-
Wood rat	1	-	-	-	-	-	-	-	-	-	-	-
Dog and coyote	1	-	-	-	-	-	-	1	-	-	-	-
Dog	-	-	-	-	-	-	-	-	-	-	-	-
Badger	-	-	-	-	-	-	-	-	-	-	-	-
Bobcat	-	-	-	-	-	-	-	-	-	-	-	-
Deer	-	-	1	-	-	-	-	1	-	-	1	-
Antelope	-	-	-	-	-	-	-	-	-	-	-	-
Bighorn	-	-	-	-	-	-	-	-	-	-	-	-
Bison	-	-	-	-	-	-	-	-	-	-	-	-
Total	8	2	4	1	1	1	3	4	1	3	5	1

Table 76.   (continued)

Species	Features								Total
	106	107	112	114	115	116	119	B-7	
Jackrabbit	-	1	-	-	1	1	-	1	69
Cottontail rabbit	-	-	2	-	1	-	-	-	41
Ground squirrel	-	-	1	-	-	-	1	-	11
Pocket gopher	-	-	-	-	-	-	-	-	9
Pocket mouse	-	-	-	-	-	-	-	-	3
Kangaroo rat	-	-	-	-	-	-	-	-	0?
Cotton rat	-	-	-	-	-	-	-	-	5
Wood rat	-	-	-	-	-	-	-	-	2
Dog and coyote	-	1	-	-	-	-	-	-	8
Dog	1	-	-	-	-	-	-	-	1
Badger	-	-	-	-	-	-	-	-	1
Bobcat	-	-	-	-	-	-	-	-	1
Deer	-	-	-	-	-	-	-	-	6
Antelope	-	-	-	-	-	-	-	-	1
Bighorn	-	-	-	-	-	-	-	-	5
Bison	-	-	-	1	-	1	-	-	2
Total	1	2	3	1	2	2	1	1	165*

*Does not include eight specimens of unknown provenience.

APPENDIX D

BONE ARTIFACTS FROM LAS COLINAS

by Sandra Olsen*
Arizona State Museum
University of Arizona

Introduction

Only eleven bone artifacts were recovered during the excavations at Las Colinas. Four types of artifacts are represented: a tubular bead, a needle, splinter awls, and hairpins.

Artifacts Recovered

Tubular Bead

The tubular bead (Figure 145, a) was manufactured from the left femur of a kit fox, Vulpes macrotis. The articular ends of the femoral shaft were removed by the "groove and snap" technique. Annular grooves were made at both ends of the bone to a sufficient depth that pressure of the hand could snap the bone apart along the scored line. Transverse scratches created by the scoring tool are still visible near both ends. The ends of the bead were ground smooth with a piece of sandstone. The entire external surface of the bead has been abraded, perhaps to prepare it for polishing.

This bead was recovered from Level 11 of the area delineated by the massive adobe walls, and below the historic house foundation. The bead measures 39 mm in length and 6 mm in diameter.

Needle Fragment

The needle fragment (Figure 145, b) consists of the basal half of a long thin implement, drilled 19 mm from the rounded end. The unusual cross-section of this finely manufactured tool is D-shaped, with one side planed completely flat.

None of the manufacturing marks remain, and the edges and the convex side show considerable polish from handling. The piece was undoubtedly shaped by scoring two tapering grooves along a limb bone of a large mammal. After the rough preform was removed from the whole bone, it was probably smoothed and shaped into its final form by abrasion.

---

*Draft completed: April 1979

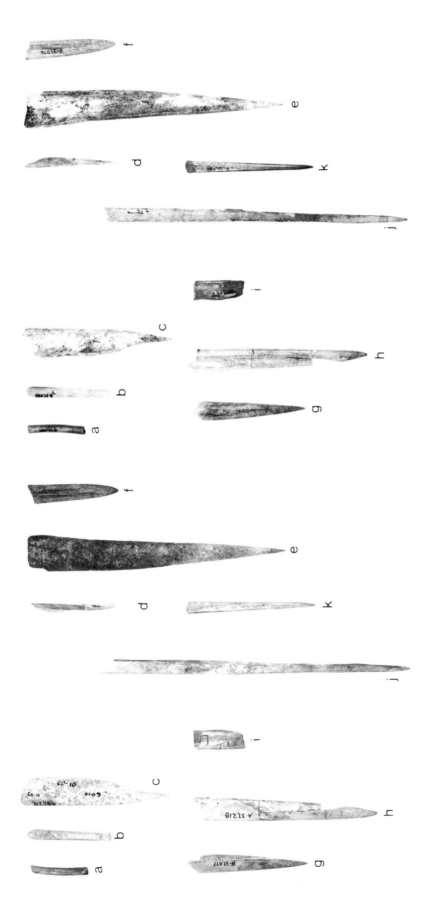

Figure 145. Bone artifacts from Las Colinas: exterior (left) and interior (right) views. Length of a is 4 cm

The needle fragment came from the upper fill of the area delineated by the massive adobe walls, below the historic house foundation. Its present length is 57 mm, but its total length, inferred from the angle of the tapering sides, would have been approximately 100 to 120 mm. The width of the base is 7 mm.

Splinter Awls

Two splinter awls made from fragments of mammal long bones were recovered at Las Colinas. The larger of the two (Figure 145, c) was made from the radius or femur of a large mammal. The only alteration of the splinter was the creation of a fine point at one end. This was accomplished by a few strokes with an abrader. The sharp point is round in cross-section, and very slightly polished from use. The awl was recovered from the lower fill of Feature 60. It measures 99 mm in length, 19 mm in width, and 1.3 mm in diameter at the tip. Measurements of the diameters of awl and hairpin tips were taken 1 mm from the end for consistency.

The smaller splinter awl (Figure 145, d) was made from a fragment of a large mammal long bone, and was sharpened to a very fine point on one end. The sharp point is round in cross-section. The tip is highly polished from wear for a distance of 11 mm from the end. The presence of diagonal striae above this point is evidence that the bone was sharpened with a sandstone abrader. The raised areas of the tool's surface are polished from handling. This awl came from the level below the basement in Feature 45. It is 68 mm in length, 6 mm in width, and .8 mm in diameter at the tip.

Hairpins

Five of the bone artifacts from Las Colinas are best described as hairpins. These long, tapered implements are not typed as awls because the tips are stout and blunt, the shafts are generally longer and larger than those of most awls, and they have been deliberately polished over the entire surface. These distinctions are derived from a study comparing Mogollon awls and hairpins with ethnographic basketry awls (Olsen 1979).

One of these hairpins (Figure 145, e) is nearly complete and measures a full 168 mm in length. The width of the squared-off base is 24 mm and the flattened tip is 1.1 mm wide. Heavy surface damage from root etching has obliterated most of the evidence of manufacturing and polishing. The edges are slightly uneven and show some traces of abrasion near the tip. This hairpin was found in the area south of the cement pad that covers the well, and east of the main massive adobe wall.

There are three tip fragments (Figure 145, f, g, h) made from the metatarsals of artiodactyls. This is the most common type of hairpin known from the Southwest. The double condyle at the distal end of the metatarsal or metacarpal is usually retained and is often embellished with ornate carving. The proximal articular surface, and part of the shaft have been removed from two of the fragments (Figure 145, f, g). Each of these hairpins tapers from the handle (the distal end of the metatarsal) to a blunt point.

The shorter of the two (Figure 145, f) is 60 mm in length, is 2.5 mm in diameter at the tip, and was recovered from the area of Feature 17 in the lower section of the fill. The larger hairpin (Figure 145, g) is 78 mm in length and is 1.4 mm in diameter at the tip. The provenience of this artifact is uncertain.

The third tip fragment (Figure 145, h) is from a hairpin made by longitudinally bisecting the shaft along the vascular sulcus and along the centerline of the posterior surface. Either the proximal or distal end may be retained with hairpins of this sort, though often both articular surfaces have been removed. Since the base is missing, it is not possible to determine the style of this particular hairpin. Eleven diagonal intersecting lines are incised at the tip, apparently with decorative intent. This hairpin is 118 mm in length, is 2.2 mm in diameter at the tip, and was recovered from the general fill of Feature 3. All three of these hairpin fragments have polished surfaces and stout, blunt tips.

The fifth hairpin (Figure 145, i) was made from an unidentified long bone of a mammal. It is incised with two figures resembling the letter S. They face in opposite directions, and each is composed of five straight segments. This hairpin was made in the conventional manner of grooving and snapping, abrading the edges, and polishing the surfaces. The length of the fragment is 34 mm and its width is 13 mm. This piece came from Level III of the room below Feature 8, south of the barn.

Ambiguous: Awls or Hairpins

The last two bone artifacts (Figure 145, j, k) may have been used as either awls or hairpins. One (Figure 145, j) is 198 mm long but only 10 mm wide. The tip is rectangular and tapers to a point that is only 1.5 mm thick. Although the convex outer surface of the bone is highly polished, manufacturing marks are quite distinct. The edges still bear the longitudinal striations formed during the grooving process, as well as the irregular protuberances on the inner surface caused by breaking the bone at the grooves. Fine diagonal striations above the tip are indications that the edges were smoothed by abrasion. Normally this abrasion would have continued along the edges up to the broad end. This piece is unique in that it appears to have been polished on the convex outer surface prior to separation from the entire bone. The manufacturing marks and the rough edges were not smoothed, giving the impression that the tool was not finished. There is, however, limited wear polish at the tip, indicating that it may have served as an awl. Other features, such as the extreme length, surface polish, and flattened cross-section of the tip, would place it in the category of hairpins.

The other tip fragment (Figure 145, k) may have been either an awl or a hairpin. Although the entire surface is highly polished, the point, which is round in cross-section and very sharp, would have made it an excellent awl. Light handling polish over the broken surface of the shaft suggests that the object was used after breakage occurred.

The provenience of this tool was the fill below floor Level I, in the room below Feature 8. It measures 83 mm in length and about 1.3 mm in diameter at the tip.

Considering the quantity of pottery and lithic material collected from Las Colinas, bone artifacts are rare. Those that were recovered are common types that span hundreds of years of occupation in Arizona and connote no specific cultural affiliations.

APPENDIX E

AVIAN REMAINS FROM LAS COLINAS

by Amadeo M. Rea[*]
Natural History Museum
San Diego, California

Introduction

A mere double handful of bird bones was recovered from the Las Colinas site. Over two-thirds of the bones are of Eurasian origin, and are intrusive from the period of Anglo settlement of the lower Salt River Valley in the past century. Seventeen identifiable bird bones appear to be associated with the Hohokam occupation, in contrast with the more than nine hundred identifiable mammal bones that are believed to be prehistoric (see Johnson, this volume).

List of Species

Anatidae

Anas platyrhynchos

Domestic Mallard (complete femur). The specimen measures more than 64 mm and is far too massive for a wild male Mallard (maximum length 50.5 mm). Charmion R. McKusick, who has studied the osteology of domesticated fowl, has told me that this specimen is "like Rouen, not Pekin, not that domestic; male size range; not as meaty as modern Pekin; could be an earlier, lighter Pekin." A second specimen (distal end femur) is similar in characters and is referred to domestic Anas platyrhynchos.

Anser (Compare A. cygnoides)

Domestic Chinese Goose (humerus). The characters are different from those of large Branta canadensis races. A female-sized coracoid is larger than in male wild and domestic Anas platyrhynchos. The head has a different shape entirely from that of Cairina moschata. This also is referred to A. cygnoides.

_____

[*]Draft completed: May 1980.

Cairina moschata

Domestic Muscovie Duck (mandible, missing articular ends). This neotropical species has long been domesticated. The archaeological specimen matches the size of a very large, old domesticated male.

Psittacidae

Ara macao

Scarlet Macaw (humerus, head damaged). The specimen was taken from above the cap of the mound. Two species of macaws were brought into the Southwest in prehistoric times (Hargrave 1970), so correct species determination is critical. The bicipital crest (usual diagnostic feature separating A. macao from A. militaris, the Military Macaw; see Hargrave 1970:13-14) was completely excised during excavation. From the curvature of the shaft below the bicipital crest, it appears to have been shaped as in A. macao. Separation was made on the basis of the small attachment of the anterior ligament

Table 77. Comparison of anterior ligaments of A. militaris and A. macao

Species	Sex	Collection	Measurements
A. militaris	F	U of A	5.4 mm x 3.5 mm
A. militaris	M	U of A	5.85 mm x 4.0 mm
A. macao	F	L. Hargrave	4.4 mm x 3.15 mm
A. macao	-	L. Hargrave	4.5 mm x 3.15 mm
Las Colinas 4-24	-	-	4.3 mm x 3.05 mm

(see Table 77). Though the Scarlet Macaw ranges farther south in Mexico than does the Military Macaw, the majority of macaws recovered from archaeological sites in the Southwest belong to the former group (Hargrave 1970; Rea 1980).

Phasianidae

Meleagris gallopavo

Common Turkey (coracoid, missing sternal articulatory end). It is probable that all prehistoric turkeys were brought into the Southwest by agricultural peoples, as the Pleistocene species found broadly throughout the Southwest is the entirely unrelated species M. crassipes (Rea 1980). At least two breeds were imported, the Small Indian Domestic and the Large Indian Domestic (McKusick 1974; McKusick 1980). The latter is thought to have become feral and to have given rise to the present local subspecies M. g. merriami, a large, white-rumped race. The prehistoric bone is smaller than in the domestic turkey and is smaller even than in wild females of M. g. merriami taken in Arizona mountains. It appears to represent a female Small Indian Domestic (see Figure 146). It is distinguishable from M. crassipes, the Pleistocene species, by the configuration of the head (Rea 1980). In addition, M. crassipes is distinguished from the modern species by its thicker sternal facet, shape of coraco-humeral surface, blunt procoracoid, more oval scapular facet, and overall more blunt, compact configuration of the head. In all these characters the Small Indian Domestic agrees with M. gallopavo, but is smaller than the wild population. Modern domestic breeds are larger and heavier than the wild ones. Turkeys occur rarely in Hohokam archaeological sites, and many of the supposed turkey bones reported from earlier excavations have now been lost. Few zooarchaeologists appear to appreciate the similarities between the bones of turkey and Sandhill Crane, Grus canadensis (Hargrave and Emslie 1979).

The coracoid was compared with those of M. crassipes, wild M. g. merriami, Centrocercus urophasianus (Sage grouse), and Gallus gallus. Measurements are: width across triosseal canal 9.3 mm, width across scapular facet 12.55 mm, and depth of shaft 7.5 mm.

Callipepla (Lophortyx) gambelii

Gambel's Quail (five humeri, one femur, all from different proveniences). The femur (37.8 mm long) is mature but is the minimum size for modern Phoenix area females. The humerus (33.05 mm long) is smaller than in four modern Gila River Indian Reservation females (33.7 mm to 34.5 mm) but matches those of three females from the Tucson area. The species occurs commonly in brushy Lower Sonoran Desert areas and probably its numbers were increased by aboriginal farming methods in the Salt River and Gila River valleys (Rea 1979).

Gallus gallus

Domestic Chicken (ten elements, five from the same provenience). All the chicken bones, with one possible exception (see Appendix J), were taken outside any Hohokam features and are certainly intrusive from the overlying farm, as are bones of the other barnyard birds.

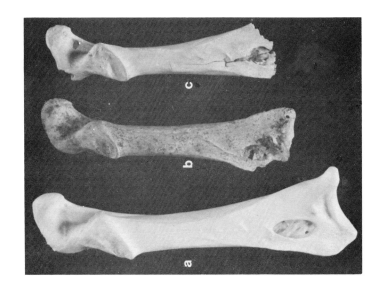

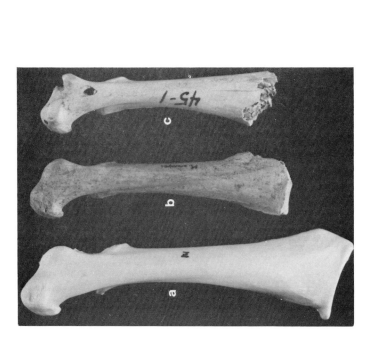

Figure 146. Coracoids of wild female turkey (a), extinct Pleistocene turkey (b), and Las Colinas domestic turkey (c); ventral (left) and dorsal (right) views

Accipitridae

Buteo (compare B. jamaicensis)

Red-tailed Hawk (two unguals, one partial sternum; each from different proveniences within the site). These bones are too large and heavy for B. swainsoni (Swainson's Hawk), or Parabuteo unicinctus (Harris' Hawk). The elements are not diagnostic, however, and might represent some other large buteonine hawk. They are referred to this species because it is widespread in the Sonoran Desert and appears frequently in Hohokam sites.

Parabuteo unicinctus

Harris' Hawk (ungual, blackened). This might also be Buteo swainsoni on the basis of size. However, the toe bone is relatively slender both laterally and in its basal articulation, therefore excluding the more massive buteonine species such as B. jamaicensis. It differs in characters from Buteogallus anthracinus (Black Hawk), a Sonoran Desert riparian species that might be expected in Hohokam sites.

Cuculidae

Geococcyx californicus

Greater Roadrunner (distal end of tarsometatarsus). Whether this species was captured for ceremonial or utilitarian purposes cannot be determined, but the bone was recovered from part of the mound that yielded the Scarlet Macaw (as well as intrusive duck and chicken). Roadrunner tail feathers in particular are used ceremonially by a number of Pueblo tribes. Historic Pima tabooed this bird, which figures in a number of their narrations (Rea, in press; Bahr and others, 1974).

Corvidae

Corvus corax

Common Raven (two femora, proximal one-third of ulna). The two femora, though from separate but superimposed Civano phase features within the site, match perfectly and are certainly from the same bird. The complete femur measures 66.7 mm, within the size range of modern C. c. sinuatus, the race inhabiting most of the interior of North America. The largest male C. c. clarionensis of coastal California is 63.5 mm, the smallest female C. c. principalis of mainland Alaska is 69.2 mm. The ulna has a remarkably short olecranon, but is too large for Corvus cryptoleucus, the other raven species inhabiting the Southwest. The length of the external cotyla, parallel to the shaft, is 5.9 mm, compared to 5.8 mm for the smallest of 15 C. c. sinuatus and 4.8 mm for the largest of 11 C. cryptoleucus. There are ethnographic references (Rea 1977) to a second, colonial corvid in the Riverine Pima country (Salt-Gila valley). It is to be hoped that some archaeological site may solve the question of whether this was C. brachyrhynchos or C. cryptoleucus. So far, only the Common Raven has been reliably reported from Hohokam sites.

Icteridae

Xanthocephalus xanthocephalus

Yellow-headed Blackbird (humerus, missing distal articulation). This icterid is quite dimorphic in size and the archaeological specimen is in the size range of males.

Discussion

Occasionally an attempt is made to argue for a pre-Columbian distribution in the New World or even the Southwest of the chicken, or domesticated form of the Asian Red Junglefowl, Gallus gallus (Carter 1971). The Las Colinas site was overlaid with a historic farm, and the domestic birds (Muscovie, Chinese Goose, Mallard, chicken) as well as the domestic mammals (domestic cat, domestic pig: see Johnson this volume) are simply intrusive. I have also identified chicken bones together with the domestic barnyard pigeon or European Rock Dove, Columbia livia, from Pueblo Grande ruins, Phoenix, a site contemporaneous with Las Colinas. Extreme caution must be exercised in interpreting the presence of Eurasian domesticates in prehistoric sites that have been subsequently inhabited by Europeans (Hargrave 1972:6-14; Hamblin and Rea 1979:31).

The turkey bone might also be considered intrusive except for the fact that it is not only smaller than the bones of heavy-bodied domestic breeds, but even smaller than the bones of the female of the wild subspecies (Merriam's Turkey) from local mountains. The remaining avian bones recovered at Las Colinas are typical of almost every Hohokam site. Except for the Scarlet Macaw, a common trade item, and the Small Indian Doemstic Turkey, undoubtedly Salado in origin, the birds are characteristics of the ecology of the area before the destruction of the watersheds and drying of Arizona rivers.

APPENDIX F

THE LAS COLINAS SHELL ASSEMBLAGE

by Sharon F. Urban*
Arizona State Museum
University of Arizona

Introduction

Shell from prehistoric sites has often received inadequate consideration in final excavation reports. This may in part be due to the small size of the shell assemblage from many sites. The Hohokam, however, were accomplished workers with shell and used large quantities of shell as raw material. Although shell working is known from Hohokam sites dating back as far as 300 B.C., shell utilization and manipulation burgeoned in the Santa Cruz and Sacaton phases (A.D. 700 to A.D. 1100). In Classic period sites (A.D. 1150 to A.D. 1450) shell continues to be abundant, although there are some changes, the details of which are discussed in this report.

At the end of this chapter is a list, by artifact type, of the total number of shell items found in each feature at Las Colinas (Table 79). Most of the shell artifacts from the site were recovered from three trash-filled retaining cells: Features 45, 49, and 62. The material used for the fill was most likely obtained from nearby trash mounds. Since much of the material comes from the retaining cells, it is not possible to document changes in the shell assemblage.

Haury (1976) has suggested that the origin of the Hohokam shell tradition may be found in the Río Balsas area of Guerrero, Mexico (Figure 147). There, a developed shell industry existed prior to the arrival of Hohokam peoples in the Southwest. It is possible that the shell tradition of the Río Balsas area may have formed part of the foundation of Hohokam shell working. The origin of the Hohokam shell industry is a special problem in itself and will only be commented on here. The inhabitants of Las Colinas either traded for their shell, or obtained it directly from the Gulf of California or the Pacific coast. Perhaps as a result of exploiting several sources, a relatively large number of species is represented in the Las Colinas collection. Characteristics of these species are discussed below, as are aspects of the shell industry at Las Colinas.

Species Identification

Seventeen marine species and three freshwater species were identified in the collection of shell from Las Colinas. Marine species were probably obtained for raw material rather than as a source of

*Draft completed: August 1973

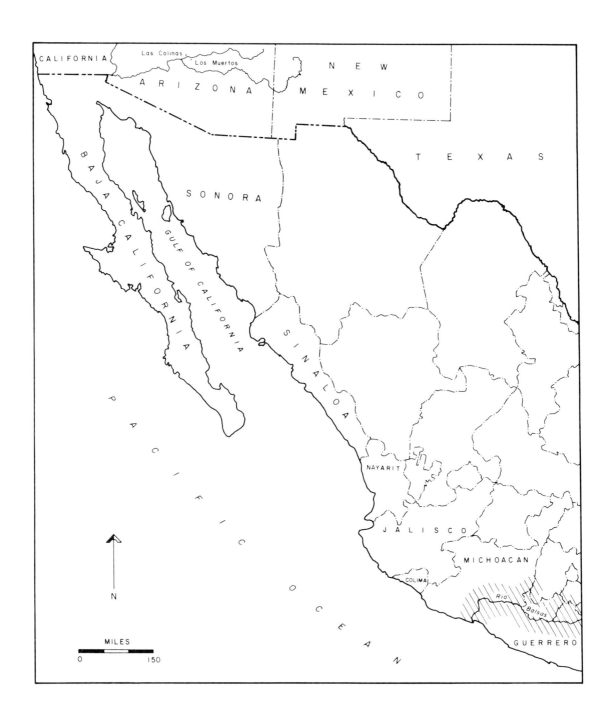

Figure 147. Origin of Hohokam shell industry (hatching)

food, although at least four of the marine species found at Las Colinas are edible (as is one of the freshwater species). All these marine species can be found in the Gulf of California (Figure 148) except Haliotis or abalone, which is only found on the Pacific coast. The Pteria (winged oyster) and the Laevicardium may be found either on the Pacific coast or in the Gulf of California.

One of the snail forms is a terrestrial gastropod that lives in decaying vegetation. The remaining species inhabit a riverine environment and were known to inhabit the Gila when it was a free-flowing waterway. The shell species identified at the site are presented in Table 78.

It should be noted that Anodonta is an edible freshwater clam. Presumably this species was gathered primarily as a food resource, and the utilization of its shell was of only secondary importance. This particular shell is highly nacreous and extremely fragile, making it most difficult to work. However, it was used to a limited extent by the inhabitants of Las Colinas.

Unworked Raw Material

The term "raw material" is used to designate whole shells or significant fragments of larger shells--such as those of the bivalves Laevicardium and Glycymeris - that exhibit no intentional modification from grinding, cutting, polishing or allied processes.

Whole Shell

This category is represented by three species: Laevicardium, Olivella, and Turritella. The Laevicardium and the Turritella were recovered in an unmodified condition. The Olivella shells, however, have been bleached white, either deliberately or through exposure to the elements. Although some shells bleach naturally while lying on the beach, others retain their colors. Some shells in the Las Colinas collection have retained vivid colors despite five centuries of burial. Unfortunately, we do not know if the Olivella shells were obtained in this bleached condition or whether the inhabitants of Las Colinas bleached them intentionally.

The Seri of the northwest coast of Mexico bleach Olivella shells deliberately by rolling them around in hot sand (Johnston 1970). Once the spire has been removed, the shells are used in making necklaces.

Nineteen specimens of non-marine snails (Physa and Helisoma) were found at Las Colinas. Neither species was found in large enough concentrations to indicate purposeful acquisition for use in the shell industry.

Table 78. Species of shell recovered from Las Colinas

Marine

Aequipecten circularis Sowerby

Cerithidea albonodosa Gould and Carpenter

Conus perplexus Sowerby

Conus regularis Sowerby

Glycymeris gigantea Reeve

Glycymeris maculatus Broderlip

Haliotis cracherodii Leach

Haliotis fulgens Philippi

Laevicardium elatum Sowerby

Lyropecten subnodosus Sowerby

Olivella dama Mawe

Pecten vogdesi Arnold

Pteria sterna Gould

Pyrene major Sowerby

Spondylus princeps Broderlip

Strombus galeatus Swainson

Turritella leucostoma Valenciennes

Freshwater

Anodonta californiensis Lea

Physa virgata Gould

Helisoma tenue Dunker

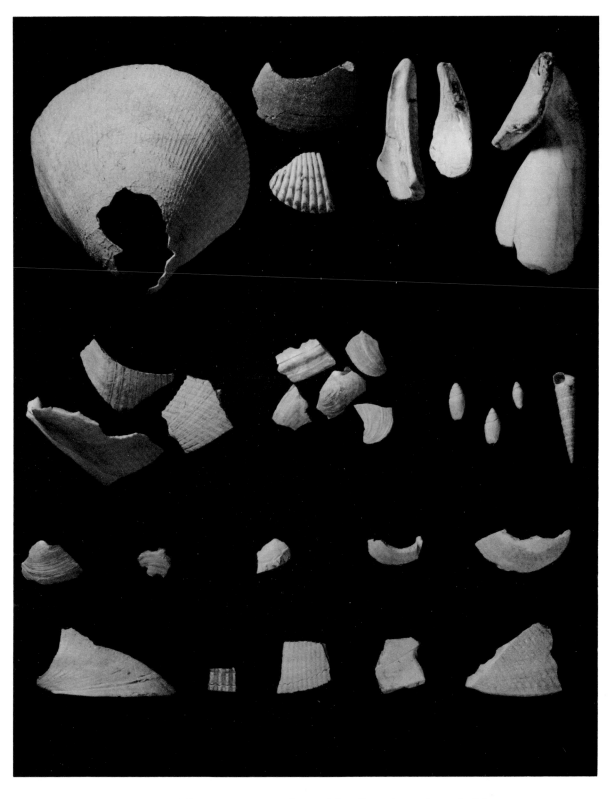

Figure 148.   Species of shells found at Las Colinas

Fragments

Fragments were found of the following six species: Anodonta, Laevicardium, Glycymeris, Haliotis, Pecten, and Strombus. There has been no alteration of the edges or surfaces of these specimens. Three pieces of the Haliotis appear to be beach-worn sections of the rim rather than worked fragments. The Anodonta fragments are quite small and very fragile, with rough and irregular edges.

Worked Shell

Most of the shell from the site of Las Colinas is from Laevicardium, Glycymeris, and Anodonta. Sixty-one fragments of Laevicardium shell (ground or cut) were identified. All parts of the shell were utilized, including lateral edges, beak and umbonal regions, medial sections of the body, and the outer margins. Grinding and polishing were the most frequent forms of surface or edge alteration. However, several specimens have cut edges that were made by snapping the shell along a groove cut into its surface with a graving tool. This technique produces a slightly ragged lip on the surface opposite that into which the groove was cut.

Only six specimens of Glycymeris were found. Five specimens have been ground on a bevel, with the lateral margin worn and containing several shallow U-shaped notches. The remaining piece had been cut on one edge in the manner described above for the fragments of Laevicardium.

The fragile Anodonta shell, of which 59 specimens were found, lends itself well to cutting but not to grinding. On most of these specimens the edges are cut to shape, and there is no surface treatment. Fifteen specimens show cut edges, while only three with ground edges were observed. Probably the shell could not withstand the abrasive action of grinding.

One small piece of Strombus has been chipped to shape. This is the only example of shell chipping encountered in the Las Colinas material.

Utilitarian Items

Awl - Hairpin

There are eight specimens of Glycymeris shell from Las Colinas that superficially resemble the shell needles found at Los Muertos and Snaketown (Haury 1945; Gladwin and others 1965). However, each of the eight specimens lacks the eye that characterizes needles from the above mentioned sites, and it is not clear just how they were used (Figure 149). At least some of these items appear to be fragments of shell bracelets that have had one or both ends reworked. Some of the reworked ends have been sharpened into points; however, others have been rounded or squared off. It seems certain that whatever their function, the fragility of these shell implements would have limited their usefulness.

Scoops

Four Laevicardium fragments--all showing worn, ground edges--may have been used as scoops. The specimens exhibit bevelled outer margins, that could have been produced by using the shell as a scoop for grain or some other material (Figure 149). Two specimens of whole Laevicardium shells showing comparable wear patterns were recovered from the Escalante Ruin, a large Classic period Hohokam site near Florence, Arizona (Debowski 1974:165, Plate 41).

Miscellaneous

Three specimens of Laevicardium are notched along one edge. One has clearly been cut to shape. The smallest piece has been ground on one edge, suggesting that it broke while being worked and was discarded.

A complete Haliotis shell was recovered with a section of the rim cut away and the entire bead and umbonal region knocked out. The interior has a black, pitch-like stain, while the exterior is stained with rust as though it had been in association with metal. Since this piece may be historic in context, it cannot be considered significant.

Beads

Whole Shell Beads

There is a total of 48 examples within this group, manufactured from Olivella (Figure 150). Shell beads were made in two ways: first by snapping off or grinding away the spire to leave a perforation; and second, by removing the spire and canal ends to leave only the medial section of the body. In either case, the beads could then be strung end to end.

Disc

Fourteen specimens (Figure 150) were included in this category. It is difficult to determine the species from which these beads were made since many natural diagnostic shell features have been eliminated. However, color can be an indicator--in this case, a most helpful one. The magenta and orange samples may be Spondylus and Strombus. The buff-colored ones may be Laevicardium, Glycymeris, and perhaps Strombus.

The beads are either biplano or biplano-converging in cross section. Only two specimens are of the same size, but each bead is uniformly shaped. Both biconical or straight-sided perforations were noted.

Bi-lobed

There are four examples of this bead style (Figure 150); only one specimen is complete. Two fragments are from the solid basal section, and

Figure 149. Shell, awls, and scoops

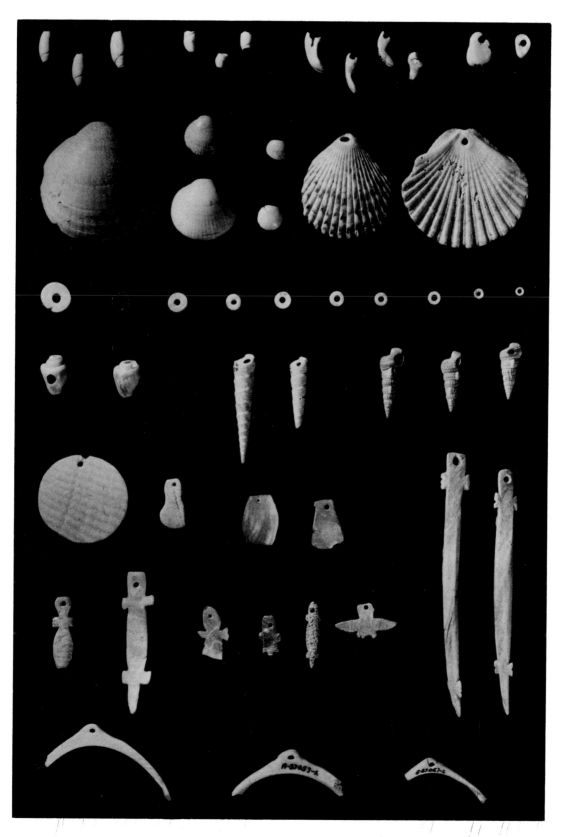

Figure 150. Shell beads, pendants, and bracelets

one is from the perforated upper section of the original shell. All are biplano-converging in longitudinal section. The two perforations are biconical. The shell species could not be determined for this category of beads.

Claw-shaped

There are six specimens in this category. Four of them were made from Spondylus. Three specimens are elongated and curved with biconical perforations at one end (Figure 150). Two specimens are globular in shape; one has a biconical hole, and the other a straight-sided hole. The sixth specimen is nearly flat with a barb at one end.

Pendants

Whole Shell

This category includes 21 specimens representing six species: Cerithidea, Glycymeris, Nassa, Pecten, Pyrene, and Turritella. In the Glycymeris examples, the beaks have been ground flat to cause perforation. One of the Pecten specimens (scallop) has a ground hole in the umbo, and the lateral wings have been removed. In another Pecten specimen there is a biconical drill perforation at the hinge, just below the beak. This particular shell is the upper valve, as indicated by its flatness and slight concavity. In general, however, the lower valve is the one used.

The other species represented are characterized by elongated or turriform shells. Either the lip or the whorl just behind the lip is perforated. These ornaments required only minor modification before use. Grinding was the most common form of perforation: removal of the beak, spire, or canal sections of the shell resulted in a hole through the shell.

Cut and Ground

Shell species modified by cutting and grinding included Anodonta, Laevicardium, Haliotis, and Pteria. Of 35 specimens, four are of geometric design and nine are zoomorphic. The latter include representations of lizards and birds, with perforation at the head of the figure in each case. The balance of the artifacts are plain.

Two specimens warrant special mention. Each was made in the form of a lizard with an exceptionally elongated body, and is perforated at the head (Figure 150). These specimens may be either pendants or earrings. A similar artifact was recovered at Los Muertos (Haury 1945:151).

Bracelets

Bracelets and their fragments are the most abundant shell artifacts at Hohokam sites. At Las Colinas, 324 fragments were recovered. Unfortunately, no complete specimens were found.

The only shell utilized for making bracelets was Glycymeris, except for one specimen of Lyropecten. Glycymeris is sturdy and can withstand the stress of manufacture, and it is naturally round in shape. A bracelet can easily be made by cutting out the midsection of the body and smoothing the edge. A more detailed account of the manufacturing process can be found in Gladwin and others (1965:138) and Haury (1945:154; 1976). Figure 151 illustrates the various parts of a bracelet.

Waste materials from bracelet manufacturing processes were not abundant at the site. It may be that many of the bracelets were not manufactured at Las Colinas (Figure 152, e).

Two kinds of bracelets--Type A and Type B--were identified in the analysis. Type A is smaller than Type B and is better made and more delicate in appearance, and has a thin band. Type B is not as well made in many cases, has a wider band, and is more massive in appearance.

Type A

This category consists of 282 specimens. Of this total, 191 examples are portions of the band. Another 41 specimens contain some part of the beak. This part has usually been ground away to produce a perforation.

Since sections containing the beak/umbo are so few, measurements were recorded only for the plain band examples. Average thickness is 5.2 mm while the average width is 4.5 mm. Cross-section shapes and tallies are listed below (Figure 153).

Of the total number of bracelet fragments for this class, 44 are burned. All of these are from areas of trash fill (Figure 152, a).

Type B

This is a small sample consisting of 30 specimens (Figure 152, b) of which 26 are band fragments and four are beak/umbonal sections. One specimen from this second group is nearly half a bracelet, the closest example to a complete piece. This category contains the larger style of bracelet where the band is quite thick (wide) and the beak/umbo has not been much altered. The beak has been perforated in one specimen as a result of grinding. The large bands are well polished and have been nicely formed.

Fragments are crescentic in plan, except for one beak/umbonal section that is rectangular. Cross-sections are pictured below (Figure 153). Average thickness is 11.3 mm and the average width is 4.5 mm. Five specimens have been burned; they were recovered from trash-filled areas.

Carved

The 12 carved bracelet fragments found at the site are not as detailed as those from Snaketown (Gladwin and others 1965:143). They more closely resemble those from Los Muertos (Haury 1945:156). They are crescentic in plan

COMPLETE

BROKEN

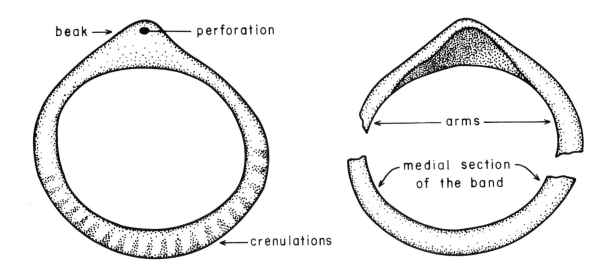

beak → perforation

arms

medial section of the band

crenulations

REVERSE

OBVERSE

Figure 151. Parts of a bracelet

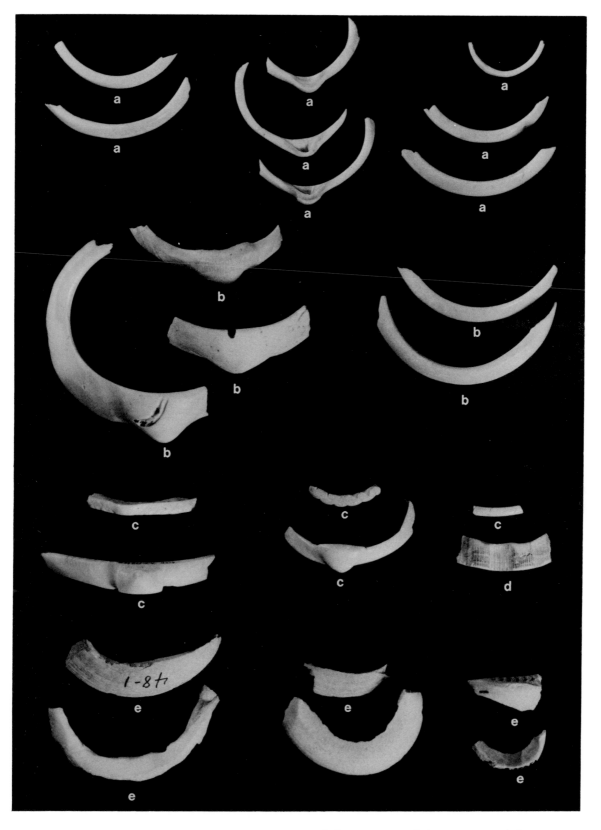

Figure 152. Bracelets: Type A (a), Type B (b), Carved (c),
Lyropecten (d), broken during manufacture (e)

SHAPE	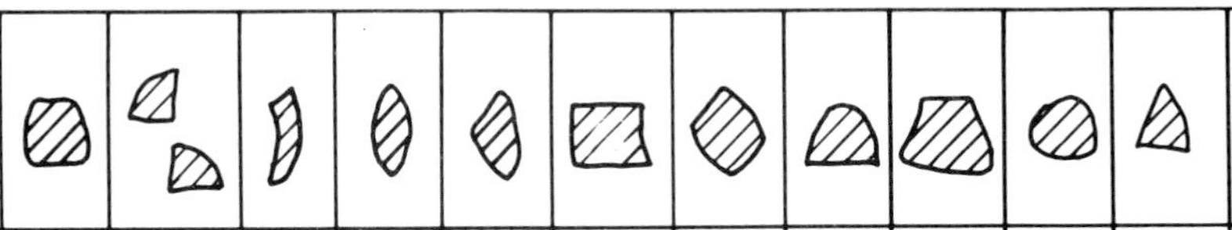											Ind.
TOTAL	73	26	14	22	25	1	13	8	1	1	2	96

SHAPE	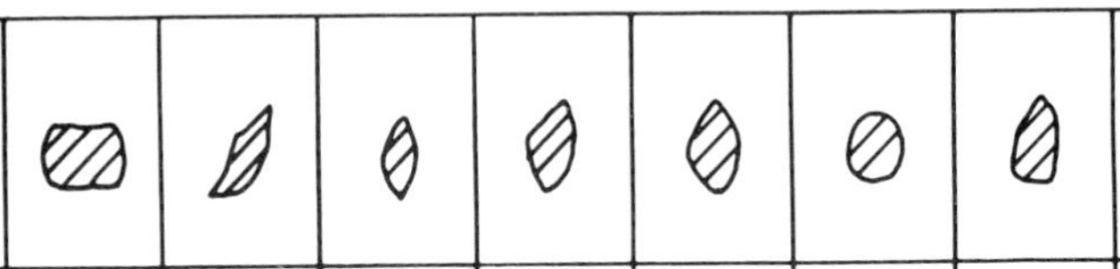							Ind.
TOTAL	1	5	7	8	1	1	3	4

SHAPE	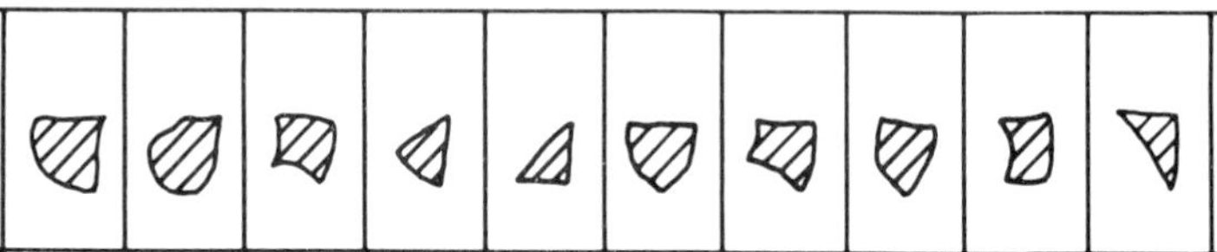										Ind.
TOTAL	1	1	11	1	1	1	1	1	3	1	4

Figure 153. Frequencies of different bracelet cross-sections:
Types A (top) and B (middle) and rings (bottom)

with well-formed and polished bands. Carving (Figure 151,c) takes the form of geometric designs and stylized zoomorphic figures. One small medial fragment contains a series of diagonal, parallel lines and is the only example of geometric design. Two specimens are stylistic snakes with one band being carved in the round in a zigzag or wavy line pattern. Another band is done in a running diamond pattern with the center of each diamond containing a "dot" (depression). The remaining eight bands are plain; however, their umbonal areas have been considerably altered. Here the edges of the umbo where it meets the band has been cut away (Haury 1945:154), causing the umbo to stand out. This isolated umbo may represent a stylized frog.

One additional bracelet fragment requires discussion. This artifact is somewhat unusual because of the shell (Lyropecten subnodosus). It appears that this bracelet (Figure 152,b) was constructed in the same manner as the others. Unfortunately, all that remains is a medial section of the band, leaving open the possibility that the shell was used for some other purpose, such as an open-center pendant.

Rings

Excavations at Los Muertos (Haury 1945:frontispiece, 158) and San Cayetano del Tumacacori (Di Peso 1956:95) have produced some of the most elaborate rings ever recovered from a Southwestern archaeological context. Those from Los Muertos contained colored inlays of paint and stone, while those from San Cayetano were incised in a geometric design and the channels filled with colored paints.

Seven fragments and one complete ring made of Conus shell were recovered (Figure 154,c). All of these were manufactured by removing the spire and the lower portion of the shell body. What remains is a circular section of the body (similar to a barrel bead, but on a larger scale) that varies in width. The surfaces are highly polished and the edges have been well finished.

A second variety of ring (Figure 154,a-b) is made from a juvenile Glycymeris shell. In a sense they are miniature versions of the bracelets. Twenty-six examples are represented, of which two are complete. Ten specimens contain umbos, four are not perforated, three were perforated during the manufacturing processes, and three are deliberately perforated higher up on the umbonal bulge. Though similar to the bracelet, a vast size difference does exist. On the average, thickness of the band is 2.9 mm while the width is 2.8 mm. As can be seen from the chart (Figure 153) below, cross-sections are varied and bear little similarity to bracelet sections.

Although this kind of artifact has traditionally been referred to as a "ring" in the literature, Pailes (1963:174) is doubtful of this usage since "thinness and fragility would cause their breakage rather quickly under normal use." Only some of the rings are of the proper size to be worn on fingers; others are exceptionally small and could only fit an infant. A quick search of a fraction of the literature on prehistoric burials has failed to produce a photograph or any reference to a Glycymeris ring found in situ on a phalanx. Perhaps the term "ring" might be expanded to "ring-pendant."

Figure 154. Rings (a-c), frogs, tinklers, zoomorphs,
and geometrics

Miscellaneous

Frogs

The riverine environment provided the popular frog motif for Hohokam shell carvers. Frog-effigies are always carved from a single valve of Glycymeris. Several examples (Figure 154 were recovered during the Las Colinas excavations. One artifact was rendered in a very realistic manner with prominent legs and backbone. Other specimens are more subtly rendered with incised lines. In all instances, the umbo has been ground flat, resulting in a large perforation.

Tinklers

A tinkler is made from a complete Conus shell. The spire is removed by grinding, and there is a perforation in the lip near the canal. This perforation may take one of two forms. In one case there is a V-notch perpendicular to the lip; in the other, there is a rounded hole through the lip. In either case, there is a hole through which a string may be threaded to hang the artifact.

Excavations at the site turned up 11 whole or nearly whole specimens (Figure 154). The Las Colinas examples do not have a perforation in the lip, presenting the possibility that these specimens may have been used for something other than making sounds. One possibility is that these are ring blanks, although a groove through the body would be needed to separate the ring from the rest of the shell. However, no other preparations have been observed.

Zoomorphic

This category consists of fragments of five zoomorphic forms made from Laevicardium or Glycymeris (Figure 154). Two specimens may be tails, while two others have tail and hind leg bulges, possibly representing (anteriorly) a lizard (see Haury 1945:150, Figure 92m; 151, Figure 93k, m and p). One specimen is a block-shaped head of an animal with a drilled eye depression, while another appears to be the head and upper body of a lizard.

The final specimen is the head from what is called Cipactli, or "The Mythical Monsters" (Haury 1945:152, 153, Figure 94i; 184-185; Meighan 1969:18-21; Wasley and Johnson 1965:103, Figure 76). Cipactli is a composite of several animals based on the alligator, and it can be traced in various forms from the southwest United States through Mesoamerica and into Peru. This motif occurs on pottery as well as in shell.

Geometric Forms

This category includes all miscellaneous pieces of worked shell. All of the specimens except one are Laevicardium. Some of the shapes represented are elongated rectangular, rectangular ovate, and circular (Figure 154). Surfaces and edges are ground smooth, although edges may originally have been cut and grooved to separate the pieces from the original shell mass.

These pieces may be pendant blanks awaiting perforation. Flat specimens could serve as mosaic inlay tiles. Two of the specimens have been burned. Geometrics range from 9 mm to 36 mm in size.

Discussion and Conclusions

Only three Classic period sites have yielded significant quantities of shell: Los Muertos, Escalante, and Las Colinas. The total number of shell pieces recovered from Los Muertos is unknown; Las Colinas produced 953 specimens, and the Escalante total is 303 pieces. In comparison, other Classic period sites have produced much lower shell counts: Mesa Grande (193+), the Fitch Site (83), University Indian Ruin (53), and Pueblo del Monte (16).

Haury summarized his thoughts regarding the Los Muertos shell assemblage as follows:

> ...[A]nd particularly during the occupation of Los Muertos, the present evidence indicates that there were more shells and more shell artifacts proportionate to earlier time, although there was some reduction in the number of species and in the number of kinds of things made.
> A notable technique not present at Los Muertos or in other Classic Period sites so far dug, was etching. On the other hand, inlaying as described here, has not been certainly reported from pre-Classic sites (1945:159).

Except for the lack of inlay work, this description also fits the Las Colinas shell assemblage. One of the few differences is that no evidence of inlay work was observed in the Las Colinas material.

In general, fewer species are utilized during the Classic period; however, Conus was initially used during the Classic period. Conus continued to be a popular shell into the post-Classic, as evidenced by the numerous examples at San Cayetano del Tumacacori (Di Peso 1956).

Cardium, Glycymeris, and Olivella continued to be extensively used throughout the occupation of Las Colinas. Pecten (sp.) is reported by Haury (1945:159) as becoming scarce in Classic times. This is true at Las Colinas, as only six pieces were found.

According to Haury, claw-shaped beads (1945:149) were uncommon at Los Muertos but were relatively frequent in earlier phases at Snaketown. As noted, six specimens were recovered from Las Colinas. An interesting note is that Di Peso (1956:107) excavated five similar specimens from the Hohokam component at San Cayetano, but none from the overlying Pima occupation. It would appear that, at least in this area, the manufacture and use of claw-shaped beads had definitely ended by post-Classic times.

One item that was popular was the cut pendant of either geometric or zoomorphic form. Laevicardium and Haliotis were extensively used for both types. Haury (1945:152) states that "the tendency to depict life forms on Colonial pottery was to a certain degree perpetuated in the shell carving of the Classic period when animal figures in ceramic decorations were no longer in style." This aptly describes the situation at Las Colinas.

Several common traits of the Classic period are engraving, inlay, and painted shell work. Los Muertos, Pueblo Grande, San Cayetano and probably La Ciudad, Mesa Grande, and Casa Grande all produced this elaborate art form. However, the Fitch Site, Pueblo del Monte, Las Colinas, and the University Indian Ruin failed to turn up any shell of this description. The only possible exception among the Las Colinas collection is a bracelet fragment that has circular depressions as a part of a running diamond pattern. These depressions may have contained an inlaid stone or shell in the past.

A characteristic primarily associated with the Classic period is the presence of large, wide-banded bracelets. Gladwin and others (1965:142) and Haury (1945:154) think that this style of bracelet originated in the Sacaton phase and carried on into Classic period times. The bracelet fragments recovered from Las Colinas do not fit this description well as most of them were of a thinner style. Di Peso (1956:87, 97) excavated many bracelets of the larger Classic style from his upper occupation at San Cayetano del Tumacacori. However, they were all worn on the upper arm and technically should be called armlets. The thin variety of bracelet was found exclusively in the underlying occupational zone.

Table 79. Frequency of shell artifacts by feature

	Feature									
	0	1	2	3	4	5	6	7	8	9
Unworked Raw Material										
Laevicardium	1	1	1	1	3	7	–	1	4	1
Glycymeris	–	–	–	–	–	–	–	–	–	–
Anodonta	–	–	1	–	–	–	–	–	–	–
Cerithidea	–	–	–	–	–	–	–	–	–	–
Haliotis	–	–	–	–	–	–	–	–	–	–
Olivella	1	–	–	–	1	1	–	–	–	1
Pecten	–	–	–	–	–	1	–	–	–	–
Turritella	–	–	–	–	–	–	–	–	–	–
Strombus	–	–	–	–	–	–	–	–	–	–
Miscellaneous	–	1	–	–	1	–	–	–	–	–
Freshwater Snail	–	–	–	–	–	–	–	–	–	–
Worked Shell										
Fragments										
Ground or Polished										
Laevicardium	–	2	–	1	2	2	–	–	1	–
Glycymeris	–	–	–	–	–	–	–	–	–	–
Anodonta	–	–	1	–	–	–	–	–	–	–
Miscellaneous	–	–	–	–	–	1	–	–	–	–
Cut										
Laevicardium	–	–	–	–	–	–	–	–	–	–
Glycymeris	–	–	–	–	–	–	–	–	–	–
Anodonta	–	–	–	–	1	1	–	–	–	–
Miscellaneous	–	–	–	1	–	–	–	–	–	–
Utilitarian Items										
Awls	–	–	–	–	–	–	–	–	–	–
Scoops	–	–	–	–	–	–	–	–	–	–
Miscellaneous	–	–	–	–	–	3	–	–	–	–
Beads										
Whole Shell	2	1	1	1	–	1	–	–	–	–
Barrel	–	–	–	1	–	1	–	–	–	–
Disc	–	–	–	–	–	1	–	–	1	–
Bi-lobed	–	–	–	–	–	–	–	–	–	–
Claw-shaped	–	–	–	–	–	–	–	–	–	–
Pendants										
Whole	–	–	–	–	–	–	–	–	–	–
Cut/Ground	2	–	–	–	–	1	–	–	1	–
Indeterminate	–	–	–	–	–	–	–	–	–	–
Effigy	–	–	1	–	–	–	–	–	–	–
Bracelets										
Type A	12	9	2	2	6	4	–	–	6	4
Type B	–	–	–	–	–	1	–	–	–	–
Carved	–	–	–	–	–	–	–	–	–	–
Rings										
Conus	2	–	–	–	1	–	–	–	–	–
Glycymeris	–	–	–	–	–	–	–	–	–	–
Miscellaneous										
Frogs	1	–	–	–	–	–	–	–	–	–
Tinklers (?)	–	–	–	1	–	–	–	–	–	–
Zoomorphic	1	–	–	–	–	–	–	–	–	–
Geometric Forms	–	–	1	–	–	–	–	–	–	–
TOTAL	22	14	8	8	15	25	0	1	13	6

Table 79. (continued)

	Feature									
	10	11	12	13	14	15	16	17	18	19
Unworked Raw Material										
Laevicardium	3	-	-	3	-	-	1	1	-	2
Glycymeris	-	-	-	-	-	-	-	-	-	-
Anodonta	-	-	-	-	-	-	-	-	-	-
Cerithidea	-	-	-	-	-	-	-	-	-	-
Haliotis	1	-	-	-	-	-	-	-	-	-
Olivella	1	1	-	1	-	-	-	1	-	1
Pecten	-	-	-	-	-	-	-	-	-	-
Turritella	-	-	-	-	-	-	-	-	-	-
Strombus	-	-	-	-	-	-	-	-	-	-
Miscellaneous	-	-	-	-	-	-	-	-	-	-
Freshwater Snail	-	-	-	-	-	-	-	-	-	-
Worked Shell										
Fragments										
Ground or Polished										
Laevicardium	1	-	-	-	-	-	2	-	-	-
Glycymeris	-	-	-	-	-	-	-	1	-	1
Anodonta	-	-	-	-	-	-	-	-	-	-
Miscellaneous	-	-	-	-	-	-	-	-	-	-
Cut										
Laevicardium	-	-	-	1	-	-	-	-	-	-
Glycymeris	-	-	-	-	-	-	-	-	-	-
Anodonta	-	-	-	-	-	-	-	-	-	-
Miscellaneous	-	-	-	-	-	-	-	-	-	-
Utilitarian Items										
Awls	-	-	-	-	-	-	-	-	-	1
Scoops	-	-	-	-	-	-	-	-	-	-
Miscellaneous	-	-	-	-	-	-	-	-	-	-
Beads										
Whole Shell	1	1	-	1	-	-	-	-	-	-
Barrel	-	-	-	-	-	-	-	-	-	-
Disc	-	-	-	2	-	-	-	-	-	-
Bi-lobed	-	-	-	-	-	-	-	-	-	-
Claw-shaped	-	-	-	-	-	-	-	-	-	-
Pendants										
Whole	1	-	-	1	-	-	-	-	-	-
Cut/Ground	1	-	1	-	-	-	-	-	-	1
Indeterminate	-	-	-	-	-	-	-	-	-	-
Effigy	-	-	-	-	-	-	-	-	-	-
Bracelets										
Type A	5	1	-	5	-	-	1	5	-	3
Type B	-	-	-	-	-	-	-	-	-	-
Carved	-	-	-	-	-	-	-	-	-	1
Rings										
Conus	-	-	-	-	-	-	-	-	-	-
Glycymeris	-	-	-	-	-	-	-	-	-	-
Miscellaneous										
Frogs	-	-	-	-	-	-	-	-	-	-
Tinklers (?)	1	-	-	1	-	-	-	1	-	-
Zoomorphic	-	-	-	-	-	-	-	-	-	-
Geometric Forms	-	-	-	-	-	-	-	-	-	-
TOTAL	15	3	1	15	0	0	4	9	0	11

Table 79.   (continued)

	20	21	22	23	24	25	26	27	28	29
Unworked Raw Material										
Laevicardium	-	-	-	-	-	-	1	-	-	1
Glycymeris	-	-	-	-	-	-	-	-	-	-
Anodonta	-	-	-	-	-	-	-	-	-	1
Cerithidea	-	-	-	-	-	-	-	-	-	-
Haliotis	-	-	-	-	-	-	-	-	-	-
Olivella	-	-	-	-	-	-	6	-	-	-
Pecten	-	1	-	-	-	-	-	-	-	-
Turritella	-	-	-	-	-	-	-	-	-	-
Strombus	-	-	-	-	-	-	1	-	-	-
Miscellaneous	-	-	-	-	-	-	-	-	-	-
Freshwater Snail	-	-	-	-	-	-	-	-	-	-
Worked Shell										
Fragments										
Ground or Polished										
Laevicardium	-	-	-	-	1	-	-	-	-	-
Glycymeris	-	-	-	-	-	-	-	-	-	-
Anodonta	-	-	1	-	-	-	-	-	-	-
Miscellaneous	-	-	-	-	-	-	-	-	-	-
Cut										
Laevicardium	-	-	-	-	-	-	-	-	-	-
Glycymeris	-	-	-	-	-	-	-	-	-	-
Anodonta	-	-	-	-	-	-	-	-	-	-
Miscellaneous	-	-	-	-	1	-	-	-	-	-
Utilitarian Items										
Awls	-	-	-	-	-	-	-	-	-	-
Scoops	-	-	-	-	-	-	-	-	-	-
Miscellaneous	-	-	-	-	-	-	-	-	-	-
Beads										
Whole Shell	1	-	-	-	-	-	3	-	-	2
Barrel	-	-	1	-	-	-	-	-	-	-
Disc	-	-	-	-	-	-	-	-	-	-
Bi-lobed	-	1	-	-	-	-	-	-	-	-
Claw-shaped	-	-	-	-	-	-	-	-	-	-
Pendants										
Whole	-	-	-	-	-	-	-	-	-	-
Cut/Ground	1	2	-	-	-	-	1	-	-	1
Indeterminate	-	-	-	-	-	-	-	-	-	-
Effigy	-	-	-	-	-	-	-	-	-	-
Bracelets										
Type A	3	-	1	-	2	-	2	1	1	4
Type B	-	-	-	-	-	-	-	-	-	-
Carved	-	-	-	-	-	-	-	-	-	-
Rings										
Conus	-	-	-	-	-	-	-	-	-	-
Glycymeris	-	-	-	-	-	-	-	-	-	-
Miscellaneous										
Frogs	-	-	-	1	-	-	-	-	-	-
Tinklers (?)	-	-	-	-	-	-	-	-	-	-
Zoomorphic	-	-	-	-	-	-	-	-	-	-
Geometric Forms	-	-	-	-	-	-	1	-	-	-
TOTAL	5	4	3	1	4	0	14	1	1	9

Table 79.   (continued)

	Feature									
	30	31	32	33	34	35	36	37	38	39
Unworked Raw Material										
Laevicardium	-	-	-	1	-	-	-	-	-	-
Glycymeris	-	-	-	-	-	-	-	-	-	-
Anodonta	-	-	-	-	-	-	-	1	-	-
Cerithidea	-	-	-	-	-	-	-	-	-	-
Haliotis	-	-	-	-	-	-	-	-	-	-
Olivella	-	-	-	-	-	-	-	-	-	-
Pecten	-	-	-	-	-	-	-	-	-	-
Turritella	-	-	-	1	-	-	-	-	-	-
Strombus	-	-	-	-	-	-	-	-	-	-
Miscellaneous	-	-	-	-	-	-	-	-	-	-
Freshwater Snail	-	-	-	-	-	-	-	-	-	-
Worked Shell										
Fragments										
Ground or Polished										
Laevicardium	-	-	-	-	-	1	1	1	-	-
Glycymeris	-	-	-	-	-	-	-	-	-	-
Anodonta	-	-	-	-	-	-	-	-	-	-
Miscellaneous	-	-	-	-	-	-	-	-	-	-
Cut										
Laevicardium	-	-	-	-	-	-	-	-	-	-
Glycymeris	-	-	-	-	-	-	-	-	-	-
Anodonta	-	-	-	-	-	-	-	-	-	-
Miscellaneous	-	-	-	1	-	-	-	-	-	-
Utilitarian Items										
Awls	-	-	-	-	-	-	-	-	-	-
Scoops	-	-	-	-	-	-	-	-	-	-
Miscellaneous	-	-	-	-	-	-	-	-	-	-
Beads										
Whole Shell	-	-	-	-	-	3	-	-	-	1
Barrel	-	-	-	1	-	1	-	-	-	-
Disc	-	-	-	-	1	1	-	-	-	-
Bi-lobed	-	-	-	-	-	-	-	-	-	-
Claw-shaped	-	-	-	-	-	-	-	-	-	-
Pendants										
Whole	-	-	-	-	-	-	-	-	-	-
Cut/Ground	-	2	-	-	-	-	1	-	-	-
Indeterminate	-	-	-	-	-	-	-	-	-	-
Effigy	-	-	-	-	-	-	-	-	-	-
Bracelets										
Type A	-	2	-	2	1	1	1	-	-	-
Type B	-	-	-	-	-	-	-	-	-	-
Carved	-	-	-	-	-	-	-	-	-	-
Rings										
Conus	-	-	-	-	-	-	-	-	-	-
Glycymeris	-	-	-	-	-	-	-	-	-	-
Miscellaneous										
Frogs	-	-	-	-	-	-	-	-	-	-
Tinklers (?)	-	-	-	-	-	1	-	-	-	-
Zoomorphic	-	-	-	-	-	-	-	-	-	-
Geometric Forms	-	-	-	-	-	-	-	-	-	-
TOTAL	0	4	0	6	2	8	3	2	0	1

Table 79. (continued)

	Feature									
	40	41	42	43	44	45	46	47	48	49
Unworked Raw Material										
Laevicardium	1	-	1	-	-	21	-	1	1	38
Glycymeris	-	-	-	-	-	-	-	-	1	-
Anodonta	-	-	-	-	-	4	-	-	1	16
Cerithidea	-	-	-	-	-	-	-	-	-	-
Haliotis	-	-	-	-	-	-	-	-	-	-
Olivella	-	-	1	-	-	-	-	-	-	-
Pecten	-	-	-	-	-	1	-	-	-	-
Turritella	-	-	-	-	-	-	-	-	-	-
Strombus	-	-	-	-	-	-	-	-	-	-
Miscellaneous	-	1	-	-	-	-	-	-	1	-
Freshwater Snail	-	-	-	-	-	-	-	-	1	5
Worked Shell										
Fragments										
Ground or Polished										
Laevicardium	-	-	-	-	-	4	-	1	-	3
Glycymeris	-	-	-	-	-	-	-	-	-	2
Anodonta	-	-	-	-	-	-	-	-	-	-
Miscellaneous	-	-	-	-	-	-	-	-	-	-
Cut										
Laevicardium	-	-	-	-	-	-	-	-	-	-
Glycymeris	-	-	-	-	-	-	-	-	-	-
Anodonta	1	-	-	-	-	2	-	-	-	3
Miscellaneous	-	-	-	-	-	-	-	-	-	-
Utilitarian Items										
Awls	-	-	-	-	-	-	-	-	-	1
Scoops	-	-	-	-	-	-	-	-	-	-
Miscellaneous	-	-	-	-	-	-	-	-	-	-
Beads										
Whole Shell	-	-	-	-	-	2	1	-	-	3
Barrel	-	-	-	-	-	1	-	-	-	1
Disc	-	-	-	-	-	1	-	-	-	1
Bi-lobed	-	-	-	-	-	-	-	-	-	1
Claw-shaped	-	-	-	-	-	-	-	-	-	-
Pendants										
Whole	-	-	-	-	-	-	-	-	-	-
Cut/Ground	-	-	-	-	-	-	-	-	1	1
Indeterminate	-	-	-	-	-	-	-	-	-	-
Effigy	-	-	-	-	-	1	-	-	-	-
Bracelets										
Type A	6	1	1	-	-	20	2	-	7	33
Type B	-	-	-	-	-	1	-	-	-	-
Carved	-	-	-	-	-	-	-	-	-	1
Rings										
Conus	-	-	-	-	-	-	-	-	-	-
Glycymeris	-	-	-	-	-	-	-	-	-	-
Miscellaneous										
Frogs	-	-	1	-	-	-	-	-	-	1
Tinklers (?)	-	-	-	-	-	-	-	-	-	-
Zoomorphic	1	-	-	-	-	-	-	-	-	1
Geometric Forms	-	-	-	-	-	-	-	-	-	-
TOTAL	9	2	4	0	0	58	3	2	12	111

Table 79. (continued)

	Feature									
	50	51	52	53	54	55	56	57	58	59
Unworked Raw Material										
Laevicardium	1	1	-	-	-	1	-	1	-	-
Glycymeris	-	-	-	-	-	-	-	-	-	-
Anodonta	-	-	-	-	-	-	-	-	-	-
Cerithidea	-	-	-	-	-	-	-	-	-	-
Haliotis	-	-	-	-	-	-	-	-	-	-
Olivella	-	-	-	-	-	-	-	2	-	-
Pecten	-	-	-	-	-	-	-	-	-	-
Turritella	-	-	-	-	-	-	-	-	-	-
Strombus	-	-	-	-	-	-	-	-	-	-
Miscellaneous	-	-	-	-	-	-	-	-	-	-
Freshwater Snail	-	-	-	-	-	-	-	-	-	-
Worked Shell										
Fragments										
Ground or Polished										
Laevicardium	-	-	-	-	-	-	-	-	-	1
Glycymeris	-	-	-	-	-	-	-	-	-	-
Anodonta	-	-	-	-	-	-	-	-	-	-
Miscellaneous	-	-	-	-	-	-	-	-	-	-
Cut										
Laevicardium	-	-	-	-	-	-	-	-	-	-
Glycymeris	-	-	-	-	-	-	-	-	-	-
Anodonta	-	-	-	-	-	-	-	-	-	-
Miscellaneous	-	-	-	-	-	-	-	-	-	-
Utilitarian Items										
Awls	-	-	-	-	-	-	-	-	-	2
Scoops	-	-	-	-	-	-	-	-	-	-
Miscellaneous	-	-	-	-	-	-	-	-	-	-
Beads										
Whole Shell	-	2	-	-	-	-	-	1	-	-
Barrel	-	1	-	-	-	-	-	-	-	-
Disc	-	-	-	-	1	-	-	-	-	-
Bi-lobed	-	-	-	-	-	-	-	-	-	-
Claw-shaped	-	-	-	-	-	-	-	-	-	-
Pendants										
Whole	-	-	-	-	-	-	-	-	-	-
Cut/Ground	-	2	-	-	-	-	1	-	-	-
Indeterminate	-	-	-	-	-	-	-	-	-	-
Effigy	-	-	-	-	-	-	-	-	-	-
Bracelets										
Type A	-	1	-	-	-	1	-	3	-	2
Type B	-	-	-	-	-	-	-	-	-	-
Carved	-	-	-	-	-	-	-	-	-	1
Rings										
Conus	-	-	-	-	-	-	-	-	-	-
Glycymeris	-	-	-	-	-	-	-	-	-	-
Miscellaneous										
Frogs	-	-	-	-	-	-	-	-	-	-
Tinklers (?)	-	-	-	-	-	-	-	-	-	-
Zoomorphic	-	-	-	-	-	-	-	-	-	-
Geometric Forms	-	-	-	-	-	-	-	-	-	-
TOTAL	1	7	0	0	1	2	1	7	0	6

Table 79. (continued)

	Feature									
	60	61	62	63	64	65	66	67	68	69
Unworked Raw Material										
Laevicardium	-	2	42	7	-	-	-	-	-	-
Glycymeris	-	-	1	-	-	-	-	-	-	-
Anodonta	-	-	26	-	-	-	-	-	-	-
Cerithidea	-	-	-	-	-	-	-	-	-	-
Haliotis	-	-	1	-	-	-	-	-	-	-
Olivella	-	-	-	-	-	-	-	-	-	-
Pecten	-	-	-	-	-	-	-	-	-	-
Turritella	-	-	1	-	-	-	-	-	-	-
Strombus	-	-	-	-	-	-	-	-	-	-
Miscellaneous	-	-	-	-	-	-	-	-	-	-
Freshwater Snail	-	1	2	-	-	-	-	-	-	-
Worked Shell										
Fragments										
Ground or Polished										
Laevicardium	2	1	13	1	-	-	-	-	-	-
Glycymeris	-	-	-	-	-	-	-	-	-	-
Anodonta	-	-	2	-	-	-	-	-	-	-
Miscellaneous	-	-	-	-	-	-	-	-	-	-
Cut										
Laevicardium	-	-	-	-	-	-	-	-	-	-
Glycymeris	-	-	1	-	-	-	-	-	-	-
Anodonta	-	-	2	-	-	-	-	-	-	-
Miscellaneous	-	-	-	-	-	-	-	-	-	-
Utilitarian Items										
Awls	-	-	1	-	-	-	-	-	-	-
Scoops	-	-	-	-	-	-	-	-	-	-
Miscellaneous	-	-	1	-	-	-	-	-	-	-
Beads										
Whole Shell	-	-	5	-	-	-	-	-	-	1
Barrel	-	1	2	-	-	-	-	-	-	-
Disc	-	-	1	-	-	-	-	-	-	-
Bi-lobed	-	-	2	-	-	-	-	-	-	-
Claw-shaped	-	-	-	-	-	-	-	-	-	-
Pendants										
Whole	-	-	-	-	-	-	-	-	-	-
Cut/Ground	-	1	5	2	-	-	-	-	-	-
Indeterminate	-	-	1	-	-	-	-	-	-	-
Effigy	-	-	2	-	-	-	-	-	-	-
Bracelets										
Type A	5	7	37	6	-	1	1	-	-	-
Type B	-	-	-	-	-	-	-	-	-	-
Carved	-	-	1	-	-	-	-	-	-	-
Rings										
Conus	-	-	1	-	-	-	-	-	-	-
Glycymeris	-	-	-	-	-	-	-	-	-	-
Miscellaneous										
Frogs	-	-	-	-	-	-	-	-	-	-
Tinklers (?)	-	-	-	-	-	-	-	-	-	1
Zoomorphic	-	-	-	-	-	-	-	-	-	-
Geometric Forms	-	-	1	-	-	-	-	-	-	-
TOTAL	7	13	151	16	0	1	1	0	0	2

Table 79.   (continued)

	Feature									
	70	71	72	73	74	75	76	77	78	79
Unworked Raw Material										
Laevicardium	-	3	1	-	-	1	-	1	2	-
Glycymeris	-	-	-	-	-	-	-	-	-	-
Anodonta	1	-	5	-	-	-	-	-	-	-
Cerithidea	-	-	-	-	-	-	-	-	-	-
Haliotis	-	-	-	-	-	-	-	-	-	-
Olivella	-	-	-	-	1	-	-	-	-	-
Pecten	-	-	1	-	-	-	-	-	-	-
Turritella	-	-	-	-	-	-	-	-	-	-
Strombus	-	-	-	-	-	-	-	-	-	-
Miscellaneous	-	-	-	-	-	-	-	-	-	-
Freshwater Snail	-	-	-	-	-	1	-	-	-	-
Worked Shell										
Fragments										
Ground or Polished										
Laevicardium	-	-	2	-	-	-	-	1	-	-
Glycymeris	-	-	-	-	-	-	-	-	-	-
Anodonta	-	-	-	-	-	-	-	-	-	-
Miscellaneous	-	-	-	-	-	-	-	-	-	-
Cut										
Laevicardium	-	-	1	-	-	-	-	-	-	-
Glycymeris	-	-	-	-	-	-	-	-	-	-
Anodonta	-	-	1	-	-	1	-	-	-	-
Miscellaneous	-	-	-	-	-	-	-	-	-	-
Utilitarian Items										
Awls	-	-	-	1	-	-	-	-	-	-
Scoops	-	-	-	-	-	-	-	-	-	-
Miscellaneous	-	-	-	-	-	-	-	-	-	-
Beads										
Whole Shell	-	-	-	-	1	-	-	-	-	-
Barrel	-	1	-	1	-	-	-	-	-	-
Disc	-	-	1	-	-	-	-	-	1	-
Bi-lobed	-	-	-	-	-	-	-	-	-	-
Claw-shaped	-	-	-	-	-	-	-	-	-	-
Pendants										
Whole	-	-	-	-	-	-	-	-	-	-
Cut/Ground	-	-	2	-	-	-	-	-	-	-
Indeterminate	-	-	-	-	-	-	-	-	-	-
Effigy	-	-	-	-	-	-	-	-	-	-
Bracelets										
Type A	2	1	4	1	3	2	-	2	1	-
Type B	-	-	-	-	-	-	-	-	-	-
Carved	-	-	-	1	-	-	-	-	-	-
Rings										
Conus	-	-	-	-	-	-	-	-	-	-
Glycymeris	-	-	-	-	-	-	-	-	-	-
Miscellaneous										
Frogs	-	-	-	-	-	-	-	-	-	-
Tinklers (?)	-	-	1	-	-	-	-	-	-	-
Zoomorphic	-	-	-	1	1	-	-	-	-	-
Geometric Forms	-	-	-	-	-	-	-	-	-	-
TOTAL	3	5	19	5	6	5	0	4	4	0

Table 79.   (continued)

			Feature							
	80	81	82	83	84	85	86	87	88	89
Unworked Raw Material										
Laevicardium	-	-	9	2	-	-	1	-	1	-
Glycymeris	-	-	1	-	-	-	-	-	-	-
Anodonta	-	-	-	-	-	-	-	-	-	-
Cerithidea	-	-	1	2	-	-	-	-	-	-
Haliotis	-	-	-	-	-	-	-	-	-	-
Olivella	-	-	4	-	2	-	-	-	2	-
Pecten	-	-	-	-	-	-	-	-	-	-
Turritella	-	1	-	-	-	-	-	-	-	-
Strombus	-	-	-	-	-	-	-	-	-	-
Miscellaneous	-	-	-	-	-	-	-	-	-	-
Freshwater Snail	-	-	2	-	-	-	-	-	-	-
Worked Shell										
Fragments										
Ground or Polished										
Laevicardium	-	-	2	-	-	1	-	-	-	-
Glycymeris	-	-	-	-	-	-	-	-	-	-
Anodonta	-	-	-	-	-	-	-	-	-	-
Miscellaneous	-	-	-	-	-	-	-	-	-	-
Cut										
Laevicardium	-	-	2	-	-	-	-	-	-	-
Glycymeris	-	-	-	-	-	-	-	-	-	-
Anodonta	-	-	2	-	-	-	-	-	-	-
Miscellaneous	-	-	-	-	-	-	-	-	-	-
Utilitarian Items										
Awls	-	-	-	-	-	-	-	-	-	-
Scoops	-	-	-	-	-	-	-	-	-	-
Miscellaneous	-	-	-	-	-	-	-	-	-	-
Beads										
Whole Shell	-	-	1	-	-	-	1	-	-	1
Barrel	-	-	-	1	-	-	-	-	-	-
Disc	-	-	-	1	-	-	-	-	-	-
Bi-lobed	-	-	-	-	-	-	-	-	-	-
Claw-shaped	-	-	-	-	-	-	-	-	-	-
Pendants										
Whole	-	-	-	-	1	-	-	-	-	-
Cut/Ground	-	-	-	-	-	-	-	-	-	1
Indeterminate	-	-	-	-	-	-	-	-	-	-
Effigy	-	-	-	-	-	-	-	-	-	-
Bracelets										
Type A	-	-	11	-	-	1	-	-	-	-
Type B	-	-	1	-	-	-	-	-	-	-
Carved	-	-	-	-	-	-	-	-	-	-
Rings										
Conus	-	-	1	-	-	-	-	-	-	-
Glycymeris	-	-	-	-	-	-	-	-	-	-
Miscellaneous										
Frogs	-	-	-	-	-	-	-	-	-	-
Tinklers (?)	-	-	1	1	-	-	-	-	-	-
Zoomorphic	-	-	-	-	-	-	-	-	-	-
Geometric Forms	-	-	-	-	-	-	-	-	-	-
TOTAL	0	1	38	7	3	2	2	0	3	2

Table 79.   (continued)

	Feature									
	90	91	92	93	94	95	96	97	98	99
Unworked Raw Material										
Laevicardium	-	-	-	-	5	-	-	-	-	1
Glycymeris	-	-	-	-	-	-	-	-	-	-
Anodonta	-	-	-	-	1	-	-	-	-	-
Cerithidea	-	-	-	-	-	-	-	-	-	-
Haliotis	-	-	-	-	-	-	-	-	-	-
Olivella	-	-	-	-	-	-	-	-	-	-
Pecten	-	-	-	-	-	-	-	-	-	-
Turritella	-	-	-	-	-	-	-	-	-	-
Strombus	-	-	-	-	-	-	-	-	-	-
Miscellaneous	-	-	-	-	-	-	-	-	-	-
Freshwater Snail	-	-	-	-	-	-	-	-	-	-
Worked Shell										
Fragments										
Ground or Polished										
Laevicardium	-	-	-	-	2	-	-	-	-	-
Glycymeris	-	-	-	1	-	-	-	-	-	-
Anodonta	-	-	-	-	-	-	-	-	-	-
Miscellaneous	-	-	-	-	-	-	-	-	-	-
Cut										
Laevicardium	-	-	-	-	-	-	-	-	-	-
Glycymeris	-	-	-	-	-	-	-	-	-	-
Anodonta	-	-	-	-	-	-	-	-	-	-
Miscellaneous	-	-	-	-	-	-	-	-	-	-
Utilitarian Items										
Awls	-	-	-	-	-	-	-	-	-	-
Scoops	-	-	-	-	-	-	-	-	-	-
Miscellaneous	-	-	-	-	-	-	-	-	-	-
Beads										
Whole Shell	-	-	-	-	1	-	-	-	-	-
Barrel	-	-	-	-	-	-	-	-	-	-
Disc	-	-	-	-	-	-	-	-	-	-
Bi-lobed	-	-	-	-	-	-	-	-	-	-
Claw-shaped	-	-	-	-	-	-	-	-	-	-
Pendants										
Whole	-	-	-	-	-	-	-	-	-	-
Cut/Ground	-	-	-	-	-	-	-	-	-	-
Indeterminate	-	-	-	-	-	-	-	-	-	-
Effigy	-	-	-	-	-	-	-	-	-	-
Bracelets										
Type A	-	-	-	1	-	-	-	-	-	2
Type B	-	-	-	-	-	-	-	-	-	-
Carved	-	-	-	-	-	-	-	-	-	-
Rings										
Conus	-	-	-	-	-	-	-	-	-	-
Glycymeris	-	-	-	-	-	-	-	-	-	-
Miscellaneous										
Frogs	-	-	-	-	-	-	-	-	-	-
Tinklers (?)	-	-	-	-	-	-	-	-	-	-
Zoomorphic	-	-	-	-	-	-	-	-	-	-
Geometric Forms	-	-	-	-	-	-	-	-	-	-
TOTAL	0	0	0	2	9	0	0	0	0	3

Table 79. (continued)

	Feature									
	100	101	102	103	104	105	106	107	108	109
Unworked Raw Material										
Laevicardium	1	-	1	1	-	-	-	-	-	-
Glycymeris	-	-	-	-	-	-	-	-	-	-
Anodonta	-	-	-	-	-	-	-	-	-	-
Cerithidea	-	-	-	-	-	-	-	-	-	-
Haliotis	-	-	-	-	-	-	-	-	-	-
Olivella	1	-	1	-	-	-	-	-	-	-
Pecten	1	-	-	-	-	-	-	-	-	-
Turritella	-	-	-	-	-	-	-	-	-	-
Strombus	-	-	-	-	-	-	-	-	-	-
Miscellaneous	-	-	-	-	-	-	-	-	-	-
Freshwater Snail	-	-	-	-	-	-	-	-	-	-
Worked Shell										
Fragments										
Ground or Polished										
Laevicardium	-	1	2	1	-	-	-	-	-	-
Glycymeris	-	-	-	-	-	-	-	-	-	-
Anodonta	-	-	-	-	-	-	-	-	-	-
Miscellaneous	-	-	-	-	-	-	-	-	-	-
Cut										
Laevicardium	-	-	-	-	-	-	-	-	-	-
Glycymeris	-	-	-	-	-	-	-	-	-	-
Anodonta	-	-	-	-	-	-	-	-	-	-
Miscellaneous	-	-	-	-	-	-	-	-	-	-
Utilitarian Items										
Awls	-	-	-	-	-	-	-	-	-	-
Scoops	-	-	-	-	-	-	-	-	-	-
Miscellaneous	-	-	-	-	-	-	-	-	-	-
Beads										
Whole Shell	5	1	-	-	-	-	-	-	-	-
Barrel	3	-	-	-	-	-	-	-	-	-
Disc	-	-	-	-	-	-	-	-	-	-
Bi-lobed	-	-	-	-	-	-	-	-	-	-
Claw-shaped	-	-	-	-	-	-	-	-	-	-
Pendants										
Whole	-	-	-	-	-	-	-	-	-	-
Cut/Ground	1	-	-	-	-	-	-	-	-	-
Indeterminate	-	-	-	-	-	-	-	-	-	-
Effigy	-	-	-	-	-	-	-	-	-	-
Bracelets										
Type A	8	-	6	2	-	-	-	-	1	1
Type B	-	-	-	-	-	-	-	-	-	-
Carved	-	-	-	-	-	-	-	-	-	-
Rings										
Conus	-	-	-	-	-	-	-	-	-	-
Glycymeris	-	-	-	-	-	-	-	-	-	-
Miscellaneous										
Frogs	-	-	-	-	-	-	-	-	-	-
Tinklers (?)	1	-	-	-	1	-	-	-	-	-
Zoomorphic	-	-	-	-	-	-	-	-	-	-
Geometric Forms	-	-	-	-	-	-	-	-	-	-
TOTAL	21	2	10	4	1	0	0	0	1	1

Table 79. (continued)

	Feature									
	110	111	112	113	114	115	116	117	118	119
Unworked Raw Material										
Laevicardium	-	-	-	-	-	2	-	-	-	1
Glycymeris	-	-	-	-	-	-	-	-	-	-
Anodonta	-	-	1	-	-	-	-	-	-	1
Cerithidea	-	-	-	-	-	-	-	-	-	-
Haliotis	-	-	-	-	-	-	-	-	-	-
Olivella	-	-	-	-	-	-	-	-	-	-
Pecten	-	-	1	-	-	-	-	-	-	-
Turritella	-	1	-	-	-	-	-	-	-	-
Strombus	-	-	-	-	-	-	-	-	-	-
Miscellaneous	-	-	-	-	-	1	-	-	-	-
Freshwater Snail	1	-	-	-	-	1	-	-	-	-
Worked Shell										
Fragments										
Ground or Polished										
Laevicardium	-	-	1	-	-	-	-	-	-	2
Glycymeris	-	-	-	-	-	-	-	-	-	-
Anodonta	-	-	-	-	-	-	-	-	-	-
Miscellaneous	-	-	-	-	-	-	-	-	-	-
Cut										
Laevicardium	-	-	1	-	-	-	-	-	-	-
Glycymeris	-	-	-	-	-	-	-	-	-	-
Anodonta	-	-	-	-	-	-	-	-	-	-
Miscellaneous	-	-	-	-	-	-	-	-	-	-
Utilitarian Items										
Awls	-	-	-	-	-	-	-	-	-	-
Scoops	-	-	-	-	-	-	-	-	-	-
Miscellaneous	-	-	-	-	-	-	-	-	-	-
Beads										
Whole Shell	-	-	-	-	-	-	1	-	-	-
Barrel	-	-	-	-	-	-	-	-	-	-
Disc	-	-	1	-	-	-	-	-	-	-
Bi-lobed	-	-	-	-	-	-	-	-	-	-
Claw-shaped	-	-	-	-	-	-	-	-	-	-
Pendants										
Whole	-	-	-	-	-	-	-	-	-	-
Cut/Ground	2	-	-	-	-	1	-	-	-	-
Indeterminate	-	-	-	-	-	-	-	-	-	-
Effigy	-	-	-	-	-	-	-	-	-	-
Bracelets										
Type A	-	-	2	1	-	2	1	-	-	3
Type B	-	-	-	-	-	-	-	-	-	-
Carved	-	-	-	-	-	-	-	-	-	-
Rings										
Conus	-	-	-	-	1	-	-	-	-	-
Glycymeris	-	-	-	-	-	-	-	-	-	-
Miscellaneous										
Frogs	-	-	-	-	-	-	-	-	-	-
Tinklers (?)	-	-	-	-	-	-	-	-	-	-
Zoomorphic	-	-	-	-	-	-	-	-	-	-
Geometric Forms	-	-	-	-	-	-	-	-	-	-
TOTAL	3	1	7	1	1	7	2	0	0	7

Table 79.   (continued)

	Feature									
	120	121	122	123	124	125	40a	72a	72b	B4
Unworked Raw Material										
Laevicardium	-	-	-	-	-	-	-	-	-	-
Glycymeris	-	-	-	-	-	-	-	-	-	1
Anodonta	-	-	-	-	-	-	-	-	-	-
Cerithidea	-	-	-	-	-	-	-	-	-	-
Haliotis	-	-	-	-	-	-	-	-	-	-
Olivella	-	-	-	-	-	-	-	-	1	-
Pecten	-	-	-	-	-	-	-	-	-	-
Turritella	-	-	-	-	-	-	-	-	-	-
Strombus	-	-	-	-	-	-	-	-	-	-
Miscellaneous	-	-	-	-	-	-	-	-	-	-
Freshwater Snail	-	-	-	-	-	-	-	-	-	-
Worked Shell										
Fragments										
Ground or Polished										
Laevicardium	-	-	-	-	-	-	-	-	-	-
Glycymeris	-	-	-	-	-	-	-	-	-	-
Anodonta	-	-	-	-	-	-	-	-	-	-
Miscellaneous	-	-	-	-	-	-	-	-	-	-
Cut										
Laevicardium	-	-	-	-	-	-	-	-	-	-
Glycymeris	-	-	-	-	-	-	-	-	-	-
Anodonta	-	-	-	-	-	-	-	-	-	-
Miscellaneous	-	-	-	-	-	-	-	-	-	-
Utilitarian Items										
Awls	-	2	-	-	-	-	-	-	-	-
Scoops	-	-	-	-	-	-	-	-	-	-
Miscellaneous	-	-	-	-	-	-	-	-	-	-
Beads										
Whole Shell	-	-	1	-	-	-	1	-	-	-
Barrel	-	-	-	-	-	-	-	-	-	-
Disc	-	-	-	-	-	-	-	-	-	-
Bi-lobed	-	-	-	-	-	-	-	-	-	-
Claw-shaped	-	-	-	-	-	-	-	-	-	-
Pendants										
Whole	-	-	-	-	-	-	-	-	-	-
Cut/Ground	-	-	-	-	-	-	-	-	-	1
Indeterminate	-	-	-	-	-	-	-	-	-	-
Effigy	-	-	-	-	-	-	-	1	-	-
Bracelets										
Type A	1	-	-	-	-	-	-	-	-	1
Type B	-	-	-	-	-	-	-	-	-	-
Carved	-	-	-	-	-	-	-	-	-	-
Rings										
Conus	-	-	-	-	-	-	-	-	-	-
Glycymeris	-	-	-	-	-	-	-	-	-	-
Miscellaneous										
Frogs	-	-	-	-	-	-	-	-	-	-
Tinklers (?)	-	-	-	-	-	-	-	-	-	-
Zoomorphic	-	-	-	-	-	-	-	-	-	-
Geometric Forms	-	-	-	-	-	-	-	-	-	-
TOTAL	1	2	1	0	0	0	1	1	1	3

Table 79.   (continued)

	Feature				Totals
	B6	B14	Cr1	Unk	
Unworked Raw Material					
Laevicardium	-	-	-	-	184
Glycymeris	-	-	-	-	4
Anodonta	-	-	-	-	59
Cerithidea	-	-	-	-	3
Haliotis	-	-	-	-	2
Olivella	-	-	-	-	31
Pecten	-	-	-	-	6
Turritella	-	-	-	-	4
Strombus	-	-	-	-	1
Miscellaneous	-	-	-	-	5
Freshwater Snail	-	-	-	-	14
Worked Shell					
Fragments					
Ground or Polished					
Laevicardium	-	-	-	-	56
Glycymeris	-	-	-	-	5
Anodonta	-	-	-	-	4
Miscellaneous	-	-	-	-	1
Cut					
Laevicardium	-	-	-	-	5
Glycymeris	-	-	-	-	1
Anodonta	-	-	-	-	14
Miscellaneous	-	-	-	-	3
Utilitarian Items					
Awls	-	-	-	-	8
Scoops	-	-	-	-	4
Miscellaneous	-	-	-	-	4
Beads					
Whole Shell	-	-	-	-	48
Barrel	-	-	-	-	17
Disc	-	-	-	-	14
Bi-lobed	-	-	-	-	4
Claw-shaped	-	-	-	-	6
Pendants					
Whole	-	-	-	18	21
Cut/Ground	-	1	-	-	35
Indeterminate	-	-	-	-	1
Effigy	-	-	-	-	5
Bracelets					
Type A	-	1	1	-	282
Type B	-	-	-	27	30
Carved	-	-	-	7	12
Rings					
Conus	1	-	-	1	8
Glycymeris	-	-	-	26	26
Miscellaneous					
Frogs	-	-	-	-	4
Tinklers (?)	-	-	-	-	11
Zoomorphic	-	-	-	-	5
Geometric Forms	-	-	-	-	3
TOTAL	1	2	1	79	953

APPENDIX G

POLLEN STUDIES AT LAS COLINAS

by Jamie Webb*
Department of Geosciences
University of Arizona

Part I: Analysis and Interpretation

Introduction

        Pollen analyses of archaeological sites have, in the past, been
interpreted in three ways: as reflecting paleoclimate or environment (Schoenwetter 1962; Hevly 1964), as indicating cultural disturbance (Kelso 1971), and
as indicating the presence of introduced species of plants (Bohrer 1970; Hill
and Hevly 1968). The present study at Las Colinas demonstrates aspects of all
three interpretations. First, a feature of the environment during occupation
that differs from present conditions is reflected by the presence of cattail
type pollen (Typha angustifolia type). On the other hand, Cactaceae pollen as
well as other desert types are found in both modern and site occupation samples
indicating little overall change in environment. An hypothesis of disturbance
at the site is supported by the high frequency of Cheno-am (members of the
Chenopodiaceae or goose-foot, and Amaranthaceae or pig-weed families) grains.
Cultural activities, such as agriculture and the introduction of new plants,
are demonstrated by the presence of Zea mays and Cucurbita pollen.

        The pollen analysis from Las Colinas is significant because it is from
a Hohokam site (A.D. 1180 to A.D. 1450) in which pollen sufficient for 200-grain
counts was found in all slides analyzed. Bohrer's (1970) study at Snaketown
found sufficient pollen for analysis only in trash mounds. Differences in
pollen quantities between Las Colinas and other areas may be due either to
preservation, or to different methods of extraction.

        Palynology has only recently been applied in Southwestern archaeological
studies. It is through studies such as Las Colinas that we are learning the
limitations of its application and the ways to derive the most information
possible within these limitations. Presently the greatest need is to plan the
sampling strategy ahead of time. The archaeologist and the palynologist should
decide before excavation begins what problems are presented by the site and
what types of samples could be used to help solve these problems.

Method

        Soil samples for the pollen analysis were collected by L. Hammack, the
project director, during excavation of the site. All samples were taken with

*Draft completed: September 1973

a clean trowel. Stratigraphic samples were collected from the bottom to the top of the stratigraphic column. The wall was freshly cleaned before each sample was selected. Samples from pits consisted of the dirt in the bottom of the pits. The samples were placed in plastic bags, sealed, and stored.

Pollen was extracted by the method commonly used for Southwestern alluvial samples as outlined in Mehringer (1968). In all, 37 samples were analyzed. Fourteen were samples from "puddling" pits, two from floors, 17 from two stratigraphic columns, two from burial vessels, and one from a nonassociated vessel. A 200-grain count was made of each slide on a Zeiss binocular microscope with 12x eyepieces and a 40x lens. In addition, each slide was scanned using a 20x lens. Pollen found on a slide but not in the 200-grain count is marked with a check on the pollen diagram (Figures 155-158).

Interpretation of Samples According to Provenience

Floor Samples

The pollen spectra in the two floor samples show no discernible trend. Of note is the absence of Zea mays pollen. Emil Haury suggests that most cooking occurred outdoors. However, the number of floor samples at this site is too small to make a statistically valid statement.

Samples from Burials

There are two interesting features in the pollen spectra of the burials. The Cheno-am frequency in Burial 4 was very high (90 percent). This could be related to general disturbance in the area or to the presence of an anther(s) in the grave.

A sample from a vessel associated with Burial 14 contained the highest incidence of oak pollen in the site (4 percent). Oak pollen corrodes quickly in an oxidizing environment and is present only in very small percentages in the rest of the site. One possible explanation for its occurrence in Burial 14 is that it is the residue of an offering of acorns, or stew made from the nuts. It could also be that conditions favored preservation.

Pit Samples

The appearance of cattail type pollen in "puddling" pits would indicate the use of water or mud that contained this pollen. This indicates that these pits were indeed used to mix plaster or mortar.

Storage Pit Sample

Cucurbita pollen occurs only in a pit previously identified by Hammack as a storage pit. The presence of squash pollen supports this identification.

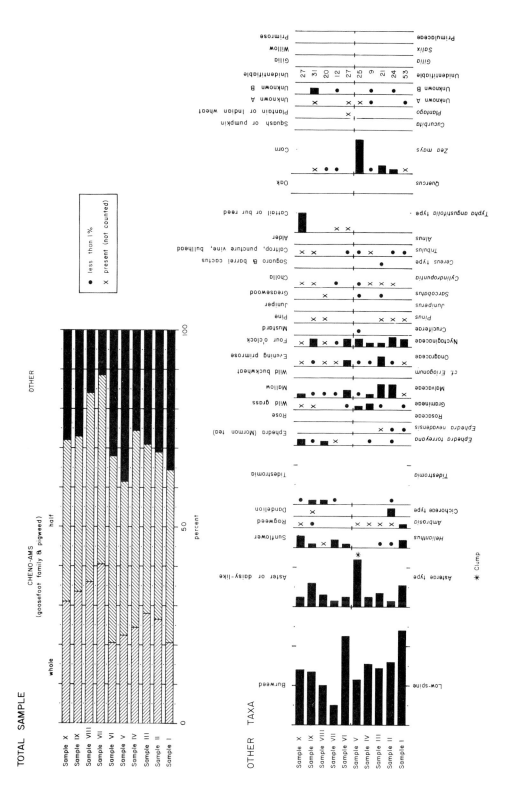

Figure 155. Percentages of pollen species from Feature 57

340

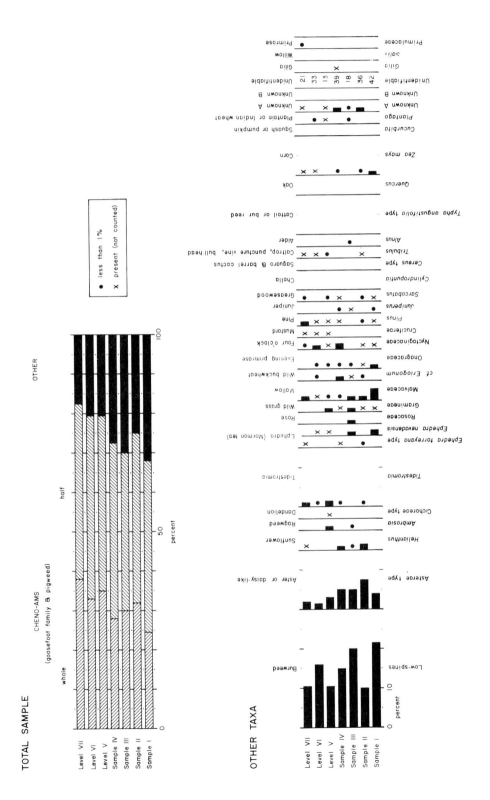

Figure 156. Percentages of pollen species from Feature 68

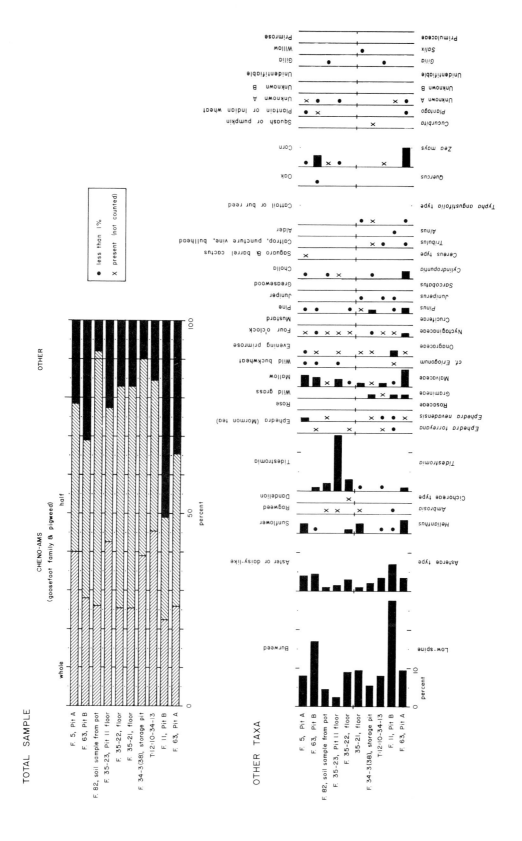

Figure 157. Percentages of pollen species from pits and floors

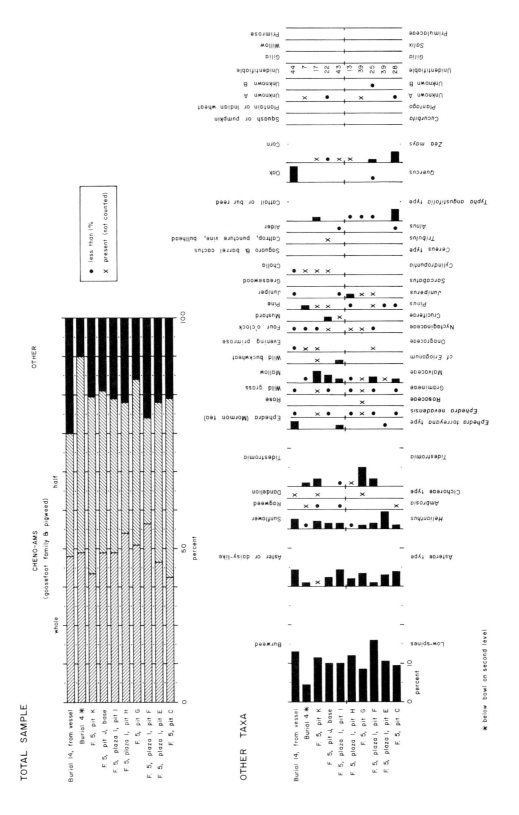

Figure 158. Percentages of pollen species from pits in Feature 5 and Burials 4 and 14

Samples from Stratigraphic Columns

Samples from Features 57 and 68, two dirt-filled pits inside a mound, were taken from stratigraphic columns. Hammack hypothesized that both features represented a single period of deposition, for it appeared that the prehistoric inhabitants had brought the dirt and packed it themselves. This is neither supported nor disproved by the pollen analysis.

There is no clear trend in the pollen spectra from either column; each is variable in both the major and minor pollen types. In Feature 68, Cheno-am pollen varied from 68 percent to 80.5 percent, and Compositae pollen varied from 10.5 percent to 21.5 percent. While these differences may seem large, the number of unidentifiable grains (from 4 to 42) makes a more detailed interpretation impossible. In Feature 57, the variation of percentages of both Cheno-am and Compositae pollen (61.5 percent to 88.5 percent, and 8 percent to 24 percent, respectively) is greater than that of Feature 68. In addition, samples in Feature 57 contained the highest percentage of Zea mays (14 percent in Sample V) found in the site as well as the highest percentage of cattail pollen (8 percent in Sample X). These irregularities do not support the hypothesis of a single period of deposition. It is possible, however, that uneven mixing of materials from different sources might account for these anomalies.

General Comparison of Pits, Floors, Vessels, Burials,
and Stratigraphic Columns

The pollen spectra of the various features exhibit no immediately apparent anomalies. No statistical tests were performed on the data. Two similarities in the spectra are notable: the Cheno-am/Compositae ratio, and the regular occurrence of pollen from three insect-pollenated plants in the families Malvaceae, Onagraceae, and Nyctaginaceae. It should be noted that some insect-pollenated plants may also be pollenated by birds, bats, and other animals, and that they may, on occasion, be pollenated by grains carried by the wind.

In comparison to modern surface samples, Cheno-am pollen is over-represented and Compositae pollen under-represented in all samples from Las Colinas. Two reasons are suggested for this difference. First, according to Martin (1963), plants of the Cheno-am group favor heavily disturbed ground. Since the area around a village and its fields would be heavily disturbed, one might expect an increase in the frequency of these plants. Second, there is a likelihood that the prehistoric inhabitants of Las Colinas used these types of plants for food. Castetter and Bell (1942:33) report the discovery of Amaranth seeds at Snaketown. And while modern Hopi do not cultivate weeds in their fields, there are certain plants that are encouraged when they do occur. Emory Sekaquaptewa has said that these plants are not pulled up but are watered and hoed along with the corn. Since it is possible that the Hohokam similarly encouraged grain Amaranthus or other Cheno-ams and gathered them for food, this could account for the increased percentages of Cheno-am pollen.

Pollen from three insect-pollenated plants are found in small but regular quantities (<10 percent) in the samples. Onagraceae (evening primrose) pollen occurs in 75.7 percent (28 of 37 samples), Malvaceae (mallow) in 97.3 percent (36 of 37 samples), and Nyctaginaceae (four-o'clock) in 86.5 percent (32 of 37 samples). Paul S. Martin has told me that the occurrence of pollen from insect-pollenated plants in quantities less than 10 percent is not unusual in modern studies. However, the regular occurrence of these three types of pollen introduces the possibility of their use, and invites additional study.

Flowers in the evening primrose family produce large amounts of pollen that is very viscid, that tends to stick together, and that is, therefore, not readily windblown. A seed of the genus Gaura was found in the site, but the majority of the pollen grains were Oenothera type. The highest percentages of evening primrose pollen were found in the stratigraphic columns. If the evening primroses were used one would expect to find the higher percentages in vessels or on floors. The data do not suggest that the evening primrose was used.

Mallow pollen was found in 19 samples in greater than trace amounts (but still less than 10 percent). Plants in the mallow family are reported to be used by both the Hopi and the Pima. However, the plants produce such quantities of pollen that it is visible on the anthers. High percentages are found in the samples from the stratigraphic columns as well as in other samples. Though the use of mallow is possible, this conjecture is not supported by the data.

Like the evening primrose, higher percentages of four-o'clock pollen are found in the stratigraphic columns than in the other samples. Small percentages of this pollen are commonly found in modern pollen rain studies.

While present evidence does not support the conjecture that these three plants were in use, it should be remembered that little is known about the medicinal or ceremonial use of trees, shrubs, and herbs. It is possible that by comparing samples from many sites, a pattern indicating this kind of use will emerge.

Missing Pollen Types

Pollen types of some plants that are known to have been used by aboriginal groups are missing. Pollen from Gossypium sp. (cotton), Phaseolus sp. (beans), and Prosopis sp. (mesquite) were not identified in the analysis.

To the author's knowledge (confirmed by discussion with colleagues at the University of Arizona), there is no occurrence of pollen from cotton or beans in soil samples from Southwestern archaeological sites. Bohrer (1970) found cotton seeds and charred beans in the trash mounds at Snaketown, but no mention of their pollen was made. Both plants are insect-pollenated. It may be that the pollen is very viscid, so that very little of it is released to the soil or wind. Another factor is susceptibility to corrosion. Pollen grains are not equally resistant to corrosion. Some corrode much more readily than others, and therefore they may not be identifiable.

Pollen from mesquite generally resembles many other pollen types, especially those in the same family (Leguminoseae). If the grain is crushed or corroded, identification may be difficult or impossible. Pollen in soil samples from Southwestern archaeological sites is usually corroded, probably due to oxidation and to the alkaline nature of the soil.

Chronological Interpretation

One important contribution of pollen analysis to archaeology is the possibility of interpreting changes in the pollen with time. This was not possible at Las Colinas for two reasons: lack of floor samples and inappropriate stratigraphic samples. A comparison of floor samples can be used for chronological interpretation if there are many samples available from each floor. Studies (Bohrer 1968) have shown that samples taken from the same floor are variable, so more than one sample is necessary to get a true picture of the pollen that is present. Only two floor samples were taken at Las Colinas.

Samples from vessels, burials, and pits are inherently biased. It is assumed that something happened in these areas that was different than events in ordinary living areas. The pollen samples should reflect this difference. Anomalies between samples can be attributed to differences in cultural use as well as to differences in time.

Samples from stratigraphic columns can also be used for chronological interpretations. A pit is dug in material that is known (or thought) to have accumulated over a period of time. This may be a trash mound, an early house, or some other place deemed suitable. Soil samples are taken from the side of the pit according to the stratigraphy or, if no strata are apparent, at arbitrary intervals. Changes in the pollen spectra should reflect changes over time in the pollen rain.

Stratigraphic columns from Features 57 and 68 were sampled at Las Colinas, but these features were pits which had apparently been purposely filled. Thus no information on change through time could be derived from them.

Conclusions

Pollen reflecting three different aspects of the total pollen rain--environment, disturbance, and cultural activity--was present in the samples from Las Colinas. Perennial water, not present in the modern environment, was indicated by the presence of cattail pollen in eleven samples. Cactaceae and other desert-plant pollen in site samples demonstrates a similarity to the modern environment. Percentages of most other types of pollen are either consistent with modern pollen rain studies or are not considered anomalous. Disturbance during occupation of the site and/or use of grain Amaranths or Chenopodiaceaes is indicated by the high Cheno-am/Compositae ratio found in all samples. Agricultural activity is reflected by Zea mays pollen. The presence of oak in a burial vessel may indicate an offering of some type.

One or two pollen types cannot be fully interpreted. Studies of the pollen rain in modern agricultural villages have not been made. Such studies are necessary to determine how the presence of a given pollen type is related to the regional pollen rain, to disturbance, and to cultural activity.

The present study and previous work in the Southwest form a preliminary base upon which interpretations can be built. As work continues and as the data base grows, the interpretations can be more comprehensive and stable. More intensive sampling with rigorous controls will enable investigators to use comparative data to determine trends not only within single sites, but within the Hohokam culture as a whole.

Part II: Ethnobotanical Implications of the Las Colinas Material

Introduction

This section of the appendix presents an alphabetized listing of the pollen species identified from samples recovered from the Las Colinas excavations. Accompanying each species description is a brief discussion of its known use based on ethnographic accounts of contemporary southwestern Indian groups and comparisons involving similar material recovered from archaeological contexts.

List of Pollen Types

Alnus sp.

While pollen of the wind-pollenated alder family is not common in the modern pollen rain of southern Arizona, Paul S. Martin has told me that it is not unusual to find a few pollen grains in the samples. This is especially true when the site is located near water which may carry the pollen from higher elevations. Schoenwetter and Doerschlag (1970) found one alder grain in their fifteen samples.

Library research indicates no known use.

Cactaceae: Cylindropuntia and Cereus Types

Plants in the family Cactaceae are insect-pollinated. Cylindropuntia refers to cholla-type cactus. Cereus includes a variety of cactus plants, among them the barrel cactus, the saguaro, and the organpipe cactus.

Schoenwetter and Doerschlag (1970) record only one Opuntia type pollen (which includes cholla) in their fifteen samples. This pollen occurs in percentages lower than 3 percent in modern samples of a transect of the Sonoran Desert (Hevly and others 1965). In the trash mounds at Snaketown, Bohrer (1970) found up to 5.5 percent Cylindropuntia type pollen grains. She interpreted this as indicating aboriginal use of the cholla. Cereus type pollen was found infrequently and in small amounts (0 to .25 percent) in lower bajada and flood-plain samples (Hevly and others 1965).

As is well known, the Papago collect the saguaro fruit in the summer to make an intoxicating liquor and a jam preserve. Hopi collect and eat the fruit of the hedgehog cactus and the cholla (Whiting 1939:86). The Papago eat the fruit of the cholla and also make a medicinal syrup from it (Castetter 1935:37). Various species of Echinocereus are eaten by different Pueblo Indians (Castetter 1935:26).

Cheno-am Type Pollen

The category Cheno-am consists of pollen from the family Chenopodiaceae (goose-foot family) and the genus Amaranthus of the family Amaranthaceae (the pig-weed family). With a few exceptions (such as Sarcobatus), the pollen of these plants is virtually indistinguishable from one another. Both groups are wind-pollenated. Common genera of Chenopodiaceae are Chenopodium or goose-foot and Atriplex or salt-bush.

Generally, pollen grains that are damaged or incomplete are counted as whole grains if they can be identified at all. Because many of the Cheno-ams were split, it was feared that they would be over-represented if they were given the same value as whole grains. Half grains of Cheno-ams were therefore counted separately from whole grains. Two half grains equal one whole grain in the final percentages.

Martin's (1963) Cheno-am grain counts for the modern pollen rain in the Sonoran Desert were 47 percent and 48 percent. With one exception, Schoenwetter and Doerschlag (1971) record percentages of Cheno-am type pollen of less than 15 percent in samples from floodplains. In samples taken from a plowed area the Cheno-am content jumped to about 35 percent. Nearly the same percentage of Cheno-am pollen was found in a floodplain deposit further south (Hevly and others 1965).

Seeds of the Chenopodium leptophyllum Moq. Nutt. are eaten by the Zuni, while the seeds and flowers of C. cornutum are eaten by the Hopi. The Pima consume the seeds of both C. murale L. and Atriplex Lentiformis (Torr.) Wats. (Castetter 1935:18). Whiting (1939:73) reports that the young leaves of certain species of goose-foot are cooked and eaten as greens by the Hopi. Castetter and Bell (1942:33) cite the recovery of gallons of charred Amaranth seeds from Snaketown, a Hohokam site 35 miles south of Phoenix. Bohrer (1962:109) suggests that Amaranthus sp. might have been cultivated by the Hohokam as well as by other aboriginal groups. For a more detailed discussion of this subject, see Bohrer (1962).

Compositae: Low-spine, Ambrosia, Asterae, Helianthus and Cichorae

The sunflower family is a large and complex group. In this family, plants which produce low-spine pollen are wind-pollinated. Some of the more common are the bur-sages and Ambrosia, or ragweed. Asterae and Helianthus pollen are commonly combined in the high-spine group. Asterae type plants (daisy-like) may be either wind-pollenated or insect-pollenated. Those plants related to the sunflower (Helianthus) are commonly insect-pollenated. Cichorae, also insect-pollenated, includes those plants related to the common dandelion.

Low-spine Compositae pollen is generally the most common type found in analyses of surface samples from the lower bajadas and floodplains of the Sonoran Desert. Percentages for southern Arizona range from 21.5 percent to 73 percent (Hevly and others 1965:129). In central Arizona the range is 28 percent to 49 percent (Schoenwetter and Doerschlag 1970).

The sunflower has been cultivated by the Pueblo, Apache, and Navajo for its edible seeds (Castetter 1935:30). The Pima use the sap of the brittle-bush (Encelia farinosa Gray) as a chewing-gum (Castetter 1935:31). The Hopi use many genera of Compositae plants as dyes, teas, medicines, emetics, and panaceas (Whiting 1939:94-99).

The significance of the proportion of Cheno-am to Compositae type pollen has generated much controversy among palynologists in the Southwest. These proportions have been variously interpreted as reflecting climate or environment (Schoenwetter 1962 and 1967), disturbance (Martin and Byers 1965, Jelinek 1966, Kelso 1971), or other cultural factors (Hill and Hevly 1968). One reason for the confusion is that the environmental implications of these two pollen groups have not been thoroughly studied. Concerning the proportion in the modern pollen rain, Martin (1963:21) states:

> The ratio of cheno-ams to Compositae...appears to change with alti-
> tude. Cheno-ams reach a maximum between 1,200 and 1,300 m., where
> they may exceed 90 percent of the total pollen count. At lower
> elevations they are replaced by Franseria, Hymenoclea, and various
> high-spine pollen types.

Of the occurrence of Cheno-ams he said:

> With rare exceptions the flood plain environment at present is
> dominated by cheno-am pollen. The cheno-ams reflect a low water
> table in the flood plain, a high soil salt content, and a climate
> characterized by heavy summer rain (Martin 1963:69).

He also indicates that Cheno-ams prefer disturbed ground (Martin 1963:49). Compositae plants are seen as occupying an environment that directly contrasts to that of the Cheno-ams (Martin 1963:23), "...a relatively undissected flood plain with a high water table and non-saline soil..."

The key to the interpretation of Cheno-am and Compositae type pollen in Southwestern archaeological sites may be in the amount of disturbance a site would have experienced. In an area near fields that were being irrigated, one might expect a fairly high water table which would favor the growth of Compositae plants. But the constant disturbance in the fields and around the village would encourage the growth of Cheno-am type plants. I predict that if a modern Indian village were studied palynologically, one would find a rise in Cheno-am percentages near the village of 20 percent to 40 percent.

A new dimension in the interpretation of Cheno-am and Compositae pollen has been recently introduced by studies of the correlation between monthly precipitation and pollen production (Solomon and Dayes 1972). Compositaes that produce pollen during the spring are strongly related to rainfall which occurs between November and March. On the other hand, spring pollen production of Cheno-ams is quite low. With summer Compositae production there is a "remarkably consistent lack of response...to monthly moisture" (Solomon and Dayes 1972:29). Summer Cheno-am pollen production is directly related to summer moisture and inversely related to winter moisture. Compositae pollen production has both a spring and a summer peak, while Cheno-am production occurs mainly in summer, equalling more than twice the Compositae production for that reason. The implications of this data for alluvial and archaeological palynology have not been fully studied.

Cruciferae

Plants in the mustard family, which are insect-pollenated, are a common sight in the Sonoran Desert in the spring. Sometimes their blooms cover large fields. Small percentages of mustard pollen were occasionally found by Martin (1963).

The tender plants of the tansy mustard , Sophia sp., are eaten by the Pueblo Indians of New Mexico (Castetter 1935:25). (This genera is probably Kearney and Peeble's [1960] Descurainia.) The Hopi eat two species of Stanleya as greens in the spring (Whiting 1939:77). They use Descurainia pinnata (Walt.) Britton in the preparation of paint for pottery and as a spring green (Whiting 1939:77).

Cucurbita sp.

Corrosion of the surface of the pollen grain prevented the identification of the species of the Cucurbita (squash or pumpkin family) found. Cucurbita species are insect-pollenated.

Cucurbita spp. occur as both native plants in the Sonoran Desert and as cultivated gourds (Whiting 1939:92-93). Their meaning as an economic indicator is therefore ambiguous.

Ephedra torreyana and Ephedra nevadensis

Both types of Ephedra (the joint fir family, includes Mormon tea) are wind-pollenated. Both are commonly found in the modern pollen rain of the lower elevations in southern Arizona (Martin 1963; Schoenwetter and Doerschlag 1970; Hevly and others 1965).

The Hopi used E. torreyana, as did later settlers, to treat syphilis (Whiting 1939:63). E. nevadensis is made into a tea drunk for refreshment by the Papago (Castetter and Underhill 1935:27).

Eriogonum

The wild-buckwheat of the Polygonaceae family is both wind- and insect-pollenated.

Eriogonum grains occur in small amounts with regularity in Schoenwetter and Doerschlag's samples from floodplains in central Arizona (1970).

The Hopi combine the boiled leaves of E. corymbosum with corn to form a type of bread (Castetter 1935:29). Some species of wild-buckwheat are also used by the Hopi to relieve menstrual pain and during childbirth (Whiting 1939:73).

Gilia sp.: Polemoniaceae or Phlox Family

Gilia is a common, showy, insect-pollenated plant. Native species in the phlox family are presently cultivated in gardens.

Neither Martin (1963) nor Schoenwetter and Doerschlag (1970) record Gilia in their modern counts, but small percentages are not considered unusual.

Two species of Gilia are used by the Hopi for medicinal and ceremonial purposes (Whiting 1939:87).

Gramineae and Zea mays

The pollen of cultivated grasses is, in theory, similar to that of wild grasses in all characteristics except size. The upper limit for classification as Zea mays is arbitrarily taken to be 60 microns to 70 microns. In practice, Zea was identified by a larger annulus (collar) and pore, as well as by the size difference. Corn pollen is indistinguishable from the pollen of the other cultivated grasses. Zea is assumed to be the only grass cultivated by the Hohokam at this site.

Juniperus

Juniper is wind-pollenated, and is a common, though minor, component of the pollen rain in the Sonoran Desert.

Malvaceae

The Malvaceae or mallow family is insect-pollenated. Two types of pollen from this family could be identified, though not with consistency. These were most like reference slides of the genera Sphaeralcea or globe mallow, and Malvastrum. Other types not identifiable as to genera were also present.

Martin (1963) occasionally found mallow pollen in very small percentages (.5 percent to 2 percent). Schoenwetter and Doerschlag (1970) do not mention it at all in their study of surface samples in the Sonoran Desert. Mallow pollen was also found in small percentages (less than 1 percent) in lower bajada and floodplain samples near Tucson (Hevly and others 1965).

Hopi chew the stems of Sphaeralcea angustifolia (Cav.) G. Don (Castetter 1935:31). "The Pima Indian name of these plants signifies 'a cure for sore eyes '" (Kearney and Peebles 1960:541).

Nyctaginaceae

The plants of the four-o'clock family, which are common in many parts of the Sonoran Desert, are insect-pollenated. Small amounts of four-o'clock pollen were found in surface samples from the lower bajadas and floodplains in southern Arizona (Hevly and others 1965:129).

The genus _Boerhaavia_, which the majority of the pollen grains in the samples most closely resemble, is used by the Hopi to swat flies (Whiting 1939:75).

Onagraceae

These plants are insect-pollenated herbs, or shrubs, in the evening-primrose family. After favorable rains, their flowers are a common sight on the desert floor.

The Mescalero Apache Indians gather the fruit of one genus for food (Castetter 1935:17).

Pinus

Pine trees are wind-pollenated and are prolific producers of pollen. It is not unusual to find pine pollen hundreds of miles from the nearest pine tree. Small percentages of pine are consistent with studies of the modern pollen rain in the desert (Martin 1963; Schoenwetter and Doerschlag 1970; Hevly and others 1965).

Plantago sp.

Plantain or Indian-wheat is a common plant found in much of Arizona (Kearney and Peebles 1960:802-805). Though some species have been introduced (Plantago _major_ L.), native ones are also abundant. It is both wind- and insect-pollenated.

Martin (1963) and Hevly and others (1965) found some plantain in their modern samples. Schoenwetter and Doerschlag (1970) have no record of _Plantago_.

Castetter (1935:42) says that the young leaves of _P. major_ (the introduced species) are used for food by the Acoma and Laguna.

Primulaceae

The insect-pollenated plants in the primrose family are not common to the lower desert regions but do occur occasionally. Many are found in the wet soil along streams, though Kearney and Peebles (1960) have no report or record of the plant in Maricopa County. This may be a misidentification.

Quercus sp.

Pollen from oak trees is often found in small percentages in the modern pollen rain. Quercus sp. grains were found in four of five samples taken from floodplains in central Arizona (Schoenwetter and Doerschlag 1970). Small percentages of oak were found in all modern samples taken from lower elevations in southern Arizona (Martin 1963). In the study of an archaeological site near Tucson (Lytle 1971), it was found that modern surface samples contained up to 7.5 percent oak pollen, while site samples contained less than 3 percent. The difference was thought to be due to the rapid corrosion of oak under oxidizing conditions (Havinga 1964). Such deterioration makes identification impossible.

Acorns are eaten or used by many Indian groups. In Arizona, acorns are boiled or roasted by the Navajo (Castetter 1935:47) and the Apache. The Pima obtain acorns from the Papago, then parch and grind them to make flour (Castetter 1935:47). The Hopi make use of oak for various utensils and weapons (Whiting 1939:72).

Rosaceae

The rose family contains a variety of insect-pollenated herbs, shrubs, and trees. Plants of this family present in Maricopa County are Vauquelinia californica (Torr.) Sarg., Rubus arizonensis Focks (R. oligospermus Thornber.), Cowania mexicana D. Don (Kearney and Peebles 1969). Rosaceae pollen is not common in the pollen record of southern Arizona.

Cowania stansburiana was used by the Hopi to make cradle boards and arrows, and served as an emetic, and as a wash for wounds (Whiting 1939:78).

Salix sp.

Willow trees are both wind- and insect-pollenated. Though neither Martin (1963) nor Schoenwetter and Doerschlag (1970) report occurrences of Salix in modern pollen rain from the Sonoran Desert, it might be expected in a site associated with water. Aspects of the grains and the lack of corrosion indicate that this occurrence is a modern contaminant.

Sarcobatus sp.

Sarcobatus sp. (greasewood) is one of the few identifiable pollen types in the family Chenopodiaceae. It is found in Maricopa County and grows at elevations ranging from 1000 feet to 6000 feet in moist, saline soil (Kearney and Peebles 1960:262). Spaulding has told me that Sarcobatus is not unusual in the pollen record of the Sonoran Desert.

Greasewood is used by the Hopi for fuel in kivas, for making rabbit sticks and planting sticks, and for general construction (Whiting 1939:74).

Tidestromia

Tidestromia is a small, insect-pollenated annual in the family Amaranthaceae. Library research indicates that it is not used. High percentages of Tidestromia in site samples may occur because the plant favors disturbed ground.

Tribulus sp.

Tribulus, an insect-pollenated weed found throughout the state, is known as caltrop, puncture vine, bull-head, or bur-nut (Kearney and Peebles 1969:491).

It is not recorded in modern sediments by Martin (1963) or Schoenwetter and Doerschlag (1970).

Library research indicates that it is not used.

Typha angustifolia

Pollen of Typha angustifolia (cattail) and Sparganium sp. (bur-reed) are difficult to distinguish, especially if some corrosion has occurred. However, they grow in similar environments. Cattails are found in marshy or wet places. Bur-reeds are aquatic or semi-aquatic herbs. Solomon has told me that although they are both wind-pollenated, the pollen is most common in moist or semi-moist environments. The mature heads of T. angustifolia are used by the Hopi Indians as chewing gum, and the children chew the stems much as Hawaiian children chew sugar cane (Whiting 1939:64).

Unknowns and Unidentifiables

Unknowns are pollen grains that cannot be identified, even though they are intact and undamaged. Pollen grains listed as unidentifiables are so corroded or mangled that they cannot be identified. The number in the unidentifiable column was in addition to the 200-grain count. The percentage of unidentifiable grains is given by this formula:

N = number unidentifiable grains in the slide

$$\frac{N}{200 + N} = \text{percent of N in total count}$$

The number of grains that could not be identified is an index of the corrosion of the samples and must be considered in interpretation and comparison of pollen counts. With large numbers of unidentifiable grains present, one should be cautious in drawing conclusions from the pollen data.

Unknown A is a fairly large (30 microns to 50 microns), periporate, echinate grain with a very thick exine. Its features are closest to the four-o'clock family. Reference slides of Nyctaginaceae genera were studied, but no grain was found which matched. Photographs of pollen grains taken by electron microscopy were also viewed. Unknown A is tentatively identified as a four-o'clock because of its general resemblance to pollen in this family.

Uknown B is a small (13 microns), micro-reticulate, tricolpate grain with no visible wall. This may be an example of a corroded grain that has lost its identifying features and that might be better classified as Unidentifiable.

APPENDIX H

IDENTIFICATION OF CHARCOAL FROM LAS COLINAS

by William J. Robinson*
Laboratory of Tree-Ring Research
University of Arizona

Feature Number	Location	Species	Comments
8	Loose disturbed fill above cap	Pinyon	
29	2 meters west of Feature 35, surface	Mesquite or Ironwood	Prehistoric?
34	Floor	Ocotillo?	
40a	Fill - east section	Palo verde?	
45	Level I fill	Ironwood	
48	Fill - west end	Mesquite	
61	Level II	Rodent bone	
77	-	Ironwood	
84	Floor contact	Ocotillo	
103	Fill above cap	Ironwood	
108	Fill above cap	Mesquite	

*Draft completed: June 1973

HISTORIC MATERIAL FROM LAS COLINAS

by Edward Staski*
Department of Anthropology
University of Arizona

Introduction

The historic material from Las Colinas includes the adobe house built on top of Mound 8, and the artifacts of modern or historic origin recovered from features elsewhere in the site. The purpose of this Appendix is to provide available documentation about the historic adobe house and to describe the character of the artifacts recovered from the excavations.

The Historic Adobe House

The most prominent historic feature associated with Mound 8 was certainly the historic adobe house constructed on top of the mound in the 1880s (Figure 159). The presence of this historic structure was perhaps the main reason that the mound survived as long as it did; much of the rest of the Las Colinas ruins group has been destroyed by the expansion of the Phoenix metropolitan area. The house was destroyed by fire in 1956; except for the depredations of vandals, the character of the site has not changed substantially since then.

The presence of the house affected both the excavation and interpretation of Las Colinas in ways that have been discussed by Hammack earlier in the volume. To recapitulate: a four-foot-deep basement (rare in this area) had been dug into the center of the mound, causing considerable damage to the prehistoric features there; and, after the house burned, the basement served as a convenient pit for the disposal of contemporary garbage and trash from nearby residences.

Documentation of the structure is incomplete because of the lack of historic records. Unlike cities and towns in the east, cities in the west often did not keep street atlases showing types of structures present and their street numbers. The adobe house at Las Colinas can be easily located since it was built on top of the prehistoric mound, but its original address is unknown. Various departments of the Phoenix city government were consulted on this question, but were unable to provide any information since the area in which the house stood was not incorporated into the City of Phoenix until 1959, three years after the structure burned.

The present owner of the land (the Arizona Department of Transportation) provided a description of the property. The description is as follows:

---

*Draft completed: August 1978

Figure 159. Historic adobe house on top of Mound 8

N2N2SW4NW4 except W 600' except E 30' of the N 30' except any point lying N of the following line: beginning 33' E of the NW corner SW4NW4 than S 23.1' E 1279.62' N 22.7' to N line SW4NW4.

The Artifacts

Many different kinds of material are represented in the collection of historic artifacts from Las Colinas. Unfortunately, the collection is so small that statistically accurate statements about the character of late nineteenth century Southwestern society cannot be derived from the available material.

There follows a descriptive listing, by feature number, of the historic artifacts recovered during the excavations. The frequencies of these artifacts are presented in Table 80.

List of Artifacts by Feature

Feature 0

1. Two-piece metal military button with a loop shank (Luscomb 1967:126); eagle and shield design in front; inscription on back: "...VILL"; ASM catalog number A-37,211. This is an enlisted man's button of the U.S. Army, and it is thought to postdate 1850. The style continues to the present (Luscomb 1967:11). Provenience: house basement.

2. Indian Head nickel, minted in 1919. ASM catalog number A-37,213. Provenience: surface stripping, northwest corner of mound.

Feature 1

1. Complete small brown glass bottle; 5 cm long; cylinder shaped; screw cap neck with a bore diameter of .7 cm; writing on base: "7". Provenience: general upper fill south of the eastern portion of the massive wall.

2. Neck and finish of a green bottle; two-piece mold with a seam that does not extend; bore diameter is 1.3 cm, outside diameter is 2.2 cm. Provenience: general fill north of massive wall.

3. Fragment of clear bottle glass with molded lettering: "[G]ARRE...," "ESTABLISHED," "1835," "...IRG...," "...REG...." Provenience: general fill, east side of mound.

4. Fragment of purple bottle glass; patinated. Provenience: fill east of massive wall.

5. Fragment of clear bottle glass; patinated. Provenience: fill east of massive wall.

6. Fragment of brown beer bottle glass; melted. Provenience: general fill.

7. Fragment of clear window pane. Provenience: general fill east and south of concrete well cap.

8. Two earthenware rim sherds; white glaze on both sides; both slightly burned. Provenience: fill along northeast wall.

9. Earthenware rim sherd; orange pastoral scene interior; underglaze; gilding along rim; burned. Provenience: fill along northeast wall.

10. Earthenware sherd; cobalt blue floral design exterior. Provenience: fill along northeast wall.

11. Stoneware rim sherd; salt glaze with blue design exterior. Provenience: fill along northeast wall.

12. Stoneware rim sherd; gray salt glaze exterior. Provenience: fill along northeast wall.

13. Brick fragment with some mortar attached. Provenience: general fill south of conrete well cap.

14. Fragment of aluminum. Provenience: Feature 1, south.

15. Cast iron stove fragment; 2.6 cm by 1.9 cm. Provenience: fill east wall, south of well.

16. Black, round object; not identifiable due to the effects of burning. Provenience: general fill, east side of mound.

Feature 2

1. Red agate marble. Agate marble production for the most part was restricted to Germany, where production began about 1869 and reached a peak in the 1880s. Agate marbles are rare today (Baumann 1970:22-23; Randall 1971). Provenience: southeast top of mound.

Feature 3

1. Earthenware sherd, possibly from a tile; gray salt glaze one side. Provenience: loose fill from vicinity of the board-lined latrine pit.

2. Early cat's-eye type marble; clear, with blue and red spirals in center; probably machine made (Randall 1971). Provenience: loose fill from vicinity of the board-lined latrine pit.

3. Clay marble; no decoration. Clay marbles were produced primarily in the late 19th and early 20th centuries in Europe and the United States. Commercially produced clay marbles in the United States are dated from 1884 to the end of the First World War (Baumann 1970:29; Randall 1971:103). Provenience: general fill.

4. Spherical lump of burned green glass; probably a marble. Provenience: loose fill from vicinity of board-lined latrine pit.

5. Button from a Navy pea coat; 3.1 cm in diameter; anchor design on front; four holes. Provenience: loose fill near northeast corner of house.

6. Brass button with textured "zig-zag" line design; 1.6 cm in diameter; two holes. Provenience: loose fill from vicinity of board-lined latrine pit.

7. Large fragment and numerous small fragments of a hollow, thin, and fragile glass bead; drilled, with .2 cm bore diameter; overall diameter is 1.3 cm. Provenience: loose fill from vicinity of board-lined latrine pit.

8. Fragment of percussion lock from the left side of a gun. Provenience: loose fill from vicinity of board-lined latrine pit.

9. Skeleton key. Provenience: loose fill from vicinity of board-lined latrine pit.

10. Two spoons. Provenience: loose fill from vicinity of board-lined latrine pit.

11. Miniature plate, white glaze; child's toy; diameter is 5.3 cm. Provenience: loose fill from vicinity of board-lined latrine pit.

12. Porcelain doll's head; 2.8 cm high; painted black hair, and features. Provenience: loose fill from vicinity of board-lined latrine pit.

13. Rodent tooth. Provenience: loose fill from vicinity of board-lined latrine pit.

Feature 4

1. United States Lincoln penny; San Francisco Mint, 1939; ASM catalog number A-37,212. Provenience: top of wall.

Feature 5

1. Earthenware sherd; green design one side. Provenience: general fill, exterior area north of mound.

2. Complete oval eye piece from spectacles. Provenience: general stripping outside north massive wall.

3. Glass portion of an eye dropper; almost complete; patinated; 5.5 cm long. Provenience: general stripping outside north massive wall.

4. Fragment of historic whetstone. Provenience: general stripping north of Feature 25.

5. Iron wire handle. Provenience: general stripping area north of massive wall.

Feature 7

1. Fragment of clear bottle glass. Provenience: trash area east of mound.

2. Fragment of purple bottle glass. Provenience: trash area east of mound.

3. Fragment of clear window pane. Provenience: trash area east of mound.

4. Earthenware sherd; white glaze both sides. Provenience: trash area east of mound.

5. Porcelain sherd; white; soft paste. Provenience: trash area east of mound.

6. Basal sherd of earthenware; blue transfer design on interior. Provenience: trash area east of mound.

7. Iron horseshoe. Provenience: trash area east of mound.

Feature 8

1. Basal fragment of a light green bottle patinated. Provenience: general upper fill, top of mound, south of house.

2. Earthenware rim sherd; white glaze, both sides. Provenience: general upper fill, top of mound, south of house.

3. Basal sherd of stoneware; gray salt glaze, both sides. Provenience: loose disturbed fill above last adobe cap.

Feature 10

1. Copper or brass plaque; floral border around a tram and station scene; 8 cm by 5.9 cm; rectangular shape; writing on front: "SUMMIT HOUSE PIKES PEAK," "ALTITUDE 14147 FEET"; writing on back: "MADE IN JAPAN." Provenience: general upper fill.

Feature 13

1. Fragment of clear jelly jar glass with red and pink design. Provenience: west of house, general upper fill above last adobe cap.

2. Gold peery marble; melted. Provenience: west of house, general upper fill.

3. Lump of potmetal (?). Provenience: general upper fill on top of mound near southwest corner of house.

Feature 17

Miscellaneous small pieces of iron. Provenience: general stripping south of Feature 40A.

Feature 21

1. Neck and finish of a light green bottle; patinated; no clear evidence of mold seam; wide mouth, possibly used for condiments; bore diameter is 3.2 cm; outside diameter is 3.8 cm. Provenience: general fill.

2. Fragment of light green bottle glass; patinated. Provenience: fill.

3. Basal fragment of a dark green wine bottle with kick-up; patinated. Provenience: west of Feature 23.

4. Fragment of purple bottle glass; patinated. Provenience: fill.

5. Stoneware sherd; gray salt glaze, both sides. Provenience: fill.

6. Stoneware sherd; dark brown glaze, both sides; ribbing on interior. Provenience: west of Feature 27, fill.

7. Five stoneware sherds; dark brown glaze, both sides; ribbing on interior. Provenience: fill.

Feature 25

1. One early glass marble with blue and black spiral design; burned and highly pot-lidded; opaque with evidence of cutting and grinding at one end; early machine made, dating from 1901 to 1926 (Randall 1971:105). Provenience: floor fill.

Feature 26

1. Eight fragments of brown bottle glass from a patent medicine bottle; patinated. Provenience: fill, subfloor Pit A, south side.

Feature 42

1. Fragment of brown beer bottle. Provenience: general fill.

Feature 43

1. Earthenware rim sherd; red and green floral design, interior; gilding along rim. Provenience: pit house, upper fill.

Feature 45

   1. U-shaped fragment of iron. Provenience: fill just below basement floor.

   2. Two fragments of copper tubing. Provenience: fill below basement.

Feature 48

   1. Iron rod fragment. Provenience: below basement.

   2. Two fragments of iron. Provenience: fill west of cross wall.

Feature 49

   1. Small blue glass bead; almost spherical; .7 cm in diameter. Provenience: upper fill.

   2. Two cut shell coat buttons; two holes in each (one has a brown thread intact); shell polished in front; 2 cm diameter. Provenience: upper fill.

Feature 69

   1. One mangled iron fence staple. Provenience: fill.

Feature 72

   1. Lump of melted lead. Provenience: Level 3, Area B.

Feature 82

   1. Several fragments of a pocket knife. Provenience: upper fill.

Feature 84

   1. Iron buckle. Provenience: fill.

Feature 114

   1. Fragment of light green bottle glass; patinated. Provenience: upper fill.

Fill of House Foundation

1. Pistol, 44 caliber. Barrel and cylinder are badly rusted, and most of the underlying metal is probably oxidized also. The handle is in good condition, as is the trigger guard, which has turned green. A screw is missing from the butt. The trigger is also missing. Part of the thumb cock of the hammer is missing. A few rounds remain in the chambers of the cylinder. Bruce Huckell has told me that the small trigger guard is diagnostic of an early model Navy Colt, predating 1863. The serial number 6479 appears on the butt near the screw hole. It is reported that Broyles, the last person to live in the house, told the archaeologists that he could not remember ever having seen the pistol. The weapon may have been stuck in a joist in the basement, and may have become part of the foundation fill after the fire. ASM catalog number A-37,209.

Unknown Provenience

1. Numerous scraps of paper, many with illegible handwriting, were recovered, including a letter and an envelope. The envelope has a green 2-cent stamp, and the cancellation mark: "Chi... Feb 6   4 PM   AA   1888." Printed letterhead has the following notation: "149 Wabash Ave., Chic...." The contents of the letter are handwritten and are illegible.

2. Bone toothbrush handle. Inscription: "6 4 M   JOHN GOSNELL & CO. LONDON."

3. Gray button; 1.8 cm in diameter.

4. Two coat buttons; black and brown line design on front; one hole in front opens to two holes in back--the so-called "whistle button" arrangement of holes (Luscomb 1967:221); 2.4 cm in diameter.

5. Black shank button; loop shank with shank plate (see Luscomb 1967: 127); engraved flower design on front; 1.5 cm in diameter.

Summary

This appendix has presented a description of the historic artifacts found at the Las Colinas site and an outline of the available history concerning the adobe house on Mound 8. The archaeology of late nineteenth century Southwestern sites is not well understood. Since the excavation of Las Colinas, the archaeological investigations of this region and historical period have grown in number and in sophistication (see R. McGuire 1979; T. McGuire 1980).

Table 80.   Historic artifacts recovered from Las Colinas

Artifact Type	Frequency
Beads	
Fragile, whole	1
Blue glass	1
	2
Buttons	
Metal military (ASM Cat. No. A-37,211)	1
Navy pea coat type	1
Brass	1
Cut shell	2
Coat	2
Black shank	1
	8
Ceramics	
Earthenware Sherds	
White glaze	3
Orange pastoral scene	1
Cobalt blue floral	1
Gray salt glaze--tile	1
Red and green floral, interior design	1
Green design	1
Interior blue transfer design	1
Stoneware Sherds	
Salt glaze with interior blue design	1
Gray salt glaze	2
Dark brown glaze	6
	18
Coins	
Buffalo Indian Head nickel, minted 1-1919 (ASM Cat. No. A-37,213)	1
U.S. Lincoln penny, minted 1-1939 (ASM Cat. No. A-37,212)	1
	2

Table 80.   (continued)

Artifact Type	Frequency
Firearms	
Fragment of a percussion lock	1
Forty-four caliber pistol (ASM Cat. No. A-37,209)	1
	2
Glass	
Brown bottle fragment	1
Brown medicine bottle fragments	4
Brown beer bottle fragments	2
Light green bottle fragments	4
Green bottle necks	2
Dark green wine bottle	1
Purple bottle glass fragments	2
Purple glass fragments	1
Clear glass fragments	2
Clear window fragments	2
Clear bottle fragment	1
Clear jelly glass fragment	1
Oval eyepiece	1
Eye dropper	1
	25
Marbles	
Red agate	1
Early cat's eye	1
Green lump, burned	1
Peery	1
Early opaque	1
Clay	1
	6
Metal Objects	
Copper or brass plaque	1
Copper tubing	2
Iron buckle	1
Iron horseshoe	1
Cast iron stove fragment	1
Iron fence staple	1
Iron wire handle	1

Table 80.   (continued)

Artifact Type	Frequency
Metal Objects (continued)	
Iron rod fragment	1
U-shaped iron fragment	1
Unidentified iron fragments--several	2+
Potmetal lump	1
Lead lump	1
Skeleton key	1
Pocket knife fragments--several	2+
Spoons	2
Aluminum fragment	1
	20+
Toys	
Miniature plate, white glaze	1
Porcelain doll's head	1
	2
Miscellaneous	
Brick fragment	1
Unidentified black, round caked object, burned	1
Toothbrush handle	1
Whetstone fragment	1
Rodent tooth	1
Paper scraps with undecipherable writing--several	2+
	7+
TOTAL	92+

APPENDIX J

ARIZONA STATE MUSEUM PHOTOGRAPHIC NEGATIVE NUMBERS
AND SPECIMEN NUMBERS OF CATALOGUED ARTIFACTS
FROM LAS COLINAS

by Kim E. Beckwith and Benjamin W. Smith
Arizona State Museum
University of Arizona

Chapter 3 - Architecture

Page Number	Figure Number	ASM Negative Number
16	5	Not assigned
16	6	Not assigned
19	7	33089
22	9	33272
22	10	32493
24	11	33142
26	12	33160
26	13	33297
32	16	33239
32	17	33235
33	18	33047
54	29	33187
56	30	32599
57	31	32549
57	32	32548
58	33	32977
66	34	33198
66	35	33052
68	36	32799
68	37	33024
71	38	33287
73	39	33221
73	40	32469
76	41	32512
76	42	32522
78	43	33279
80	44	38431
80	45	32611
81	46	32667
81	47	32671

Chapter 4 - Analysis of the Las Colinas Ceramics

Page Number	Figure Number	ASM Catalog Number
152	99	a = A-49,080-x; b = same; c = same; d = A-49,081-x; e = same; f = same; g = A-49,082-x; h = same; i = same
156	100	a-i = A-49,090-x
156	101	a-h = A-49,089-x
157	102	a-h = A-49,091-x
163	106	A-37,254
166	109	a = A-49,097; b = A-49,095; c = A-49,096; d = A-37,203-x-6; e = A-37,203-x-5; f = A-37,203-x-15; g = A-37,203-x-16
166	110	a = A-37,245; b = A-49,092; c = A-49,093; d = A-49,094

Chapter 5 - The Las Colinas Flaked Stone Assemblage

Page Number	Figure Number	ASM Catalog Number
174	111	a = A-37,093-x-2; b = A-37,104-x-1; c = A-37,095-x-1; d = A-37,097-x-1; e = A-37,092-x-2; f = A-37,111-x-2; g = A-37,098-x-1; h = A-37,090; i = A-37,106-x-2; j = A-37,100-x-1; k = A-37,111-x-1; l = A-37,088; m = A-37,101-x-1; n = A-37,087
174	112	a = A-37,094-x-1; b = A-37,091-x-1; c = A=37,109-x-1; d = A-37,099-x-2; e = A-37,099-x-1; f = A-37,089; g = A-37,091-x-2; h - A-36,086; i = A-37,085; j = A-37,118; k = A-37,092-x-1
179	114	b = A-37,214; d = A-37,122
184	116	a = A-37,215; c = A-37,116; 3 = A-37,117
195	122	d = A-37,119

Chapter 6 - The Nonflaked Stone Artifacts from Las Colinas

Page Number	Figure Number	ASM Catalog Number
203	126	A-37,190
208	127	a = A-46,728; b = A-46,726; c = A-46,727; d = A-46,725; e = A-46,729
208	128	a = A-37,178; b = A-37,177
215	129	mano = A-37,197
215	130	a = A-37,188

Page Number	Figure Number	ASM Catalog Number
220	131	A = A-37,134; B = A-37,159; C = A-37,151-x-3; 1 = A-37,146-x-3; 2 = A-37,145; 3 = A-37,146; 4 = A-37,147-x-3; 5 = A-37,161; 6 = A-37,162-x-1
223	132	a = A-37,125; b = A-37,126-x-1; c = A-37,132; d = A-37,133; e = A-37,134; f = A-37,135; g = A-37,140; h = A-37,136; i = A-37,137; j = A-37,138-x-8; k = A-37,142; l = A-37,141; m = A-37,217-x; n = A-37,131-x-2; o = A-37,131-x-1; p = A-37,131-x-3; q = A-37,144; r = A-37,137; s = A-37,138-x-1; t = A-37,138-x-4; u = A-37,138-x-3; v = A-37,138-x-5; w = A-37,138-x-2; x = A-37,138-x-7; y = A-37,138-x-6
226	133	a = A-37,127; b = A-37,130-x-2; c = A-37,130-x-1; d = A-37,165-x-3
226	134	a = A-37,180; b = A-37,179; c = 37,181
227	135	A-37,121
227	136	a = A-37,124; b = A-37,123
229	137	a = A-37,201; b = A-37,198; c = A-37,198-x-2

Appendix B - Disposal of the Dead at Las Colinas

Page Number	Figure Number	ASM Negative Number
262	140	32574
265	141	32502

Appendix C - Mammalian Remains from Las Colinas

Page Number	Olsen's (1968) Specimen Numbers
276	1-31; 1-107

Appendix D - Bone Artifacts from Las Colinas

Page Number	Figure Number	ASM Catalog Number
292	145	a = A-37,082; b = A-37,083; c = A-37,219; d = A-37,079; e = A-37,081; f = A-37,076; g = A-37,077; h = A-37,218; i = A-37,084; j = A-37,078; k = A-37,080

Appendix E - Avian Remains from Las Colinas

Page Number	Description	Feature - Artifact Number
	Anatidae	
297	Anas platyrhynchos	
	(complete femur)	49-64
	(distal end femur)	100-42
297	A. cygnoides	
	(humerus)	5-30
	(coracoid)	30-3
298	Cairina moschata	
	(mandible)	1-79
	Psittacidae	
298	Ara macao	
	(humerus, 4.3 mm x 3.1 mm)	4-24
	Phasianidae	
299	Meleagris gallopavo	
	(coracoid)	45-1
299	Callipepla	
	(5 humeri, 1 femur)	different pro- veniences
299	Gallus gallus	
	(10 elements)	49-26
	Accipitridae	
301	Buteo	
	(2 unguals, 1 partial sternum)	different pro- veniences
301	Parabuteo unicinctus	
	(ungual)	83-22
	Cuculidae	
301	Geococcyx californicus	
	(distal end of tarsometatarsus)	49-76

Page Number	Description	Feature - Artifact Number
	Corvidae	
301	*Corvus corax*	
	(femora)	22-7
	(femora)	5-62
	(partial ulna)	114-8
	Icteridae	
	Xanthocephalus xanthocephalus	
302	(humerus)	62-87

REFERENCES

Ahler, S.A.
1971   Projectile Point Form and Function at Rodgers Shelter, Missouri.
        Missouri Archaeological Society Research Series 8. Columbia.

Allen, G. M.
1920   Dogs of the American Aborigines. Bulletin of the Museum of
        Comparative Zoology 63(9). Cambridge.

Bahr, D., J. Gregorio, D. I. Lopez and A. Alvarez.
1974   Piman Shamanism and Staying Sickness (Kà:cim Mùmkidag). The
        University of Arizona Press, Tucson.

Bancroft, H. H.
1889   History of Arizona and New Mexico, 1530-1888, Volume 17. The
        History Company, San Francisco.

Bartlett, K.
1933   Pueblo Milling Stones of the Flagstaff Region and Their Relation to
        Others in the Southwest, A Study in Progressive Efficiency.
        Museum of Northern Arizona Bulletin 3. Flagstaff.

Bass, W. M.
1971   Human Osteology: A Laboratory and Field Manual of the Human
        Skeleton. Missouri Archaeological Society, Columbia.

Baumann, P.
1970   Collecting Antique Marbles. Mid-America Book Company, Leon, Iowa.

Binford, L. R.
1968   Archaeological Perspectives. In New Perspectives in Archaeology,
        edited by S. R. Binford and L. R. Binford, pp. 5-32. Aldine,
        Chicago.

1972a   An Analysis of Cremations from Three Michigan Sites. In An
        Archaeological Perspective, pp. 373-382. Seminar Press, New York.

1972b   Analysis of a Cremated Burial from the Riverside Cemetery,
        Menominee County, Michigan. In An Archaeological Perspective,
        pp. 383-389. Seminar Press, New York.

Bohrer, V. L.
1962   Nature and Interpretation of Ethnobotanical Materials from Tonto
        National Monument, 1957. In Archaeological Studies at Tonto
        National Monument, Arizona, by C. R. Steen, L. M. Pierson, V. L.
        Bohrer, and K. P. Kent. Southwestern Monuments Association
        Technical Series 2. Globe, Arizona.

Bohrer, V. L.
 1968   Paleoecology of an Archaeological Site near Snowflake, Arizona.
         Ph.D. Dissertation. University of Arizona, Tucson.

 1970   Ethnobotanical Aspects of Snaketown, a Hohokam Village in Southern
         Arizona. American Antiquity 35(4):413-430.

Brand, D. D., F. M. Hawley and F. C. Hibben
 1937   Tseh So, A Small House Ruin. The University of New Mexico Bulletin
         2(2). University of New Mexico Press, Albuquerque.

Breternitz, D. A.
 1960   Excavations at Three Sites in the Verde Valley, Arizona. Museum
         of Northern Arizona Bulletin 34. Flagstaff.

 1966   An Appraisal of Tree-Ring Dated Pottery in the Southwest. Anthro-
         pological Papers of the University of Arizona 10. University of
         Arizona Press, Tucson.

Brothwell, D.
 1963   Digging Up Bones. The British Museum, London.

Brothwell, D. and A. T. Sandison, editors.
 1967   Disease in Antiquity. C. C. Thomas, Springfield, Illinois

Burt, W. H. and R. P. Grossenheider
 1964   A Field Guide to the Mammals. The Riverside Press, Cambridge.

Carter, G. F.
 1971   Pre-Columbian Chickens in America. In Man Across the Sea, edited
         by C. L. Riley, J. C. Kelly, C. W. Pennington and R. L. Rand, pp.
         178-218. University of Texas Press, Austin.

Castetter, E. F.
 1935   Uncultivated Native Plants Used as Sources of Food. University of
         New Mexico Bulletin 4(1), pp. 7-62. University of New Mexico
         Press, Albuquerque.

Castetter, E. F. and W. H. Bell
 1942   Pima and Papago Indian Agriculture. Inter-American Studies I.
         University of New Mexico Press, Albuquerque.

Castetter, E. F. and R. M. Underhill
 1935   The Ethnobiology of the Papago Indians. University of New Mexico
         Bulletin 4(3). University of New Mexico Press, Albuquerque.

Cockrum, E. L.
 1960   The Recent Mammals of Arizona: Their Taxonomy and Distribution.
         University of Arizona Press, Tucson.

 1962   Introduction to Mammalogy. Ronald Press, New York.

Colton, H. S.
   1941   Winona and Ridge Ruin Part II: Notes on the Technology and Taxonomy of the Pottery. Museum of Northern Arizona Bulletin 19. Flagstaff.

Colton, H. S. and L. L. Hargrave
   1937   Handbook of Northern Arizona Pottery Wares. Museum of Northern Arizona Bulletin 11. Flagstaff.

Cosgrove, H. S. and C. B. Cosgrove
   1932   The Swarts Ruins: A Typical Mimbres Site in Southwestern New Mexico. Peabody Museum Papers 15(1). Cambridge.

Coues, E.
   1867   The Quadrupeds of Arizona. American Naturalist i:281-292, 351-363, 393-420, 531-541.

Crabtree, D. E.
   1972   An Introduction to Flintworking. Occasional Papers of the Idaho State University Museum 28. Pocatello.

Cushing, F. H.
   1890   Preliminary Notes on the Origin, Working Hypothesis and Primary Researches of the Hemenway Southwestern Archaeological Expedition. Congress International Des Americanistes, Compte-Rendu de la Septieme Session, pp. 151-194. Berlin.

Dalquest, W. W., E. Roth and F. Judd
   1969   The Mammal Fauna of Schulze Cave, Edwards County, Texas. Bulletin of the Florida State Museum 13(4), pp. 206-276.

Daly, P.
   1969   Approaches to Faunal Analysis in Archaeology. American Antiquity 34(2): 146-153.

Danson, E. B.
   1954   Pottery Type Descriptions. In Excavations, 1940, at University Indian Ruin, by Julian Hayden. Southwestern Monuments Association Technical Series 5, pp. 219-231. Globe, Arizona.

Danson, E. B. and R. M. Wallace
   1956   A Petrographic Study of Gila Polychrome. American Antiquity 22: 180-183.

Dean, J. S. and W. J. Robinson
   (1973)   Dendrochronology of Grasshopper Pueblo. Multidisciplinary Research at Grasshopper Ruin, edited by M. W. Graves, S. J. Holbrook, and W. A. Longacre. Anthropological Papers of The University of Arizona (In Press). University of Arizona Press, Tucson.

Debowski, S. S.
  1974   Provenience and Description of Shell and Miscellaneous Artifacts from the Escalante Ruin Group. In Excavations in the Escalante Ruin Group, Southern Arizona, by David E. Doyel, pp. 276-298. Arizona State Museum Archaeological Series 37. University of Arizona, Tucson.

Dick, H. W.
  1965   Bat Cave. School of American Research Monographs 27. Santa Fe.

Dickie, R. T.
  1965   A Study of Physical and Chemical Methods of Archaeological Data Retrieval. M.A. Thesis, Arizona State University, Tempe.

Di Peso, C. C.
  1951   The Babocomari Village Site on the Babocomari River, Southeastern Arizona. Amerind Foundation Publications 5. Dragoon, Arizona.

  1956   The Upper Pima of San Cayetano del Tumacacori: An Archaeo-historical Reconstruction of the Ootam of Pimería Alta. Amerind Foundation Publications 7. Dragoon, Arizona.

Doyel, D. E.
  1974   Excavations in the Escalante Ruin Group, Southern Arizona. Arizona State Museum Archaeological Series 37. University of Arizona, Tucson.

  1977   Classic Period Hohokam in the Escalante Ruin Group. Ph.D. Dissertation, University of Arizona, Tucson.

Ellis, F. H. and L. C. Hammack
  1968   The Inner Sanctum of Feather Cave, a Mogollon Sun and Earth Shrine Linking Mexico and the Southwest. American Antiquity 33(1):25-44.

Fewkes, J. W.
  1912   Casa Grande, Arizona. Annual Report of the Bureau of American Ethnology 28. Washington.

Fitzhugh, W. W.
  1972   Environmental Archaeology and Cultural Systems in Hamilton Inlet, Labrador. Smithsonian Contributions to Anthropology 16. Washington.

Franklin, H. H.
  n.d.   The Use of Percentages in Ceramic Analysis: An Example from Las Colinas. Unpublished Manuscript, on file Arizona State Museum, University of Arizona, Tucson.

Fritts, H. C.
  1965   Tree-ring Evidence for Climatic Changes in Western North America. Monthly Weather Review 93(7):421-443.

Fritts, H. C., T. J. Blasing, B. P. Hayden and J. E. Kutzbach
    1971   Multivariate Techniques for Specifying Tree-Growth and Climate
            Relationships and for Reconstructing Anomalies in Paleoclimate.
            Journal of Applied Meteorology 10(1):845-864.

Genovés, S.
    1967   Proportionality of Long Bones and Their Relation to Stature Among
            Mesoamericans. American Journal of Physical Anthropology 26:67-78.

Gifford, J. C.
    1957   Archaeological Explorations in Caves of the Point of Pines Region.
            M.A. Thesis, University of Arizona, Tucson.

    1976   A Conceptual Approach to the Analysis of Prehistoric Pottery. In
            Prehistoric Pottery Analysis and the Ceramics of Barton Ramie
            in the Belize Valley. Peabody Museum Memoirs 18, pp. 1-43.
            Cambridge.

Gladwin, W. and H. S. Gladwin
    1933   Some Southwestern Pottery Types, Series III. Medallion Papers 13.
            Gila Pueblo, Globe, Arizona.

Gladwin, H. S., E. W. Haury, E. B. Sayles, and N. Gladwin
    1937   Excavations at Snaketown I: Material Culture. Medallion Papers 25.
            Gila Pueblo, Globe, Arizona.

    1965   Excavations at Snaketown: Material Culture. University of Arizona
            Press, Tucson.

Gregory, D. A. and T. R. McGuire
    1980   Research Design for the Testing of Interstate 10 Corridor Pre-
            historic and Historic Archaeological Remains between Interstate 17
            and 30th Drive (Group II, Las Colinas). Cultural Resource Manage-
            ment Section, Arizona State Museum. The University of Arizona,
            Tucson.

Guilday, John
    1970   Animal Remains from Archaeological Excavations at Fort Ligonier.
            Annals of Carnegie Museum 42:177-186.

Haas, J.
    1971   The Ushklish Ruin: A Preliminary Report on Excavations in a Colonial
            Hohokam Site in the Tonto Basin, Central Arizona. Arizona Highway
            Salvage Preliminary Report. Arizona State Museum, University of
            Arizona, Tucson.

    n.d.   Las Colinas Ceramics. Manuscript on file at the Arizona State
            Museum, University of Arizona, Tucson.

Hall, E. R. and K. R. Kelson
    1959   The Mammals of North America. Ronald Press, New York.

Hamblin, N. L. and A. M. Rea
1979   La Avifauna Arqueologica de Cozumel. Boletín, Escuela de Ciencias Antropologicas, Universidad de Yucatan 37, pp. 21-49.

Hammack, L. C.
1969   A Preliminary Report of the Excavations at Las Colinas. The Kiva 35(1):11-28.

Hargrave, L. L.
1970   Mexican Macaws: Comparative Osteology and Survey of Remains from the Southwest. Anthropological Papers of the University of Arizona 20. University of Arizona Press, Tucson.

1972   Comparative Osteology of the Chicken and American Grouse. Prescott College Studies in Biology 1. Prescott College Press, Prescott, Arizona.

Hargrave, L. L. and Steven D. Emslie
1979   Osteological Identification of Sandhill Crane vs. Turkey. American Antiquity 44:295-299.

Haury, E. W.
1936   The Mogollon Culture of Southwestern New Mexico. Medallion Papers 20. Gila Pueblo, Globe, Arizona.

1937   Stone: Palettes and Ornaments. In Excavations at Snaketown: Material Culture, edited by H. S. Gladwin, E. W. Haury, E. B. Sayles, and N. Gladwin. Medallion Papers 25. Gila Pueblo, Globe, Arizona.

1940   Excavations in the Forestdale Valley, East-Central Arizona. University of Arizona Bulletin 11 (4), Social Sciences Bulletin 12. University of Arizona Press, Tucson.

1945   The Excavation of Los Muertos and Neighboring Ruins in the Salt River Valley, Southern Arizona. Peabody Museum Papers 24(1). Cambridge.

1976   The Hohokam: Desert Farmers and Craftsmen. The University of Arizona Press, Tucson.

Haury, E. W. and others
1950   The Stratigraphy and Archaeology of Ventana Cave, Arizona. University of New Mexico and Arizona Presses, Albuquerque and Tucson.

Havinga, A. J.
1964   Investigation into Differential Corrosion Susceptibility of Pollen and Spores. Pollen et Spores 6:621-635.

Hawley, F. G.
1937   Chemical Investigation of the Incrustation on Pottery Vessels and Palettes from Snaketown. In Excavations at Snaketown: Material Culture, edited by H. S. Gladwin, E. W. Haury, E. B. Sayles, and N. Gladwin. Medallion Papers 25. Gila Pueblo, Globe, Arizona.

Hawley, F. M.
1934   The Significance of the Dated Prehistory of Chetro Ketl, Chaco
        Cañon, New Mexico. The University of New Mexico Bulletin 1(1).
        University of New Mexico, Albuquerque.

Hayden, J. D.
1957   Excavations, 1940, at University Indian Ruin. Southwestern
        Monuments Association Technical Series 5. Globe, Arizona.

Hevly, R. H.
1964   Pollen Analysis of Quaternary Archaeological and Lacustrine Sedi-
        ments from the Colorado Plateau. Unpublished Ph.D. Dissertation,
        University of Arizona, Tucson.

Hevly, R. H., P. J. Mehringer, Jr., and H. G. Yocum.
1965   Modern Pollen Rain in the Sonoran Desert. Journal of The Arizona
        Academy of Science 3:123-135.

Hill, J. N. and R. H. Hevly
1968   Pollen at Broken K. Pueblo: Some New Interpretations. American
        Antiquity 33(2):200-210.

Hodge, F. W.
1920   Hawikuh Bonework. Indian Notes and Monographs 3(3). Heye
        Foundation, New York.

Hoffmeister, D. F. and M. R. Lee
1963   Taxonomic Review of Cottontails, Sylvilagus floridanus, in
        Arizona. American Midland Naturalist 70:138-148.

Jelinek, A. J.
1966   Correlation of Archaeological and Palynological Data. Science 152
        (3278):1507-1509.

Johnson, A. E.
1964   Archaeological Excavations in Hohokam Sites of Southern Arizona.
        American Antiquity 30(2):145-161.

Johnston, B. B.
1970   The Seri Indians of Sonora. Arizona Board of Regents, Tucson.

Kearney, T. H. and R. H. Peebles
1960   Arizona Flora. University of California Press, Berkeley.

Kelly, I. T.
1938   The Hodges Site. MS, Arizona State Museum, University of Arizona,
        Tucson.

1975   The Hodges Site. Anthropological Papers of the University of
        Arizona 30. The University of Arizona Press, Tucson.

Kelso, G.
   1971   A Critical Evaluation of the Use of Pollen Data from Archaeological Sites in Construction of Environmental Sequences. Manuscript prepared for University of Arizona Seminar on Archaeology as Anthropology. On file, Arizona State Museum, University of Arizona, Tucson.

Kidder, A. V.
   1932   The Artifacts of Pecos. Papers of the Phillips Academy, Southwestern Expedition 6. Yale University Press, New Haven.

Lawrence, B.
   1951   Mammals Found at the Awatovi Site and Post-Cranial Skeletal Characters of Deer, Pronghorn, and Sheep-Goat with Notes on Bos and Bison. Peabody Museum Papers 35(3). Cambridge.

Lincoln, E. P.
   1961   A Comparative Study of Present and Past Mammalian Fauna of the Sunset Crater and Wupatki Areas of Northern Arizona. M.S. Thesis, University of Arizona, Tucson.

Lowe, C. H.
   1964   The Vertebrates of Arizona. The University of Arizona Press, Tucson.

Luscomb, S. C.
   1967   The Collector's Encyclopedia of Buttons. Bonanza Books, New York.

Lytle, J. L.
   1971   A Microenvironmental Study of an Archaeological Site, Arizona BB:10:3, Whiptail Ruin. Unpublished M.S. Thesis, University of Arizona, Tucson.

Lytle-Webb, J. L.
   1973   Unpublished paper (untitled) presented at Arizona Academy of Science meetings, Tucson.

McGregor, J. C.
   1941   Winona and Ridge Ruin, Part I. Architecture and Material Culture. Museum of Northern Arizona Bulletin 18. Flagstaff.

McGuire, R. H.
   1979   Rancho Punta de Agua. Contribution to Highway Salvage Archaeology in Arizona 57. Arizona State Museum, University of Arizona, Tucson.

McGuire, T. R.
   1980   Historic Materials. In Research Design for the Testing of Interstate 10 Corridor Prehistoric and Historic Archaeological Remains between Interstate 17 and 30th Drive (Group II, Las Colinas), pp. 3-43. Cultural Resource Management Section, Arizona State Museum, University of Arizona, Tucson.

McKusick, C. R.
   1974   The Casas Grandes Avian Report. In, Casas Grandes, a Fallen
            Trading Center of the Gran Chichimeca 8, edited by C. C. Di Peso,
            J. B. Rinaldo and G. Fenner. Northland Press, Flagstaff.

Martin, P. S.
   1963   The Last 10,000 Years, a Fossil Pollen Record of the American
            Southwest. University of Arizona Press, Tucson.

Martin, P. S. and W. B. Byers
   1965   Pollen and Archaeology at Wetherill Mesa. In, Contributions of
            the Wetherill Mesa Archaeological Project, assembled by Douglas
            Osborne. Memoirs of the Society for American Archaeology 19,
            pp. 132-135.

Masse, W. B.
   n.d.   The Las Colinas Redwares: A Preliminary Analysis of the Redware
            Assemblage from AZ T:12:10, A Classic Period Hohokam Site in
            Phoenix, Arizona. Manuscript on file at the Arizona State Museum,
            University of Arizona, Tucson.

Mehringer, P. J., Jr.
   1968   Pollen Analysis of the Tule Springs Site, Nevada. Ph.D. Disserta-
            tion, University of Arizona, Tucson.

Meighan, C. W.
   1959   New Findings in West Mexican Archaeology. The Kiva 25(1):1-7.

Midvale, F.
   1970   Prehistoric "Canal Irrigation" in the Buckeye Valley and Gila Bend
            Areas in Western Maricopa County, Arizona. On file at the Arizona
            State Museum, University of Arizona, Tucson.

Moorehead, W. K.
   1906   A Narrative of Explorations in New Mexico, Arizona, Indiana, etc.
            Bulletin of Phillips Academy Department of Archaeology 3. Andover,
            Massachusetts.

Morris, E. H., and R. F. Burgh
   1954   Basket Maker II Sites near Durango, Colorado. Carnegie Institute
            of Washington Publications 604. Washington.

Munsell Color Company
   1954   Munsell Soil Color Charts. Munsell Color Company, Baltimore.

O'Bryan, D.
   1950   Excavations in Mesa Verde National Park. Medallion Papers 39.
            Gila Pueblo, Globe, Arizona.

Olsen, S. J.
   1968   Canid Remains from Grasshopper Ruin. The Kiva 34(1):33-41.

   1971   Zooarchaeology: Animal Bones in Archaeology and Their Interpreta-
            tion. Addison-Wesley, Reading, Massachusetts.

Olsen, S. L.
    1979   A Study of Bone Artifacts from Grasshopper Pueblo. The Kiva 44(3).

Opfenring, D. J.
    1965   The Herbinger Site, a McDowell Mountain Hohokam Settlement. M.A.
            Thesis, Arizona State University, Tempe.

Oswalt, W. H.
    1966   This Land Was Theirs. John Wiley & Sons, New York.

Pailes, R. A.
    1963   An Analysis of the Fitch Site and its Relationship to the Hohokam
            Classic Period. M.A. Thesis, Arizona State University, Tempe.

Parmalee, P. W., A. A. Paloumpis, and N. W. Wilson
    1972   Animals Utilized by Woodland Peoples Occupying the Apple Creek Site,
            Illinois. Illinois State Museum Reports of Investigation 23.
            Springfield.

Randall, M. E.
    1971   Early Marbles. Historical Archaeology 5:102-105.

Rea, A. M.
    1977   Historic Changes in the Avifauna of the Gila River Indian Reserva-
            tion, Central Arizona. Unpublished Ph.D. Dissertation, University
            of Arizona, Tucson.

    1979   The Ecology of Pima Fields. Environment Southwest 484:8-13.

    1980   Three Groups of Turkeys from Southwestern Archaeological Sites.
            Los Angeles Contributions to Science (in press).

    in   Resource Utilization and Food Taboos of Sonoran Desert Peoples.
    press

Reed, E. K.
    1955   Bison Beyond the Pecos. Texas Journal of Science 7:130-135.

Robinson, W. J. and J. S. Dean
    1969   Tree-ring Evidence for Climatic Change in the Prehistoric Southwest
            from A.D. 1000 to 1200. Laboratory of Tree-ring Research, University
            of Arizona, Tucson.

Roe, F. G.
    1970   The North American Buffalo: A Critical Study of the Species in its
            Wild State. Unversity of Toronto Press, Toronto.

Rogers, R.
    n.d.   Letter and report to Dr. William A. Longacre. Manuscript on file,
            Department of Anthropology, University of Arizona, Tucson.

Russo, J. P.
   1956   The Desert Bighorn Sheep in Arizona. Arizona Game and Fish
             Department Wildlife Bulletin 1. Phoenix.

Sayles, E. B.
   1937   Stone: Implements and Bowls. In Excavations at Snaketown,
             Material Culture, edited by H. S. Gladwin, E. W. Haury, E. B. Sayles,
             and N. Gladwin. Medallion Papers 25. Gila Pueblo, Globe, Arizona.

Schiffer, M. B.
   1972   Archaeological Context and Systemic Context. American Antiquity
             37:156-165.

Schmidt, E. F.
   1928   Time-Relations of Prehistoric Pottery Types in Southern Arizona.
             Anthropological Papers of the American Museum of Natural History 30.

Schoenwetter, J.
   1962   The Pollen Analysis of Eighteen Archaeological Sites in Arizona,
             and New Mexico. In Chapters in the Prehistory of Eastern Arizona,
             I, by P. S. Martin, J. B. Rinaldo, W. A. Longacre, C. Cronin,
             L. G. Freeman, Jr., and J. Schoenwetter. Fieldiana Anthropology
             53:168-209.

   1967   Pollen Survey of the Chuska Valley. In An Archaeological Survey
             of the Chuska Valley and the Chaco Plateau, New Mexico, by
             Harris, J. Schoenwetter, and A. H. Warren. Museum of New Mexico
             Research Records 4:72-103, Museum of New Mexico Press, Santa Fe.

Schoenwetter, J. and L. A. Doerschlag
   1970   Surficial Pollen Records from Central Arizona I. Department of
             Anthropology Research Papers 3, Arizona State University, Tempe.

   1971   Surficial Pollen Records from Central Arizona I: Sonoran Desert
             Scrub. Journal of the Arizona Academy of Science 6:216-221.

Schreiber, K. J., C. H. McCarthy and B. Byrd
   1981   Report of the Testing of Interstate 10 Corridor Prehistoric and
             Historic Archaeological Remains between Interstate 17 and 30th
             Drive (Group II, Las Colinas). Cultural Resource Management
             Section, Arizona State Museum, the University of Arizona, Tucson.

Schroeder, A. H.
   1940   A Stratigraphic Survey of Pre-Spanish Trash Mounds of the Salt
             River Valley, Arizona. M.A. Thesis, University of Arizona, Tucson.

   1952   The Bearing of Ceramics on Developments in the Hohokam Classic
             Period. The Southwestern Journal of Anthropology 8:320-335.

Sellers, W. D.
   1960   Arizona Climate. University of Arizona Press, Tucson.

Smith, C. E. Jr.
    1950   Prehistoric Plant Remains from Bat Cave. Botanical Museum
                Leaflets 14(7). Cambridge.

Smith, W., R. B. Woodbury and N. F. Woodbury
    1966   The Excavations of Hawikuh by Frederick Webb Hodge. Contributions
                from the Museum of the American Indian 20. Heye Foundation, New
                York.

Soloman, A. M. and H. D. Dayes
    1972   Qualitative Influence of Moisture. Interim Research Report 4,
                Department of Geosciences, University of Arizona, Tucson.

Speth, J. D.
    1972   Mechanical Basis of Percussion Flaking. American Antiquity 37:
                34-60.

Stanislawski, M. B.
    1969   The Ethno-archaeology of Hopi Pottery Making. Plateau 24(1):27-33.

Steen, C. R.
    1965   Excavations in Compound A, Casa Grande National Monument, 1963.
                The Kiva 31:213-222.

Steen, C. R., L. M. Pierson, V. L. Bohrer, and K. P. Kent
    1962   Archaeological Studies at Tonto National Monument, Arizona. South-
                west Monuments Association Technical Series 2. Globe, Arizona.

Stein, W. T.
    1962   Mammals from Archaeological Sites, Point of Pines, Arizona. M.A.
                Thesis, University of Arizona, Tucson.

    1963   Mammal Remains from Archaeological Sites in the Point of Pines
                Region, Arizona. American Antiquity 29(2):213-220.

Steinbock, R. T.
    1976   Paleopathological Diagnosis and Interpretation. C. C. Thomas,
                Springfield, Illinois.
Stewart, K. M.
    1967   Excavations at Mesa Grande, a Classic Period Hohokam Site in
                Arizona. The Masterkey 41:14-23.

Thompson, R. H.
    1958   Modern Yucatecan Maya Pottery Making. Society for American Archae-
                ology Memoir 15.

Turney, O. A.
    1924   The Land of the Stone Hoe. Arizona Republican Print Shop, Phoenix.

    1929   Prehistoric Irrigation in Arizona. Arizona State Historian,
                Phoenix.

Wagner, Phillip
1960 The Human Use of the Earth. The Free Press, New York.

Wasley, W. W.
1957 The Archaeological Survey of the Arizona State Museum. Arizona State Museum, University of Arizona, Tucson.

1960 A Hohokam Platform Mound at the Gatlin Site, Gila Bend, Arizona. American Antiquity 26(2):244-262.

1966 Classic Period Hohokam. Manuscript, Arizona State Museum, University of Arizona, Tucson.

Wasley, W. W. and A. E. Johnson
1965 Salvage Archaeology in Painted Rocks Reservoir, Western Arizona. Anthropological Papers of the University of Arizona 9. University of Arizona Press, Tucson.

Weaver, D. E., Jr.
1972 Investigation Concerning the Hohokam Classic Period in the Lower Salt River Valley, Arizona. M.A. Thesis, Arizona State University, Tempe.

1973 The Site Characterization Program. In Definition and Preliminary Study of the Midvale Site, edited by J. Schoenwetter, S. W. Gaines, and D. E. Weaver, Jr. Arizona State University Anthropological Research Papers 6, pp. 92-154. Arizona State University, Tempe.

Weaver, D. E., Jr., S. S. Burton and M. Laughlin, editors
1978 Proceedings of the 1973 Hohokam Conference. Contributions to Anthropological Studies 2. Center for Anthropological Studies, Albuquerque.

Weed, C. S.
1972 The Beardsley Canal Site. The Kiva 38(2):57-94.

1973 Classic Period Hohokam Lithic Assemblages. Paper presented for the Annual Meeting of the Society for American Archaeology.

n.d. Preliminary Report on the Las Colinas Ceramics (1974). Manuscript on file at the Arizona State Museum, University of Arizona, Tucson.

Weed, C. S. and A. E. Ward
1970 The Henderson Site: Colonial Hohokam in North Central Arizona: A Preliminary Report. The Kiva 36(2):1-12.

Wheat, J. B.
1972 The Olsen-Chubbuck Site: A Paleo-Indian Bison Kill. Society for American Archaeology Memoir 26.

White, T. E.
1953 A Method of Calculating the Dietary Percentage of Various Food Animals Utilized by Aboriginal Peoples. American Antiquity 18: 396-398.

Whiting, A. F.
    1939   Ethnobotany of the Hopi. Museum of Northern Arizona Bulletin 15.
            Flagstaff.

Woodbury, R. B.
    1954   Prehistoric Stone Implements of Northeastern Arizona. Peabody
            Museum Papers 34. Cambridge.

Zahniser, J. L.
    1966   Late Prehistoric Villages Southeast of Tucson, Arizona, and the
            Archaeology of the Tanque Verde Phase. The Kiva 31:103-204.

Zaslow, B. and A. E. Dittert
    1977   Pattern Mathematics and Archaeology. Arizona State University
            Anthropological Research Papers 2. Arizona State University, Tempe.